W9-BLN-297

WAR AND PEACE THROUGH WOMEN'S EYES

WAR AND PEACE THROUGH WOMEN'S EYES

A Selective Bibliography of Twentieth-Century American Women's Fiction

SUSANNE CARTER

Bibliographies and Indexes in Women's Studies, Number 14

GREENWOOD PRESS
New York • Westport, Connecticut • London

Library of Congress Cataloging-in-Publication Data

Carter, Susanne.
  War and peace through women's eyes : a selective bibliography of
twentieth-century American women's fiction / Susanne Carter.
    p. cm.—(Bibliographies and indexes in women's studies,
ISSN 0742-6941 ; no. 14)
  Includes bibliographical references and index.
  ISBN 0-313-27771-0 (alk. paper)
    1. American fiction—Women authors—Bibliography. 2. Women and
literature—United States—Bibliography. 3. American fiction—20th
century—Bibliography. 4. War stories, American—Bibliography.
5. Peace in literature—Bibliography. I. Title. II. Series.
Bibliographies and indexes in women's studies ; no. 14.
Z1231.F4C37 1992
[PS374.W6]
016.813'5080358—dc20   91-33399

British Library Cataloguing in Publication Data is available.

Library of Congress Catalog Card Number: 91-33399
ISBN: 0-313-27771-0
ISSN: 0742-6941

First published in 1992

Greenwood Press, 88 Post Road West, Westport, CT 06881
An imprint of Greenwood Publishing Group, Inc.

Printed in the United States of America

The paper used in this book complies with the
Permanent Paper Standard issued by the National
Information Standards Organization (Z39.48-1984).

10 9 8 7 6 5 4 3 2 1

Contents

Preface

This bibliography is the culmination of an research effort to collect and analyze American women's literary interpretations of war and peace through fiction during the twentieth century. In each of the novels and short fictions included in the bibliography war and/or peace is a dominant theme. The bibliography is divided into five chapters—World War One, World War Two, The Vietnam War, Nuclear War, and War and Peace. The final chapter includes novels and short fictions from the Korean War and various foreign wars, American Indian war fiction, writings not specific to a particular war as well as those which include more than one war, and utopian fictions which visualize idealistic, peaceful societies where war no longer exists. While the majority of these writings take place during this century, some novels and short stories included in the nuclear war and war and peace chapters are futuristic in nature and leap forward in time to predict what war—as well as the state of the universe and its inhabitants—may be like during the centuries to come. A chapter to include women's literary responses to the Persian Gulf War, fought against Iraq during the early months of 1991 as this bibliography was compiled, remains unwritten as we await the novels and short stories which will eventually be published both by the women in the United States military who served in the Middle East during Operation Desert Storm and by those women who experienced the war from afar waiting on the homefront.

Each chapter of the bibliography begins with an introductory overview of the war literature included in that chapter. Annotations of the novels and short fiction pertaining to each chapter's theme follow, concluded by a list of sources of literary criticism and bibliographic resources cited within that chapter and/or consulted for the compilation of the chapter. The annotations offer a critical summary of each novel or short fiction, including excerpts from many of the novels and short fictions included, partial reviews, and synopses of literary criticism published about the works and their respective authors.

Because this is a literary bibliography, war fiction written by women of a more popular than literary nature has not been included. All novels and short stories included in this bibliography were written by women who were either born in the United States or have established residency in this country. The collection includes women who are well known among twentieth century literary circles, such as Edith Wharton, Willa Cather, Cynthia Ozick, Dorothy Parker, Toni Morrison, and Bobbie Ann Mason, as well as more obscure writers with less extensive publishing histories. The bibliography includes fiction authored by concentration camp survivors, former military nurses and relief workers, war journalists, a Quaker, and one First Lady. The book also includes several short stories written by one science fiction writer who disguised herself using the pen-name of a male writer during much of her publishing career to gain acceptance in a male-dominated field.

Each individual citation of the bibliography has been numbered and includes complete bibliographic information presented in the format of the <u>MLA Handbook for Writers of Research Papers</u> (Third Edition, 1988). Quotations included within individual annotations have been referenced according to MLA standards as well. For those novels which have been reprinted from earlier editions, both years of publication have been given. The author and title indices at the end of the book reference these citations by number. The subject index references citations by item number and introductory pages of each chapter by page number.

Acknowledgments

My sincere thanks to the Reference and Circulation Departments of Southwest Missouri State University Library, the Interlibrary Loan staff of Southwest Missouri State University Library, especially Francie Rottmann, the Reference and Circulation Departments of Springfield-Greene County Library, the librarian and publications staff of the University of Madison-Wisconsin Women's Studies Program, all of the libraries across the country which loaned materials to me through the interlibrary loan network, Larry Rottmann, Dr. Jim Jones, Lynne Freeman, Ed DeLong, Robert Jordan, J. R. Robinson, and my understanding family.

Introduction

War has been a continual theme woven through women's literature since the beginning of history. In ancient Sumeria 4,300 years ago one of the world's first poets, Enheduanna, railed at war in her poem "Lament to the Spirit of War" as a "fiery monster" filled with a "spirit of hate, greed and anger" (199). Writing 2,500 years ago in ancient Greece, Sappho maintained that the power of love was far superior to military strength in her poem "To An Army Wife in Sardis" (249).

"Women writers have persisted in making war a part of their writing because historically war has insisted on making women part of its story," contends Dorothy Sauber in her thesis "Historical Context/Literary Content: Women Write About War and Women" (197). "Through the centuries," she writes, "women have patronized, participated in, and been part of the upheaval and chaos created by war" (197). Women's literary interpretations which depict war in diverse ways as a "glorious adventure, patriotic necessity, a time when life becomes a living death, and an evil threatening the future of the human race," evidence that war has significantly affected the lives of women throughout history (197).

Although war has traditionally been considered the province of men, as Hope Norman Coulter writes in the introduction to <u>Civil War Women</u>: <u>American Women Shaped by Conflict in Stories by Alcott, Chopin, Welty and Others</u>, there has always "been another side to war—the women's view." She explains:

> Someone packs the knapsacks of those warriors and bids them goodbye. Someone turns back to mundane labors, to the day-to-day responsibilities of a life that has suddenly, drastically changed. Someone runs the small farms and businesses that feed the hyperactive economics of wartime. Someone rears the next generations, and answers its questions about the killing of this one. (7)

In her <u>Women and War: An Appeal to the Women of All Nations</u>, written as World War One began in 1914, Frances S. Hallowes expressed regret that "the sufferings of women through war and militarism are seldom dwelt upon. Books and treaties dealing with arguments against war," she contends, "almost invariably omit to mention the damage done to one half of the human race by this remnant of barbarism" (3). War seems to be a "concentration of crimes," she writes. "Under its standard gather violence, malignity, fraud, rage, perfidy and lust" (4). During war women suffer physically from "starvation, disease, violation, loss of home, poverty, sometimes death, slavery and imprisonment" (4). But the mental anguish they have to endure is even harsher, she explains:

> And who can describe adequately the slow torture of fear and suspense, the long agonies of anticipation; the sleepless nights and fevered imagination, the pitiless hours of barren loneliness; the visions of butchered bleeding boldies! And who but those who experience it, can tell of the blow of bereavement, the broken heart of wife or mother or daughter! What must the mental suffering be, in receiving back the sons and husbands, alive indeed, but mulitated or diseased, life-long cripples, or weakened and unable to work.

> We can picture the agonised watching of mothers over starving children, the slow death of the dear ones, their heart-rending cries, or their visible fading from the mothers' arms; or the premature births of infants who frequently are neurotic or idiotic, due to ghastly frights and anxieties of mothers in time of war. Their homes burnt, their furniture used for fuel, their crops taken, bedding and clothes stolen; homeless, naked, starved, widows, orphans, childless, such are the victims of war. And do men care? Do they ever think of the stupendous misery they produce in the other half of their nation by their support of war? (4 – 5)

While war literature may have a long history, it is only during the twentieth century that war fiction written by both men and women has matured as a genre in its own right. The novels and short stories of this century differ from literary interpretations of wars waged during the past because of the vast difference in the way wars have been fought during this century and the reactions of twentieth century men and women to war as a social phenomenon. In his <u>World War One and the American Novel</u>, Stanley Cooperman describes the change in Americans' relationship to war which has occurred during this century—a change which continues to be reflected in American war literature as the century draws to a close:

> Love, death, and war have always been the great raw materials of literature. Men still love and die in very much the same way that their ancestors—including their literary ancestors in the Homeric and epic patterns—loved and died. They do not, however, make war the same way; indeed, one might say that in the twentieth century war is made upon them. (193)

War is "made upon" both men and women, as Marge Piercy convincingly points out in her essay "Of Arms and the Woman": "Bombs do not fall only upon men from the ages of eighteen to forty-five," she writes. "They kill and maim women, old people, children, babies, cats, dogs, tigers, and water buffalo; birds, reptiles, and the landscape and future of a place" (30). The writings of twentieth century women give recognition to the fact that females are participants—and often victims—of the furor and turmoil of war, even if they have never experienced combat. "War is not suspended in time, something outside a woman's experience of life," writes Sally Hayton-Keeva in her introduction to <u>Valiant Women In War and Exile</u>. "It is part of life, woven into all the rest" (iv). Sauber elaborates further:

> The written history of war may include a few deeds and words of women who publicly acted out their sentiments about war, but for the most part it excludes the largest groups of women affected by the social phenomenon called war. Millions of women of all ages never went to battle or actively supported war or publicly protested war, and yet their lives became part of the history of war. (101)

As the end of the century approaches, the genre of war literature continues to evolve with both men and women making significant contributions to this still growing body of literature. As women have gained a more authoritative voice and recognition for their literary endeavors, they have exercised more freedom to write about—and even question—the phenomenon of war once considered exclusively male. American women have explored the concepts of war and peace through a myriad of fictional interpretations both traditional and experimental. While most men's war fictions written during the twentieth century have focused on the combat experience and military strategy, with the exception of Vietnam War literature which analyzes the psychological impact and moral dilemma of war as well, women's writings emphasize the human dimension of war, particularly the reactions of individual women to their varied encounters with war, both real and imagined. In her essay "Of Arms and the Woman," Marge Piercy writes: "I would have to say that war is too important in our time to leave only to men to write about, especially in the limited ways that men have often thought about and felt about war" (30). Women's writings have broadened the scope of war literature once defined predominantly by men.

War literature written during this century by American women offers a realistic representation of the homefront experience of women who have sent sons, husbands, fathers, and lovers off to war with no assurance of their return. The emotional agony of separation and loss endured by these women can be considered "the female equivalent of the agony of the trenches" endured by men in combat, Nosheen Khan explains in <u>Women's Poetry and the First World War</u>. The reactions of the mothers, wives, lovers, sisters, and daughters in these novels and short fictions to the emotional strain of anxious waiting on the homefront substantiate Khan's belief that "courage is manifest not only in brilliant attack, but also in patient waiting and patient endurance" by women who "go to battle" in their own private ways during wartime (138).

World War One short fiction is especially illustrative of this theme. In her story "On the Edge" Dorothy Canfield Fisher portrays one woman's solitary war to save her sanity as she tries to cope with single parenting six children forced to live in one room while the war is ongoing. The protagonist of another story written by Fisher, "La Pharmacienne," delivers her own child even as invading German troops occupy her home. Helen Mackay depicts a homefront wife in "Their Places" who is so isolated from the reality of war and so absorbed in managing the family's farm business while her husband is away at war that she can no longer relate to him when he does return. Similarly, the wife in Mackay's "Second Hay" is forced to choose between trying to reestablish intimacy with her soldier-husband or harvesting the hay crop during his short furlough home from the front.

These novels and short stories illustrate that the suffering inflicted by war ranges far beyond the battlefront. The concentration camp survivor in Cynthia Ozick's World War Two story "The Shawl" witnesses the brutal death of her infant daughter by a camp guard as she stands frozen by the knowledge that to try to rescue her child would precipitate her own death as well. Another Holocaust victim characterized in Elzbieta Ettinger's Kindergarten eventually loses her tenuous grasp on sanity and disintegrates into an "inhuman madwoman" who is never able to recover from her war experience. Japanese women in Edita Morris' World War Two novels who survive the atomic bombing of their country suffer the physical and psychological after-effects of radiation exposure and later give birth to deformed children. A young Chinese revolutionary is put to death for her progressive ideas in Pearl S. Buck's "Singing—to Her Death." And despite her indifference to her veteran-husband's war experience, the homefront wife in Bobbie Ann Mason's "Big Bertha Stories" begins to experience the same recurring nightmares of war that have disturbed him since he returned from the Vietnam War. Fictions written by Martha Gellhorn, Joyce Reiser Kornblatt, and Sadie Roberson document the lonely isolation of immigrants forced from their homelands by war who remain outcasts on American soil. None of these characters engages in combat, yet each endures physical and emotional pain that originates in war.

Although women often suffer from their encounters with war, the experience can also foster growth and self-discovery, as illustrated in this literature. The French women in Dorothy Canfield Fisher's World War One story "What Goes Up . . ." pool their resources and bond together to build a communal strength that enables them to survive more than four years in a German prison camp without loss of self respect and dignity. The protagonist of Katharine Fullerton Gerould's World War One story "A Moth of Peace" discovers within herself the courage to go forth alone out of hiding to face approaching German troops, unaware of what the encounter will bring. When her husband volunteers for World War Two duty and she is left alone to support her family, the war wife in Laura Kalpakian's "Wine Women and Song" discovers a self-assuredness never before realized and refuses to sacrifice this newfound competence once her husband returns and discovers his prewar wife has become an independent woman. For the war widow in Bessie Breuer's World War Two story "Home is a Place" the death of her husband at war also represents an opportunity for her to become more than "someone else's wife" and establish her own self-identity for the first time. The mother in Maxine Kumin's Vietnam War story "The Missing Person" learns she is capable of handling crises calmly and independently and can finally admit to herself that her son, declared Missing in Action in Vietnam for several years, is dead through her encounter with war. Women characters in several of this century's utopian fictions learn they can survive quite adequately—and much more peacefully—by living independently without men.

This literature also documents the experiences of women who have served in support positions during war. These women discover that to endure war requires an emotional numbing which usually promises a lengthy postwar readjustment, prolonged by painful memories and feelings of loss. The nurse-protagonists of Mary Lee's World War One novel "It's a Great War!" and Elizabeth Ann Scarborough's Vietnam War novel The Healer's War both return from war feeling like alien misfits who can no longer blend comfortably into civilian life because their witness to the atrocities of war has set them apart. The relief worker in Dorothy Canfield Fisher's autobiographical World War One novel The Deepening Stream eventually reaches the disheartening conclusion that her personal contribution to the war effort has only furthered a game of murder and perpetuated war's cycle of death and destruction by keeping murderers alive. The narrator of Dorothy Canfield Fisher's World War One short story "Vignettes from Life at the Rear," weary from administering to so many blinded soldiers, cannot look at her own children without seeing the "scarred, mutilated, sightless faces of young men in their prime, with long lives of darkness before them" (81). The perception of the nurse who narrates Helen Mackay's World War One story "The Cauldron" may be representative of many behind-the-scenes support workers who come to view war's casualties as a despairing cycle of nameless faces that is never-ending.

Few women who have written about war during this century have visualized women in combat. Two World War One writers fantasize European women as warriors in their fictions. In Gertrude Atherton's The White Morning the women of Germany rise in revolt against the men of their country who have prolonged war for too long and subjugated them in subservient positions. Frances Gilchrist Wood envisions the women of France taking arms in revenge for the death of their husbands killed in battle in her "The White Battalion." Maxine Kong Kingston fantasizes herself as a woman warior chosen to lead a people's rebellion against the reigning emperors of China in "White Tigers." The heroine of her narrative ceases fighting long enough only to give birth before she rejoins the battle, her newborn son's umbilical cord waving proudly as her flag. In her bizarre, satirical lampoon on war, "The Lincoln-Pruitt Anti-Rape Device," Vietnam War writer Emily Prager envisions former American prostitutes sent to Southeast Asia as warriors to test the effectiveness of a vaginally inserted weapon designed to inflict death upon seduced Viet Cong soldiers. In Pamela Sargent's futuristic "Shadows," alien female warriors descend upon earth to conquer the human race. But such visions of women taking up arms are rare in twentieth century American literature.

A minority of women writers view war from a male perspective.   These writers characterize soldiers above all as human beings instead of military automatons, men who are often victimized by their own war experiences. The young World War One soldier in Hetty Hemenway's "Four Days" returns home on leave wearing the "numb, dazed look" his bride has recognized on the faces of so many other soldiers. He describes himself as one among many robot-like cogs in the wheel of war to his new bride. As a soldier, he confides to his wife, "You're just one in a great big machine called England," (582).   Susan M. Boogher envisions a World War One soldier visiting Westminster Abbey in her story "An Unknown Warrior" who is surprisingly reassured that the peaceful, contemplative part of life he values so highly has not been erased by the brutality of war he has witnessed.   Alison Stuart contrasts soldiers' varied attitudes toward fighting in her World War Two story "Sunday Liberty." While two sailors in the story eagerly anticipate their chance to fight, a third attempts to drown himself because he would rather end his own life than someone else's. The protagonist of Susan Schaeffer's epic <u>Buffalo Afternoon</u>, like many young men who served during the Vietnam War, starts his tour of duty enthusiastically but soon becomes disillusioned and repulsed by the atrocities he witnesses and the seeming futility of the American strategy in Southeast Asia. The engineer who helps to design a nuclear bomb in Kate Wilhelm's "Countdown" faces his assigned task with moral ambivalence and a heavy conscience. He questions himself as well as mankind, as he stands horrified and ashamed shortly after the bomb is launched: "My God, what have we done?"

If soldiers are victimized by the experience of war, many men are also infatuated with war as an alluring game, these fictions illustrate. To Claude Wheeler, the lure of the battlefield represents a romantic diversion from the mediocrity of his agrarian lifestyle in Willa Cather's World War One novel <u>One of Ours</u>. Similarly, in Ethel Yates' Vietnam War story "The Seeds of Time" young Harry Hartley joins the military to prove that he is a man. "And to him the fastest, simplest, and surest way is to join the Marines!" (263).   The combat photographer in Martha Gellhorn's World War Two story "Till Death Us Do Part" may abhor the loss of life associated with war but admits he thrives on its diversity and intensity so much that he refuses to set down permanent roots so that he can continue to follow the path of war.   The men in Martha Gellhorn's "Week End at Grimsby" predict that the peaceful respite following the end of World War Two in Europe will only last a few years because men cannot bear to live in peace for long periods of time. Men start wars, one veteran explains, "so they get some excitement first before they die; or they only live and die, that is nothing much" (71). A young Chinese warrior in Pearl S. Buck's <u>Sons</u> chooses warring as a way of life and builds his self-esteem through the attainment of power and continued conquest.

Deena Metzger's innovative novella <u>The Woman Who Slept with Men to Take the War Out of Them</u> contrasts the aggressive drives of men which perpetuate the game of war, personified by the General, with the pacifist attitudes of women personified by the Woman, blended into a caring harmony during the act of making love. Women sleep with the enemy "to make him their own, to assert their commitment to life over death,"

Barbara Myerhoff writes in the foreward to the novella, "in final refusal to believe that anyone who understands can continue to destroy" (vi – vii).

The veterans of all wars fought during this century are characterized in these novels and short stories as men who suffer both emotionally and physically long after their official tours of duty have ended. The feelings voiced by the distressed Vietnam War veteran in Bobbie Ann Mason's In Country are typical, especially among veterans of the Vietnam War. "There's something wrong with me," Emmett cries. "I'm damaged. It's like something in the center of my heart is gone and I can't get it back" (225).

After he witnesses the decapitation of a fellow soldier, the World War One veteran in Toni Morrison's Sula can't remember who or what he is; at age 22 he is an outcast in his own community, dismissed as a lunatic while he embarks on a quest for self-discovery. The American Indian veteran in Leslie Marmon Silko's World War Two novel Ceremony faces an equally difficult postwar readjustment because of his sensitivity and painful memories of combat. Julia Thacker's Vietnam War short story "A Civil Campaign" portrays the distress of a veteran who faces postwar life both incontinent and potentially impotent. Although the World War Two veteran in Pearl S. Buck's "Begin to Live" returns home to a faithful fiancee and caring family, he is hindered in his readjustment by apprehension and indecisiveness. His father, who served during World War One, explains that the most difficult part of becoming a civilian again is trying to "recapture reality. That's because war is unreal," his father says. "You lose the habit of feeling, in war" (146 – 147). Several veterans portrayed in Vietnam War literature, such as Maxine Kumin's "These Gifts" and Laurie Alberts' "Veterans," cannot sustain intimate relationships once they return from the war. Other Vietnam War veterans, such as those characterized in Diane Taylor's "The Skull" and Stephanie Vaughn's "Kid MacArthur," only discover a sense of peace by living in isolation. Still others who fail to develop an inner peace, such as the veterans depicted in Joyce Harrington's "A Letter to Amy" and Jane Bradley's "What Happened to Wendell?", end their lives violently with the skills they have perfected at war turned tragically inward upon themselves.

Children are also frequently victims of war, as these novels and short stories illustrate again and again. A young Belgian lad in Madeleine Z. Doty's World War One story "Little Brother" becomes the sole survivor of his family after he flees with his newborn sister at his mother's request as German forces advance toward their village. While his sister survives only three days, he returns home to learn that everyone in his village has been slaughtered and his father killed at the front. The young war victim in Diana Chow's "The Village" witnesses the heinous butchering of her mother and father before invading soldiers discover her hiding place and she too becomes a victim of their savage violence. The pre-adolescent character in Rita-Elizabeth Harper's story "Survivors" learns that in order to provide for her siblings after her mother has become a casualty of war, she must sell her own body to the "protector" who rations her family's provisions. Adolescent orphans in Kay Boyle's "The Lost" adopted during World War Two as GI mascots are left behind with unfilled promises of a home and family when American troops evacuate Europe. Young sons in Linsey Abrams' "Secrets Men Keep" and Bobbie Ann Mason's "Big Bertha Stories" both develop psychological problems originating from their veteran-fathers' disturbing war experiences in Vietnam. The experiences of children reared in military families where war becomes a way of life are relived in short fictions authored by Ellen Gilchrist and Stephanie Vaughn.

While some of these writings, especially those published during the first half of the century, such as Ellen Glasgow's The Builders and Edith Wharton's A Son at the Front, were written in support of American involvement in war, blurring the distinction between propaganda and literature with their patriotic—even didactic—messages, the majority of war fiction authored by American women during this century has obviously been written in opposition to war. In the preface to her World War One novel "It's a Great War!" Mary Lee states that the "Chief Protagonist" of any war novel is "always war itself, with its stupidity, its carelessness of human life" (vii). The fiction written by many American women during this century verifies Lee's assertion. Although Edith Wharton viewed American involvement in World War One as a necessity to preserve western civilization, she defines war in The Marne as "an unfathomable thing that suddenly escaped out of the history book like a dangerous lunatic escaping from the asylum" and cries out against the destructive power of this runaway lunatic:

> This was what war did! It emptied towns of their inhabitants as it emptied veins of their blood; it killed houses and lands as well as men. Out There, a few miles beyond the sunny vineyards and the low hills, men were dying at that very moment by hundreds, by thousands—and their motionless young bodies must have the same unnatural look as these wan ruins, these gutted houses and sterile fields . . . War meant Death, Death, Death—Death everywhere, and to everything. (25)

A strong antiwar bias is evident in other fiction written by women as well. The young lieutenant in Beulah Marie Dix's The Battle Months of George Daurella enters war with expectations of invincibility but soon learns that war reduces all of humanity to the same level of vulnerability and "unravels" the advances made by civilization as it regresses to aggressive primitivism. The combat photographer in Martha Gellhorn's World War Two story "Till Death Us Do Part" considers leaving his career in war photography because during war, he says, men are "engaged in losing what they loved, and destroying what others loved, and there was no help for this, it was the nature of man and the real shape of history" (243). In her story "Memorial Day" Dorothy Canfield Fisher fantasizes veterans buried in a cemetery crying out a warning to the young men decorating their graves above not to waste their lives in the senseless act of war. The Chinese father in Pearl S. Buck's Dragon Seed denounces one of his sons who becomes full of "zest for war." Ling Tan declares: "A man who kills because he loves to kill out to die for the good of the people, though he is my own son. Such men are always tyrants and we who are the people are ever at their mercy" (251).

Whereas the writings of Pearl S. Buck and Roberta Silman examine the rationalizations of the American scientists who perfected the atomic bomb with the ultimate aim of world peace as their motivation, the novels of Edita Morris document the long-term pervasive effects of this bombing upon successive generations of Japanese victims. For the majority of the scientists' wives in Silman's Beginning the World Again the desire to give birth becomes the most paramount mission in their lives. "For when your husband is working on a weapon capable of unknown and perhaps unprecedented destruction," writes Silman, "perhaps the only thing a woman can do to convince herself of a future is to have a child. A kind of balancing act, really" (233). For Japanese women, however, giving birth carries a high risk of deformity due to the pervasive, long-term effects of radiation exposure.

American women writing during this century have objected to the inconsistency between their maternal role as life givers and compassionate nurturers of life and the sacrifice of life they are expected to make during wartime. While the mothers characterized in many short stories and novels published during World War One send their sons to a war of necessity they feel is being fought for a just cause, the women in Fanny Kemble Johnson's "The Strange-Looking Man" vow not to give birth to any more children because they fear they might bear sons who will eventually be sent to war. The protagonist of Mary Lee's "It's a Great War!" begins to wonder if war is a game that was invented by men to "even the score" between birth and death: "Women suffered, through the centuries, to bring men into this crazy world," she writes. "Was it by War that the score of suffering between man and woman even up, then? "(246). If so, she reasons, then women should refuse to bring any more children into a world destined to continue warfare. The daughter of a Vietnam War casualty who never knew her father in Bobbie Ann Mason's In Country questions a society where each generation of males seems compelled to prove its masculinity in battle and a country where war seems to have become man's "basic profession." "I don't get it," she confesses. "If there wasn't a war for fifty years and two whole generations didn't have to fight, do you mean there should have been a war for them? Is that why we have wars—so guys won't miss out?" (87) Several utopian fiction writers such as Pamela Sargent and Joanna Russ even envision all-female societies as the only assured solution to war and protection of the peaceful lifestyle women in these novels and short fictions establish when separated from men.

During the second half of the century women have become more vocal in their stated opposition to war. Influenced by contemporary psychology and feminist ideology, these writers look inward in self-examination of our own behavior for explanations to the causes of war and are less inclined than women who wrote earlier during the century to search for justifications to armed conflict. More assertively than during previous years, the writings of American women during the latter half of the century question the male fascination with power and weaponry as well as the traditional ritual of battle which have been a part of the American culture since its inception. Many blame a patriarchal system which has largely excluded the pacifist voices of women as the source of our continued warfare and arms escalation. Short stories written by Eleanor Clark during World War One and more recently by Valerie Miner, Katharine Haake and Maureen Brady feature women as active participants in antiwar protests.

Twentieth century antiwar fiction is also frequently critical of the American military system. The soldier personified in Dorothy Parker's World War Two story "The Lovely Leave" becomes such a model warrior he cannot make the transition from soldier to civilian-husband during his brief leave at home. Through the strict demands of his military indoctrination, Steve loses his ability to become human again and play the role of a caring husband, if only temporarily. As her father dies, the narrator of Stephanie Vaughn's "Able, Baker, Charlie, Dog" mourns the father-daughter relationship the two of them never had the chance to develop because his absorption in his military career precluded such intimacy. American soldiers in Kate Wilhelm's "The Village" efficiently carry out their orders to murder unsuspecting small town Southerners without questioning, exemplifying a military system that can request the unthinkable and expect compliance without resistance. Alice Hastings Sheldon (as James Tiptree, Jr.) foresees an American military institution of the future in "Yanqui Doodle" that freely dispenses drugs to its servicemen in order to coat the horrific reality of war they are about to experience with a euphoric sense of "all-rightness" that will sustain their motivation and insure victory. Vietnam War literature authored by women is especially critical of the Veteran Administration's lack of sensitivity toward the needs of veterans. Writings such as Corinne Brown's Body Shop and Pat Taylor Ellis' "Descent Into Brotherland" document the neglect of veterans who are offered only impersonal treatment in a system where individual needs are frequently overlooked.

In a similar manner many of these fictions are critical of Americans' attitudes toward war and the propensity of this country to resort to war so readily for conflict resolution. As early as 1922 in her novella The Aerial Flight To The Realm of Peace, Martha Kayser envisioned a utopian planet free of war where earth's inhabitants might travel and then vow "Never! NEVER!! NEVER!!!" to return to earth again. Dorothy Canfield Fisher criticizes Americans' indifference toward the threat of Hitlerism spreading throughout Europe in her World War Two story "Americans Must Be Told." Americans, she warns, "are like people working nice and quiet in their vegetable gardens, while somebody back of the house is putting poison into their well" (229). In "Seeds of Conflict" Kathryn Kramer is critical of Americans' complacent beliefs that they are immune to war when the seeds of conflict that breed war are so obviously being sewn in their very own homes.   Kathryn Kramer satirizes Americans' seeming need for war in our lives in her A Handbook for Visitors from Outer Space which depicts war as a state of mind that has become an addictive game among Americans. "Everything tastes so much better when one is listening for boots on the stairs," one soldier confesses (10). The protagonist of Ursula K. Le Guin's The Lathe of Heaven whose "effective" dreams can change the course of history fails to end war because, even in his dreams, he cannot begin to imagine a warless world because war has become so ingrained in the collective unconscious of every American.

Mary Arkley Carter's The Minutes of the Night predicts how Americans might react to the advent of a nuclear holocaust. The cooperation and mutual support that would be necessary to survive such a crisis are found lacking in the Americans she envisions who panic in a frenzy of self-centeredness that is counterproductive to survival. The invading aliens in Dorothy De Courcy's "Rat Race" are so repulsed by the warlike behavior they discover among the human race which inhabits earth, they decide to explore other planets in the universe for possible conquests. From a futuristic perspective in "Atlantis Discovered: Meet the Skyscraper People of the Burning West," Grace Shinell concludes that humans destroyed themselves during the second millennium because "in the final analysis they were over-achievers of self-destruction" (126). In her World War Two novel Her Human Majesty Kay Boyle traces the roots of warfare to the "absence or failure of human bonds" but expresses her belief that everyone has within a "human majesty" enabling us to reestablish those bonds that will assure peace.

The writings of these women illustrate the changes in attitude toward war that have occurred during the century. Daughters' attitudes toward war in Pam Durban's "Notes Toward an Understanding" and Shirley Ann Grau's "Homecoming" are decidedly different from their parents'. In Martha Lacy Hall's "Lucky Lafe" a World War Two veteran who loses a brother during the Korean War and sends his own son to Vietnam expresses the dubious hope that the warring tradition will not be passed on to his own grandson. Sara Vogan contrasts three generations of males' perspectives on war in her "Scenes From the Homefront," the father and grandfather's fascination with war contrasted with the son's refusal to serve in the Vietnam War. Marti Kristen's Vietnam War story "The Guard" compares a seasoned veteran's attitude toward war, sobered by experience and death, with a young soldier's eager but naive anticipation of combat.

These fictions emphasize too that the "enemy" during war is a human being with emotions and needs very much like our own. The American pilot in Margaret Applegarth's "Every Mother's Son of Them" regrets the killing of a German pilot when he realizes there is a human being similar to himself behind the "enemy" he has shot down. "I suppose I'm his enemy," he writes in a letter to the aviator's mother, "yet I'd give my life to have him back" (89). The Japanese physician in Pearl S. Buck's World War Two story "The Enemy" who harbors nothing but animosity toward Americans risks his life to heal a wounded American prisoner of war who escapes. The doctor later questions himself in bewilderment, "I wonder why I could not kill him?" (126). The young French protagonist in Leslie Brownrigg's World War Two story "Man Gehorcht" falls in love with a German "enemy" although she eventually betrays him in allegiance to her country. The Philippino general in Cecilia Manguerra Brainard's "The Black Man in the Forest," left alone to contemplate the black American corpse he has shot, begins to realize that this giant of a man is an individual who could easily have been himself.

Through the century minority women have interpreted war and peace through the eyes of fictionalized minority characters. The writings of

Odella Phelps Wood, Alice Childress, Toni Morrison, and Ann Petry emphasize the Black American experience through war while writers such as Leslie Marmon Silko, Louise Erdrich, Elizabeth Cook-Lynn, and Anna Lee Walters focus on the experiences of American Indians during war and their attitudes toward war. These women's writings explore the special impact that war has upon members of minority groups. In Ceremony Leslie Marmon Silko illustrates how military service during war elevates all Americans, regardless of ethnic background, to a hero status, but once wars end, former prejudices resurface and minority members are once again shunned as inferior citizens. The writings of Alice Childress and other Black writers indicate that to Black Americans, the definition of peace extends beyond the absence of war. To be genuine and lasting, peace must also guarantee equality for all Americans, regardless of race.

American women's fictional versions of war and peace written during this century also reach beyond the experience of American women only. Fictions written by Agnes Smedley, Adet Lin, and Pearl S. Buck examine the effect of war on Chinese women while the writings of Dorothy Canfield Fisher, Helen Mackay, and Kay Boyle focus on European women's encounters with war during the first two world wars. The short stories of Toni Cade Bambara, Diana Chow, Evelyn Lee, and Gloria Oberst document the tragic effect of war on Southeast Asian women.

Visions of a nuclear holocaust are common images in contemporary American women's war writings. These writers anticipate nuclear war as an inevitable consequence of our civilization's uncontrolled aggressive drives and disregard for the future of the planet. The narrator of Grace Paley's "Anxiety" admonishes a young father for his impatience with his young daughter's behavior, warning that hers may be the "last generation of humankind" because "mad men intend to destroy this beautifully made planet" with nuclear weapons (193). The novels and short stories authored by these women envision a world that is bleak and barren with few, if any, survivors. In one representative novel, The Last Day: A Novel of the Day After Tomorrow, Helen Worrell Clarkson McCloy (as Helen Clarkson) details the destruction of earth over a duration of six days following a nuclear explosion. The last survivor on earth who narrates the novel carefully records her experiences and accompanying emotions as the number of survivors dwindles day by day. At last she is the only human left who bears the guilt of her generation for breaking the chain of life in a careless act of self-destruction.

While American women have written about war throughout this century, they have also authored novels and short stories in which peace is a dominant theme. Utopian fiction, which originated during the nineteenth century, continues as an enduring vision of what life might be like in an idealistic society where war is considered a barbaric, antiquated notion, and cooperation and harmony have replaced aggression and violence. While some of these writers envision separatist all-female utopias, others such as Mary Alice White and Charlotte Perkins Gilman, picture a restructuring of society where men and women share the best of their respective traits and dwell in peace.

The overwhelming majority of women who have published war fiction during this century have written in the tradition of realism, striving to portray war and its pervasive effects and aftereffects as accurately as possible. World War One fictions authored by Helen Mackay and Dorothy Canfield Fisher present a realistic portrayal of the war experience in Europe among the "plain men and women in whom the horrors and crises of an invaded homeland uncovered new strength of spirit" (Washington 160). Fiction written by women during the first two world wars frequently has autobiographical roots originating from the experiences of American women who visited or lived in Europe during these war periods. World War Two literature, especially the fiction of the Holocaust, attempts to recreate the war experience in realistic detail. During this war period the writings of Martha Gellhorn also introduced the genre of journalistic fiction into women's war literature.

During the second half of the century experimentation and innovation have become more evident in the war fiction written by women. Many of these women have rejected traditional form and content as too confining for their expansive interpretations of war which often move both backward and forward in time while moving far away from the parameters set by traditional realism. Authors such as Catherine L. Moore, Ursula K. Le Guin, and Alice Hastings Sheldon (as James Tiptree, Jr.) have often written in the science fiction genre which seems especially appropriate for war fiction, when applied to the definition offered by Jacqueline Pearce in her essay "Feminist Utopian Vision and Social Change." She writes: "Science fiction literature in particular invites us to imagine what it would be like to be in a very different situation, to feel and think within a different reality, and to question ideas we may have accepted as given" (50).

The common thread which binds together this diverse body of literature is the consistent reminder that women as well as men are victims of war, whether or not they are exposed to direct combat. The mother in Della Thompson Lutes' World War One novel My Boy in Khaki who would rather go to war herself than send her son to his possible death but cannot because of her gender is a victim of war. The war wife in Dorothy Parker's World War Two story "The Lovely Leave" whose life constricts in lonely isolation while her husband's expands in the camaraderie and heroism of war is a victim of war. The Japanese mother in Edita Morris' Seeds of Hiroshima who leaps to her death from a mountaintop with her infant son, born deformed from atomic radiation exposure, is a victim of war. The Holocaust survivor of Susan Schaeffer's Anya whose recollections of her war experience, even years later, are replayed instantly "like scenes from a movie" is a victim of war. The wartime prostitute in Pearl S. Buck's "Duet in Asia" trapped between Korean and American cultures is a victim of war. The nurse in Patricia Walsh's Forever Sad the Hearts who feels her "humanity draining from me like the sweat that trickled down my extremities" during the war in Vietnam is a victim of war. The mother in Carol Amen's "Testament" who buries two children and awaits the inevitable death of her third child as well as her own resulting from nuclear fallout is a victim of war. All of these fictional characters exemplify how pervasively war affects women, whether they play an actual part in the war effort or stand waiting on the homefront.

Most importantly there is an unspoken thread of commonality among most of these novels and short stories expressing the belief that war is a manifestation of our own inadequacies as human beings to live together cooperatively. More and more, it seems, we resort to armed conflict to solve our differences when human negotiations fail, and violence has become an expected outgrowth of our indifference toward the value of life. Jean Bethke Elshtain describes the precarious state of our antagonistic existence in her Women and War, as she writes:

> We live today, at the end of the twentieth century, in a world increasingly polarized, between light and dark, between "them" and "us," between women and men, with nuclear war looming as the most terrible form of potential collective destruction, but with group violence occurring all over the world, always with one justification or another. (3)

In her biography Daybreak, Joan Baez predicts that if planet Earth survives beyond this century, historians of a more peaceful time will record the twentieth century as an era dominated by violence. She writes:

> Perhaps there will be another century of living things . . . children and green grass, summer insects and old people . . . not a burned-out planet floating about the universe, forsaking as a windy moon crater. If, by God's sudden grace, and a chain of miracles, a new intelligence, and a tremendous effort, we survive the nuclear age and 1967 is a page in some future child's history book, the page might look something like this . . .
>
> "By the middle of the twentieth century men had reached a peak of insanity. They grouped together in primitive nation-states condoning organized murder as the way to deal with international differences. Between 1914 and 1960, one hundred and fifty million people had died as a result of wars and violent revolutions. Some of the larger nations spent as much as 83 percent of the national budget to build weapons which everyone agreed were too destructive ever to be used. In spite of the fact that violence had failed to bring the things that men said they longed for—peace, freedom (which means 'peace and love'), a brotherhood of man, etc., men continued to cling to violence. . . . When the concept of organized nonviolence was first introduced it was, naturally, misunderstood and rejected for many years, its proponents written off as unpatriotic, unrealistic, idealistic, evil, or just plain crazy. . . ." (148 – 149)

If we can begin to understand why war has been such a pervasive force in our culture, only then can we begin to understand ourselves and hope for peace. As the wise Chinese father in Pearl S. Buck's "The Courtyards of Peace" tells his son-in law, peace is a state of mind that comes from within, that must be discovered by each individual for himself. But peace is not a passive process. Just as war "as armed conflict between nations shades into civil war and wars of liberation and then into violence and its control in society, and finally into individual violence," as explained in the introduction to My Country is the Whole World, "peace is something more than mere absence of war. Peace has to be sought actively" (4). In her essay "Pacifying the Forces: Drafting Women in the Interests of Peace," Sara Ruddick theorizes that if peaceful women were drafted into military service and joined forces with "reluctant male soldiers," the violence of war might be abated. In Vietnam, she points out, "we occasionally saw that while one can lead an army to battle one cannot always might it fight" (487). But unless peaceful women are put in positions of power traditionally dominated by men, she concedes, "it is unlikely that reluctant solders or even reluctant generals will change war policies" (487). Women's most promising opportunities for cultivating peace are within pacifist organizations, she proposes. "Given the extreme dangers posed by our violent state," Ruddick writes, "we should cultivate any resource for peace. Appealing to women on the basis of their peacefulness, organizing them in traditional care for others but with clear transforming self-respect, seems good for women and promising for peacemakers" (489).

In her essay "Women and War" Janna Thompson traces women's peace efforts to ancient Greece to the period when the Greek poet Aristophanes pictured the women of Athens withholding sexual favors from their husbands until these men made peace in his play Lysistrata. Throughout history, she points out, the question has been raised of "whether women, because of an aversion to war, might not sabotage the war effort of their country by discouraging their men from participating, or by not offering them encouragement and moral support" (64). During this century Thompson contends that American involvement in wars has given American women more independence and "an entry into public life," both of which can benefit peace efforts. While men have served in combat roles, women have competently assumed traditional male roles left vacant on the homefront and have become more active in effecting social and political changes. She elaborates:

> The developments associated with the requirements of modern war have meant not only the entry of women into public life, but also the transformation of the domestic concerns of women into public concerns. Education, welfare, childrearing, care of the sick and the old are no longer merely private family concerns, but have come to be regarded as matters of social concern and subjects of political decision-making. Family life has become more and more open to public scrutiny and control, and the domestic has become the political. (74)

Thompson believes that as American women become more involved in all areas of political life, their influence "will help to alter the nature of social organizations and make them less prone to hatred and violence" (74). As the writings included in this bibliography indicate, twentieth century American women's involvement in instigating social change and shaping our thoughts concerning war and peace can be literary as well. A genre once considered primarily male is being reshaped by alternative visions offered by women writers.

The young Japanese war victim in Edita Morris' The Seeds of Hiroshima considers her suicidal leap a "gift of peace" to the women of the world in hopes that her self-sacrifice will awaken women who will "cry out" worldwide in active protest against war. The vast majority of writings included in this bibliography represent American women's attempts to understand war, and thus the nature of ourselves, through literature with the tacit hope that understanding may be the first step toward establishing a lasting peace on earth. Their writings too may be considered "gifts of peace."

Sources:

Baez, Joan. "History Book." Daybreak. New York: Dial Press, 1968. 148 – 149.

Cambridge Women's Peace Collective. Introduction. My Country is the Whole World. London: Pandora Press, 1984. 1 – 9.

Cooperman, Stanley. World War One and the American Novel. Baltimore: Johns Hopkins Press, 1968.

Coulter, Hope Norman. Introduction. Civil War Women: American Women Shaped by Conflicts in Stories by Alcott, Chopin, Welty and Others. Eds. Frank McSherry, Jr., Charles G. Waugh and Martin Greenberg. Little Rock: August House, 1988. 7 – 11.

Dougall, Lucy. War and Peace in Literature: Prose, Drama and Poetry which Illuminate the Problem of War. Chicago: World Without War Publications, 1982.

Elshtain, Jean Bethke. Women and War. New York: Basic Books, 1987.

Enheduanna. "Lament to the Spirit of War." Women on War: Essential Voices for the Nuclear Age. Ed. Daniela Gioseffi. New York: Simon and Schuster, 1988. 199 – 200.

Hallowes, Frances. S. Women and War: An Appeal to the Women of All Nations. London: Headley Brothers, 1914.

Hayton-Keeva, Sally. Introduction. Valiant Women in War and Exile. San Francisco: City Lights Books, 1987. i – iv.

Khan, Nosheen. Women's Poetry and the First World War. Lexington: University Press of Kentucky, 1988.

Lee, Mary. Preface. "It's a Great War!". Boston: Houghton Mifflin, 1929. vii – viii.

Myerhoff, Barbara. Foreward. The Woman Who Slept With Men to Take the War Out of Them. By Deena Metzger. Culver City, CA: Peace Press, 1978. v – viii.

Pearce, Jacqueline. "Feminist Utopian Vision and Social Change." Alternatives. 16.3 (1989) 50 – 54.

Piercy, Marge. "Of Arms and the Woman." Harper's Magazine. June 1987: 30 – 31.

Ruddick, Sara. "Pacifying the Forces: Drafting Women in the Interests of Peace." Signs: Journal of Women in Culture and Society. 8.3 (1983): 471 – 489.

Sappho. "To An Army Wife in Sardis." Women on War: Essential Voices for the Nuclear Age. Ed. Daniela Gioseffi. New York: Simon and Schuster, 1988. 249.

Sauber, Dorothy A. "Historical Context/Literary Content: Women Write About War and Women." Thesis. Hamline University, 1988.

Thompson, Janna. "Women and War." Women's Studies International Forum 14.1 – 2 (1991): 63 – 75.

WAR AND PEACE
THROUGH
WOMEN'S EYES

1

World War One

INTRODUCTION

Considered one of the catastrophic turning points of the twentieth century, World War One marked the end of one long-standing literary and historical cycle and the birth of another. In her novel <u>A Son at the Front</u>, Edith Wharton pictured the threatened defeat of France as the subsequent demise of the entire western civilization, a belief that indicated just how strong American cultural ties were with Europe during the second decade of the century. The cultural history of both Europe and America would never be the same after the war as Americans would struggle to establish their own cultural identity independent of Europe. Those who lived during the war period of 1914 – 1918 "witnessed the collapse of four empires, the slaughter of nearly ten million men, the imposition of state controls on public opinion and the economy, the emerging horror of war as an industry employing a nation's entire population, and radical transformations in all aspects of society," events that rendered all things unstable (Johnston 1). In his <u>Heroes' Twilight, a Study of the Literature of the Great War</u>, Bernard Bergonzi characterizes the war as one that "started as a war to end wars, but instead it pointed forward to the totalitarian state, to an even greater war and a concept of unlimited conflict in which not merely uniformed armies but whole populations, down to the smallest child, are regarded as appropriate victims for destruction on a scale that makes the slaughter on the Somme appear ordinary" (222).

Writers of the postwar years would wrestle with these events in an effort to define the war and the changes it wrought for society in literary dimensions. While men's writings would emphasize the combat experience of this country's first technologically sophisticated war and the disillusionment that became so pervasive following the war, women would offer literary interpretations of the war unique to their own experiences either on the homefront or behind the scenes in relief work— experiences often overlooked in the traditional male-dominated canon of war writing. Women's fiction would emphasize the reaction of civilians under stress experiencing the twentieth century's first major conflict.

Much of the literature of World War One written by women has autobiographical roots. Katherine Anne Porter's <u>Pale Horse, Pale Rider</u> is based, in part, upon the author's illness with influenza which almost resulted in her death near the end of World War One. Dorothy Canfield Fisher, Willa Cather, and Edith Wharton all lived in Europe during at least part of the war. Edith Wharton was active in establishing humanitarian and relief efforts even before the United States officially entered the war. While writing descriptive essays of life in wartime France, she also distributed medical supplies to ambulances and hospitals (Price 96). Dorothy Canfield Fisher was also exposed to the gruesome details of war while working as a relief worker in France. Her experiences were later fictionalized in the novel <u>The Deepening Stream</u>. Assuming the character of Matey Gilbert, Fisher realizes and admits to readers that although she has been exposed to the brutality of combat while administering to the wounded, she can never totally comprehend the experience of soldiers who have been to the front—men who remain so curiously silent in their attempt to hide their pain and memories of war. Instead of attempting to recreate the experiences of these soldiers in her war fiction, Fisher turned her attention instead to depicting the strength of character of the French civilians she observed and their attempts to endure a war fought on their own homeland. In her short stories Fisher "focused her attention on plain men and women in whom the horrors and crises of an invaded homeland uncovered new strength of spirit. The series of sketches that make up her two war books display a search for the springs of strength in these ordinary people" (Washington 160).

Even before the United States entered World War One, American writers of both genders espoused the French cause. To Edith Wharton, France exemplified the epitome of western culture, and her writings reflect a strong sense of moral responsibility toward saving France and subsequently, the civilized world. The authors of these writings depict the French as a courageous and enduring people, even in defeat. In Dorothy Canfield Fisher's "The Permissionaire," a French soldier returns from the front to find his home has been destroyed by the Germans and all the trees and vines of his garden have been "neatly, dexterously murdered and their corpses left hanging on the wall as a practical joke" (304). As he and his family begin plans to rebuild what war has ravaged, sprouts start to appear above the soil. The soldier's wife testifies to her own strength and optimism as she points out the evidence of life reborn to her husband, proof that "what was in the ground alive they couldn't kill" (301). Three other short stories written by Fisher—"What Goes Up. . .," "La Pharmacienne," and "France's Fighting Woman Doctor"—pay tribute to French women whose exceptional strength sustains them through the adversities of war.

Although Willa Cather and Edith Wharton both visited the front, neither was able to accurately portray the male combat experience in their novels, often criticized as sentimental and naively simplistic with their unrealistic depictions of technological warfare and trench life. Claude Wheeler, the martyred hero of Willa Cather's <u>One of Ours</u>, and Troy Belknap, the heroic protagonist of Edith Wharton's <u>The Marne</u>, never really reach realistic proportions. Both remain romantic characterizations of heroic fantasy and agents of propaganda for their creators.

Several short fictional narratives included in Helen Mackay's Chill Hours relate the experiences of women who served in various medical capacities during the war. These women learned they had to develop an emotional distance to endure the continuous cycle of suffering that became their daily task during war. During the height of the military campaign at the Battle of Verdun, the resilient doctor in Dorothy Canfield Fisher's "Frances Fighting Woman Doctor" administers to 18,000 wounded soldiers during the span of one week. To one nurse in Mackay's "The Cauldron," the continuous storm of nameless casualties eventually seems to blend into one, their wounded bodies "coming and going, going and coming, until sometimes it seems that all these men are just one man to whom these things happen eternally, round and round" (96). While Matey Gilbert experiences a "certainty of wholeness" as a relief worker in Dorothy Canfield Fisher's The Deepening Stream, Anne Wentworth's nursing experiences in Mary Lee's "It's a Great War!" leave her with a frustrated bitterness and sense of alienation while she tries to reintegrate into civilian life following the war. Life becomes a "plate of soup, grown cold" for this young woman who witnesses a myriad of war's behind-the-scenes horrors.

The women characterized in these novels and short stories often make discoveries about themselves revealed through their individual encounters with the adversities of war. The women prisoners portrayed in Dorothy Canfield Fisher's "What Goes Up . . ." discover a life-sustaining strength inside each of themselves that thrives through their communal support and enables them to endure the dehumanization of prison camp experience. The introverted protagonist in Katharine Gerould's "A Moth of Peace," who has never experienced war during her young lifetime, is forced out of her hibernation in a French manor and must choose either surrender or direct confrontation with the approaching Germans. She discovers within herself the will to venture forth into the unknown with confidence, unaware of what her first encounter with the enemy will bring. The protagonist of Alice Hegan Rice's "The Reprisal" discovers she is incapable of taking the life of another human being—even the life of an enemy she claims to despise—when an opportunity arises for revenge. The elderly French woman personified in Frances Huard's "Mademoiselle Prune" chooses to endure the social ostracism of her community rather than reject the "enemy"—a polite, young German officer—she has befriended. Each of these women experiences growth and self-awareness through her experiences.

The homefront experience of women left to manage by themselves while their husbands are at war is a recurring theme in this body of fiction. Madeleine Brismantier, a sheltered middle-class wife in Dorothy Canfield Fisher's "La Pharmacienne," makes the first major decision of her life on her own when war invades her village. She refuses to leave, despite the invasion of the reputedly brutal Germans, delivers her third child by herself, and resolves to rebuild her husband's ransacked pharmaceutical business. Women characters in several of Dorothy Canfield Fisher's wartime sketches learn to manage their family farms and households alone while their husbands are at the front, often repressing their needs as women and forgetting their roles as wives, even as their husbands return. The stifling condition of the homefront wife is especially vividly illustrated in Dorothy Canfield Fisher's "On the Edge." With only meager resources and six dependent children, the female protagonist of this story comes close to the edge of insanity when she foresees no relief from the stressful monotony of her daily survival routine other than her husband's cherished letters from the front.

Women writers of the World War One experience also explore the effect of war on women's relationships with men. While the separation of war strengthens some relationships, it can also be a divisive factor, as these writings suggest. The husband and wife in Dorothy Canfield Fisher's "Their Places" become so estranged by their respective experiences while he is away at war and she is managing their homestead that he forfeits one of his furloughs rather than face another awkward reunion. Similarly, the wife in Fisher's "Second Hay" views her husband's short leave from military duty more as an opportunity for him to help her harvest the hay crop than a chance for the two of them to reestablish their marital relationship. Only as her husband is about to leave once more does she realize—and then regret—her misguided priorities. Yet the husband and wife in "La Pharmacienne," also written by Fisher, grow closer as they mourn the destruction of their homestead and make a mutual commitment to press forward and rebuild where war left off.

Mother-son relationships form the basis of several novels and short stories of the World War One era written by women. The prevailing sentiments of American mothers toward their soldier-sons is presented in Anne Douglas Sedgwick's "Hepaticas." As the stalwart mother in this story sends her son off to war, she faces the possibility of his death as a widow might accept her husband's, acknowledging that if he does return, it will be "a gift of grace, unexpected and unclaimed" (47). When her son fails to return, this mother assures herself he has died gloriously, freeing himself from the burden of the future, which is now fully hers to bear. Della Thompson Lutes offers a more realistic portrayal of a mother's ambivalent feelings toward her son's military duty in the novel My Boy in Khaki. While she approves of her son being "Over There" doing his duty to "deal out justice," she admits she also longs for him to be at home, safe from the "treacherous enemy." Although this mother tries to reassure herself that thousands of soldiers throughout history have "come back unscathed from the bloodiest wars," she recognizes that even if her son does return, he will surely leave his innocence and boyhood spirit behind on the battlefield. For the distraught mother in Hetty Hemenway's "Their War," the romantic lure of the battlefield finalizes the alienation which has been building between mother and son ever since he erected a barrier of self-absorbed aloofness around himself during his adolescent years.

The effect of war on children's lives is also a dominant theme in this literature, illustrated brilliantly in Fanny Kemble Johnson's "The Strange Looking Man." In this story a three-year-old boy who has never lived during a peaceful time screams in terror at his first glimpse of a "whole man" who lacks the scars and deformities of war that he has associated with the male gender all of his life. The young boy in Madeleine Z. Doty's "Little Brother," like many European children, is left orphaned and homeless by war, while the children in Dorothy Canfield Fisher's "Their Places" shy away from their returning father whose role as a soldier of war makes his return home seem strangely awkward and disruptive to their lives.

While these writings illustrate that children are not immune to the war experience, they also indicate how children can be a source of strength for many survivors of war. The overburdened mother in Dorothy Canfield Fisher's "On the Edge" who comes close to the edge of madness raising six children alone while her husband is away at war also derives renewed strength from the realization that the future of these children depends upon her own will to survive. The birth of a child in Fisher's "What Goes Up . . . " represents an affirmation of life for women prisoners of war determined to survive the concentration camp experience.

These women novelists and short fiction writers also explore beneath the surface of the experiences of combat soldiers in search of the human being who exists behind the uniform. Margaret Applegarth portrays a sensitive American pilot in "Every Mother's Son of Them" who so poignantly regrets his killing of a skilled German pilot in retrospect that he writes the soldier's mother a letter of consolation, begging forgiveness. Susan Boogher presents a nameless soldier in "An Unknown Warrior" whose love of poetry and beauty resurfaces while he visits the peaceful Westminster Abbey, giving him reassurance that the literary and philosophical dimensions of his life have miraculously remained unblemished despite the ugliness of war which has interrupted his life. Helen Mackay characterizes the human nature of soldiers in "The Nine and the Ten" who are willing to put aside social class distinctions while they fight side by side during wartime but allow their prejudices to resurface once the threat of war is removed. Toni Morrison sensitively portrays the dilemma of a veteran in Sula who returns from the trauma of war uncertain of who or what he is and suffers from the ostracism of unsympathetic civilians who merely regard him as insane.

For several women writers, these novels and short stories provide a forum for political discussion that ranges from antiwar in authorial attitude to unquestionably supportive of American involvement in the war. The fine distinction between what is literature and what is propaganda often becomes blurred in these writings. In his essay "Edith Wharton's War Story," Alan Price points out that it was not uncommon for American authors to turn from fiction to propaganda to boost support for war charities. This altered the complexion of literature produced by such writers as Wharton, for whom the war was most unsettling, as Price explains:

> The convergence of historical forces that temporarily transformed Wharton from an ironic social novelist into a partisan war reporter provides one of the few moments in her life when she was not in control of what happened. The war was not just a shock; it was a catastrophe that threatened anyone's ability to make a world. For a

novelist who made fictional worlds and for a woman who created aesthetic spaces, the loss of control was potentially devastating. (96)

The integration of literature and political commentary is evident in such works as Ellen La Motte's "Civilization" which questions whether a society that wages war can consider itself civilized and Dorothy Canfield Fisher's "It is Rather For Us To Be Here Dedicated" which questions if war ever justifies the loss of life. The protagonist of Mary Lee's "It's a Great War!" becomes so cynical she begins to wonder if war is actually a game designed by men to eliminate life and thus "even the score" with women whose role has traditionally been to continually bring forth new life into the world. If this scheme is true, she concludes, then women should put an end to war by refusing to give birth anymore. The French women in Fanny Kemble Johnson's "The Strange-Looking Man" vow not to bear any more children because they fear if they have sons, they will be sent to war and return "limbless and mad" like so many veterans of this war. Women characters in Eleanor Clark's "Call Me Comrade" actively protest the war despite the imprisonment and social stigma that results from their public demonstration.

In a few of these writings, war is portrayed as a glorious adventure—a chance for young men to prove themselves heroic in battle, or at least achieve manhood, as the novels of Willa Cather and Edith Wharton illustrate. Members of a lower-class family in Mary Brecht Pulver's "The Path of Glory" gain overnight respect and self-esteem for the first time in their lives when their soldier-son's death in Europe instantly elevates their social reputation in the community. The cobbler in Margaret Sherwood's A World to Mend echoes the prevailing American attitude during this time period that war was a justified means to quell the force of the Germans ravaging Europe and preserve freedom for western civilization. Ellen Glasgow depicts the conflict as a war "not of materials, but of ideals" deeper than nationality in her political novel The Builder. A soldier in Dorothy Canfield Fisher's "Vignettes from Life at the Rear" justifies the carnage of war as a necessity for the beginning of a new, more cooperative world when he states:

> "When a mother gives birth to a child, she suffers, suffers horribly. Perhaps all the world is now trying to give birth to a new idea, which we have talked of, but never felt before; the idea that all of us, each of us, is responsible for what happens to us all . . . " (75)

Della Thompson Lutes ends My Boy in Khaki with a vision that embodies the attitude of the majority of American women during World War One who saw themselves as necessary to the war effort but secondary in importance to the men they chose to follow: "Guns booming and shells bursting alone the fighting-line; men sweating, men dropping, men bleeding, men dying. And behind them, close behind them, rank upon rank and file upon file, are women; women feeding, women nursing, women clothing, women cheering" (194).

Only two of these authors present a non-traditional vision of women as direct participants of war. Curiously, the fictions written by American women which place women in combat roles depict European—not American—women as warriors. Francis Wood's "The White Battalion" visualizes French women avenging the loss of their dead husbands in battle while Gertrude Atherton envisions the women of Germany rising in arms against male domination and continued warfare in their country in her novel The White Morning.

Wood and Atherton are among a small minority of American women whose fictional interpretations of the World War One experience deviate from the tradition of realism. Alice Brown's supernatural fantasies, "The Flying Teuton" and "Empire of Death," which include images of phantom ships and charging trees, are also nontraditional in approach. Much of Katherine Anne Porter's Pale Horse, Pale Rider is written in an innovative stream-of consciousness style that uses dream sequences as its major structure. But these experimentations with fiction are rare exceptions to the realistic novels and short stories which dominate this genre.

The novels and short stories authored by American women, which differ from men's literary interpretations of the World War One experience in their perspective and treatment of war, emphasize the human condition battered and anguished by the war experience. At the center of most of these fictions are women characters who are either left on the homefront or join the war effort behind the front lines working in various capacities— women who may not actually experience combat in the traditional sense but nevertheless experience war—the loneliness, the pain of separation, the anxiety of daily uncertainty, the burden of responsibility, the fear of the unknown, the pain of loss. The characters in these stories are represented above all as human beings caught in the storm of war who retain their humanity and dignity despite the ignominy of the situation imposed upon them by war, whether that be through surviving concentration camp, facing an unknown enemy, giving birth alone, or celebrating the re-emergence of life symbolized by sprouting leaves among the ruins. These writings celebrate the strength and persistence of women whose encounters with war have been largely overlooked by male writers of the World War One era but nevertheless deserve critical attention as a documentation of women's experiences and attitudes toward this catastrophic event which changed the course of history and literary thought.

NOVELS

1.   Atherton, Gertrude.   The White Morning.   New York: Frederick Stokes, 1918.

In this novel Atherton fantasizes a war within a war, waged by the longtime subservient but dissatisfied German women against their warring male comrades in the midst of World War One. Feeling restless and betrayed by the promises of their male leaders for a short, triumphant war that has instead dragged on for more than three years and caused widespread malnutrition and starvation among their children, these once passive women, inspired by the feminist movement for equality in the United States, band together to stage a revolution that will end both war and inequality among the sexes:

> They have suffered too much at the hands of men. They have no illusions left. Love and marriage are ghastly caricatures to women who have lived in a time when men are slaughtered like pigs in massed formation; when their little boys are driven to war; when young girls—and widows!—are forced to bring more males into the world with the sanction of neither love nor marriage; when those too young for the trench or the casual bed of any but legal dominion is over. (96)

These women are in an ideal position to stage a revolution, for they now outnumber the men of Germany and have assumed key positions in industry, including German munitions factories. And who would expect women to revolt—these silent females who have accepted their subservient roles without protest for so long?

Gisela Doring, chosen leader of the revolution, puts country and womanhood above her personal desires and stabs her own lover through the heart as he sleeps to begin the war: "A gallant gentleman, a brave soldier, and a great lover had the honor to be the first man to pay the price for his country's crime, on the altar of the Woman's Revolution" (134). For Gisela the revolution that is won is also paradoxically lost, for the "sacrifice of life that gave meaning to her own" leaves her ultimately alone with her victory.

The revolution envisioned by Atherton is not a peaceful one; nor is it without bloodshed. Entering the factories, these traditionally non-aggressive females "made a concerted rush and disposed of the terrified offenders as remorselessly as their own men had punished the desperate civilians of the lands they had invaded" (148). The women of Germany do not hesitate to use the same violence usually associated with male soldiers in order to make sure their revolution succeeds.

Atherton, who lived in Germany for several years, based her novel on the subservience of the German women she witnessed first hand. In the afterword to the novel, entitled "The Women of Germany: An argument for my The White Morning," she writes of the German female population: "These women have lost their fathers, sons—well, that is the fortune of any war; but they are beginning to understand that they have lost them, not in a war of self-defense, but to gratify the insane ambitions and greed of a dynasty and a military caste that are out of date in the twentieth century" (191). Although Atherton acknowledges that no German male would believe "in anything so unprecedented as German women taking the law into their own hands, uniting, and overthrowing a dynasty," she dismisses the idea that the content of her novel is totally unrealistic:

"No one knows what the future holds, or what unexpected event will suddenly end the war; but I should not have written The White Morning if I had not been firmly convinced that a Gisela might arise at any moment and deliver the world," she writes (195).

A review of The White Morning published in The New York Times Book Review describes the novel as "a book—a dream, maybe a prophecy perhaps!". Although the novel is "powerfully pro-Ally," the reviewer writes that Atherton's work also simultaneously "celebrates Germany—a Germany asleep, cowed, downtrodden, but full of tremendous powers, the Germany of its women" ("The War in England" 1). A White Morning foresees the undeniable force of women who have been wearied by the sacrifices of war and visualizes a better society based upon gender equality and peace.

2. Cather, Willa. One of Ours. New York: Alfred Knopf, 1922.

Winner of the 1923 Pulitzer prize, One of Ours was Cather's fifth novel and the one which severed her link with earlier novelists such as Henry James and built a new kinship with later writers who were concerned with postwar alienation and lost values such as Ernest Hemingway and F. Scott Fitzgerald. "At the moment when (Jon) Dos Passos and his followers in the cult of experience were making the Great American Novel something that a woman as noncombatant could never write," Frederick T. Griffiths points out in his essay "The woman warrior: Willa Cather and One of Ours," "Cather reasserted the great tradition of war narrative as the province of artists more than of warriors" (263). Although One of Ours is generally recognized as one of Cather's least successful novels artistically, receiving mixed reviews from literary critics, it is considered one of her most significant in terms of social commentary. The novel won Cather the Pulitzer Prize, Elizabeth Shepley Sergeant theorizes in Willa Cather: A Memoir, because it stood in contrast to many of the much bleaker postwar novels published at the same time. She explains:

> In her story there are a few smelly corpses, but no profanity, no sex no rebellion no chaos are even hinted at. Avaricious French peasants, whom we used to hear of during the First World War, as exploiting our doughboys, are absent. Instead, we meet comprehending French people of the upper and lower bourgeoisie. The sense of order, veracity, and *politesse* are such that the army as an institution is fully upheld, and Claude's fulfillment in heroic death suffers no disillusion, till the last pages and sentences of the book.
>
> This is no doubt, why Willa Cather received the Pulitzer Prize for One of Ours. Thousands of American parents and many American veterans, too, saw the rewards of their sacrifices here displayed gloriously. The intellectual and more humanly or philosophically conscious, veteran found the war narrative "off the beam." (181)

In World War One and the American Novel, Stanley Cooperman finds One of Ours valuable "not so much as a treatment of war, but rather as an examination of particular psychological needs which helped fashion the bold journey into war" (136 – 137).   For Claude Wheeler, going to war is a personal necessity, not a political one—an alluring escape from the rigidity of midwestern farm life, adolescent restlessness, and a sterile marriage (Cooperman 129).   At war Claude's life takes on a new, more meaningful dimension.   "The army, the war, and France combined to give Claude the youth he never had" (Brown 225).   As Claude becomes enamored with both the "virility-through-violence" experience of war and the simplicity of rural French life, he concludes that for the French "to be alive, to be conscious and have one's faculties, was to be in the war" (416).   He dreams of living in France once the war ends, disengaging himself from American society, which he criticizes as emotionally shallow and overly dependent upon technology and monetary gain.   But Claude is killed in combat before his dreams have a chance for fulfillment.   As his mother reads the letters that keep arriving after his death, Cather speaks through her, raising the "disquieting question of whether idealism can, after all, survive in the modern world" (458).   Claude's mother, echoing the beliefs of the author, concludes it was better for her son to have died with his "vision" than to return to a "terrible disillusion" that has driven other returning war veterans to suicide. The hopes and beliefs Claude discovered in France "may enable one to die meaningfully, but they do not enable one to live" (McFarland 60).

In her thesis "The Mud in God's Eye: World War One in Women's Novels," Tamara Jones points out that like many women during the World War One era, Claude's mother wanted to believe the war was noble because her son was a part of it.   As a woman, she was sheltered from many of the horrors of a war fought so far away.   It was not until the soldiers began to return home that the truth became clear—the war had solved none of Europe's problems and had left a generation of young men bruised by devastating disappointment that war was not the heroic adventure they had envisioned (60).   The ending of One of Ours, writes Jones, "manages to capture the particular disappointment of thousands of women who hoped that the War would be a quick one, and that it would finally eliminate war, that incomprehensible institution that had always threatened their sons and sons-to-be" (60).

One of Ours presents "a minutely balanced symmetry of peace and war" with its two distinctive parts which take place on American and later, European soil, Griffiths explains (268).   While Claude fails to find the garden of Eden he is searching for in Nebraska, he paradoxically discovers a pastoral paradise in the "waste land of France." "To a large extent," Griffiths writes, "the two parts of the novel exist in the mode of paradox: To fulfill his Americanness— that is, to have purpose and usefulness—Claude must discover and die for France. The culturally exhausted New World somehow finds renewal in the Old.   The disintegration of family life in Nebraska is compensated for by the army as (for Claude, at least) a nurturant community" (269).

The character of Claude originated in G. P. Cather, one of Cather's cousins killed in World War One combat. His letters written to his mother during the war first inspired Cather to write One of Ours. While she was writing the novel, Cather remarked, "I always felt it was presumptuous and silly for a woman to write about a male character but by a chain of circumstances I came to know that boy better than I know myself" (Sergeant 172).

The writing of One of Ours represented the beginning of Cather's feelings of estrangement from modern American life that were to grow more acute as she grew older (Brown 226). If war is glorified as heroic and the reality of combat softened in her prose, this flaw in her writing reflects both her limited knowledge of technological warfare and lack of exposure to life in the trenches. The novel also strongly reflects her criticism of what she termed the American "gadget civilization," a society she felt was too dependent upon machinery and too oblivious to pastoral beauty.

3.   Doolittle, Hilda. Bid Me to Live. New York: Grove Press, 1960.

Written by the American expatriate poet H.D., this highly autobiographical novel recalls the lives of those of the lost generation —the "war generation" as H.D. describes them—adrift during wartime in London, 1917 when relationships were ephemeral and values seemed to hold little permanence. Several times during the course of the war Doolittle repeats: "The war will never be over," as if a life of uncertainty and unrest has become a permanent state of being. The all-encompassing nature of war as it impacts on the novel's main character, a fictionalized version of H.D., is evident in this passage: "It was allright in the beginning. But as the war crept closer, as it absorbed everything, the thing that bound body and soul together seemed threatened, so that she seemed to tune-in to another dimension. . . " (60).

Titled after the first line in one of Robert Herrick's seventeenth century British poem "To Anthea," Bid Me to Live is a "poet's novel, an avant garde piece of literature," according to reviewer Horace Gregory (31 – 32). "It is a work of rare art that has caught and preserved the essential spirit and atmosphere of the First World War," he writes (32). Although Bid Me to Live was not published until 1960, the writing of the novel began shortly after World War Two, "when suddenly everything came back to me," H.D. explained during an interview. "In a sort of intense state I wrote it off" ("Life in a Hothouse" 92).

4.   Fisher, Dorothy Canfield. The Deepening Stream. New York: Harcourt, Brace and Company, 1930.

This highly autobiographical novel was written ten years after the end of World War One. By that time, writes biographer Ida Washington, Dorothy Canfield Fisher "was able to see the intense pain of the war years and the troubled postwar period—together with the earlier conflicts of her childhood home—as parts of a larger life experience and to give this new understanding fictional form" (97). Although the novel traces Fisher's life from early childhood on, it is in the second half of the book, set in wartime France, where Fisher (characterized as Matey Gilbert in the novel) experiences "personal and social maturation against the backdrop of war" (Washington 99). As a relief worker Matey discovers in herself a "certainty of wholeness" while her pacifist husband, who drives an ambulance during the war, becomes more severely disillusioned as the war progresses, even to the point of voicing regret that Matey and he brought children into a world which condones warfare. In her thesis "The Mud in God's Eye: World War One in Women's Novels," Tamara Jones explains the transitions that Adrian and Matey undergo as they both encounter war for the first time:

> By the end of The Deepening Stream, both Matey and Adrian are despairing; but Matey, who before the War had to be shown life by her husband, now has life to give back to him, who can see nothing but waste and horror. . . .
>
> Matey, too, tries to make Adrian realize that life has not disappeared; it has only gone underground. Like the stream of the title, the sources are still there, but deep, and it is the women who are able to tap them. (77 – 78)

While serving in France, Matey begins to understand that as a woman her encounters with war are vastly different from those of combat soldiers. Although she is exposed to the horrors of war through her relief work, Matey realizes that she cannot fully comprehend or internalize the feelings of soldiers who have been to the front—soldiers who remain so curiously silent with their memories and pain. It is not until the end of the war when the intensity of life begins to slow down that Matey is able to gradually distance herself and view the war more objectively.

Eventually she comes to the despairing conclusion that war is actually a form of murder, and that with her contributions as a relief worker, she has personally contributed to war's cycle of death and destruction by keeping murderers alive:

> She had drugged herself to unconsciousness of what they were all doing by the traditional woman's narcotic of small personal services. She had assumed to the fighting men she knew the domestic relation of sister and mother and so had seen them, as sisters always see their brothers and mothers their sons, as victims, never as the butchers they punctually took their turn at being. (355)

The Deepening Stream is significant both as a fictionalized account of one life of an American fiction writer who experienced war as closely as any woman during World War One and an analysis of a woman's maturation against the background of war.

5.   Glasgow, Ellen. The Builders. Garden City: Doubleday, 1919.

Ellen Glasgow's first political novel, considered one of her least successful, reflects the prevailing political thoughts of many Americans as the United States entered the first World War. Americans, writes Glasgow in the novel, "realized that this was a war not of men, not of materials, but of ideals—of ideals which are deeper than nationality since they are the common heritage of the human race. . . . The cause was the cause of humanity, therefore it was America's war" (23). The national interest surpassed any personal or regional interests men and women may have had, uniting the country as never before. War "has done what nothing has been able to do before—it has made us one people," declares Caroline, the female protagonist of The Builders. The impending war and America's entrance into it allows Glasgow the opportunity for a theoretical analysis of the war within the framework of the novel. The adamant nationalistic beliefs expressed by several characters are undoubtedly her own, reflective of a time when war was viewed as a moral obligation for a higher cause than individual need. Glasgow's novel also reflects how war affects male-female relationships and their attitude toward the permanence of their relationships as well as the moral standards governing them. War imposes its own set of ethics based upon the urgency of the moment.

6.   Lee, Mary. "It's a Great War!". Boston: Houghton Mifflin, 1929.

Co-winner of the Houghton Mifflin award for the best novel of World War One, this lengthy novel was written by a woman who served with a French hospital unit during the war. In his review Herschel Brickell commends the novel as the first that "undertakes to tell the truth about war from the point of view of a noncombatant who remained behind the lines. . . " (3). The novel "is also distinguished," he writes, "by the fact that Miss Lee carries her story into the occupation of German territory and even into the post-war period in America" (3).

Using an episodic, staccato rhythm of prose which reproduces the stream of consciousness thoughts of the protagonist, a rhythm which the author felt matches the natural rhythms of war, Lee relates the feelings and reactions of a young woman who trades her cultured American home for the mud of France and experiences "the gigantic bewilderment of those days in France, the seamy and sordid and disillusioning side of war, the bitterness and waste of life" (Wallace 459). Anne Wentworth's experiences reinforce Lee's assertion, voiced in the preface to the novel, that the "Chief Protagonist" of any war novel is "always war itself, with its stupidity, its carelessness of human life" (vii). Anne's increasing pessimism and realization that war has permanently altered her perspective of life and childbirth are evident in this passage from the novel, also illustrative of the staccato rhythm of the narrative:

> How could things look the same? Anne did not feel the same. Knew she would never feel the same, as long as she lived. . . . She ate the cold food, chewing the hard grease. What did food matter: If only shoes were not so hard to pull off. . . . Feet, swollen. . . . That did not matter, either. . . . Stretchers full of men, men with names lost, identity gone from them. . . . Men crying out, clutching with lonely hands at darkness. . . . Men suffering. . . . Women suffered, through the centuries, to bring men into this crazy world. . . . Was it by War that the score of suffering between man and woman evened up, then? Women ought not to have children. . . . That would stop it. . . . Men, dying, in agony, alone there. . . . (246)

Like thousands of other men and women who served during the war, Anne loses her youthful idealism as the war begins to assume a variety of metaphors, all of them disparaging. World War One, for her generation, becomes "a great war, a great carnage, a shambles, and a universal crucifixion of the highest and noblest of their youthful emotions" (Gilman 2). At the war's end, Anne attempts to bury one life and assimilate herself back into an alien civilian life that seems meaningless and empty compared to the intensity of her life during war. She has become a misfit who cannot relate with civilians whose lives during the war retained a sense of normalcy while hers took such a deviant turn into a far-removed world that defies explanation for those who have never been there. "Life must be somewhere," she keeps insisting to herself, but seems so distant now. "Life, a plate of soup, that had grown cold. . . . Without salt. . . . There had been hot soup, once. . . . And salt, that War put,—Go on!" (661).

Lee's novel, writes Harry Hansen, "brings home to every one the smells, the indecencies, the obscenities, the incongruities that are a part of war," making it "pertinent propaganda against war" (17). Although literary critics of the day generally lauded the realistic contents of the novel, many found fault with the excessive length (250,000 words) and confusing, jerky style. Anticipating that her novel might be criticized for its length and style, Lee defended both characteristics of her writing in the novel's preface:

> A book with the war as a background cannot be a short book. For those who are in it, war is interminably long, and only a long book can create the impression of interminable length. Those who lived through the war in Europe have lived two lifetimes: one the lifetime in France; the other, that connected existence which took place before they went and resumed its pace after they came home. A book about war cannot move smoothly, swiftly. War moves in jerks. Jerks which consist in moments of intense excitement, punctuated by hours and weeks and months on end of boredom. A book which would

picture war faithfully must not fail to give that alternating sense first that living has become more real, more vivid, and then that the whole pace of life has been made suddenly sluggish and dull. Nine-tenths of war is waiting. A book which eliminates the waiting, eliminates nine-tenths of what the people who go to war live through. (9)

7. Lutes, Della Thompson. My Boy in Khaki. New York: Harper and Brothers, 1918.

This novel examines a mother's ambivalent feelings when her son heads to war for the first time. Although she tries to convince herself—and readers—that it is a mother's patriotic duty to let her son go gracefully, the narrator also recognizes the loneliness of separation and fear for her son's fate as he faces combat at the age of 19. Although, like many mothers, she would willingly take her son's place in battle in order to protect his life, she accepts the fact that as a woman she cannot. Remembering that her son's interest in hunting died quickly after he shot only one rabbit, she consoles herself that in battle he "will not destroy except to save" (11). And she optimistically reminds herself of his favorable odds for survival: "Men, thousands of them, do come back unscathed from the bloodiest wars" (104). Although he may survive, this mother also realizes that her son will undoubtedly shed his youthful innocence at war. Even if he should return physically, her young son will never return in spirit, his carefree nature "shut into the past along with childish things, while the soul of the Man is called forth, full stature, to take its place" (22). Ambivalent emotions keep tormenting her resolve to remain strong as she battles her own conflicting feelings toward her son, now a soldier: "My blood runs cold—and hot. I want my boy at home—safe from danger and the barbarous cruelties of that treacherous enemy—and I want him Over There helping to deal out justice. I should even prefer to be with him" (58 – 59). Despite the "thrill of newly stirred patriotism" felt as the first American soldiers parade by, bound for Europe, she admits that she is among many American mothers who undoubtedly feel lost at the moment "reeling about in a world that holds no familiar landmarks" (11).

The novel includes letters flowing to and from mother and son, the son's letters carefully worded to avoid any revelation of truth about combat life, dwelling instead on innocuous small talk and reassuring platitudes carefully chosen so as not to further disturb an already worried mother. Her letters—and thoughts expressed in the text—are much more honest than his in their representation of the concern, grief, confusion, and anxiety of war mothers who watch their sons march off into the unknown and must live with the uncertainty of their return. Although her moods vary throughout the novel—wavering between patriotic sacrifice and maternal protectiveness of her only son—ultimately it is her firm religious commitment (she takes offense at those so disillusioned with the world at war to declare that "God is dead") and equally strong anti-German sentiment prevalent during the time—which sustains

her through her son's military service. The novel ends with a vision
which embodies this mother's acceptance of women's expected roles
in war and acknowledges the importance of their supportive strength
as they join soldiers in the march of war:

> Women behind and men at the front. That is the line of action.
> Long lines of stern, determined men, marching, marching,
> marching across the trampled fields of France to where the
> very soil groans and heaves and belches forth its ghastly
> secrets beneath a shocked and saddened Heaven. Behind them
> long lines of brave, unflinching women marching, marching,
> marching—to whatever duty may befall their hands; nor
> thought of rank or station, ease, or fine accustomedness.
>
> Guns booming and shells bursting along the fighting-line;
> men sweating, men dropping, men bleeding, men dying. And
> behind them, close behind them, rank upon rank and file upon
> file, are women; women feeding, women nursing, women
> clothing, women cheering. (193 – 194)

Lutes offers a realistic analysis of a mother's varied feelings and
emotional defenses as her son parts with his youth and innocence
and sheds his childhood dependence upon her as he goes to war. The
novel portrays the vacillation between logical rationalization of
maternal duty and sensitive outcry of emotion which women on the
homefront must resolve who give up their sons to war.

8.   Sherwood, Margaret. A World to Mend. Boston: Little, Brown and
Company, 1920.

Written in a journal-diary format, this novel records the experiences
and philosophical contemplations of a middle-aged New England
cobbler during the last two years of the war. Although Wentworth
Masters condemns war in general as "savagery" and wonders if we
are nearing the "end of civilization, dying as Rome died" as the
penalty for our predilection for war, he rationalizes America's
entrance into World War One as a necessary means to end all
war and preserve freedom as well as "our faith, and the integrity of
home and family" (333). He records his justification of American
involvement in the war in his journal:

> The fact that we of America had long outgrown war is no
> reason for shirking our responsibility of helping save for
> mankind that liberty which we have won for ourselves.
> Growth is an uneven thing; progress is an uneven thing, yet
> the marching host must go together; we cannot leave behind
> those who have struggled and fallen from the line. They who
> retard, as Germany does now, retard the whole; they who drag
> down drag down the whole,—for a time only, for certain
> months and days. (259)

Masters envisions an idealistic world free of war based upon a foundation "of understanding and sympathy and trust between man and man," a society based upon the worth of human souls instead of "material and mechanical progress" (15). According to a reviewer for The New York Times Book Review, Sherwood's novel affirms "that the virtues which required war for their evocation in man, that is, the unity of human brotherhood, the sense of fair play, heroism, and altruistic regard, all these are more important in the battles of peace than in those of war" ("A World to Mend" 23).

9.   Wharton, Edith. The Marne. New York: D. Appleton, 1918.

As both literature and propaganda, this novel combines "gentility with bloodthirst," as Stanley Cooperman writes in The American Novel and World War One, and "the mannerisms of the social novelist with the matter of a recruiting poster" (41). Although the novel voices a strong antiwar sentiment (Wharton describes war at one point in the novel as "an unfathomable thing that suddenly escaped out of the history book like a dangerous lunatic escaping from the asylum"), her sense of loyalty toward the preservation of her adopted country, France, which she considered the apex of all that is cultural, was much stronger (9). Her endorsement of the war effort is evident in this passage from the novel describing the United States' entrance into the war: "America tore the gag of neutrality from her lips, and with all the strength of her liberated lungs, claimed her right to a place in the struggle. The pacifists crept back into their holes. . ." (45).

Wharton's feelings of obligation toward the defense of France are exemplified in the symbolic character of Troy Belknap, a young American who spends much of his boyhood in France and later longs impatiently for his eighteenth birthday to arrive so that he can join the Allied cause. In France Troy serves as an ambulance driver but becomes more directly involved in the war effort when faced with an unexpected opportunity to test his courage in combat, personifying the possibility for heroism at war which lured many young American males to volunteer for the war effort.

Critics have pointed to Wharton's oversimplification of the issues involved in World War One and her inability to distance herself from her subject in order to write more objectively. Fueled by her "passionate Francophilia" and fear for the survival of Western civilization under attack by the barbaric Huns as she wrote The Marne, Wharton's "artistic taste, detachment, and skill were temporarily, but fully, eclipsed by her passionate engagement in the Allied cause" (Buitenhuis 497). If Wharton's views in The Marne are considered naive and sentimental, as most critics would agree, it should also be remembered that her opinions are reflective of an era when women were sheltered from the reality of war and pro-Ally sentiment was extremely strong. Wharton wrote out of a sincere conviction that civilization was in danger and war, no matter how repugnant, was justifiable to insure the protection of France and ultimately, the continuation of civilized mankind.

10.   Wharton, Edith. A Son at the Front. New York: Scribners, 1923.

Wharton first conceived of the idea of this novel in 1917 but felt she could not objectively deal with her emotions toward war until time had distanced her from it. She began writing the novel five years later but even then, she recalls in her autobiography, A Backward Glance, she found herself writing "in a white heat of emotion" (369). In neither A Son at the Front nor The Marne was Wharton able to separate her emotions from her artistry. A Son at the Front was written during a time when the lost generation was coming to maturity and novels of disillusionment, such as Jon Dos Passos' Three Soldiers and E. E. Cummings' The Enormous Room, were considered representative of novelists' retrospective views of the great war. Ironically, as Tamara Jones discusses in her thesis "The Mud in God's Eye: World War One in Women's Novels," "Instead of moving from optimism and patriotic fervor to a dark cynicism as most war novels do, A Son at the Front reverses that movement" (48). The protagonist's initial opposition to war "changes to a conviction that the War is a noble and necessary one" as the novel progresses. Although Wharton may have been ahead of her time with the feminist viewpoints expressed in her prewar novels, the attitudes expressed in her two World War One novels placed her behind the times, as Ann Maret Jones explains in her thesis "Three American Responses to World War I: Wharton, Empey, and Bourne":

> Far ahead of the times before the war, she was left behind in the immediate post-war years. Her problem was not so much that she held positions untenable in themselves, as her critics so often seem to think; her beliefs were almost always remarkably logical and consistent, but she so often held them before others had taken them up or, more fatally, after they had been discarded. (81)

A Son at the Front focuses on a father's struggle to resolve his conflicting loyalties to his son and to his adoptive country, France. John Campton's two passions in life are his art and his son; both are threatened by the war. When his attempts to prevent his American son from conscription in the French military fail, he immerses himself in self-absorption of his work, disregarding the war outside. Gradually his attitude changes from artistic aloofness to a strength of conviction that no one can ignore the gravity of the crisis at hand:

> Yes, they were all being swept into it together—swept into the yawning whirlpool. Campton felt that as clearly as all these young men; he felt the triviality, the utter unimportance, of all their personal and private concerns, compared with this great headlong outpouring of life on the altar of conviction. (397)

In her thesis "The Cultural Legacy of World War I: A Comparative Study of Selected War Novels," Judith Lynne Johnston explains that Campton's vacillation between neutrality and endorsement of the war effort "mirrors the intense crises many parents suffered when the demand to sacrifice their children put to the test their belief in the war aims" (205). Through Campton, Wharton was "able to create a feeling of terrible pathos in the situation of a man who has to see his son fight and be killed in what he believed for a long time to be another country's war" (303). "Another country's war" becomes symbolic of the combined Allied effort to withstand the threatened destruction of the culture of Europe. Campton (voicing Wharton's convictions) comes to believe that "if France went, western civilization went with her, and then all they had believed in and been guided by would perish" (133 – 134). Despite the changes resulting from the war, this novel shows that Wharton still embraced a romantic vision of Europe she hoped war would sustain, but hers would prove to be "a defiant yet hopeless stand against the course of history" (Clough 13).

SHORT FICTION

11. Applegarth, Margaret. "Every Mother's Son of Them." And So He Made Mothers. New York: Richard R. Smith, 1931. 89 – 90.

This short narrative explores the feelings of a soldier who realizes in retrospect there is a human being much like himself behind the "enemy" he has killed and the emotions of a soldier's mother who must accept the loss of her son. Regretting his actions, an American pilot composes a letter to the mother of the German aviator whose plane he has shot down. "I suppose I'm his enemy," he writes. "Yet I'd give my life to have him back. I didn't think of him or of you when I shot at his machine. . . . He handled his plane magnificently. I thought how I should like to fly with him. But he was the enemy and had to be destroyed" (89). In a return letter of forgiveness, the German mother assumes part of the guilt of the war because she is a woman as she writes: "To women brotherhood is a reality. For all men are our sons. That makes war a monster, that brother must slay brother. Yet perhaps women more than men have been to blame for this world war. We did not think of the world's children, our children" (90). In both characters of this story, readers glimpse a nontraditional view of war—the soldier who regrets his supposed heroic feat when he realizes the enemy is some other mother's son, just as he is—and the mother who is able to grant forgiveness and look beyond her personal loss to view war in a more global sense as a needless loss of many sons who should be united in "oneness" instead of divided by armed conflict.

12. Boogher, Susan M. "An Unknown Warrior." Best Short Stories of 1922. Ed. Edward J. O'Brien. Boston: Small, Maynard, and Company, 1923. 42 – 48.

An unnamed soldier in this narrative reaffirms that his personal values have remained unchanged despite his war experience when he makes a tranquil visit to Westminster Abbey. In the dim and quiet of the peaceful Abbey he comes to the conclusion that war is an "interruption, a suspension, a holding of one's breath" in his life while the intangibles that mean the most to him—"poetry and beauty"—have been preserved, unaltered in their purity by his three years of "mud and blood." Imagining himself as a medieval knight, he becomes a warrior "for poetry and peace—tranquility like the silence here in Westminster, where dreams unfold" (44). Boogher's short story demonstrates that the literary, contemplative side of man can survive despite the trauma of the war experience, if given the opportunity and atmosphere to awaken.

13.   Brown, Alice. "Empire of Death." The Flying Teuton and Other Stories. New York: MacMillan, 1918. 48 – 68.

In this supernatural fantasy, narrated as a story within a story, a German and American soldier, once friends before the war, meet once again on a European battlefield where Hugo, who has chosen to fight on the German side, has been slain and the narrator lies injured. The narrator, a writer and fruit tree farmer, abhors the wholesale destruction of life and property the Germans have reaped upon the European continent but objects most strongly to the "arboricide" he witnesses—the unnecessary butchering of trees "by the hundred sawed two-thirds through and then broken down, split, mangled, murdered" (59). In their imaginary conversation Hugo defends the part he has played in the murder of men and trees as his military obligation to follow orders as instructed. The trees soon rise in retaliation, chasing the two young soldiers who have entered a "hell of trees." The trees, writes the narrator, "ran beside us, they pursued us, they waved their branches—it was their own volition, mind you—there was no wind—they outran us and beckoned us on, they pelted us with blooms that hurt like ice-pellets and suffocated like wool. It seemed millions of years that we were running—for we ran fast now, as if we spurned the undergrowth, ran through the air—but never, never could we outrun the racing trees" (67). The two men eventually part, Hugo back to his death as the narrator returns to life, carrying with him this haunting vision of a hell only war could create.

Brown explores the effect of war on friendships and allegiances in this story. She also uses the bleak imagery of slaughtered trees rising in retaliation to criticize the German "empire of death" for its indiscriminate destruction of life in all forms.

14.   Brown, Alice. "The Flying Teuton." The Flying Teuton and Other Stories. New York: MacMillan, 1918. 1 – 23.

In this fantasy tale, World War One has ended, and Germany has been granted the right to trade internationally without penalty as before the war under the terms of the final peace agreement. But a "higher Power" intervenes on the high seas, offering divine retribution for the sins of the Germans. Using the technique of a story within a story, a newspaper correspondent aboard the first commercial German liner to sail the Atlantic following the war recalls the haunting sensation when he learned he was aboard an invisible vessel, through which other ships could pass without recognition or harm. He explains:

> "We were invisible on the seas. We were practically non-existent. . . . We were marooned—if you can be marooned on the high seas. Civilization had put us on an island of silence and invisibility. Civilization wasn't going to play with us any more. But it wasn't civilization at all. It wasn't any punitive device of man. It was something outside." (10)

In the course of his story, the journalist-narrator explains the irony and justice of this bizarre phenomenon. Although German ships have been given "full possession" of freedom of the sea under the peace terms, just as before the war, they are ironically unable to use this freedom, for there is not "a port on the surface of the globe that could receive them" in their invisibility (20). They have no recourse but to head back to Germany. Although the German fleet eventually gains visibility, one submarine is left as a lone wanderer of the seas, permanently condemned to invisibility as a warning for the future "against pride and cruelty and lust of power."

15. Clark, Eleanor. "Call Me Comrade." New Letters in America. Ed. Horace Gregory. New York: W. W. Norton, 1937. 151 – 169.

This narrative visualizes a union of women who band together to publicly protest against the war, despite the risk of antagonizing those who might view them as radical and outspoken. Although they are jailed for staging their protest on private property, these women rise above the indignity of imprisonment in a communal spirit that is strengthened by their antiwar convictions. Their strong commitment to peace also erases the class barriers which would have otherwise socially segregated these women. For each woman, there is a price to pay for her public protest against war, as Dorothy A. Sauber explains in her thesis "Historical Context/Literary Content: Women Write about War and Women":

> For some of the women their public protest had cost them their dignity. For others it had cost them their livelihood. Miss Knowlesworth represents the many women who have devoted their lives to the pursuit of peace through organizing and speaking out publicly in protest. Miss Hinckley represents the women who perhaps only once in their lifetime feel the empowerment of community with other women in organized action. The women are comrades in this story because of their common belief that peace requires of each and every one of them a personal commitment to speak out against war. (142)

16.   Cook-Lynn, Elizabeth. "Loss of the Sky." The Power of Horses and Other Stories. New York: Arcade Publishing, 1990. 7 – 11.

The grief of an Indian father for his son killed in combat is illustrated in this war narrative. Seven years before his tribesmen become official United States citizens, the Dakotah Indian in this story loses his middle (of five) sons to a white man's war in distant Europe. Joseph views "the marauding German armies and the war clouds hanging over the capitals of Europe" with indifference until Teo enlists in the Army and lands on the shore of France with 14,000 other troops during the summer of 1917, never to return (9). "Joseph kept the paper which told of his son's bravery and his death and that his body would not be coming back. It was the last part of that message which made Joseph an old man" (10). Mourning for the loss of their son, Teo's mother cuts her hair and clashes her legs, never to wear pretty beaded shawls and bright moccasins and hair pieces again while his father grows old before his time and indifferent to life. Cook-Lynn writes:

> The old man seemed somehow compelled to sit and gaze into the distance, as if he might see Teo, tall and straight in the saddle, the middle son, the finest rider anywhere around, come over the rise, his arm lifted gently in greeting.
>
> Joseph seldom went into the hills to pray and sing anymore, but when he did, he never failed to weep that the bones of his son, the middle son, the finest rider anywhere around, could not mingle with the bones of his grandfathers. (11)

17.   Doty, Madeleine Z. "Little Brother." The Atlantic Monthly. April 1916: 461 – 465.

The plight of children tragically orphaned by war is told in this story within a story. A young Belgian lad flees with his newborn sister, at the request of his mother, while German forces advance toward their village. While his sister only survives three days, despite her brother's solicitous care, he learns that everyone in his village has been slaughtered and his father killed at the front. "Little Brother" illustrates how children are involuntarily swept into the turmoil of war and often left alone in their attempt to survive.

18.   Fisher, Dorothy Canfield. "The Day of Glory." The Day of Glory. New York: Henry Holt and Company, 1919. 139 – 149.

In this short narrative Fisher describes the ecstasy of the moment when the armistice was signed and peace was declared for France:

> The war was over. The accursed guns had ceased tearing to pieces our husbands and our sons and our fathers. . . . The horrible weight on the soul that had grown to be a part of life dissolved away in that assuaging flood; the horrible constriction around the heart loosened. We wept with all our might; we

poured out once for all the old bitterness, the old horror. We felt sanity coming back, and faith and even hope, that forgotten possession of the old days. (140)

The "dreadful past" and inevitable "terrible problems of the future" are put aside as Fisher describes a scene of French citizens converging onto the streets, integrating as one large family in celebration of long-awaited peace.

19. Fisher, Dorothy Canfield: "France's Fighting Woman Doctor." The Day of Glory. New York: Henry Holt, 1919. 39 – 88.

This is a narrative portrait of Dr. Nicole Girard-Mangin, "mobilized and sent to the front by mistake," who spends two years of the war administering to wounded soldiers, sustained by her "coolness under fire, her steadiness under overwhelming responsibilities, her astonishing physical endurance. . ." (86). Separated from her 14-year-old son for the first time, Dr. Girard-Mangin follows her brother into military service. "This is no place for a woman" is the initial reaction of the all-male regiment to her arrival, followed closely by the more rational afterthought and mutual plea: "But, good God! if you know anything about surgery, roll up your sleeves and stay!" (44). Stay she does, according to Fisher's account, witnessing as many as 18,000 wounded passing through the hospital in one week following the German invasion of Verdun. Fisher's portrayal is of a woman who rises above gender distinctions to serve her country in a traditionally male capacity during a crisis when survival necessitates the setting aside of customary peacetime conceptions of women's roles.

20. Fisher, Dorothy Canfield. "A Honeymoon . . . Vive l' Amerique." Home Fires in France. New York: Henry Holt and Company, 1918. 227 – 258.

This is a sketch of French war victims in need and a rich, benevolent American couple who spend their honeymoon in France financing humanitarian projects. A war widow who loses both son and husband in the war and opens her home to war orphans is one recipient of their generosity. Describing how war has affected her existence, the widow says: "It is the punishment we have called down on ourselves. I see now that the war has only intensified everything that existed before, it has *changed* nothing fundamentally. We were living as hideously in a state of war before as now, except that it was not physically bloody" (249). In the midst of so much unhappiness, Fisher describes the honeymoon couple as "possibly the only happy human beings left" (258).

21. Fisher, Dorothy Canfield. "It Is Rather For Us To Be Here Dedicated." The Day of Glory. New York: Henry Holt and Company, 1919. 133 – 137.

In this narrative Fisher contrasts the tragic sight of an American soldier lying dead in a golden wheat field with the comparative triviality of life that continues to dominate the concerns of civilians despite the presence of war—a rich French woman complains of bon bon deprivation, an alcoholic lies passed out on a park bench while another young man eagerly checks the stock market report—each seemingly oblivious to the war at hand. Contrasting the American soldier to the countryside surrounding his body, "ghostly quiet after the four-days' din of battle," Fisher writes: "Compared to his stillness, the wheat stalks, broken and trampled as they were, seemed quivering conscious life; the trees, although half-shattered by shell-fire, fluttered their bright leaves, wounded, mutilated, disfigured, but they had survived. They were alive. Only the soldier had not survived" (133). Fisher questions if his—and other lives lost at war—have been given in vain to a cause that seems unjustified.

22. Fisher, Dorothy Canfield. "Lourdes." The Day of Glory. New York: Henry Holt and Company, 1919. 89 – 103.

This short narrative is a description of an annual pilgrimage to a famous shrine of healing at Lourdes. Many of the "pilgrims" are wounded victims of war in search of physical and spiritual healing and a renewed faith in humanity at a time when mankind's inhumanity is so glaringly obvious.

23. Fisher, Dorothy Canfield. "Notes from a French Village in the War Zone." Home Fires in France. New York: Henry Holt and Company, 1918. 1 – 26.

Fisher sketches a poetic illustration of a typical prewar French village that has changed little during the past century and continues to fascinate American visitors with its pastoral charm. The tranquil character of the small village changes overnight with the advent of war and infiltration of soldiers outnumbering the inhabitants, who try to "make themselves small, move over to the edge, and make the necessary room" to accommodate their troops (22). Underlying this descriptive narrative are the unspoken questions dominating the author's mind: In what ways will war change—or even destroy—this village? Will its unique character ever be the same? Will peace ever return to this and so many other villages identical to it throughout France?

24. Fisher, Dorothy Canfield. "October, 1918." Raw Material. New York: Harcourt, Brace, and Company, 1923. 255 – 264.

"October, 1918" provides a comparison of three generations of Americans toward war. A member of the oldest generation believes that "without the soldier in every man (and that means love of force and submission to force—you must swallow that!) there would be no order in the world. . . . There would be anarchy in the twinkling of an eye" (258). A younger woman, whose generation is still at war, anticipates a pacifist world to emerge that will have outgrown war.

She objects to a display of cannons in Paris the older man admires, denouncing the cannons as "hideous instruments of torture," symbolic of a barbaric era she would hope is now past tense. A third generation—her own children playing in a park—fantasize the overthrow of ancient monarchies by ordinary people thirsty for freedom. To this generation, war is but innocent play-acting, the brutal consequences still far beyond the capacity of their youthful comprehension.

25. Fisher, Dorothy Canfield. "On the Edge." The Day of Glory. New York: Henry Holt and Company, 1919. 3 – 38.

This is the portrayal of one woman's solitary war on the homefront to save her sanity as she attempts to cope with single-parenting six children living in one room. This French woman does daily battle with limited heating resources, inadequate food and clothing, inflated war prices for basic necessities, and the always hovering threat of death for her soldier-husband. The only event sustaining Jeanne through the monotonous struggle for survival each day is the arrival of the postman and the possibility of a letter from her husband. "It was the only moment of the day when she felt herself wholly alive" (17). At times when Andre's letters are infrequent, Jeanne feels herself drifting "over the edge," near madness with the anxiety of uncertainty and burden of homefront responsibilities which she must bear alone. When her husband returns unexpectedly from the front for only a few hours' leave, she worries later that the wonderful interlude and confirmation of love and life was only a hallucination of her distraught frame of mind and considers suicide as an escape from her misery. But like many war wives, Jeanne's will to live is preserved by the thought of the future of her children—the innocent victims of an adult-made war who would suffer needlessly even more should they lose their mother as well: "In all that was left alive of her, she knew that she must try to go on living for the children. She turned her back on escape, and in a spiritual agony like the physical anguish of childbirth, she put out her hands to grope her way back to the fiery ordeal of life" (36). This narrative describes with realistic detail how war affects women and children who wage their own domestic battles for physical and emotional survival and attempt to cope with the adverse changes wrought by war, always uncertain if and when the hardships will all end.

26. Fisher, Dorothy Canfield. "The Permissionaire." Home Fires in France. New York: Henry Holt, 1918. 27 – 59. Reprinted as "In the Eye of the Storm." A Harvest of Stories. New York: Harcourt, Brace, and Company, 1927. 289 – 308.

This story recounts with realistic accuracy the plight of the French left homeless following the German invasion which ravaged their country. With similar accuracy, Fisher's writing also grasps the determined strength and persistence of the French people to survive the ignominy of war with their dignity and self-respect still intact.

A French soldier granted a three-week furlough heads home not knowing if his family or home still remains. The Germans have reportedly taken prisoner all women under the age of 45 and placed them in munitions factories while they have devastated the French countryside. Although Nidart's home is in ruins, he discovers that his family is still alive. It appears that his beloved garden, too, has been spared until he looks closer to find that all the trees and vines "had been neatly and dexterously murdered, and their corpses left hanging on the wall as a practical joke. . . . He felt something like an inward bleeding, as though that neat, fine saw had severed an artery in his own body" (304). During his leave he and his wife sustain each other's strength with plans for rebuilding what war has taken away. Sprouts start to appear through the loosened earth. "You see," his wife points out to Nidart. "I told you what was in the ground alive they couldn't kill!" (301). At times Nidart slips into a depression of self pity, convinced that his family will never regain its self respect "which had been ravished from them, which the ravishers still enjoyed." Although a part of him longs to give up the struggle to survive, "something deeper than his conscious self was at work. The tree had been cut down, but something was in the ground, alive" (301). With mutual support and love for their land, Nidart and his family begin the slow, tedious process of rebuilding what they have lost until all too soon he must trade his rake for a gun and return to the front as a soldier once more.

27. Fisher, Dorothy Canfield. "La Pharmacienne." Home Fires in France. New York: Henry Holt, 1918. 259 – 306. Reprinted as "Through Pity and Terror." A Harvest of Stories. New York: Harcourt, Brace, and Company, 1927. 261 – 288.

In this narrative Fisher portrays the courage and independence of a French woman, accustomed to the comforts of middle-class life and protective hand of her husband, who must face adversity and make her own life-dependent decisions during the war for the first time in her life. When Germany assaults France during the summer of 1914, Madeleine Brismantier's life takes a dramatic turn away from her accustomed comfort and security. Alone she faces the protection of her two children and the delivery of her third child with the threat of invading German troops—reputed to be harsh and insensitive—close at hand. As families make a mass exodus from Mandrine, Madeleine too must decide to flee or stay: "Madeleine wrung her hands, walking up and down the room, literally sick with indecision. What ought she to do? It was the first great decision she had ever been forced to make alone" (266). Although she and her children are unharmed by the invading Germans, they destroy her home, ransacking and plundering the contents of it and her husband's pharmacy. Once the Germans leave and the streets of Mandrine are quiet once more, the women of the town begin organizing and rebuilding, assuming the roles their husbands at war once occupied. Madeleine vows to restore her husband's pharmacy and reassemble her shattered life with the newly discovered competence she has gained independently as her only support.

In a letter to editor Paul Reynolds, Fisher described the character of Madeleine Brismantier as "a Frenchwoman, typical nice, housekeeper, good-mother variety, who is hard hit by the war, living in the war-zone, and is little by little transformed out of being a house-cat, into being one of the stern, unconsciously heroic obscure heroines of France" (Washington, 159).

In her thesis "The Mud in God's Eye: World War I in Women's Novels," Tamara Jones refers to this story as an example of a war narrative in which Fisher "has combined many of the unique qualities of women's writings on the War—"the recognition of social injustices on 'the home front,' the new abilities that many women discovered during the War, the strength and confidence that using those abilities encouraged, and the importance of creating and caring for life" (85).

28.   Fisher, Dorothy Canfield. "The Refugee." Home Fires in France. New York: Henry Holt, 1918. 111 – 131.

A French woman recounts life under German occupation in this narrative as "a nightmare similar to an unimaginably huge roller advancing slowly, heavily, steadily, to crush out our lives" (114). Her recorded experience describes the repression, suspicion, dehumanization, and hopelessness that characterized French existence during the German occupation. Although the proud French never wept in front of the Germans, the refugee remembers that a nearby insane asylum "was filled to overflowing with new cases of madness" spreading among the French citizenry during that time (131).

29.   Fisher, Dorothy Canfield. "Reunion." Taken at the Flood: The Human Drama as Seen by Modern American Novelists. Ed. Ann Watkins. New York: Harper and Brothers, 1946. 184 – 191.

In this excerpt from the autobiographical novel The Deepening Stream, Fisher focuses on the feelings of a woman anticipating her husband's first furlough from driving an ambulance at the front. Matey wonders if she will ever recognize her husband (the days since his departure seem to have been transformed into years) and fears that their separation may have changed the intimate closeness they once enjoyed.

> From his letters, it had been evident that he had been profoundly affected by what he saw at the front. Perhaps he had grown away from her, would feel that her wildness of longing for him was grasping and personal, indecorous in the midst of tragedy. In a flash she imagined him grown like his father, old, remote, disembodied, beyond passion, beyond her, lost to her. . . . (190)

But Adrian's experience at war has not diminished his feelings for his wife, for he approaches her when they are alone for the first time since his homecoming "trembling like a bridegroom," allaying all of her imagined fears (191).

30. Fisher, Dorothy Canfield. "Some Confused Impressions." The Day of Glory. New York: Henry Holt and Company, 1919. 105 – 132.

Fisher offers contrasting impressions of war, from both American and French soldiers' and civilians' viewpoints in this narrative. An elderly French couple whose village has been destroyed still desires to return home even under shell-fire to save what they can of their crops. Young American troops yet to see the front look forward to combat experience with romanticized idealism. A young war widow accepts her loss with "courage and steadfastness," grateful the war has spared her daughters, if not her husband. Walking amid fresh graves in a nearby cemetery, Fisher notes the irony of a large monument's inscription—"Love ye one another"—with the hatred that characterizes war. The sacrifices often demanded by war seem too harsh and unjustifiable.

31. Fisher, Dorothy Canfield. "Vignettes from Life at the Rear." Home Fires in France. New York: Henry Holt, 1918. 60 – 83.

These short character sketches depict several varied perspectives on war. Narrated first is a one-armed soldier's "heartsick desolation of the uprooted exile, the disintegrating misery of the home-loving man without a home" who cannot go back to the trenches but doesn't know if he has a family or home to return to either (61). Next, Fisher presents an effervescent soldier whose "good-natured acceptance of the present insane silence of the universe" seems curiously incongruous to the story's narrator. A first-line stretcher-carrier of three years spares none of the graphic horror of war as he recounts his experiences and bitterly resents the complacency of many civilians. He describes himself as a "rat in a hole, surrounded by other rats putrefying" and confesses: "When I come back to Paris on furlough and look at the crowds in the Paris streets, the old men with white collars, and clean skins, the women with curled hair and silk stockings, I could *kill* them, when I think that they will have a voice in the future, will affect what will be done hereafter about war. . . " (73 – 74). His brother, who has undergone similar experiences, justifies the carnage with an abstract philosophical rationalization:

> "When a mother gives birth to a child, she suffers, suffers horribly. Perhaps all the world is now trying to give birth to a new idea, which we have talked of, but never felt before; the idea that all of us, each of us, is responsible for what happens to us all. . . ." (75)

A glass-blower remains as silent about his experience and humble about his heroism as the stretcher-barrier is vocal. The last vignette is the narrator's own story, the story of a woman weary from many days of administering to so many war blind, who despairs of life in "such a wicked and imbecile world" (81). As she watches her children playing in the sunshine, what she sees instead are the "scarred, mutilated, sightless faces of young men in their prime, with long lives of darkness before them" (81). She experiences a renewed faith however, when she enters a cathedral with her children and recognizes that this magnificent structure is also man's creation:

> Men had made this beauty, imperfect, warring, doubting, suffering, sinning men had upreared this perfect creation. They had created this beauty out of their faith in righteousness, and they would again create other beauty, out of other manifestations of righteousness, long after this war was a forgotten nightmare. (83)

32. Fisher, Dorothy Canfield. "What Goes Up . . . " Raw Material. New York: Harcourt, Brace and Company, 1923. 37 – 68.

"What Goes Up . . ." is a portrait of a group of French women, led by one particularly ingenious one, who survive more than four years in a German prison camp without losing self respect and dignity. Under Octave Moreau's direction and inspiration ("Nobody can help us but ourselves!" she proclaims. "But if we give all we have, they can never conquer us"), these prisoners pool their meager resources and varied talents in a rigorous battle for survival that includes the successful delivery of a new life whose birth becomes a "shout of triumph"—an affirmation of life—for these war-weary women (47). With communal support these prisoners of war find the strength to endure a system designed to break that strength, and return after four years of incarceration "lean and worn and pale, but stronger, better, finer human beings than they had been before," ready to continue their lives where war intervened (66). Fisher's story offers an accurate depiction of the dehumanization of the German prison camp system and an equally realistic analysis of the determined will to survive which sustains these victims of war.

33. Freeley, Mary Mitchell. "Blind Vision." The Best Short Stories of 1918. Ed. Edward J. O'Brien. Boston: Small, Maynard and Company, 1918. 85 – 91.

The narrator of this story wrestles with his conscience and grief after the loss of his best friend at war. Following an airplane crash, Esme is taken prisoner of war by the Germans. To save his own life, Esme finally succumbs to his captors' demand that he fly his reconstructed airplane over western Europe so that the Germans can survey the French and British fronts. When he escapes back to his own unit, however, his best friend rejects him as a murderer and traitor. Esme disappears, leaving a note behind that he intends to cross the German lines "to give them at least my death, since I can no longer offer even that proudly to France" (91). The narrator is left to bear the guilt of his best friend's death and compare his own lack of integrity to Esme's selfless heroism.

34. Gerould, Katharine Fullerton. "A Moth of Peace." The Atlantic Monthly. January 1915: 14 – 24.

Gerould illustrates the way war shatters innocence and idealism as well as the security of peace in this story. An introverted American woman isolates herself from the ongoing war in an old French manor in the Marne Valley while she awaits her British fiancee. As rumors of an imminent German invasion reach the manor, Anne faces the end of her own protected and naive past:

> She must, for life or death,—for honor, at all events,—respond to a situation for which nothing, since her birth, had prepared her. Peace had been to her as air and sunlight—the natural condition of life. This was like being flung into a vacuum; it was death to her whole organism. Yet, somehow, she was still alive. (24)

As Anne tries to mentally prepare herself for her first direct encounter with war, she is strengthened by the natural instinct to survive and the innate courage she has inherited from previous generations. Dismissing the option of surrender, she steps forward confidently to meet the approaching German troops with all the fortitude she can gather propelling her forward for her first unpredictable encounter with the enemy.

35. Hart, Frances Noyes. "Contact." O. Henry Memorial Award Prize Stories of 1920. Ed. Blanche Colton Williams. Garden City: Doubleday, Page and Company, 1921. 23 – 42.

The stress of war upon waiting women on the homefront is vividly illustrated in this story. Succumbing to the stress of uncertainty about her wayward lover's fidelity while he is away at war, Janie begins to hallucinate. As she burns her soldier-lover's letters in an effort to forget him as she believes he has forgotten her, she hears a distant airplane "hovering and throbbing like some gigantic bird" that no one else seems to hear (26). The phantom sounds heard only by Janie continue until she learns that Jerry's own airplane has been shot down and that he will never walk again. This time the "gigantic humming" she has heard grows louder and closer in her imagination, bringing with it a vision of Jerry in which she sets him free in the midst of a storm with the assurance, "Now you can fly!" "Contact" illustrates a bizarre variation of the emotional strains of war on women who cope in their own individual ways with the frustration of uncertainty in their lives and relationships imposed by war.

36. Hemenway, Hetty. "Four Days." The Atlantic Monthly. May 1917: 577 – 593.

"Four Days" shows the strains of war on young, idealistic soldiers encountering the reality of combat for the first time and men and women who are forced to make the most of their limited hours of intimacy during warfare. The young bride in this story recognizes the "numb, dazed look" on her young soldier-husband's face. It is the same look she has seen in the eyes of other young soldiers on their first leaves—"mute young eyes that contained the unutterable secrets of the battlefield, but revealed none" (580). Marjorie wonders about these secrets she may never know because she is a woman:

> What had they seen, these silent youngsters—sensitive, joyous children, whom the present day had nurtured so cleanly and so tenderly? Their bringing-up had been the complex result of so much enlightened effort. War, pestilence, famine, slaughter, were only names in a history book to them. They thought hardship was sport. A blithe summer month had plunged them into the most terrible war of the scarred old earth. The battlefields where they had mustered, stunned, but tingling with vigor and eagerness, were becoming the vast cemeteries of their generation. (580)

Leonard describes himself as one among many robot-like cogs in the wheel of war. As a soldier, he confides to his new bride, "You're just one in a great big machine called England" (582). Marjorie senses in her soldier-husband a groping "for an explanation, an inspiration deeper than anything he had known before—a something immense that would make it all right, this gigantic twentieth-century work of killing. . . " (585). But when his four days of furlough have expired, Leonard leaves for the front with stoic resolution, expecting the same attitude from his fearful wife as he dreams of a possible son-to-come as one of his few comforts.

37. Hemenway, Hetty. "Their War." The Atlantic Monthly. April 1918: 444 – 458.

Hemenway examines war's effect on mother-son relationships in this story. At 17, Edwin immerses himself in adolescent aloofness, slipping away from his mother as he becomes a "curious alien in a far-away country, lonely and rejoicing in his loneliness" (444). When he volunteers for service in the Canadian military, Edwin's mother tries to take advantage of her chance to regain the closeness they shared during his boyhood, but her attempts to approach him are awkwardly ineffectual. Even as he leaves, Edwin "had nothing to say to her but what he would say to a stranger" (451). The only real mother-son bond that survives is her memories of him as a young boy dependent upon her strength and responsive to her affections. War becomes the final wedge solidifying her alienation from her son, whom she has lost to a younger woman and a far-away battlefield that lures eager young men such as Edwin toward the possibility of heroism or death.

38. Huard, Frances Wilson. "Mademoiselle Prune." Lilies, White and Red. New York: George H. Doran, 1919. 9 – 103.

In this character sketch an aging French woman faces two moral dilemmas imposed by war. As the Germans invade and occupy her village, she befriends a wounded young German officer whose gentility and admitted abhorrence of war contradicts the stereotypical image of most German soldiers. As the two forget they are "enemies," Mademoiselle Prune suffers rebuke and ostracism from the community for associating with—and even defending—a German. Mademoiselle Prune faces the dilemma of allegiance to country or to her own feelings. Blaming her predicament on the intrusion of war in her life, a violent disruption of her peaceful routine about which she admittedly knows very little, she defends her actions to the local priest: "It is war with all its hateful consequences; war about which I know nor understand nothing; nor about which all those whom I esteem know aught—save that we must belittle, insult, hate our enemies. I cannot bring myself to this. . . " (43).

A second moral choice presents itself when a French aviator carrying a message to the front seeks refuge in Mademoiselle Prune's apartment to escape the searching Germans. Mademoiselle Prune chooses to lie to the very German officer she has befriended in order to save the life of the French soldier. War—a nebulous idea so far removed from the sheltered life of Mademoiselle Prune—wedges itself into her life as an opportunity to defend both her homeland and way of life:

> War, to her, had always seemed a thing belonging to men and soldiers; a brutal murderous combat caused by political and financial disagreements, of which it had been almost a duty to remain ignorant. Men fought to hamper or promote certain commercial possibilities. To this little woman war had always appeared an impious, cruel, unchristian, detestable proceeding created to satisfy the pride and vanity of mankind.

> Then suddenly a new light had burst upon her. Beyond man's worldly interest stood out the struggle between races and sentiments; between customs and civilisations. (84)

This story demonstrates how women—even those who consider themselves isolated from war—can become unwilling participants of war with difficult moral choices to confront.

39. Hughes, Llewellyn. "Lady Wipers—Of Ypres." The Best Short Stories of 1928. Ed. Edward J. O'Brien. New York: Dodd, Mead and Company, 1928. 166 – 179.

In this narrative a London cleaning woman relates her story of how she momentarily gains fame as "Lady Wipers" when she makes a lone pilgrimage to Wipers to touch the name of her husband engraved on a memorial dedicated to the 58,000 British soldiers who died in combat there, whose bodies were pounded into the soil by German troops and never returned home. Although she was an abused wife whose husband provided no financial income during their brief marriage, she recalls their life together fondly and considers her husband a fallen hero and herself a proud war widow as she continues her menial livelihood and tells her "war story" to anyone who will listen.

40. Hughes, Llewellyn. "The Spy." C'est La Guerre! The Best Stories of the World War. Ed. James G. Dunton. Boston: Stratford Company, 1927. 286 – 306.

The identity—and nationalistic allegiance—of a spy is not revealed until the end of this story where the identity of a female accomplice and admirer who engineered his escape is disclosed as well. The spy who exists under three identities—the French Favieres, the German Von Kedor, and the American Sinclair—comes to realize it is not the military that has determined his fate, and very possibly saved his life—but this mysterious woman.

41. Hurst, Fannie. "Humoresque." O. Henry Memorial Award Prize Stories 1919. Ed. Blanche Colton Williams. Garden City: Doubleday, Page and Company, 1921. 148 – 179.

Hurst compares a mother's grief at her son's parting for war with his commitment to the war cause in this narrative. A musical genius, Leon trades his violin for weaponry as he enlists against his mother's wishes, who feels his musical talent should exempt him from military service. "You wouldn't want me to hide behind my violin," Leon says in defense of his choice to enlist. "Know what I'm fighting for?" he asks his family. "Why this whole family knows! What's music, what's art, what's life itself in a world without freedom?" (175). As Leon leaves for service, his mother mourns his departure as a kind of poetic-musical "rendezvous with death," acknowledging that if he does not return from war, his musical talent will be forever silenced.

42. Johnson, Fanny Kemble. "The Strange-Looking Man." The Best Short Stories of 1917. Ed. Edward J. O'Brien. Boston: Small, Maynard and Company, 1918. 361 – 364.

Four years into the war, the French village depicted in this story has been stripped of all male inhabitants except the very aged, incapacitated (left to starve so that "there might be food for the useful"), and war disabled: "To go through that village after the war was something like going through a life-sized toy village with all the mechanical figures wound up and clicking. Only instead of the figures being new, and gay, and pretty, they were battered and grotesque and inhuman" (362). Many women who live in the village have vowed not to bear any more children because they might give birth to "sons who might one day be sent back to them limbless and mad, to be rocked in cradles—for many years, perhaps" (362). One mother's young son discovers a strange man swimming naked in a nearby mountain stream. Despite the German's attempts to befriend the young boy, he screams as if terrified. His mother attempts to apologize for her son's fear of the stranger. "He is quite small," she explains, "and it is the first time he has ever seen a whole man" (364). This story poignantly illustrates how war can ironically alter what is considered normal and familiar to a child who knows only war and not peace—half-men but not whole.

43. Kalpakian, Laura. "Lavee, Lagair, Lamore, Lamaird." Winter's Tales: New Series 5. New York: St. Martin's Press, 1989. 79 –146.

The 42-year-old St. Elmo, California spinster in this short story travels to France in 1918 to join the war effort as a French translator and do her part to "make short work of the horrible Hun." There, in humiliation, Mabel Judd learns that the governess who taught her to speak French during her childhood actually taught her only a collection of vulgar phrases—"words such as you and I, our sisters, our parents, would never have dreamed of speaking, not if devils sloshed our eyes with burning oil would we have uttered such phrases," she confesses in a letter home to her sister. In horror, Mabel realizes that when she repeated the well-rehearsed phrase "Lavee, Lagair, Lamore, Lamaird" instead of saying "Life, War, Love and Peace," as she was led to believe by her governess, she was actually saying "Life War, Love and Shit" in French. When Mabel is relieved of her translator post, she is arrested and interrogated by both French and American officials until she proves that she is a "victim of a cruel, cruel jest and not an agent of the Hun" (126).

Instead of returning home in "folly and disgrace," Mabel begs for any position available (she even volunteers to "go into the trenches") to allow her to contribute to the war effort. In one of several letters included in the narrative, she describes the duties she has been assigned to her sister in St. Elmo:

> I have no training as a nurse, but need none to do the work they have assigned me. The lowest of the low. I carry bedpans of bloody urine and I wash bloody rags and burn bloodied bandages and boil bloodied scalpels. I beat down beds that men had died in. I throw disinfectant on the floors where they have vomited. I pull the soiled pants from their blasted legs. (127)

Eventually Mabel advances to the rank of nurse. Her letters home continue to describe her weary despair of "this mire of blood and squalor" which has robbed so many young men of their lives. She writes: "The waves of the dead are inexorable and still there is no peace. No life. No love. Only blood and slaughter. *Lagair, Lamaird.* Only those obscenities and shelling and gas and barbed wire and bombs and rockets. It is endless" (132). The obscene combination of words once learned in pure innocence now seems entirely appropriate for the hideous reality of war Mabel has witnessed.

But in the midst of "all this carnage, this colossal wreck of humanity," a miracle unfolds for Mabel. She meets her future husband—a British soldier "gentle by nature, who has lost his arm, but not his soul" (143). The vulgar combination of words again resurface with new significance: "*Lagair* has taught me *Lamore* may flourish in the midst of *Lamaird*," Mabel writes. "The body you are loving tonight may, on the morrow, be a blasted bit of blackened flesh impaled on barbed wire. But love such as ours is not fragile as flesh" (143).

Leaving the serenity of her sheltered existence behind at an age many would consider too old for such daring, Mabel plunges into the unknown when she joins the war effort and begins to understand the connectedness of life's most basic elements—*Lavee, Lagair, Lamore,* and *Lamaird*—for the first time. If Mabel had never left St. Elmo and gone to war, Kalpakian's story suggests, she might never have lived.

44. La Motte, Ellen. "Civilization." <u>Civilization: Tales of the Orient</u>. New York: George Doran Company, 1919. 93 – 117.

La Motte probes the question "What is civilization?" in this ironic short story of war. In France, where "civilization" is at war, a middle-aged, irascible shopkeeper blames his conscription on his wife for not producing a fifth child, which would have assured him a deferment from military service:

> He would not be placed on active service—he was too old for that. Nevertheless it meant a horrid jarring out of his usual routine of life, consequently he was angry and resentful, and there was no fine glow of pride or patriotism or such-like feeling in his breast. Bah! All that sort of thing had vanished from men long and long ago, after the first few bitter weeks of war and of realisation of the meaning of war. War was now an affair—a sordid, ugly affair, and Maubert knew it as well as any man. (94 – 95)

In a French colony near the equator, "civilization" consists of primitive villages of natives who live in peaceful simplicity. Drafted by the war effort, these natives are "pressed into service" and forced to wear uniforms of war as their first official clothing. It is with "difficulty and pain" that they are trained in the foreign "ways of Europe" to defend France during their first encounter with a supposedly higher form of "civilization." One native, who does not adapt well enough to survive the first European winter, nevertheless fathers a child by the shopkeeper's wife, who is intrigued with his exotic appearance. This child's birth enables Maubert to leave his monotonous military post. As he returns home, he must decide whether to kill his wife for her adulterous sin—and consequently be returned to the front as punishment—or accept the child that is not his own and forgive his wife's infidelity in order to buy his own freedom. La Motte offers a critical look at the kind of society we have labelled as our "civilization" and seems to question "Is it really civilized?"

45.   Mackay, Helen. "At the End." Chill Hours. 1920. Freeport, NY:
       Books for Libraries Press, 1971. 3 – 19.

One of war's ironic effects on male-female relationships is poignantly
illustrated in this story. The young wife of a French prisoner of war
learns to love her husband more during his absence than she did
when they were together at the beginning of their marriage, while
he apparently becomes less assured of the strength of their marital
bond during their period of separation. After three years of
imprisonment and limited communication with his wife, Blaise is
released and sent home to die with consumption. Instead of
requesting that his wife meet his homecoming train, he writes
instead to a cousin and lifelong companion. Facing death, he needs
unconditional love and unqualified acceptance which he apparently
feels he his wife may not be able to assure him. To comfort Blaise's
wife, his cousin tries to explain how he must feel: "If he were going
to be well, to live on, he might want—I don't know whom—somebody
beautiful, somebody brilliant," she says. "But when he is going to die,
he wants me" (19). In this story Mackay illustrates how the war
experience alters perceptions and changes relationships through
separation and war's ever-present threat of death.

46.   Mackay, Helen. "The Cauldron." Chill Hours. 1920. Freeport, NY:
       Books for Libraries Press, 1971. 95 – 106.

This story documents the emotional toll of war on military nurses
who endure a continuous cycle of suffering, watching soldiers come
and go but never learning their names or knowing their fate once
they leave the hospital's protective environment. The nurse-narrator
of this narrative describes a despairing cycle in which all of the
wounded soldiers seem to blend into one in her mind: "Always and
always and always, coming and going, going and coming, until
sometimes it seems that all these men are just one man to whom
these things happen eternally, round and round" (96).

47.   Mackay, Helen. "He Cost Us So Much." Chill Hours. 1920. Freeport,
       NY: Books for Libraries Press, 1971. 154 – 159.

This is a sketch of grief of an elderly couple for their only son, for
whom they have labored hard and sacrificed much in order for him
to have an education. Their mourning for his death in combat is as
much over the loss of their "investment" as it is for the loss of their
only child. "He cost us so much to bring up," his mother laments, as
she rocks and sobs (159).

48.   Mackay, Helen. "Here Are the Shadows." Chill Hours. 1920.
       Freeport, NY: Books for Libraries Press, 1971. 160 – 163.

This short narrative describes the abrupt ending of a relationship
severed by the unnatural and often cruel circumstances of war. A
woman receives numerous letters from her soldier-lover at war,
letters that "would have Titine think he was never in danger, always

well, living in idleness and luxury, far from battle" (161). Even on the morning of his death, he composes a letter to Titine. Only when he writes the words "Here are the shadows gathering" and fails to sign his name to his last letter is there a foreshadowing that death may be approaching. This story illustrates how men in combat often protect women from the harsh realities and dangers of war in an effort to be protective of those they love.

49. Mackay, Helen. "I Take Pen in Hand." Chill Hours. 1920. Freeport, NY: Books for Libraries Press, 1971. 172 – 177.

"I Take Pen in Hand" is a comparative sketch of two young soldiers suffering with meningitis brought to die in a French hospital While one succumbs to death surrounded by his family members who plan an elaborate funeral, the other soldier's family does not respond to telegraphed communications reporting their son's critical condition. Unaware that his nightshirt is decorated with honorary medals the day before his death, the second soldier is given a simple burial with no one in attendance to accept his medals. In this short story Mackay portrays perhaps the most severe form of loneliness suffered by soldiers during warfare—to die totally alone.

50. Mackay, Helen. "Little Cousin of No. 12." Chill Hours. 1920. Freeport, NY: Books for Libraries Press, 1971. 148 – 153.

This sketch depicts a soldier's last reunion with his family before his death. As the unnamed patient—"No. 12"—is brought into the hospital, his right arm and right leg both amputated, the nurse-narrator describes his condition:

> He was whiter than any of the dead I had ever seen, and so transparent that it was as if he were not real at all, as if, trying to touch him, one's hand would pass through. There was nothing of him that seemed any more to belong to life, and yet he was terribly alive. It was with the intensity, almost the exultation of life, that comes, sometimes, just before death, the last, too high, too bright flaring up of the flame in a lamp that will shortly break. (148)

The soldier's mental clarity, too, vacillates as he imagines the nurse narrating the story to be a close cousin. Despite the shock of the severity of his wounds to his family, his beloved cousin is the one who unhesitatingly comes forward to greet him:

> It was she who moved. She gathered herself all together, and it was as if, through the horror that had been in her face, there shone out, covering the horror that he might never know of it, a brightness just pleasant and commonplace, to make as if there were no tragedy at all. (153)

This story is a depiction of the horror of war reduced to an intimate level and the emotional strength of a family coping with the death of a son.

51.   Mackay, Helen. "Madame Anna." Chill Hours. 1920. Freeport, NY: Books for Libraries Press, 1971. 143 – 147.

The anguish of waiting mothers with sons at war is rendered in this character sketch of a woman who waits four years to hear word from her son at war, only to learn after the armistice that there will never be any letters forthcoming from him. Mackay captures the agony of uncertainty and tediously long waiting periods women must endure as they watch their sons leave for war with no assurances of their return.

52.   Mackay, Helen. "The Moment." Chill Hours. 1920. Freeport, NY: Books for Libraries Press, 1971. 188 – 191.

The nurse-narrator of this short sketch depicts the hospital and surrounding environment the morning after the armistice is signed. For many people of the working class, life's routines remain unchanged. Many soldiers stand idle "who still suffered too much to care to do anything" (188). Two soldier-patients rejoice at the news of peace but can think of no appropriate words, feeling "suddenly confused, shy, as if the moment were an awkward one" (189). After five years of war, the prospect of peace brings to the narrator's mind more idealistic times now past. She writes:

> Climbing the stairs I was homesick for a sight of that something of which we used to get rare glimpses. I was homesick for the time when one was happy just in the thought of dying, of being perhaps granted the privilege of giving one's life for the faith one had; when ideals were voices and banners and wings, and torches and stars, and sacrifice was ecstasy, and courage was singled out, and glory was a thing seen, lifted up, called by its shining name. (190)

53.   Mackay, Helen. "The Nine and the Ten." Chill Hours. 1920. Freeport, NY: Books for Libraries Press, 1971. 178 – 187.

This short sketch compares the adversity of young men inherent in their different social classes that disappears in the trenches when they are fighting side by side but resurfaces when the threat of war is lifted. A hospital patient of noble birth speaks condescendingly of a poorer veteran-patient: "The more we do for them, the more they hate us. They hate us even for what we do for them" (185). The working-class veteran expresses a decidedly different view of his fate in life compared to those of the privileged class: "In the trenches we were all together, they and we, it was to die, any one like any other. But when it comes to living, they think they have a right to all of it, and we to none" (187). Through these expressed attitudes, Mackay illustrates how a life-or-death crisis can temporarily erase class prejudice which invariably reappears once that crisis passes.

54.   Mackay, Helen. "Nostalgia." Chill Hours. 1920. Freeport, NY: Books for Libraries Press, 1971. 107 – 140.

"Once upon a time there was a mood that beautiful things brought about, and that was like a place one's spirit could go away into, quite, quite away; a place of refuge" (107). Thus begins this narrative which offers a poetic vision of prewar France at peace with imagery that is serene and therapeutically comforting to remember in the midst of war and its associated grief. Mackay writes: "It was beautiful, long ago, before the war, to be a little afraid, of nothing, and a little sad, for no reason at all" (125).

55.   Mackay, Helen. "Odette in Pink Taffeta." Chill Hours. 1920. Freeport, NY: Books for Libraries Press, 1971. 20 – 34.

A mother grows closer to her daughter when a telegram arrives announcing the death of her younger brother's tutor in combat, and the mother realizes by her daughter's reaction that it is he and not the young man she had envisioned her daughter marrying who has always been present in her daughter's mind. At a time when no words need to be spoken, the mother offers her daughter emotional support and maternal closeness to help soothe the pain of loss. This story illustrates how a crisis such as war can unexpectedly foster closer family ties, providing emotional strength.

56.   Mackay, Helen. "One or Another." Chill Hours. 1920. Freeport, NY: Books for Libraries Press, 1971. 72 – 94.

Unlike the wife in Mackay's "Second Hay," whose own battle to manage the homefront household alone while her husband is at war obscures her ability to recognize his emotional needs, the wife in "One or Another" feels the weight of similar responsibilities but realizes her husband's burden is much greater than her own. For two years Charlotte consoles herself that in managing alone, she "was somehow fighting, as Philip was, and been proud. All that she could do for the estate and the people, she had felt she was doing, not only for Philip and the children, but for France" (72). But by the third year of war she has run dry of consolation. Wearied by too much tragedy and uncertainty, she longs to share that burden with her husband, but when he returns on leave earlier than anticipated, she senses that he is nearing an emotional breaking point and desperately needs a respite of peace in his life. Attempting to meet his psychological needs, Charlotte puts her own concerns on hold while she concentrates "to make every moment its best for him, so that he might have peace, and come to himself again, and be himself when he went back" (88). "One or Another" and "Second Hay," also authored by Mackay, provide an effective contrast of two women's individual reactions and responses to the familial changes and stresses imposed by the circumstances of war.

57.   Mackay, Helen. "The Second Hay." Chill Hours. 1920. Freeport, NY: Books for Libraries Press, 1971. 49 – 71.

"The Second Hay" depicts the frustration of a woman who is caught between visions of a romantic homecoming during her husband's leave and the necessity of his assistance during the hay harvest to insure the family's financial survival for the coming year. While Yvon has been away at war two years, Lise has assumed his role and hers by herself—managing a farm, parenting children, and caring for his aging parents. When he returns, she sees him most importantly as someone to help shoulder the burden and thus represses her expression of love for him. While the family talks only of the coming harvest, Yvon cannot divorce himself from visions of war that still dominate his mind: "Out there," he continues to repeat, "men fight and fight, on and on" (65). As he leaves to return to the front, Lise realizes too late she has ignored their need for intimacy. "She wanted to tell him that the dreams were not gone, the struggle had not really worn the glory off, that, behind all the hard driving on and on of necessity, there was love yet" (70). She confesses as Yvon is about to depart, "I seemed to have forgotten everything, for just the hay" (70). This story illustrates how the strains of war weigh heavily on homefront women who must assume the responsibilities left behind by their soldier-husbands, overshadowing whatever romantic feelings they once held which may necessarily become a peacetime luxury all but forgotten during war.

58. Mackay, Helen. "Their Places." <u>Chill Hours</u>. 1920. Freeport, NY: Books for Libraries Press, 1971. 35 – 48.

This story within a story examines the loneliness of a French soldier on leave in Paris who refuses to return home to his mountain farm because war has created such a compelling gap of experience between his family and himself. Michel's first eleven months at war with no leave "had been so crowded with confusion and helplessness and horror, so deadened with fatigue, that there seemed to be left of them nothing he could understand and tell. The eleven months were a wide, wide gap. He had nothing with which to fill in the gap" (39 – 40). During his first leave at home he realizes his wife knows only farm life and is contentedly oblivious to his experiences at war and its inherent dangers. Her world revolves around the farm and ends at its borders:

> There had been no one to explain to her and the three little boys what it meant that Michel was at the war. There was no one who even knew that the man who came back to them, with a rough beard, in a blue uniform, was a hero, with thousands of others. They stood about and looked at him, as if he were a stranger there among them. They had nothing to say to him, and he had nothing to say to them. (41)

The magnitude of their differing priorities becomes painfully clear to Michel on the last day of his leave as he heads back to the trenches while his wife journeys to the cattle market. That morning he lies in bed thinking, "I may be going back to be killed. Every one else is killed, and probably I shall be killed and she does not think of it at all. She is going to Barreme to the cattle-market. She thinks of the two yokes of young oxen she is going to buy" (44).

This story illustrates how the experience of war can create irretrievable distances between men, forced into life-or-death combat action, and women, left waiting on the homefront with no real awareness of the reality of warfare. The soldier in this story finds it easier to try to ignore that distance than to return home and attempt to confront it. War has forced this soldier and his wife into "their places" which may never converge again.

59. Mackay, Helen. "The Vow." Chill Hours. 1920. Freeport, NY: Books for Libraries Press, 1971. 168 – 171.

The indiscriminate nature of war's cruelty is revealed in this sketch of a hospital volunteer who works far harder than any other staff member because she has made a vow with the Blessed Virgin "that she would do anything, everything, so long as her son was spared at the war," yet loses him despite her unquestioned belief in her vow (170). This story imparts the pain of loss for war mothers and the extreme actions some may take to try to save their sons' lives when, in reality, they have so little influence over the fate of their sons.

60. Montague, Margaret Prescott. "England to America." O. Henry Memorial Award Prize Stories 1919. Ed. Blanche Colton Williams. Garden City: Doubleday, Page and Company, 1921. 3 – 20.

The heroism of a British family facing the loss of a son to war is characterized in this first place award-winning story of 1919. An American soldier spending his leave with the British family of a close friend learns at his leave's end that the friend has died in combat, but the family has spared him the news so as not to spoil his leave. "We were afraid you would go away and have a lonely leave somewhere," the mother explains. "And in these days a boy's leave is so precious a thing that nothing must spoil it—nothing" (18). The dead soldier's brother explains that there was more than friendship involved in the family's forced hospitality. In return for the aid American soldiers brought to the British, he explains, "We wanted a chance to show you how England felt. . . . You see I don't know exactly how to put it—but it was England to America" (19 – 20). Lieutenant Skipworth Cary learns in this story that heroism also takes place on the homefront among those whose altruism is sincere and who can see beyond their own grief to consider the needs of others during wartime.

61. Morrison, Toni. "1919." Sula. New York: Alfred A. Knopf, 1974. 7 – 16.

This chapter introduces a disturbed World War One veteran who becomes one of the two central characters in Sula. During combat Shadrack witnesses the decapitation of a fellow soldier in an explosion that leaves him physically and psychologically scarred. After spending a year in a mental institution, he returns home to Medallion, Ohio. Although he "survives the fire of war," he "remains a ghost of his former self" (Ogunyemi 132). At the age of 22 Shadrack is already "old, weak, hot, frightened, not daring to acknowledge the fact that he didn't even know who or what he was . . . with no past, no language, no tribe, no source, no address book, no comb, no pencil, no clock, no pocket handkerchief, no rug, no bed, no can opener, no faded postcard, no soap, no key, no tobacco pouch, no soiled underwear and nothing nothing nothing to do . . . he was sure of one thing only: the unchecked monstrosity of his hands" (12) Neither hospitalization nor incarceration cures Shadrack's craziness which the town of Medallion attributes to his traumatic war experience. But Shadrack remains an outcast in The Bottom (the section of Medallion reserved for Blacks), unsure of who or what he is.

In 1920 Shadrack institutes Medallion's First National Suicide Day which he alone celebrates annually with his one-man parade and cowbell ringing. It is a day devoted to facing the unexpectedness of death, made poignantly clear by Shadrack's war experience, and "making a place for fear as a way of controlling it" so that the "rest of the year would be safe and free" (14). Although Shadrack is the only town member who participates in the ritual, it becomes "part of the fabric of life up in the Bottom" and a necessary part of Shadrack's "quest for psychological wholeness" and self-preservation (Samuels 48).

In her essay "Sula: 'A Nigger Joke,'" Chikwenye Okonjo Ogunyemi suggests that Shadrack is symbolic of the "nihilistic and suicidal tendencies of twentieth-century man with his World Wars," a character who reflects "the spirit of the world at large," yet is denigrated by the community at large as a lunatic. "His apparent madness is Morrison's cynical commentary on a world gone awry," she writes (132).

62.   Porter, Katherine Anne. Pale Horse, Pale Rider. New York: Modern Library, 1939. 179 – 264.

Porter's response to World War One is presented in this semi-autobiographical novella set against the backdrop of war. The narrative is written in a "structured stream-of-consciousness form with Porter guiding the reader through Miranda's dreams and describing the action that holds the dreams together in a plot" (Unrue 105). It is through the interpretation of these dreams that Porter allows readers to comprehend how Miranda's childhood innocence has been shattered by war and much of her world has been "destroyed by the harsh impersonality of war and disease" (Mooney 34). In the novella World War One is presented as the "prime mover for all of the issues, since war is examined not only in its political and social implications, but particularly in its psychological or moral implications" (Hartley 130). The presence of war "creates fear and suspicion, distrust and hypocrisy, which transforms daily reality into a disturbing set of distorting mirrors" (Hartley 131). War also colors Miranda's relationship with her soldier-lover. Adam and Miranda are both "bound by obligations to society which prevent their unity, even though, ironically, the only dedications which could have value for them now in a war-world would be those based upon love for each other. They are compelled to fulfill obligations to a society operating upon hatred, not love" (Hartley 131).

The factual origin of Miranda's illness stems from a plague of influenza toward the end of World War One which almost claimed Porter's life. Because Miranda's illness is associated with the war, ending at the same time as the Armistice, "it symbolizes the spiritual malaise of the twentieth century that nurtured catastrophic world wars" (Unrue 111). While Adam dies in a military camp hospital, succumbing to the influenza he has contracted from Miranda, her life is spared. But now she faces a "joyless life, threatened and insecure, armed only with her fortitude to face the emptiness of a life to which she has heroically regained her right" (Mooney 31). The final, ironic lines of the novella express her despondent state of mind as she reenters a world that is just beginning to recover from war as she begins to recovers what is left of her own life: "No more war, no more plague, only the dazed silence that follows the ceasing of the heavy guns; noiseless houses with the shades drawn, empty streets, the dead cold light of tomorrow. Now there would be time for everything" (264).

63.   Pulver, Mary Brecht. "The Path of Glory." The Best Short Stories of 1917. Ed. Edward J. O'Brien. Boston: Small, Maynard and Company, 1918. 412 – 440.

The death of their oldest son serving as an ambulance driver in France brings new esteem to the downtrodden, socially-outcast Haynes family in this short story. Although his father was given a pauper's funeral in America, Nat is honored with an elaborate military burial in France. "Buried like a king!" his mother exclaims. "It was like some beautiful fantasy. A Haynes—despised and rejected of earth—borne to his last home with such pomp and ceremony!" (435). Although Nat was snubbed as a rebellious, restless nonconformist from a lower-class family before he secretly joined the war effort, he is elevated to the rank of hero after he dies on a French battlefield. His family suddenly gains new social standing in the judgmental eyes of the community: "These the Hayneses! These people, with hope and self-esteem once more in their hearts! These people with a new, a unique place in the community's respect!" (440). Nat's younger brother concludes that his brother is "better off than ever—safe and honored," rather than mistrusted and dishonored as he would have been had he not gone to war. Pulver's story illustrates how military service was so revered during this time period that it could completely alter a young man's reputation and his death substantially elevate his family's social standing.

64.   Rice, Alice Hegan. "Reprisal." Turn About Tales. New York: The Century Company, 1920. 153 – 174.

A woman makes a self-discovery—as well as learning something about the nature of war—in this short story set in German-occupied Belgium. In retaliation to the repressive restrictions imposed upon her village by the authoritarian Germans, Adrienne Carbonnez tricks a German sentinel into drunkenness, a breach of conduct which may cost the young soldier his life. Adrienne justifies her personal scheme for "reprisal" on his role in a war she abhors vehemently: "He was part of that damnable machine that was crushing the life out of her beloved country; that was separating her from her husband and starving her children, and making all life a hideous, continuous nightmare" (166). But just when the stage is "set perfectly for the climax," Adrienne experiences a "curious change" that convinces her to revise her original intention—"that woman's instinct to succor a helpless fellow being even though he be a foe" (168). Ultimately, and ironically, she risks her own life to save this soldier's that she nearly ended deliberately. The woman portrayed in this story discovers her own maternal instincts to nurture and sustain life, even that of an "enemy," are stronger than her hatred of the Huns.

65. Sedgwick, Anne Douglas. "Daffodils." Christmas Roses and Other Stories. Boston: Houghton Mifflin, 1920. 92–120.

"Daffodils" explores the thoughts of a dying British soldier hospitalized on the French front who relishes the thought that his heroism will bring honor to his family's name until he learns through his first encounter with his natural father as he awaits death that he was conceived out of wedlock and has no claim to the family name he has always cherished. "His life lay open before him, open from beginning to end: that beginning of tawdry sentiment and shame—with daffodils; and this end, with daffodils again, and again with tawdry sentiment and shame" (114). Although initially angered at the discovery of his true heritage, Marmaduke accepts the truth gracefully as he assures himself that "to accept the fact of being second-rate proved . . . that you were not merely second-rate" (119). As he dies, Marmaduke is comforted that his dying has brought honor to his family, regardless of the circumstances of his conception. This soldier, symbolic of many, strives to find justification that his gallantry in war and death in combat were not in vain.

66. Sedgwick, Anne Douglas. "Hepaticas." The Atlantic Monthly. August 1915: 145–157.

Douglas explores the feelings of a mother who loses her son to war while gaining a young and immature war bride and illegitimate grandson whom she will undoubtedly raise herself. As she sends her son off to war she faces the possibility of his death as a soldier's widow might, realizing that if he does return "it would be as if he were born again, a gift of grace, unexpected and unclaimed" (147). When her son fails to return, she consoles herself that he has "died the glorious death" and that "no future, tangled, perplexed, fretful with its foolish burden, lay before him. There was no loss for Jack; no fading, no waste. The burden was for her and he was free" (157). This story illustrates the prevailing attitude of women during the World War One period which gave strength and sustained mothers who sent their sons to war, facing the possibility they may never return.

67.   Silman, Roberta. "In the German Bookstore." Blood Relations. Boston: Little, Brown and Company, 1973. 65 – 80.

In this narrative a Jewish immigrant reflects upon his adolescence when he helped to manage a bookstore during the German occupation of his Polish homeland. During this period of his life Herschel was introduced to a diverse world of knowledge by the bookstore manager. Now, at age 74, financially secure by American standards, Herschel feels somehow failed that all the knowledge he acquired did not gain him the power he had envisioned:

> . . . all that knowledge had made him feel he could conquer the world. Learning was more powerful than Arabian horses. But he was no different from hundreds of immigrants from Eastern Europe who had made some money and educated their children. And worse, he had not even communicated the past. A scrap here, a scrap there, but what did it all add up to? Nothing coherent, surely—a jigsaw puzzle with pieces missing. (79)

Of all his war memories, spanning two world wars, resurrected with the discovery of a boyhood photograph taken during World War One, it is the memory of the bookstore and its treasure of knowledge discovered within that stands out foremost in his mind.

68.   Storm, Ethel. "The Three Telegrams." The Best Short Stories of 1920. Ed. Edward J. O'Brien. Boston: Small, Maynard and Company, 1920. 293 – 311.

War as perceived through the eyes of a child is envisioned by the author in this story set in France. Orphaned during early childhood, Claire Rene and her three brothers are reared by their grandmother, who is deaf and blind by the time World War One claims all of Claire's brothers' lives. War, in Claire's simplistic view, is a "great and terrible noise far away" that leaves behind only the lonely silence for children such as she who fills her days dreaming of her brothers' homecoming. Although Claire knows her brothers would have hated to kill other men, she accepts the fact that during war it is the "wicked men that had to be killed" (294). Claire is devastated when the dreaded telegram arrives ("The soil of France now covers the bodies of your three brothers," it reads), but she accepts the offer of three American soldiers to become their adopted younger sister and takes comfort that at last, like her brothers, "she was called—for France!" (311).

69. Wharton, Edith. "Coming Home." The Collected Short Stories of Edith Wharton. Ed. R. W. B. Lewis. New York: Scribners, 1968. 230 – 256.

Using the framework of a story within a story, Wharton relates one of many war stories brought back to the United States by a member of the American Relief Corps. "Some of his tales are dark and dreadful," she writes, "some are unutterably sad, and some end in a huge laugh of irony. I am not sure how I ought to classify the one I have written down here" (230). The Relief Corps member relates the story of a French calvary lieutenant who returns home during the early months of the war travelling through the war-ravaged countryside with a "sense of loneliness and remoteness," uncertain of his family's welfare or existence. Jean de Rechamp arrives home to find the fiancee his family once rejected has saved his family's chateau with her clever "coolness and courage" despite the invading Germans' "threats and insolence" (252). Rechamp later has the chance to save the life of one of the invading German officers who has been wounded but allows the German to die, perhaps as retribution for the repeated tale of "murder, outrage, torture" perpetrated by the Germans who occupied France. "Coming Home" is an illustration of the desecrating forces of war on a country and its inhabitants and the unpredictable reactions of those who face the adversities of war and its inherent moral conflicts.

In his essay "Edith Wharton's War Story," Alan Price describes this story as a "melodramatic tale of survival and retribution" which combines Wharton's fictional writing talents with her direct personal impressions of war-ravaged France. He writes:

> "Coming Home" married a formulaic revenge plot with stereotypical characters and scenes of destruction drawn from her war reportage. For her contemporary readers in the United States, it was a splendid war story with a wounded hero, an attractive heroine forced to sacrifice to save others, a vicious German officer, and an innocent American ambulance volunteer. For modern readers the story is less interesting for its structural than for its biographical and historical dimensions. Yet these biographical and historical facts argue strongly for our consideration of "Coming Home" not only in Wharton's canon of liteary achievements, but alo in the larger canon of World War I literature. (99)

70. Wharton, Edith. "Writing a War Story." The Collected Stories of Edith Wharton. Ed. R. W. B. Lewis. New York: Charles Scribner's Sons, 1968. 359 – 370.

"Writing a War Story" is a commentary on men's traditional perceptions of women, which seem unaffected by the state of war. When Miss Ivy Spang, more of a poet than a fiction writer who works as a hospital volunteer in Paris during the war, agrees to write a "rattling" war story for a magazine which will be distributed to all

British soldiers, she feels woefully inadequate for the task. She cannot decide where to begin. "Why did stories ever begin, and why did they ever leave off?" she wonders. "Life didn't—it just went on and on" (361). Not to be defeated by a genre she has rarely used or a subject she has never experienced directly, she sets out to "battle with the art of fiction" until she produces an acceptable story, based upon a true episode in the life of a wounded soldier. When the story is published, she distributes copies of The Man-at-Arms to the wounded men on her ward, eager for their reaction to her writing. But it is not her fiction that they respond to so positively, but the corresponding photograph of her dressed in a nurse's uniform, in which she appears "robed in white and monastically veiled, holding out a refreshing beverage to an invisible sufferer with a gesture halfway between Melisande lowering her braid over the balcony and Florence Nightingale advancing with the lamp" (364). Each soldier wants a framed copy—but no one mentions the story she has written. Disheartened and frustrated, Miss Spang is reminded that men value women's physical charms much more highly than their writing talents, and that perhaps these wounded soldiers—at least for the present—need a Florence Nightingale symbol of nurturing and healing in their lives more than an Edith Wharton symbol of literary excellence.

71. Willis, Connie. "Schwarzschild Radius." The Universe. Ed. Byron Preiss. New York: Bantam Books, 1987. 145 – 160.

This narrative parallels the war experience of men serving on the Russian front with the development of scientific theories exploring the unknown. If the "Schwarzschild radius" is the point of no return where nothing can stop a star from collapsing and becoming a black hole, then those who experience the horrors of war too reach a point of no return, spiralling into a trap of darkness from which there is no escape. As the German narrator of this story recalls his distant relationship with the inventor of the dark hole theory, Karl Schwarzschild, who formulated the theory as he was dying of a fatal disease during the war, he feels himself again slipping into that dark center where time ceases to exist, a prisoner of memory past the point of no return. This narrative also illustrates how the scientific, inquisitive nature of mankind never ceases, even when war intervenes.

72. Wood, Frances Gilchrist. "The White Battalion." The Best Short Stories of 1918. Ed. Edward J. O'Brien. Boston: Small, Maynard and Company, 1918. 325 – 332.

In this supernatural story French women insist upon military enlistment as the -nth Battalion of Avengers to take the place of their fallen husbands in battle. "Why," they ask, "should France be left a nation of sorrowful women only? Let the widowed women of the -nth take the place of men in the chance of death—they would welcome it—and so save men to France" (328). Both women and children take part in this phantom fight in which no blood is shed although many die, and the wrong is righted, in the minds of these revengeful widows. In this story Wood envisions women in an uncharacteristic role, not as homefront guardians, but as active warriors eager to take part in combat as revenge for their husbands' deaths.

LITERARY CRITICISM AND BIBLIOGRAPHIC SOURCES

Atherton, Gertrude. Afterword. The White Morning, by Atherton. New York: Frederick Stokes, 1918.

Bergonzi, Bernard. Heroes' Twilight, a Study of the Literature of the Great War. New York: Coward-McCann, 1966.

Brickell, Herschel. "More About the War." Rev. of "It's a Great War", by Mary Lee. The New York Herald Tribune Book Review 27 Oct. 1929: 3.

Brown, E. K. Willa Cather: A Critical Biography. New York: Alfred A. Knopf, 1964.

Buitenhuis, Peter. "Edith Wharton and the First World War." American Quarterly 18 (Fall 1966): 493 – 505.

Clough, David. "Edith Wharton's War Novels: A Reappraisal." Twentieth Century Literature 19 (1973): 1 – 14.

Cooperman, Stanley. World War I and the American Novel. Baltimore: Johns Hopkins Press, 1968.

Daims, Diva and Janet Grimes. Toward a Feminist Tradition: An Annotated Bibliography of Novels in English by Women 1891 – 1920. New York: Garland, 1982.

Egan, Maurice Francis. "Sons and Parents at the Front." Rev. of A Son at the Front, by Edith Wharton. The New York Times Book Review 9 Sept. 1923: 1.

"Ellen Glasgow, Alfred Ollivant, Walpole." Rev. of The Builders, by Ellen Glasgow. The New York Times Book Review 2 Nov. 1919: 1.

Gilbert, Sandra. "Soldier's Heart: Literary Men, Literary Women, and the Great War." Signs: Journal of Women in Culture and Society 8.3 (1983) : 422 – 450.

Gilman, Dorothy Foster. "It's a Great War—Says Mary Lee." Rev. of "It's a Great War!", by Mary Lee. Boston Evening Transcript 26 Oct. 1929: 2.

Gregory, Horace. "Love in Counterpoint." Rev. of Bid Me to Live, by Hilda Doolittle. Saturday Review 28 May 1960: 31 – 32.

Griffiths, Frederick T. "The woman warrior: Willa Cather and One of Ours." Women's Studies 11 (1984) 261 – 285.

Hanna, Archibald. A Mirror for the Nation: An Annotated Bibliography of American Social Fiction, 1901 – 1950. New York: Garland, 1985.

Hansen, Harry. Rev. of "It's a Great War!", by Mary Lee. New York World 25 Oct. 1929: 17.

Hartley, Charles. Katherine Ann Porter: A Critical Symposium. Eds. Lockwick Hartley and George Core. Athens: University of Georgia Press, 1969.

Johnston, Judith Lynne. "The Cultural Legacy of World War I: A Comparative Study of Selected War Novels." Diss. Stanford University, 1975.

Jones, Ann Maret. "Three American Responses to World War I: Wharton, Empey, and Bourne." Diss. University of Wisconsin-Madison, 1970.

Jones, Tamara. "The Mud in God's Eye: World War I in Women's Novels." Thesis. Scripps College, 1980.

Keppel, Frederick J. "More of the Truth." Rev. of "It's a Great War!", by Mary Lee. Saturday Review 2 Nov. 1929: 340.

"Latest Works of Fiction." Rev. of The Flying Teuton and Other Stories, by Alice Brown. The New York Times Book Review 24 Mar. 1918: 122.

Lauer, Kristin O. and Margaret P. Murray. Edith Wharton: An Annotated Secondary Bibliography. New York: Garland, 1990.

Lee, Mary. Preface. "It's a Great War!". Boston: Houghton Mifflin, 1929. vii – viii.

"Life in a Hothouse." Rev. of Bid Me to Live, by Hilda Doolittle. Newsweek 2 May 1960: 92 – 93.

McFarland, Dorothy. Willa Cather. New York: Frederick Ungar, 1972.

Mooney, Harry J., Jr. The Fiction and Criticism of Katherine Anne Porter. Pittsburgh: University of Pittsburgh Press, 1957.

Moore, Harry T. "The Faces Are Familiar." Rev. of Bid Me to Live, by Hilda Doolittle. The New York Times Book Review 1 May 1960: 4.

"Mrs. Wharton's Story of the Marne." Rev. of The Marne, by Edith Wharton. The New York Times Book Review 8 Dec. 1918: 1.

Nevius, Blake. Edith Wharton: A Study of Her Fiction. Berkeley: University of California Press, 1953.

Nitchie, Elizabeth, Jane F. Goodloe, Marion E. Hawes, and Grace L. McCann, eds. Pens for Ploughshares: A Bibliography of Creative Literature That Encourages World Peace. Boston: F. W. Faxon Company, 1930.

Ogunyemi, Chikwenye Okonjo. "Sula: 'A Nigger Joke.'" Black American Literature Forum 13 (1979): 130 – 134.

Phillips, Jill M. The Darkling Plain: The Great War in History, Biography, Diary, Poetry, Literature and Film. New York: Gordon Press, 1981.

Price, Alan. "Edith Wharton's War Story." Tulsa Studies in Women's Literature 8 (1989): 95 – 100.

Rev. of The Day of Glory, by Dorothy Canfield Fisher. The New York Times Book Review 24 March 1918: 122.

Rev. of Home Fires in France, by Dorothy Canfield Fisher. The New York Times Book Review 6 Oct. 1918: 422.

Rev. of My Boy in Khaki: A Mother's Story, by Delia Thompson Lutes. The New York Times Book Review 25 Aug. 1918: 366.

Rev. of A World to Mend, by Margaret Sherwood. The New York Times Book Review 14 Nov. 1920: 23.

Samuels, Wilfred D. and Clenora Hudson-Weems. Toni Morrison. Boston: Twayne Publishers, 1990.

Sauber, Dorothy. "Historical Context/Literary Content: Women Write about War and Women." Thesis. Hamline University, 1988.

Sergeant, Elizabeth Shepley. Willa Cather: A Memoir. Lincoln: University of Nebraska Press, 1963.

Tylee, Claire M. The Great War and Women's Consciousness: Images of Militarism and Womanhood in Women's Writings, 1914 – 1964. Iowa City: University of Iowa Press, 1990.

Unrue, Darlene Harbour. Understanding Katherine Anne Porter. Columbia: University of South Carolina Press, 1988.

Wallace, Margaret. Rev. of "It's a Great War!", by Mary Lee. Bookman Dec. 1929: 459 – 460.

"War at Length." Rev. of "It's a Great War!", by Mary Lee. The New York Times Book Review 17 Nov. 1929: 7.

"The War in England and Germany." Rev. of The White Morning, by Gertrude Atherton. The New York Times Book Review 27 Jan. 1918: 1.

Washington, Ida H. Dorothy Canfield Fisher: A Biography. Shelburne, VT: New England Press, 1982.

Wharton, Edith. A Backward Glance. New York: D. Appleton Century, 1934.

"A World to Mend." Rev. of A World to Mend, by Margaret Sherwood. The New York Times Book Review 14 Nov. 1920: 23.

2

World War Two

INTRODUCTION

World War Two writers expressed their fictional interpretations of war from a much less idealistic, more realistic perspective than writers of the World War One era. The literature of World War Two recognizes war as a natural part of the social environment, stripped of romantic illusions. If the soldiers who fought during World War One "expected fulfillment and suffered the impact of futility," those who fought during World War Two did so fully expecting futility (Cooperman 223). If the soldiers of World War One, such as Willa Cather's Claude Wheeler and Edith Wharton's Troy Belknap, looked forward to combat as a romantic adventure in self-fulfillment, the soldiers who fought during World War Two, such as Ann Chidester's Liam Moore, anticipated military service as "a means of accomplishing an unpleasant task" which would allow them to return home as quickly as possible (Aichinger 11). Many soldiers who eagerly entered World War One experienced the dehumanization of combat as well as the brutality of technological warfare and mechanized slaughter. These veterans returned home in a state of emotional shock, embittered by their experience, their idealism shattered. Soldiers of the World War Two era entered combat with a more realistic, if not caustic and certainly less romantic perception of war and its expected horrors. The "heroic quality of combat" that Americans found so invigorating during the World War One period had been hardened by truth by the beginning of the second World War (Aichinger 65). In particular, this war was regarded as a necessity to curb the spread of Hitlerism and protect American freedom. Comparing the nature of the two wars, Keith Nelson writes in The Impact of War on American Life: The Twentieth-Century Experience:

> If World War II seems, on the whole, to have been a less shattering experience than World War I for almost all concerned, this is probably due to the fact that it was waged by the victors with less guilt on their part, less frustration militarily, less unrealism generally, and above all, after having lived through the moral "letdown" of the previous war. Still, there is no gainsaying the unbelievable cost involved, and there is no denying the impact of the struggle. (93)

American women writers examine World War Two from a variety of perspectives—male and female, adult and child, American and foreign— and explore a variety of issues raised by a war that saw the extermination of five million Jews and the obliteration of 70,000 Japanese with the release of the atomic bomb. While a patriotic and often moralistic tone supportive of the war effort dominates some of these writings, a decidedly antiwar attitude is evident in many others.

The Holocaust experience is a dominant theme in the World War Two fiction authored by American women. Most of these writings have been published during the last quarter of the century and have been primarily authored by Jewish-American women. For a long time after World War Two ended interpretation of the concentration camp experience was considered unsuitable for artistic expression. "Art assumes meaning," writes Alan Berger in Crisis and Covenant: The Holocaust in American Jewish Fiction, "but Hitler's kingdom of death systematically destroyed the concept of rationality" (30). The experience seemed beyond the limitations of language. No words seemed inherently harsh enough to describe the concentration camp experience with authenticity. In Joyce Reisner Kornblatt's "Flo" a concentration camp survivor reveals much of her past to the young narrator of the story but stops short of her concentration camp experience, described as "the point in the world's history where conventional narrative no longer suffices, where language falters, defers to the silence in which a new alphabet struggles to form itself under the bone pits, under the eyeglass mounds" (72 – 73). Another concentration camp survivor in Zdena Berger's Tell Me Another Morning contemplates how inadequate the word "hungry" seems for the constant state of near starvation endured by camp prisoners. "No word of the time of peace can fit a time of war," she concludes (142). For many years silence was regarded as the most appropriate response of writers to the Holocaust, an atrocity "which occurred in the deepest silence of the truly abandoned," Norma Rosen explains in "The Holocaust and the American-Jewish Novelist." "The best response to it might be silence, or an endless scream," she writes. "Neither one makes art" (58).

More recently, this advocacy of silence has been challenged by writers— first European, and later American—who have come forth as witnesses to document the Holocaust experience, writers who no longer consider the Holocaust beyond the scope of artistic interpretation. These writers have proceeded cautiously to translate an experience once considered beyond words into fictional expression that neither detracts from nor somehow minimizes the actuality of the concentration camp experience. In his introduction to the 1981 O. Henry Memorial award-winning short story collection, editor William Abrahams defends the fictional interpretation of the Holocaust against the accusations of those who would argue that the atrocity defies literary interpretation, that its magnitude is best left for scholars and journalists whose expertise is in fact. Fiction, Abrahams proposes, releases writers from the "tyranny of fact" to trust in imagination to evoke emotional response. "As the facts recede into history and become the province of scholars," he writes, "art—as it expresses itself in (Cynthia Ozick's) "The Shawl"—will endure; not, if you like, as a 'story,' but as a 'memory' to haunt whoever reads it" (11).

A rebirth of interest in the Holocaust in recent years has led to the popularization and even commercialization of an experience once considered "unspeakable." Americans have traded silence for "an intense and widespread preoccupation with the Holocaust" which is potentially frightening, writes Ruth K. Angress in the afterword of Ilona Karmel's Estate of Memory. Such popularization, she explains, has created a "body of nonserious Holocaust literature which at one end of the spectrum is sentimental and at the other end pornographic, that is, books that are meant to induce an enjoyment of victimization" (445). Literary interpretations, however, rise above such simplifications to erase prior prejudices and preconceptions readers may have about life on the other side of the barbed wire fence when presented the truth of the Holocaust in starkly realistic narratives that are often emotionally shocking and cruelly authentic in fact.

Much of the Holocaust fiction written by American women is semi-autobiographical and reads similarly to non-fiction accounts. Many American writers, who received the news of the Holocaust second-hand, have adopted the role of "witnesses through imagination" with their commitment to preserve the memory of the Holocaust atrocity. These writers combine imaginative with realistic detail as they mold the Holocaust experience into fictional form (Rosen 58). During a Paris Review interview Cynthia Ozick explains how the Holocaust has continually invaded her consciousness as writer and witness so that it has becomes an inherent part of her as she writes:

> Now we, each one of us, Jew and Gentile, born during or after that time, we, all of us, forever after are witnesses to it. We know it happened: we are the generations that come after. I *want* the documents to be enough; I don't want to tamper or invent or imagine. And yet I have done it. I can't not do it. It comes, it invades. ("Art of Fiction" 184 – 85)

If Holocaust literature testifies to the horrors of the dehumanization of concentration camp existence for women, these writings also celebrate the strength of women whose future dreams were wiped out overnight with their arrest, whose mutual efforts to bond together enabled them to survive for as long as possible. These novels and short stories demonstrate how women's socialized roles as nurturers of life sustained them in mutual concern for the care and welfare of one another, even as the concentration camp experience worked to harden the sensitivity of prisoners into an egotistical battle for survival (Ezrahi 5 – 6). The concentration camp prisoner in Rebecca Goldstein's "The Legacy of Raizel Kaidish: A Story" who reports a fellow prisoner in order to gain her coveted kitchen position soon after the accused woman is sent to the gas chamber is an exception in this literature; the women who safely and covertly work together to deliver the baby of a fellow prisoner in Ilona Karmel's Estate of Memory are typical Holocaust heroines. The mother in Cynthia Ozick's "The Shawl" who stands horrified as a concentration camp guard thrashes the body of her tiny daughter against a fence but resists the overwhelming urge to intercede, maintaining a difficult silence for the sake of her own self-preservation, exemplifies the fortitude manifest by many Holocaust women.

Several women writers emphasize the post-Holocaust experience of survivors in their fictions. Female characters in both Zdena Berger's <u>Tell Me Another Morning</u> and Ilona Karmel's <u>Estate of Memory</u> anxiously await freedom, yet fear the uncertainty of the future once their freedom is assured. Even if living in a concentration camp is a dehumanizing ordeal, it offers the security of that which is known and expected compared to the frightening unknowns that lie beyond the barbed wire enclosure. The survivors returning home in Barbara Traub's <u>The Matrushka Doll</u>, greeted by awkwardly distanced neighbors, realize their postwar recovery will be an individual battle with little help offered from the seemingly indifferent outside world. One of the survivors predicts: "It's going to be hell, this our survival, that's for sure. But even if our wounds are permanent, we ourselves must stop the bleeding" (151). The husband and wife in Henia Karmel-Wolfe's <u>Marek and Lisa</u> realize their individual Holocaust experiences during two years of imprisonment in separate camps have made them different individuals and that if their marriage is to survive, they will have to learn to love one another as they have now become, not as they remember one another prior to the Holocaust.

The lasting effect of the Holocaust trauma on survivors is well documented in these writings. Elli's grandfather in Elzbieta Ettinger's <u>Kindergarten</u> predicts that the real casualties of the Holocaust will be those who survive. "Do not think, any of you," he warns his family, "that survival is the main problem or the sole target. The main problem is to be able to live when that time is over" (39). For Elli, to have died in a gas chamber might have been preferable to the madness which overtakes her life after the war. Even a quarter of a century after the war, the Holocaust replays itself over and over in the mind of the protagonist of Susan Schaeffer's <u>Anya</u>, who acknowledges that thus far during her lifespan of 52 years, she was the most alive when her concentration was focused on concentration camp survival, an experience which has minimized all of life since in comparison. At the time of Cynthia Ozick's "Rosa" 30 years have passed since the war, yet Rosa still clings to the fantasy that her infant daughter, brutally murdered by a concentration camp guard, is still alive as she worships the shawl which once sustained their tenuous life together.

Survivors often pass on their Holocaust experience to succeeding generations in these novels and short stories. In Jane Yolen's "Names" the names of Holocaust victims are carefully imprinted in the memory of young children by adult survivors who expect their offspring to continue to testify to their parents' victimization. "If you do not remember, we never lived," they warn their children. "If you do not remember, we never died" (254). The Holocaust survivor in Pamela Sargent's "Gather Blue Roses" comes to the realization that the Holocaust experience will probably be worse for her daughter to bear than it has been for herself, for her daughter has absorbed all the guilt, shame, fear, and misery passed on to her generation and has accepted this emotional burden as a natural part of her Jewish identity. The young protagonist of "Names" carries this burden one step further, starving herself to death as a self-sacrifice to appease her mother, who compulsively recites the names of Holocaust victims in a ritualized sequence of eternal remembrance. The fear of every postwar Jew that a recurrence of the Holocaust may take place reaches paranoid proportions in Leslea Newman's "Flashback" as a young woman secludes herself in protective hibernation, convinced an anti-Semitic movement has begun in the United States that will endanger the lives of all Jews.

Non-Jewish Americans are also moved by the Holocaust experience in Norma Rosen's Touching Evil. Even those who were not present can become "witnesses through imagination" who accept the moral obligation to keep the memory of the Holocaust tragedy alive. Rosen believes that anyone who has touched the evil of such a tragedy, whether directly or indirectly, can never be the same. Similarly, her novel proposes that any of us are capable of inflicting such evil upon each other. Although Holocaust literature generally depicts the Germans as merciless and inhumane, Rosen holds the entire human race responsible for the Holocaust. The behavior of the Germans toward Jews during the war only demonstrates what each of us is capable of doing to one another, she maintains. "The Germans are all of us," one of the characters in Touching Evil points out, and generations to come will "be sickened, poisoned with disgust for the human race" as the truth of the Holocaust atrocity is passed on through fact and fiction.

World War Two literature authored by American women in general is similar to the fiction of the Holocaust in its celebration of the strength of women during war. Although these women characters may not face the persecution and dehumanization that Jewish women endured during the Holocaust, their encounters with war are nevertheless often grievous and psychologically taxing. Irene Orgel characterizes a British woman of indomitable spirit in "Fish and Chips" who marches forth with her life and livelihood despite the bombs dropping all around her. In So Thick the Fog Catherine Pomeroy Stewart portrays a French woman whose strength of character holds together her family as the adversities of war threaten again and again to tear apart their unity. Kay Boyle imagines a French woman of immense courage and mysterious allure in "Let There Be Honour" who repeatedly risks her life to aid escaping soldiers in an underground connection. The American war wife of Laura Kalpakian's "Wine Women and Song" becomes one of the six million American women who entered the labor market during World War Two, many of whom moved into positions previously considered reserved for "men only." Shirley refuses to sacrifice the identity she has successfully created for herself during her husband's absence once he returns, expecting his wife to be unchanged. Although another American wife in Bessie Breuer's "Home is a Place" loses her husband to war, she gains in individuality as she realizes for the first time that she is not just "somebody's wife" anymore and is now free to create her own identity.

The losses suffered by women to war are documented in these novels and short fictions. While women characterized in Holocaust fiction frequently lose not only family and friends but their individual dignity and integrity as well, those women who did not experience the Holocaust also sustain losses. Women characters in Martha Gellhorn's "Week End at Grimsby," "Portrait of a Lady," and "Till Death Us Do Part" sacrifice lovers to war while the young WAC in Bessie Breuer's "Bury Your Own Dead" loses both her brother and the capacity to express her feelings. Although their losses may be less severe, women characters in several of these fictional works experience loneliness and isolation while their husbands go to war. The young war wife in Dorothy Parker's "The Lovely Leave" envies her soldier-husband because his life has expanded with purpose and companionship during the war while hers has contracted with loneliness and isolation. The protagonist of Josephine Johnson's "The Rented Room" longs to establish a sense of family and home but cannot because as long as the war lasts, her family remains transient and home must be a rented room. The wife and mother in M. K. F. Fisher's "The Unswept Emptiness" anticipates the return of her husband to liberate her from the continued domestic burden of childrearing and housekeeping that have characterized her banal existence during the years her husband has been at war. In her novel Beginning the World Again, Roberta Silman examines the loneliness of the wives of the scientists involved in the Manhattan Project who endured enforced isolation as well as estrangement from their preoccupied husbands while they labored under intense pressure to perfect the atomic bomb.

In several World War Two novels and short stories adolescent females are introduced to war during one of the most impressionable times in their lives. For the young protagonist in Paule Marshall's Brown Girl, Brownstones, the reality of war so distant only becomes believable as she undergoes the drastic physical changes of sexual maturation, her body "in sudden upheaval—her dark blood flowing as it flowed in the war, the pain at each shudder of her womb as sharp as the thrust of a bayonet" (57). Ellen Gilchrist's short stories explore maturing young women's emerging perceptions of war as they integrate war into their growing consciousness as one of life's many varied experiences. Frances DeArmand's "When War Came" focuses on a 16-year-old adolescent who attempts to assimilate the concept of war into her protected life but only begins to sense its reality when a classmate dies in combat.

The fictional writings in this collection which emphasize war's effect on youth illustrate that children are seldom immune to the destructive forces of war and often become innocent victims and even involuntary participants of war. The greatest crime ever committed by war, Edita Morris declares in "Heart of Marzipan," is "putting out the laughter of children." War also deprives children of their parents, as illustrated in such stories as Kay Boyle's "Winter Night" and Heather Ross Miller's "War Games," and exposes them much too soon in their young lives to horrifying realities of the often inhumane adult world, as shown by Kay Boyle in "The Lost" and Elzbieta Ettinger in Kindergarten. Stories such as Edna Blue's "Nothing Overwhelms Giuseppe" and Heather Ross Miller's "Stasia and Marek" celebrate the resilience of children to the war experience and their unflinching optimism in spite of the presence of war in their lives, while Joan Coons' "The Christmas Gift" evidences that children are sometimes forced to become active participants in the drama of war.

Although most women writers define the World War Two experience from a female viewpoint, several of these writers assume a male perspective in their writings which seek to examine the relationship of men and war and the individual effect war has upon those who experience combat. Martha

Gellhorn portrays a combat photographer in "Till Death Us Do Part" who may symbolize many men who have conflicting emotions toward war. Although Bara professes to detest the destructive, wasteful idiocy of war, he admits he is attracted with equal intensity to the thrilling diversity and freedom from commitment the game of war offers. Dorothy Parker characterizes a soldier in "The Lovely Leave" who has become so institutionalized by the military system and detached from civilian life that he cannot make the transition from soldier to husband and remains emotionally detached from his forsaken wife during his brief leave at home. Alison Stuart contrasts men's differing attitudes toward fighting in her award-winning "Sunday Liberty." While two landlocked sailors anxiously await their overseas orders, a third soldier attempts suicide to avoid military duty and the obligation to kill. Martha Gellhorn characterizes a reclusive veteran in her narrative "In the Highlands" who shuns the company of other people and ultimately discovers a purpose to his life cultivating the primitive farmland of Africa. Pearl S. Buck's "Begin to Live" describes the awkward transition of a one-armed veteran who returns home hopeful he can forget his two years of military service, "rip them out of his life, burn them up and scatter the ashes," but discovers it is difficult to shed his military indoctrination and persistent memories of war and even more difficult to express his confused feelings to civilians. In her "Letter Home," Buck analyzes the frustration of a soldier trying in vain to verbalize his war experiences in a letter home. He finally concludes that trying to compose the letter is futile, for only those who have undergone similar experiences during war could ever understand his emotions.

The creation of the atomic bomb and continued repercussions of the bombing of Hiroshima are detailed in the writings of Pearl S. Buck, Roberta Silman, and Edita Morris. Buck and Silman examine the motives and consciences of the men and women involved in the creation of the atomic bomb. Although the Americans knew the bomb had immense destructive capability, they convinced themselves that its use was morally acceptable in order to save the world from the spread of Hitlerism and end the war. But years later the moral gravity of that decision still weighs heavily on their minds. Edita Morris' novels, set in Japan following the war, emphasize the continued physical suffering of Hiroshima survivors who sustained radiation exposure that has continued to affect successive generations of Japanese. Her writings also document the mental anguish of the survivors of Hiroshima who recall the morning of August 6, 1945 with an awful clarity that refuses to fade. Morris laments that the "seeds of Hiroshima are tainted and they will blow about the world for centuries to come. . . " (Seeds 92). Her novels also testify to the strength of women whose voices rise in protest against war, even as one courageous woman in The Seeds of Hiroshima makes a suicidal leap from a mountain with her deformed son as a warning to future generations of the destructive capacity of war.

Other women's writings question the widespread anti-Japanese sentiment so prevalent in the United States during the war. Pearl S. Buck's "The Golden Bowl" illustrates how Japanese civilians living in the United States were stereotyped and persecuted against as were Americans who refused to become a part of the anti-Japanese movement and were consequently ostracized and considered suspect in their loyalty. "Nasakenai," co-authored by Candace Nosaka Ames and Louann Nosaka, illustrates how Japanese living in the United States who were once highly valued as employees were abruptly considered untrustworthy and possibly dangerous overnight as the war began, dismissed from their positions by loyal Americans caught up in a sweeping "gesture of patriotism." Gretel Ehrlich's Heart Mountain and short stories written by Hisaye Yamamoto and Marnie Mueller document the degradation of Japanese victims imprisoned in internment camps during the war, bitter at their loss of home, freedom, and personal integrity.

Leslie Silko's Ceremony exposes a similar prejudice against American Indians who were granted an inflated sense of importance and equality while serving in the war but were promptly and efficiently demoted to their original inferior position once their uniforms were removed. Ann Petry explores the themes of racism and war in her short story "In Darkness and Confusion." A black mother and father wage a private war of their own against the entire white society which they hold responsible for the unjustifiable suffering of their soldier-son.

The "enemy" is given human dimension in short stories written by Pearl S. Buck and Leslie Brownrigg. These narratives reduce war from a vast arena to an individual confrontation. In "The Enemy" the Japanese physician characterized by Buck may detest Americans but cannot ignore his commitment to healing as he endangers his own life to help an escaped American prisoner recover and eventually escape once more. The young woman in Brownrigg's "Man Gehorcht" learns to love an enemy soldier whom she discovers to be similar to herself in values and ideals, despite the fact that her country and his are at war. In Edita Morris' Flowers of Hiroshima American and Japanese citizens once considered enemies mourn together the devastation of lives caused by the atomic bombing, allied in the hope that another "Hiroshima" will never occur again.

The writings of Kay Boyle examine the impact of war on European countries, especially France. In "Defeat" and Primer for Combat Boyle captures the mood of French citizens after their defeat by the Germans in 1940, overwhelmed by loss and a sense of betrayal when their dejected veterans return, convinced their country will never be the same again. Several of her short stories, such as "Their Name is Macaroni" and "Poor Monsieur Panalitus," expose a sometimes violent prejudice on the part of the French against foreigners living in their country while "This They Took With Them" highlights a more positive side of human nature among those few humanitarians who are willing to take the time and risk their own security to help aid injured soldiers.

A patriotic, even didactic tone dominates some of these narratives which strongly support the war effort, while others question the validity of war and the inevitable losses that result. Kay Boyle's writings illustrate her lack of tolerance for those who gave personal interests a higher priority than the war effort. In her novel His Human Majesty Boyle traces the roots of war and individual conflict to the simplistic "absence of failure of human bonds" which she insists can be rebuilt through individual effort.

Dorothy Canfield Fisher criticizes Americans as an insular, protected people unwilling to face the threat of Hitlerism in "Americans Must Be Told," their indifference leaving them potentially vulnerable to invasion. The antiwar bias evident in Edita Morris' novels is also present in other women's writings of the World War Two period. Male characters in Martha Hall's "Lucky Lafe" and Martha Gellhorn's "Till Death Us Do Part" not only experience war but question war as well. War is a game, laments the combat photographer in Gellhorn's story, in which men lose what they love and destroy what others love. While friends of the female protagonist in Gellhorn's "Week End at Grimsby" predict that only a few years of peace will pass following the war before the British attack the Russians, Lily confesses she would rather move to a deserted island in the Dead Sea rather than have to live through another pointless war. The male protagonist of Ann Chidester's No Longer Fugitive defends his initial refusal to enlist in the war effort while he questions the effectiveness of war in general: "Does it profit civilization to kill men in this barbaric fashion?" he asks. "Does that solve the puzzle? It is seed for another war. Is that progress?" (146). Pam Durban's "Notes Toward an Understanding" accentuates the changing attitudes toward war within a family as the Vietnam Generation daughter becomes an ardent pacifist while her World War Two veteran father continues to define himself, even years later, through his war experience.

A strong adherence to realism is evident in these fictional works. Although the young American pilot in Pearl S. Buck's "Courtyards of Peace" crashes in a Chinese paradise isolated from war and is offered the opportunity to live in this peaceful utopia for the rest of his life, it is back to reality and the uncertainty of war that he yearns to go. Breaking with traditional form, Connie Willis experiments with the element of time in "Fire Watch" as her protagonist travels back and forth between World War Two and the twenty-first century. Elzbieta Ettinger, Barbara Fischman Traub, and Henia Karmel-Wolfe also experiment with leaps forward and backward in time in their Holocaust novels. Chelsea Quinn Yarbro's dark fantasy "Renewal" imagines casualties of war transformed into vampires with indefinite lifespans. But these deviations from the tradition of realism in form and content are definite exceptions in this body of literature.

Martha Gellhorn's writings introduce journalistic fiction into the canon of war literature, a style that is part reportage, part fiction and undoubtedly, somewhat autobiographical. Gellhorn's novels and short stories offer a realistic examination of war from the viewpoint of a woman always close to the front. In his 1948 review of Wine of Astonishment, Bennell Braunstein wrote that Gellhorn "has come closer to that subject (war) than any other American woman writer. . . . War, to her is a very human affair" (10).

Although their perceptions and themes may vary, these writers' literary interpretations emphasize the impact of war on the lives of women who may not experience direct combat but nevertheless experience war, whether they are gassed in a concentration camp at Buchenwald or showered with black atomic rain at Hiroshima or overcome with postwar grief in rural England. Their writings emphasize the pervasive, long-term effects of war far away from the front in terms of time and distance.

Long after the peace treaty has been signed, this literature illustrates,
lovers mourn soldiers who never returned, widows begin to build their
own self identities, shell-shocked soldiers struggle to readjust to civilian
life, many Japanese continue to die a slow and agonizing death from
radiation exposure while Americans who aided in designing the atomic
bomb still wrestle with their consciences, and Holocaust survivors come to
the sobering realization that surviving their ordeal was only the beginning
of a lifetime of learning to recover from the war. Like the interconnected
matrushka doll in Barbara Fischman Traub's novel, each character
portrayed in these novels and short stories has multiple layers of identity
that are separate yet part of the whole. While the experience of war is but
one of these layers, it is a predominant one that will continue to influence
these characters' visions and perspectives as they accumulate more and
more layers to their lives.

NOVELS

73.   Alexander, Lynne. <u>Safe Houses</u>. New York: Atheneum, 1985.

> <u>Safe Houses</u> contrasts the lives of two Holocaust survivors whose
> distinctive voices alternately narrate this novel. "Gerda's is sensual,
> wry and world-weary, charred by the darkest of humors; Jack's is
> childlike, occasionally mad, yet as ebullient as the pastries he
> concocts in his Brooklyn aerie" (Steinberg 56). Gerda claims to have
> once been the mistress of both Adolph Eichmann and Raoul
> Wallenberg while Jack is an escaped political prisoner who also
> served Eichmann as a hotel pastry chef. At the time of the novel both
> survivors have retreated into the safety of anonymity in a postwar
> Brooklyn apartment building. This unlikely pair of strangers is
> brought together by Gerda's daughter during her search for her
> estranged father (even her mother is unsure of his identity). Gerda
> and Jack become inseparably bonded by the remembrances of their
> World War Two experiences.
>
> Jack recalls the lonely isolation of being segregated from other
> concentration camp comrades and treated as a privileged prisoner
> because his culinary arts were valued and therefore, protected by the
> Nazis. The only consolation for his loneliness was an oak tree
> growing in the center of Buchenwald from which he derived
> strength. He explains:
>
>> "Its bark was gnarled and its boughs hung down like a house
>> of prayer around it. Many times I stood at my window and
>> prayed to it to turn me into a normal prisoner. I knew it would
>> never happen because the Kochs were enjoying the fruits of my
>> labor too much to get rid of me. But I drew comfort from the
>> tree's strength and dignity; that it could stay standing in the
>> midst of human swill and not crumble. I imagined its roots
>> went lower than the blood which was spilled daily and its
>> branches reached up beyond the bit of sky above us ringed with
>> smoke from the gas ovens. There it stood in the center of that

horrible universe just as I stood in the center of my kitchen in front of my black stove. My only comrade." (115)

Gerda, pressured into prostitution by her father, becomes a hardened, agoraphobic woman after the war who continues the only profession she has ever known and develops a caustic, cynical outlook on life, as reflected in this passage:

> "Life is a hole, that's my philosophy. One step forward and boom, up to the armpits. You grab onto a tree, somebody stretches out a helping hand, a ladder, a rope—somehow you find a way out. But you begin to notice they're all around these curious holes, you can't dance around them forever. Eventually you drop your guard and fall in again, and then see how easy it is to climb out! You are older now, your legs are not so strong; your insurance policy doesn't cover such-and-such a natural or unnatural disaster. So you decide to stay until you recover your strength; you realize you are quite safe, there are no further holes into which you can fall. Ah, soon your hole is your castle! Welcome home." (204)

From their "safe houses" in the United States these two survivors offer a "stark and unsentimental view of the Holocaust that is disturbing and often affecting," writes reviewer Laurel Graeber for The New York Times Book Review (18). Alexander's first novel, Publishers Weekly reviewer Sybil Steinberg writes, "conveys some bitter truths: that each of us bears the potential of a dangerous duality, that safe houses are the prisons of the complacent and that those who would nourish a devastated world must be hopeful, loving and a bit mad" (56).

74. Berger, Zdena. Tell Me Another Morning. New York: Harper and Brothers, 1959.

Tell Me Another Morning recounts the experience of a Jewish Holocaust survivor who spends the last years of her adolescence in a concentration camp. The novel documents the inhumane conditions of the camp and brutal nature of some German officials (one rams a cue stick into the vagina of selected female prisoners each Sunday while the others are forced to watch), balanced by the strength of endurance the women subjected to this ordeal discover within themselves and share with one another in their mutual effort to survive despite the odds carefully calculated against them.

Tania doubts there are enough words in her language to adequately describe the concentration camp experience. The word "hungry" seems so inadequate for the constant, gnawing feeling of near starvation imposed upon camp prisoners. "Maybe we do not have enough words," she speculates. "No word of the time of peace can fit a time of war" (142).

Like many camp prisoners, Tania loses track of the days, each blurring into the next in this seemingly unreal existence. She wonders if the male prisoners experience the same blurred impressions of the movement of time that the women do. Time seems to pass "by and around the four corners of the camp, not moving inside, not changing anything. I can only tell time by the color of the sky or by my body," she says (142). One spring as Tania realizes that her twentieth birthday may have recently passed, she wonders if she has left her teenage years behind while she has lived this isolated existence and has unknowingly slipped into adulthood and all that it used to signify to her before her incarceration:

> I would like to know if I am twenty or not. Twenty is a nice round figure. It almost finishes something. I don't know what. I used to think that was old. Twenty is married and powder, high heels and headaches, a certain smell and lips painted red. I don't feel twenty but maybe I am. (189)

As rumors circulate that the end of the war is near and liberation appears as a realistic possibility for the first time, Tania feels a sense of intimidation at the prospect of her long awaited freedom, departing from the security of the camp where her life has been so controlled and individual choice repressed. Leaving behind intimate friendships to enter a world that seems to have grown so much larger and stranger during the war is frightening. Like a veteran of war, Tania returns to a changed homeland feeling like a disoriented stranger for whom the resumption of a normal existence, if that is even possible, will require a lengthy period of readjustment.

Born in Prague, the author of this novel survived imprisonment in several concentration camps, including Auschwitz and Bergen-Belsen, and became an American citizen in 1955.

75. Boyle, Kay. His Human Majesty. New York: McGraw-Hill, 1949.

In this novel Boyle creates a "microcosm" of the universe in a United States military camp where American soldiers prepare for war. "While its men and women retain their idiosyncratic personalities, they represent the entire spectrum of humanity in its various fragmentations by nationality, values, and temperament" (Spanier 170). The bigotry that lies at the root of World War Two is also manifest in the prejudice American soldiers demonstrate against minority members of their own camp. The same Nazi psychology which labeled Jews as scapegoats operates here as well. "War is simply a magnification of the struggles that have raged on a personal level in the microcosm of the camp" (Spanier 171).

Boyle traces the roots of war and individual conflict to the "absence or failure of human bonds." As the soldiers in this camp head to the war in Europe, "it is as though after struggling to define their own identities—their capacities for courage or cowardice, honor or betrayal—they realize that facing evil in such a clear-cut form as the Nazis will be simply a continuation of the same struggle" (Spanier 171). But Boyle also maintains faith in each individual to discover his own "human majesty" which can enable him to rebuild those bonds of humanitarianism. During the naturalization ceremony of one of the Jewish soldiers, he speaks for Boyle as he voices the central theme of the novel:

> I believe that we are all lost, all of us, unless we can make a brotherhood of men, of all men. . . . Out of the great common suffering that has been our experience, we can make a brotherhood of man, we can make a great common love. (233)

76. Boyle, Kay. 1939. New York: Simon and Schuster, 1948.

This short novel emphasizes the impact of war on an individual level as a man and woman both face devastating changes in their lives brought on by war. As the onset of war interrupts their romantic tryst in the serenity of the Alpine Mountains, it "left Corinne alone in the high bright Alpine silence, still fighting in her mind for her lover's chance at dignity and freedom. It took Ferdl from the mountain snows, the space and solitude, and sent him, without status or identity, to a concentration camp" (Havighurst 12).

Narrated almost entirely by a flashback of moral struggle, the novel traces ski instructor Ferdl Eder's conflict to the declaration of war between France and Germany in 1939. Living as a man without a country for several years, Eder is forced at the onset of war to make a commitment to a national identity—either to his native Austria, now incorporated into Germany, or to France. As he reports to enlist in the French military forces, he is interned as an enemy alien and deported to a concentration camp. For Eder, war represents a restraint of freedom which forces him into defined choices as explained by reviewer Walter Havighurst:

> He had chosen to be both an Austrian and a Frenchman; he wanted both freedom and a woman's love. He had tried to live uncommitted, and he had failed. . . . He had been a champion at the things men do individually. He had not learned, for all his mountain climbing, that men are relentlessly roped together. (12)

Although this novel is brief and covers only a 24-hour period, it is complex in structure. "While the sentiments expressed in the novel are vintage Boyle," writes critic Sandra Whipple Spanier, "the flavor of the syntax is decidedly Faulkner," as Boyle experiments with flashbacks, shifts in time and narrative voice, interior monologues and imaginary conversations, and multiple points of view (164).

77. Boyle, Kay. Primer for Combat. New York: Simon and Schuster, 1942.

A novel written in the form of a diary of an American historian's wife, Primer for Combat covers roughly 100 days during and after the fall of France in 1940, one of the most devastating periods of time the "French have ever lived through, both as 'private persons' and as a nation, if it can be said that the French did live at all during that period" (Atlantic 152). Centered in a small French village, the novel magnifies the thoughts, both expressed and unexpressed, of its inhabitants in search of the very human side of war, "exploring a people's psychological reactions under the immense pressure of a political force majeure" (Hauser 6). Shortly after the armistice between France and Germany is signed, writes the narrator of the diary, "In every shop, in every mouth, in every face there is the one thing heard, or said, or written out: 'We have been betrayed; we have been betrayed; we have been betrayed'" (22). Although the government talks optimistically of "reconstruction," the narrator records the tone of the voices of the French people as "something quite different, for they know it can never be the same" as their soldiers return home "defeated and betrayed" to a life now defined by "restrictions and unemployment" under the oppressive German rule (22).

An Atlantic Monthly review of the novel describes Primer for Combat as "the first book written about the fall of France which conveys a sense of reality to those who were not caught in that disaster" and suggests its most important value to be "in the numerous unforgettable scenes and characters it describes, and in its authenticity." As narrator, Boyle becomes neither "journalist nor a political polemist" but always remains very much "an artist," according to the review (Atlantic 152).

78.   Buck, Pearl S. Command the Morning. New York: John Day Company, 1959.

Pearl Buck's interest in the creation of the atomic bomb which ended World War Two has demonstrated itself in several of her writings, including this novel which covers a period of five years during the creation, perfection, and eventual deployment of the atomic bomb. The novel focuses attention on the moral issues facing scientists who designed the bomb for the Manhattan Project: "whether they could in conscience devote their talents to the building of an instrument of destruction, a device which would cause untold death and suffering and, conceivably, might trigger the extinction of man" (Boatwright 4). Combining real scientists with fictional characters, Buck presents every argument against the use of the bomb that could be marshaled and regrets not only its deployment but the fact that by dropping the atomic bomb, men ignored the feelings of many women who voiced their opposition to the inhumanity of such an act and the repercussions it would have for the United States. If we drop the bomb "we'll destroy ourselves, everywhere in the world," one woman protests. "People won't believe in us any more" (276).

The morning of the bombing Buck contrasts the casual serenity of Japanese citizens in Hiroshima as they carry out their customary routines with the sudden obliteration of life forthcoming, encapsulated in a deceptively small receptacle:

> Over the city in Japan the plane floated like a butterfly above an open flower. It hovered like a fish hawk above a silver pond in the morning when the goldfish swarm to the surface to catch the light of the sun. It was a midsummer morning, the day's business just begun. Men walking to their offices, women riding in rickshas to the market, children ready to march to their classes, heard the roar of the wings above them. They lifted their faces and saw a plane in the sky, a single plane. They were reassured. One Plane. What damage could it do? Enemy planes came in hundreds to do their work. This was one—a reconnaissance plane? People smiled at each other in relief and went their way.
>
> Unnoticed, a silver thing fell out of the plane and twisted downward, a small thing in the sky, not bigger than a toy, a glittering dot, a piece torn from the sun. It was in fact a piece of the sun, a globe of fire, one third of a mile in diameter, with a temperature in the center of one hundred million degrees Fahrenheit, compressed into a small metal container. Suddenly the container burst. The air around it was forced away by the enormous pressure and out of the fierce violence winds arose at hundreds of miles an hour, even a thousand, in great waves. The mighty push, the violent blast, set aflame everything within its reach, wood, cloth, thatched roofs, great works of art, and human flesh, blood, bone and brain. (284)

Buck compares the bland reaction of the American bombardier who releases the atomic bomb as casually as if it were "like any other bomb" to the emotional response of one of the few survivors in the "dead city" who crawls from the safety of his cellar, surveys the "smoking desert of death and destruction," and howls in despair: "This—this is beyond human endurance!" (285).

In Command the Morning Buck reminds us of our limitless capacity for the destruction of life on this planet, ironically attained through continued scientific inquiry and the quest to discover during this century. Although the novel has been commended for its historical accuracy and presentation of moral dilemma, which "appeals to man's conscience for the final answer," Buck's work has been criticized for its heavy didacticism and obvious propaganda, which "pulls the story away from artistic balance" (Doyle 127). The "human interest" side of the novel has also been criticized as "thin" in plot development and characterization, detracting from the "force of the author's moral argument, which is foursquare on the side of life and against the use of the bomb for destruction. . . " (Boatwright 4).

79.   Buck, Pearl S. <u>Dragon Seed</u>. New York: John Day, 1941.

One morning while Ling Tan tends his rice fields a flight of "flying ships" suddenly appear from the east, flying much too swiftly to be geese out of season. He stops as soon as he notices them, and like every other nearby farmer working his land, "they stood, their faces turned upward not in fear but only in wonder at such speed and such beauty" (67). From one of the "silver creatures" tumbles silver eggs, one of which lands in a nearby field, delighting one of the peasants who had wanted a pond for ten years but had not found the time to dig it. Together the farmers decide that this must be the "purpose of these machines, to dig ponds and wells and waterways where they wanted" (68).

It is only when Ling Tan and his son investigate the smoke rising from a nearby city that they are introduced to the destructive power of the silver eggs and the devastating reality of war. To his young son who vomits at the sight of a woman searching for the remains of her husband in the city ruins who can only find one foot and part of a leg, Ling Tan offers words of consolation that evidence his abhorrence of war: "It is no shame to be sick at such sights as these," he tells his son. "A man if he is honorable ought to be sickened and angry. Only wild beasts cannot know shame at what has been done here to innocent people" (79).

Despite the threat to his life imposed by war, Ling Tan refuses to flee his homeland, this soil that his ancestors have toiled for centuries past, although some of his sons choose to leave. Ling Tan continues to believe in the wisdom passed down from the ancients that "no good man would be a soldier and that the warlike man was the least of men and not to be respected" while he clings tenaciously to his belief in nonviolent resistance as an alternative to fighting (113). When one of his sons rejects his father's philosophy and becomes full of the "zest for war" he so despises, Ling Tan expresses the wish that this son die before the war's end: "A man who kills because he loves to kill ought to die for the good of the people, though he is my own son. Such men are always tyrants and we who are the people are ever at their mercy" (251). Ling Tan worries that the devotion to peace which has been passed down from generation to generation in his country may be displaced by an acceptance of war as an inevitable means of conflict resolution. We must pass on to future generations who have yet to experience war the timeless concept that peace is "man's great food," he resolves.

As the novel ends, the Chinese people are uplifted by the news that their resistance against the Japanese has become "part of a worldwide struggle against evil" (Doyle 108). Although <u>Dragon Seed</u> was published before the Allied powers entered the war against Japan, Paul A. Doyle writes in <u>Pearl S. Buck</u>, the novel "was predicated on the need and desirability of more active support for China, and it definitely had been intended to arouse sympathy for the Chinese cause" (109).

The first fictionalized account of the Japanese occupation of China during the 1930s, Dragon Seed documents the "piteous and dreadful awakening" of peaceful peasants, whose simplistic existence had been rooted to the cultivation of the soil, to the aggressive and often brutal forces of war imposed upon them for more than four years by invading Japanese forces. While one of Ling Tan's sons is violated by several lust-crazed soldiers, the ancient and obese mother of a merchant is brutally raped and mutilated by Japanese soldiers. "For the first time in history these Chinese farmers witnessed destructive bombing from airplanes, the wanton killing of innocent civilians, and bestial attacks on very young and very old women" (Doyle 107). Although they were accustomed to frequent bandit skirmishes and warlord raids, "the farmers in the Nanking area had never beheld any cruelty so intense and so indiscriminate" (107).

If dragon seeds are a symbol of heroism in China, Buck's novel celebrates the heroic tenacity, humility, patience, and resilience of these Chinese peasants whose simplicity and innocent devotion to peaceful coexistence in the face of four years of Japanese oppression attests to human greatness (Woods 3). A Time review characterizes the novel as "discreet and powerful propaganda" that "makes tangible the living, the suffering, and the bravery of a great and obscure people under four years of hermetic tyranny, in a defeat which refused to stay put" ("Bloody Ballet" 80).

80. Buck, Pearl S. The Promise. New York: John Day, 1943.

The sequel to Dragon Seed, this novel is a fictionalized account of the disastrous Chinese campaign in Burma during the spring of 1942 which forever ended the sacred prestige of white men in the hearts of the common people of China and needlessly cost many Chinese lives. The Promise weaves together two "vast themes: the Chinese struggle for freedom from aggression" and "the Asiatic hope for equality with the white man" (Palmer 6). The Burma campaign, "from which China hoped for such great things and lost so sorely," Buck contends in her novel, was a "betrayal of China" on the part of self-serving British forces (Palmer 6). Although the Chinese faithfully executed the plan ordered by the British to defend their troops as they crossed a strategic bridge to safety on the Burmese border, the British then destroyed the bridge prematurely before the Chinese could reach safety, and the bulk of their troops were then slaughtered. The remaining Chinese returned home feeling abandoned and disillusioned by the carelessness of the British and "refusal of white men to treat them as genuine equals and allies" (Doyle 110).

Before the campaign in Burma, one of the Chinese leaders in the novel assures his soldiers: "We are all equals and brothers in this war, chosen because we are strong and young and because we are not afraid to die. . . . On the way in which you fight hangs more than you know. Our foreign allies must see in us what our people are, and allow to us our equal place in the world" (98). But following the tragedy, the Chinese general's thoughts reflect an entirely different attitude. "The white men are leagued together against us," he admits, "and they have let us come into their enemy country and they have not taken us as equals. "Let them cling together and we will act for ourselves since we are not to be treated as allies" (22).

The Promise, writes Paul A. Doyle in Pearl S. Buck, presents a "patriotic and stirring appeal for the Chinese cause. The prejudice of the white men, their feelings of superiority over Asians, their refusal to treat the Chinese with equality, the harm that these attitudes were causing in the war against Japan—these matters are reiterated through the novel" (111). Although the novel is best known for its historical accuracy, it is considered too dominated by propaganda and a contrived romantic relationship to be considered one of Buck's most artistic works.

81. Chidester, Ann. No Longer Fugitive. New York: Charles Scribner's Sons, 1943.

Written in a derivative style closely resembling the prose style of Thomas Wolfe, No Longer Fugitive is a bildungsroman of a young man's search for himself and clarification of his beliefs about war. Denounced as cowardly by some of his family members and friends for his refusal to enlist in the war effort, 20-year-old Liam Moore defends the logic of his antiwar position while he questions those who criticize his stance. "Does it profit civilization to kill men in this barbaric fashion?" he asks. "Does that solve the puzzle? It is seed for another war. Is that progress? I want to live and let live" (146).

To clarify his own beliefs and escape the oppressive atmosphere of home, Liam sets out from Minnesota on a solitary journey of self-discovery which can only come through experience and discovery of inner peace, a process which Liam describes in himself as a transition from "obsidian darkness into the fierce wonder of high noon" (286). Through his search for self and meaning in life, Liam comes to believe that "All men who believe and desire to believe are brothers. Their fight is my fight" (403). With great joy—and equal amounts of sorrow as well—he resolves to return home and fulfill his military obligation despite his opposition to war in general. In this novel, Chidester traces the evolution of a young man's attitude toward war and country, shaped through external experience and internal introspection, into mature thought.

82. Demetz, Hana. The House on Prague Street. New York: St. Martin's Press, 1980.

Written in the form of a memoir, this novel records the impressions of a young Czechoslovakian woman of German and Jewish parentage, who grew up during the Nazi terrorism of World War Two and loses most of the people closest in her life to war. As the only survivor of her immediate family, the narrator loses her mother when the Germans occupying her home refuse to transport a Jew to the hospital; her father dies in a similar, ironic twist of fate because the Czechs will not give medical aid to a German.

While her novel documents the fearful uncertainty which characterized the daily lives of Jews who lived during the Hitler era and their continual witness to careless acts of brutality, Demetz's writing also illustrates that the experiences and corresponding emotions associated with childhood and adolescence continue, despite the presence of war. War only makes these periods of growth more complicated and often frustrating. Newsweek reviewer Jean Strouse commends Demetz for narrating "this grim, often-told tale from a fresh angle, seeing all its ironies and victims with sympathetic dispassion" (78).

83.   Ehrlich, Gretel. Heart Mountain. New York: Viking Press, 1988.

This novel documents with compassion and a sense of shame the war experience of 10,000 Japanese-Americans who were imprisoned at Heart Mountain Relocation Camp for four years during World War Two. The novel also concerns itself with the effect of the war and sudden appearance of the camp on nearby ranchers and small-town residents whose lives were inevitably drawn together with these prisoners by the circumstances of war. In his review of the novel Garrett Hongo refers to Heart Mountain as a "richly textured and grandly romantic work about individual alienation and sexual loneliness, a novel full of immense poetic feeling for the internal lives of its varied characters and the sublime high plains landscape that is its backdrop" (37).

On February 19, 1942 President Franklin Delano Roosevelt signed an executive order giving the Secretary of War "the authority to designate military areas and exclude all or any people from them" (Author's Note xv). As a result of this order, 110,000 Japanese immigrants and Japanese-Americans innocent of any wrongdoing were removed from their homes, farms, and businesses and ordered to relocate in ten internment camps. Heart Mountain was one of these, a cluster of tarpaper shacks set up in a remote area of Wyoming. In her preface to the novel, Ehrlich explains that her writing "is a blend of fact and fiction. The Heart Mountain Relocation Camp did exist and the political realities are faithful to fact," she writes (Author's Note xv). The political realities of this war experience are translated by the author into the human suffering of many Japanese-Americans who were "swept away by the forces of history and an avalanche of racial prejudice" (Willms 100).

The novel, a blend of journal entries, letters, and narrative, focuses on one camp prisoner in particular who rebels against his imprisonment, despite the consequences involved. For Kai, the camp comes to symbolize everything he has hated in life: "exile, deviousness, injustice." Among Kai's numerous journal entries included in the novel is one in which he writes:

Sunday. Another black day. For twenty-three years I've looked in the mirror and never seen my face as "Japanese." How naive could I have been? Now I hate what I've come from. I try to appear calm and good-natured, but inside I'm seething. How can a nation that purports to fight fascism use fascist techniques to solve problems at home—and expect not to get caught in its lie. And that would be the worst thing—the hypocrisy is one thing, but getting away with it would be the real tragedy. (92)

Kai helps to lead a movement in the camp to resist the draft of interned prisoners for military service. He considers it an "outrage" to ask young Japanese prisoners to "sign up for a war which purports to protect democracy when our own democratic rights have been unconstitutionally withdrawn from us" (131). The petition Kai drafts with the assistance of other resisters reads, in part:

"Although we have yellow skins, we too are Americans. We have an American upbringing. Therefore, we believe in fair play. Our firm conviction is that we would be useless Americans if we did not assert our constitutional rights now; for unless our status as citizens is cleared and we are really fighting for the high ideas upon which our nation is based, how can we say to the white American buddies in the armed forces that we are fighting for the perpetuation of democracy, especially when our fathers, mothers, and families are in concentration camps, even though they are not charged with any crime?" (134)

This regretful chapter in American history is given human dimension in Ehrlich's novel which joins a diverse group of Americans and Japanese-Americans for whom a faraway war became an overnight nightmare invading each of their lives.

84.   Ettinger, Elzbieta. Kindergarten. Boston: Houghton Mifflin, 1970.

This novel chronicles the destruction of a wealthy Jewish family in Poland during the war. Ettinger's primary focus is on the granddaughter of the family who survives the Holocaust but later disintegrates into an "inhuman madwoman" following the experience, becoming "a mirror image of the people who murdered her fellow Jews" (Fleischer 50).

At first the eruption of war has little effect on Elli's life other than the repetition of gas-mask drills at school and the sight of weary Polish soldiers trudging by in the streets. War takes a step closer when all Jews are forced to wear yellow stars pinned to their chests and backs for identification and are forbidden to walk down certain streets. Elli and her Jewish friends learn to play a hide-and-seek game from the German officers whose authority is terrifying. At last war makes its presence painfully aware to Elli when she becomes a personal victim of its brutal force:

One morning a heavy blow in her back knocked Elli down in the street. In the course of a long diatribe she learned that the gutter was the place where she belonged, along with her filthy forefathers. She had lain awake all that night. When she got up next morning the war was "real" for her. After twenty-four hours she smiled with an air of superiority over the Elli she had been a day earlier, a mere kid with childish theories about wartime dignity and virtue. The contempt in the officer's eyes, the fury constricting his voice, and the loathing grimace distorting his face—that was The War. (21)

Elli avoids deportation to a concentration camp by crossing back and forth across Jewish-gentile barriers, disguising herself as a gentile working for the Nazis while she simultaneously attempts to secure information for Jews trapped in the ghetto. As she observes former allegiances continually betrayed by self-serving interests, Elli learns never to trust anyone. She comes to believe that the inhumane Germans may ironically be the only honest people remaining in the world whose intentions are not cloaked in dishonesty: "Poles betray Jews; Jews betray Jews; the only honest and trustworthy people left are the Germans because they were kind enough to notify us in advance that they are going to destroy us and are merely pursuing their goal" (56). Elli's learned distrust and confusion of identity have tragic psychological repercussions for her in later life. "Warned never to trust anyone, compelled to hide her real feelings from others, she is finally unable to retain her humanness, and as the mask becomes the face she is driven to madness" (Fleischer 50).

Although Kindergarten focuses on the war years of 1943 and 1944, its narrative progress is not chronological. Flashbacks and journal entries written by Elli blend the past with the present, juxtaposing the early years of the war with the later, more devastating ones for Jewish victims. By moving back and forth in time, Ettinger "is able to dramatize Elli's metamorphosis as the shocks inflicted upon her destroy first her identity, then her reason" (Fleischer 50).

Kindergarten illustrates that survival of the Holocaust is only the beginning of a lifetime of struggle against memory and fear for those such as Elli who cannot forget. Elli's grandfather, who does not survive the war, predicts before he dies that the casualties of this horrific experience will be the survivors. "Do not think, any of you, that survival is the main problem or the sole target," he warns his family. "The main problem is to be able to live when that time is over" (39). Two decades later, the prologue of the novel reveals, Elli is still haunted by recurring Holocaust nightmares and has lost the battle to retain her humanity. During the war she promised her grandfather she would never forget the experience of the Holocaust, but the price she has paid in terms of her sanity has been costly indeed.

85.   Gellhorn, Martha. <u>Liana</u>. 1944. London: Virago Press, 1987.

Set against the backdrop of war in 1940 shortly after the fall of France
to Germany, this tragic novel explores the relationship of three men
and women living on the French Caribbean island of Saint Boniface
who attempt unsuccessfully to isolate themselves from the war on the
continent.

Liana is a young mulatto woman who becomes imprisoned in a
stifling, controversial marriage to a wealthy Frenchman, too
absorbed in his own profiteering to consider the war except when an
American blockade threatens his commercial interests. Her only
hope for eventual release from the confinement and discontent of
this union is through the relationship she builds with her tutor. But
this relationship is equally doomed as Pierre eventually follows his
conscience and returns to France to join the war effort, leaving Liana
a rejected victim of circumstance with no opportunity for escape.

Pierre's decision to return to France to fight is a difficult one both
emotionally, given his love for Liana, and philosophically, given his
intellectual ideals. War is a "complete abject confused dung," in his
opinion, often waged by corrupt governmental officials who simply
use people as pawns in an ongoing test of power. If war is ever
justified, it must be for a higher ideal, Pierre believes, although he
wonders skeptically if such a war has ever been waged:

> Was there ever a decent war? Was there ever a war where in
> fact men fought for the ideas they were exhorted to fight for
> and the leaders did not lie, bargain, conceal mistakes,
> generously expend others' lives, and survive to be heroic in the
> next war? Was there ever a war in which a man could die
> without bitterness or regret or just plain disgust: where he
> could discount any personal loss, for the cause was as
> honorable as the speech-makers said? (159)

The only ideals worth fighting for, Pierre tells himself, are "dignity
and the rights of man." Although government officials may not
appear to revere such qualities, "millions of men" do, Pierre
convinces himself, as he tries to reconcile his inner conflict. "Why
then, it's like believing in God but not in the church," he concludes.
"You can refuse to believe in the war but you can believe in the people
fighting it" (160). He leaves the isolated security of Saint Boniface for
an uncertain future ahead in combat, rationalizing that Liana is still
young and capable of building a future for herself should he not
return, unaware that at the moment he slips his boat into the water
and heads for the French shore, she is slitting her wrists in lonely
despair.

In the afterword to <u>Liana</u> Gellhorn explains the circumstances
which led her to write the novel, the only one of her novels to ever
appear on <u>The New York Times</u> Best Seller List:

Liana grew from a wonderful lunatic journey through the Caribbean in 1942, about which I have written elsewhere (Travels with Myself and Another). My transport was a potato boat, a thirty-foot sloop with one sail and a hold for hauling potatoes between the islands. We were becalmed on a very small island for four days. I lived in a swoon of joy, hoping the wind would stay dead. I thought that chance had brought me to the last best place in a crazed suffering world. These little islands were always isolated, but at that time—the hurricane season and German submarines—totally isolated. I realized that Eden is a subjective state, and even here people could manage to make themselves unhappy. (255)

In her Belles Lettres review of Liana, Lorraine E. McCormack maintains that Gellhorn's "message of the pervasive evil of war is clear: No matter how remote the spit of land you call home," she writes, "the evil can infect your life" (21).

86. Gellhorn, Martha. Point of No Return. 1948. New York: New American Library, 1989.

In Point of No Return, originally published under the title The Wine of Astonishment, "the last winter of war in the European Theatre smolders and sputters and explodes in the pages of Miss Gellhorn's novel," writes reviewer Walter Havighurst (36). Point of No Return combines the talents of Gellhorn as a war correspondent and a writer of fiction as she recreates military strategy and the combat experience as effectively as the feelings and postwar dreams of men and women trapped in the miasma of war, deprived of time and certainty in their lives. In his review of the first printing of the novel in 1948, Bennell Braunstein wrote that Gellhorn "has come closer to that subject (war) than any other American woman writer. . . . War, to her is a very human affair. She never lets us forget it" (10).

Gellhorn originally intended her novel to be entitled Point of No Return, a technical phrase referring to the specific point at which an airplane pilot must turn his aircraft around and return to his original take off point or run out of fuel before reaching safe territory. For these pilots, the phrase ultimately meant "turn or die." In the afterword to the reissued version of the novel, Gellhorn explains that the editor of Scribner's in 1948 objected to the title Point of No Return as "too bleak" and "too despairing," predicting that "people would not read a novel with that grim title" (331). In retrospect, Gellhorn realized that "Giving up my true title did not alter the writing or the shape of the story; it simply spoiled the book for me," for The Wine of Astonishment seemed "ludicrously wrong with its biblically derived title," she writes. "Hitler, not God, had made the earth to tremble" (331 – 332). With the reprinting of the novel, under her originally intended title 45 years later, Gellhorn joyfully "reclaimed" the book for herself as well.

When the idea for the novel first began to "ferment," Gellhorn explains in the afterword, Jacob Levy, an American-Jewish soldier twice wounded, emerged as a "complete presence" in her mind. "I saw where he was going," she writes, "but not how he was going to get there. . . . He was so constant and so real that for an uneasy while he invaded my sleep and I thought I was dreaming his dreams not mine" (328). All of the characters and events in the novel "had to come into being because of Jacob Levy, the first invention" (330).

Of all the war atrocities Gellhorn witnessed as a journalist, her observations at Dachau, the first Nazi concentration camp, became "her own lifelong point of no return" (330). "Years of war had taught me a great deal, but war was nothing like Dachau. Compared to Dachau, war was clean," writes Gellhorn (330 – 331). As the novel materialized, Jacob Levy's visitation to Dachau became his "point of no return" as well. During one horrifying scene in the novel, Levy observes prisoners of his own Jewish heritage, completely stripped of dignity and personal freedom, impoverished beyond imagination:

> They moved about in a way that was almost like crawling even if they were walking, slow and aimless and sick. Their eyes were all the same: too big, black and empty. There was no recognition or curiosity or anything in those eyes, just sick dead eyes in yellow or grey faces. Their bodies moved, without reason, as there was nowhere to go; and they stared at him. He had never imagined people could look like this.
>
> They were all bald, too. No, their heads were shaved and the skin was so tight on the bone they seemed like bare skulls. Their teeth were rotten, with black holes where teeth were missing. You almost saw the great striped rags that covered them, creeping with lice. Jesus, their hands were enormous too, or maybe it was only because their wrists were thin as sticks. Jacob Levy stood, feeling the sweat come out on his face, and stared back at them: thousands of starved mindless men, weaving in the sunshine. Some of them sat on the ground and from time to time scratched themselves. He had no pity for these men: he had only fear. He was afraid of them, afraid of everything they showed in their eyes and their dragging bodies. He was paralyzed with fear. (272 – 273)

Overwhelmed by this glaring illustration of inhumanity displayed so masterfully, even boastfully, before him, Levy vomits uncontrollably once he leaves Dachau and trembles with rage, ashamed of his own self-centeredness in comparison to the witness of such misery.

Through the character of Jacob Levy, reviewer William Havighurst writes, Gellhorn "brings the public war to bear on a private consciousness, on a man's hopes and wishes, on his humanity. Her novel, with its unfaltering outward reality, moves significantly inward into human character and realization" (36).

87. Gellhorn, Martha. A Stricken Field. New York: Duell, Sloan and
     Pearce, 1940.

This novel is a documentation of the war experience of citizens
displaced by the 1939 German annexation of Sudetenland. Although
the novel centers mainly on the experiences of Mary Douglas, an
American woman journalist covering the event, parts of the writing
also focus on the character of Rita, a former prisoner of war who
helps fellow refugees elude the German Gestapo. In a Belles Lettres
review of the book, Laura Hapke writes that A Stricken Field is "of
historical interest as a testament to the appeasement mentality of
nations that were unwilling to take in German refugees" and could
in some ways be considered "extended reportage" (9). But, she points
out, the novel is also "equally important as a study of the woman-as-
journalist who confronts a human tragedy and is divided between
feminine compassion and masculine detachment" (9). This conflict of
feelings is illustrated in Mary Douglas' factual, yet emotional
depiction of the plight of the refugees she witnesses: "It is like being
buried alive, people deserted everywhere scattered about in empty
houses going crazy, and alone, and no one knowing who they are and
no one hearing them, and no one helping. . . . But it cannot be. It
cannot be" (71). There seems to be no end to the cycle of disaster and
defeat.

In one of the most poignant parts of the novel, an adolescent whose
life has been reduced to a constant state of fear and loneliness
commits suicide. "She was afraid of what would happen to her if she
were caught," Rita realizes in retrospect. "She did not think she
could bear it. Jacob's concentration camp, Thomas' prison, Katy's
prison, the way they tortured Hans. She was afraid to live" (147).
But Douglas discovers heroines still exist in spite of tragedy, women
who refuse to give up, who cling to life in anticipation of a better
future to come. "They have been defeated, and they will not accept
defeat. . ." she writes. "Perhaps if they will not be defeated, they
cannot be defeated" (285).

88. Karmel, Ilona. An Estate of Memory. 1969. New York: The Feminist
     Press, 1986.

Born of Karmel's experience as a survivor of three Nazi workcamps,
An Estate of Memory recreates the lives of four Jewish women who
bond together in a Polish concentration camp during the war. The
predominant theme of the novel, writes Ruth Angress in the
afterword, is "that human beings live by bonding and not in isolation.
The word 'together' dominates from the beginning. Almost every
prisoner is a part of a team, sometimes of relatives, sometimes of
friends" (446 – 447). The four women characterized by Karmel join
together as a birthing team to facilitate the safe delivery of a child
born to one of them and insure her safe deliverance to the world
beyond the barbed-wire imprisonment, giving meaning to their
own wretched lives and gaining assurance that a future does exist.
Karmel's characters, writes Angress, "survive (as long as they do

live) by holding themselves suspended between past and future, memory and hope" (446).

Although one of the women fantasizes a life of freedom once the war is over, when rumors begin to spread that the end is close, the same woman views the concept of freedom, the idea of life beyond the barbed-wire enclosure as almost inconceivable and potentially terrifying:

> Over—the war is over, Tola thought and could not understand what this meant, as though for her, unable to see herself anywhere but here in this camp, there was no war. If the war is over there will be no work tonight; the trucks won't come again if it is over; the smell will lift. And now when she began to understand, panic gripped her; she must run, must find a place to be alone, at once, before everyone burst into a jubilant shout. (403)

An Estate of Memory gives a despairingly accurate depiction of the concentration camp experience from various women's viewpoints, including survivors and non-survivors. The novel also testifies to the strength of cooperation and intimacy of bonding which can occur between women and sustain individuals, even those whose limits of endurance are put to the most severe of tests.

89.   Karmel-Wolfe, Henia. The Baders of Jacob Street. Philadelphia and New York: J. B. Lippincott, 1970.

This novel documents the experience of the Baders of Jacob Street, a typical Jewish family living in Cracow, Poland in 1940, engaged in dual struggles of survival and identity. When World War Two reaches Poland, the Baders attempt escape but return when the futility of their flight becomes apparent. Like their Jewish neighbors, the Baders derive strength from their cultural heritage and mutual will to survive. Unable to foresee the extent of the horrific devastation of their lives to come, they innocently continue their lives as usual, carrying on their traditions and daily rituals as if there really is a future for them. But there will be no future, as their lives are gradually but systematically destroyed under the increasingly oppressive Nazi domination. Stripped of their possessions and herded into the ghetto, the Jews portrayed by Karmel-Wolfe in this novel seem gracefully resigned to their predetermined fate. They accept the indifference of the outside world to their plight with similar resignation, realizing, as one character expresses it, "There is no way out" (205).

The Baders of Jacob Street is narrated from the perspective of 18-year-old Halina who is simultaneously "ashamed of her Jewishness, confused by her emerging sexuality, beset by fears over her family's fate" (Fleisher 50). Halina learns to categorize fellow Jews and their corresponding attitudes toward their bondage by the appearance of their armbands:

There were those who wouldn't give in, the orderly, the neat, the caring. Their armbands, just like the one she was wearing, were immaculate, embroidered, stitched and starched, fastened to their sleeves with snaps, to be easily removed and frequently laundered. There were those in a hurry, the practical ones, the ones who wouldn't be bothered. Their disposable armbands were made from celluloid, held by elastic, the blue star imprinted in the middle, invented by some enterprising soul and peddled at street corners by ten-year-old vendors. There were the camouflagers, the deceivers, the pretenders, who would wear their armbands down their sleeves, close to their wrists, their left hands in their pockets, making believe that they weren't wearing one at all. When stopped and asked about it, they would pull the armband up and hurry to explain, with embarrassed smiles, how it just must have slid down without their noticing. Finally there were those who had stopped caring a long time ago, the repeatedly deported, the ragged, the dirty, the poor. Their armbands were never washed, almost black, twisted to the width of a string. (80)

Ultimately, Halina proves she values her cultural identity more than her instinct for self-preservation as she rejects a fabricated Gentile identity that could have gained her freedom. Instead she chooses to remain with her family and face their predetermined fate together.

90.   Karmel-Wolfe, Henia. Marek and Lisa. New York: Dodd, Mead and Company, 1984.

Marek and Lisa narrates the experience of a young Jewish couple who survive two years in separate Nazi death camps and later search to locate one another once the war ends. Hospitalized at the beginning of the novel, Lisa slowly regains strength and memory, narrated in a series of flashbacks in the novel that trace her prewar relationship with Marek from their underground life attempting to hide from the Nazis, to their arrest and deportation to separate camps, to Lisa's almost fatal gunshot wound sustained when hunger drives her to break a camp line to retrieve a sugar beet lying in a nearby field. As she lies in the field anticipating the end of her life, Lisa's resignation to her death "came without regret, accompanied by a feeling of relief. At least she wouldn't have to march anymore" (10).

But Lisa survives. Part Two of the novel traces Marek's often frustrating attempts to locate his wife while Part Three celebrates a cautiously joyous reunion of a man and woman for whom two years has been a long period of separation, incorporating many changes and permanent fears into their still young lives. As a result of their separate Holocaust experiences, Marek and Lisa realize they may now "be different from what we thought we would be." For their marriage to survive, each realizes that "we will have to learn to love each other the way we really are" (248). Their experiences can never be blocked from memory and will forever remain an indelible part of each one's self identity. Do they still have the capacity for joy left in their lives? In spite of these uncertainties, Marek and Lisa face the future with cautious optimism and the expectation of giving birth to a child to replace the one Lisa once secretly aborted just prior to their arrest, knowing "we wouldn't have had a chance in the world with a child" (247).

91.   Leffland, Ella. Rumors of Peace. New York: Harper and Row, 1979.

This novel recounts an adolescent's reaction to the advent of World War Two as she struggles toward womanhood and a greater awareness of herself and her values. "With the verbal resources of adulthood but none of its impulses to explain or apologize," writes reviewer Harriet Rosenstein, "Leffland's heroine Suse Hansen recounts four years of her life in wartime California. . . . For Suse the war is both a hated reality and a screen onto which she projects her ambivalence about growing up" (40). Reviewer Eva Hoffman characterizes the novel as "a story of initiation into the full range of complexity of experience" which includes a perplexing introduction to war (46).

Rumors of Peace begins with the bombing of Pearl Harbor in 1941 at the time when the narrator is a junior high student living in a coastal town in California. Mendoza mobilizes its defense against possible attack, and repeated air-raid drills create an atmosphere of dreaded expectation and terror for its townspeople. War necessitates many changes in the lives of Americans, especially women:

> Everyone had money to burn; but sugar, coffee, and butter were a luxury and you stood in line at the market with your little green ration book and carried your groceries home in the same paper bag until it fell apart. Dresses were suddenly short and skimpy, with no pockets or ruffles, to conserve cloth. In place of nylon stockings, women covered their legs with tan makeup and drew on black seams with eyebrow pencil. But more often they wore pants called slacks. They worked in shipyards and defense plants. Some of them lived alone, their husbands having been drafted, and with greasy wrenches they repaired their own cars, and with hoes and mowers they cut down the lush spring grass in their backyards and planted victory gardens. (42)

Leffland lends her narrative authenticity by interspersing actual news headlines of the day with the narrative and recording Suse's reactions to the latest events. Early during the war Suse develops an intense dislike of all "Japs" common among Americans at that time. But as the war progresses Suse becomes more ambivalent and confused about her feelings. There are no simple answers for the complex questions that war provokes in her young mind. The war becomes a "moral quandary posed by history" that Suse must confront if she is to find the truth she is seeking (Hoffman 46). The

concept of victory once so simplistic—"everybody against us dead"—
becomes blurred and confused. "Something in me that had been
black as pitch and hard as a diamond, something strong and
unbreakable had broken," writes the narrator, "and in its place was a
strange spread-outness, like a thin, flickering sea, pointlessly
awash" (278). When the atomic bomb is dropped over Japan, even her
sense of allegiance is shaken. Distinctions between the good and bad
sides so clearly set in her mind when the war began have now
become confused. "A whole city of people, ceasing to exist," Suse
reflects in amazement. "And who had done it? Not the Nazis or the
Japs themselves, but us, the good ones, the ones we were supposed to
have faith in, who talked of constructive thought, creativeness,
cooperation, drawing the good out of people. They themselves were
the black beetles" (381). Events such as the atomic bombing of
Hiroshima, writes reviewer James D. Houston, lead Suse "toward
the discovery that certain traits she would like to project outward onto
'the other' are also found within herself—at which point the villain
begans to dissolve and her essential humanity is enlarged" (B3).

As Leffland traces the changes in a young woman's "emerging
social consciousness, played against the backdrop of World War
Two," her novel portrays a young girl during four years of war
"moving toward womanhood" as she gropes her way "through
youthful ignorance and communal prejudices toward moral
awakening and self-knowledge" (B3).

92.   Morris, Edita. The Flowers of Hiroshima. New York: Viking Press,
       1959.

The Flowers of Hiroshima testifies to the prolonged suffering and
innate strength of the survivors of the atomic bombing of Hiroshima
on August 6, 1945. The novel is narrated by one of the survivors who
attempts to protect a visiting American from the truth because she
does not want to offend him and feels he may be too sensitive to
accept the magnitude of misery his country's warfare inflicted upon
hers. Like many survivors, she has built a defensive wall of
protection around the bombing experience in an attempt to conceal
from the rest of the world the agony and misery that continues to
haunt those who have survived.

But the dark secrets of the aftermath of war are visible everywhere to
observant visitors. The American visitor witnesses orphans of the
bombing who now live in asylums, burned survivors barred from
public baths because of the ugliness of their scars, and other
survivors, such as the narrator's husband, who once searched
through piles of dead corpses on the day of the bombing to discover
his wife was still alive but now finds himself dying a gradual and
very painful death from radiation exposure. A Japanese doctor
explains to the American while he visits bombing victims in a
Hiroshima hospital that the damage to bombing victims is both
mental and physical. Atomic bomb patients "suffer from both
external and internal injuries," he confides. "Countless operations

can sometimes remove keloid scars and other marks of the bomb. For the internal damage there's no remedy" (120).

Once she realizes the American visitor has allowed himself to voluntarily be drawn inside the experience of war, the narrator becomes more open in discussing the bombing, relating how her mother became a "living torch" as the bomb exploded. She was one of 20,000 Japanese on the day of the bombing who jumped into a nearby river and drowned. "And now and then," the narrator explains to the American as they gaze at the river below, "people come to lay flowers on the river's surface. It's the only grave they have to decorate" (159).

Despite the aftermath of the bombing which continues to bring pain and grief to the Japanese, survivors such as the narrator of this novel derive strength from their union with other survivors. "Oh, how close we feel to one another!" she confesses to the American. "We are a special species—the radiated species—the only one of its kind on earth. We are brothers and sisters" (143).

Morris' novel joins together Japanese and Americans, once considered enemies, in a common search for greater understanding and awareness of the repercussions of war which continue to affect the lives of victims such as those described in this novel. If there are to be "No more Hiroshimas," as the narrator fervently insists, then the scars of war cannot be concealed behind a wall of shame but must be revealed as evidence of war's continued destructive force.

93.   Morris, Edita. The Seeds of Hiroshima. New York: George Brazziller, 1965.

The Seeds of Hiroshima is both a lament for the Hiroshima holocaust and a confirmation for a more peaceful earth. The Japanese narrator of the novel recalls with "awful clarity" the August morning in 1945 when the atomic bomb was dropped over Hiroshima, drenching its citizens with black atomic rain "as radio-active as the mushroom cloud itself" (96). Since the bombing, Yuka confesses, Hiroshima has become the "most sinister spot on earth, and we survivors are sinister too, with our tainted blood and bone marrow" (96).

Survivors of the bombing face not only the mental anguish of memory relived but the physical aftereffects of radiation exposure as well which will continue to manifest their imprint on generations to come. For "the seeds of Hiroshima are tainted and they will blow about the world for centuries to come. . .," Morris writes (92).

Yuka's younger sister, who gives birth to a deformed child, commits suicide by jumping from the summit of a high cliff with her son as a "gift of peace" to the women of the world in hopes that her suicide will "awaken women from their long sleep. They'll cry out," she expresses hope, "for what happened to me may happen to many—one day" (97). Ohatsu encourages her older sister to continue to fight for peace after she is gone. "For war, like that poor creature in the basket," Ohatsu declares, "is a brainless monster which cannot be allowed to survive" (106).

Through the gentle voice of Yuka, Morris conveys the pointlessness of war and futility of hate conveyed in simple and honest dialogue by a woman who has witnessed firsthand the tragedy of war and its widespread victimization of innocent civilians, including her own sister.

94.   Piercy, Marge. Gone to Soldiers. New York: Summit Books, 1987.

"World War Two was a subject I always knew I would come to take on, not in spite of being a woman, a Jew, and a writer, but because of all that I am," Piercy wrote in her essay "Of Arms and the Woman" (31). "My earliest memories are of World War II," she said during a U.S. News and World Report interview. "It's what changed the lives of everybody I knew. It's what changed—enormously—this country. So I've always known that I would eventually write a novel about it" ("A Woman Writer" 74). Gone to Soldiers is the culmination of this childhood memory, a product of seven years of research and more than four years of writing. The result is a collection of 93 chapters, each a separate entity which could stand alone as a fictional narrative, interwoven through the voices of ten different characters offering varied perspectives on the war experience.

The novel follows the lives of soldiers and civilians on both fronts, the majority of them women who play different roles but are all affected by the war in some capacity—a war correspondent, an assembly line worker, a Women's Air Force Service Pilot, and a Resistance member, among others. One of these is a French woman who begins the war with the separatist attitude that "it is not me that this vileness is aimed at" but eventually sheds her separatism to become a key member of the Resistance, leading Jewish children to safety over the mountains, experiencing rape and torture, losing her lover, and surviving Auschwitz to finally emigrate to Israel.

The most intense moments of the novel are the descriptions of the concentration camp experience, derived from 300 survivor testimonies Piercy studied to write the novel. These passages emphasize the comfort and compassionate strength of women which endures despite the brutal inhumanity of their tragic fate.

After months of concentration camp life, one woman prisoner dares to imagine what she must look like, realizing that her body must now resemble the very "apathetic creatures" she shunned with revulsion when she first came to the camp, when she first wondered, "How could people let themselves become like that?" Now she knows the awful truth because she too has become a "scarecrow":

> Daniela was a bony witch with immense eyes under a grey shaved skull, nose and chin protruding like an old woman's.

> She could imagine what she herself looked like. Boils and open
> sores covered their arms and legs. They stank from diarrhea
> because they all had dysentery. The smells, nobody got used to
> them, the fearful stench of sick unwashed starving bodies and
> piled-upwaste, of shit and blood and fear. (576)

Piercy's epic offers an eclectic examination of war on the battlefront
as well as on the homefront through the perspectives of several
characters of both genders. Each reader of the novel, Piercy
contends, "is going to encounter his or her own war" by the way
each responds to and identifies with these fictional characters whose
lives are disrupted and ultimately altered by the weariness and terror
of war ("A woman writer" 74).

In Edith Davidson's review of the novel she contends that the
structure of Gone to Soldiers prevents it from dissolving into
"abject misery" characteristic of much Holocaust literature. "Dark
alternates with light, sorrow with joy, evil with goodness, hate
with love, anti-Semitism with cooperation, trivial everyday life with
the monumental and insane to create a palatable but realistic
balance of experience," she writes (10).

95.   Rosen, Norma. Touching Evil. New York: Harcourt, Brace, and
       World, 1969.

Rosen portrays the effect of the Holocaust on non-Jewish Americans
in this novel, believing that even those who were not present should
become "witnesses through imagination" to such an atrocity.
Survival thus carries moral implications for both Jews and
Christians, Rosen believes, who are "required to live covenantally in
the tension between history and redemption" and keep the memory of
the Holocaust tragedy near-at-hand (Berger 174 – 175). In her essay
"The Holocaust and the American-Jewish Novelist," Rosen states the
central question proposed by her novel: "What kind of daily lives can
people live after they have touched an evil so absolute that it
overpowers all the old ideas of evil and good?" (60). Touching Evil
predicts "what might happen to people who truly took into
consciousness the fact of the Holocaust," not its significance for
Jewish history, but its "meaning to human life and aspiration of the
knowledge that human beings—in great numbers—could do what
had been done" (59).

The novel's two central characters, both American gentiles, never
touch the evil of the Holocaust experience directly. Their awareness
comes primarily through the televised Eichmann trials of the 1960s
during which victims testified to the violence and evil perpetrated
upon Jewish victims. Watching the Holocaust victims' testimonies
with ritual intensity, each woman discovers her own "private
symbols of horror from the welter of horror symbols" presented.
"Hattie has her pregnant women, her children, her Muslims,"
writes the narrator. "I have the woman who digs her half-dead way
up through corpses" (55).

While Jean was a college student during World War Two, young and "vulnerable to horror," she vowed as she examined a photograph of the stacked bones of Holocaust victims: "A catastrophe has changed the world. The old forms have no more meaning for me. I will never marry or have children" (74). Now she relives that horror of human cruelty as once again it is replayed on the television screen and acknowledges that her role as a "post-Holocaust individual" is not that of a victim, but a witness (Berger 174).

Hattie, too young to have remembered the incidents of World War Two, derives her perceptions of the Holocaust entirely from the television testimonies and associates her own pregnancy with the sufferings of the tortured concentration camp victims. As she labors toward the delivery of her child in a helpless and humiliated state, she "becomes in her hallucination, the women who gave birth in the camps. It is the 'taking in' of the knowledge of the Holocaust" (Rosen 59).

Hattie believes the entire human race must accept the responsibility for the Holocaust. It is too easy to curse the Germans as some sort of aberration of humanity. Their actions against the Jews only demonstrate "what people are capable of." The Germans are all of us, she insists:

> "They is the world. And us is you and me. The fathers and the mothers. The people who are supposed to carry on the loving and the giving. That's what it is you know. A poison went into the atmosphere. Just as when an atomic bomb explodes. Each generation in turn will be sickened, poisoned with disgust for the human race." (84)

96.   Schaeffer, Susan Fromberg. Anya. New York: McMillan, 1974.

Anya is an epic narrative of a survivor of the Holocaust of World War Two who was hopeful that with the passage of time and a move to the United States, the painful memory of loss of family, a medical career, and her native country might gradually be erased. But at the age of 52, she acknowledges her memory of the Holocaust is as vivid as it was a quarter of a century ago:

> I have not forgotten anything. If I am alone for even five minutes, whole sections of my life unfold in front of me. They are so vivid, they are like scenes from a movie, except the scenes are three-dimensional, and immediately the director with the small mustache casts me as the main character. (470)

As the novel's narrator and main character, Anya records in meticulous detail her life in prewar Warsaw, the complete upheaval of life for her family with the Nazi invasion. "Our whole world was destroyed," she remembers, "erased as if it were less than a spelling lesson on the blackboard." In retrospect, the story of Anya's life seems like a film "spliced one third through to an irrelevant reel by a maniac," its continuity permanently disrupted and rearranged into new and frightening patterns when war descends (470). Although the war years of her life may have been the most difficult, Anya concedes that she was most alive during that period when her concentration was focused so intently on survival. Without an attempt to make Anya a heroine or analyze the meaning of the Holocaust, Schaeffer carefully portrays a woman who has been both victimized and strengthened by her encounter with war, an experience that refuses to be placed aside and minimizes all of life since in comparison.

97.   Silko, Leslie Marmon. Ceremony. New York: Viking Press, 1977.

Ceremony chronicles the gradual recovery of an American Indian veteran of war from postwar confusion and disorientation—labelled "battle fatigue" and easily dismissed by the military—to a gradual reaffirmation of the value of life through his reorientation to the legends of customs of his own Indian heritage that explain the connections and cycles of life. Reviewer Diana Rowan writes that Silko's characters "struggle to maintain the delicate balance between fixed reference points, the moral strength they have found in the ancient tales, and the imperative necessity for continual growth and adaptation for survival in a chaotic new world" (19).

During combat Tayo discovers his sensitivity is a detriment in the drama of war where callousness toward death is demanded of soldiers. Although Tayo does not remember killing any enemy soldiers during the war, he worries later that perhaps he did shoot someone and his selective memory has repressed it. He recalls being appointed to a firing squad ordered to kill captured Japanese soldiers. When the sergeant ordered the soldiers to fire, Tayo remembers breaking out in a sweat, so anxious he "could not pull the trigger." The trauma of his war experience leaves Tayo in a state of shock with no sense of past or future and only a minimal will to live.

The novel also explores the bitter fate of the American Indian who ironically finds himself an accepted member of mainstream society for the first time as he fights the "white people's war." While the war was ongoing, Tayo explains to other equally disgruntled veterans commiserating their sorrow with drink, Indians "were America the Beautiful too" who commanded respect—and even enjoyed "cold beer and blond cunt"—while in uniform. They were awarded the same medals and honored with the same flag-draped coffins as their white counterparts. But once the war ended, the picture changed:

> First time you walked down the street in Gallup or Albuquerque, you know. Don't lie. You knew right away. The war was over, the uniform was gone. All of a sudden that man at the store waits on you last, makes you wait until all the

white people bought what they wanted. And the white lady at
the bus depot, she's real careful now not to touch your hand
when she counts out your change. You watch it slide across
the counter at you, and you know. Goddamn it! You stupid
sonofabitches! You know! (43)

The structure of the novel recreates the Indian ceremony, shifting in
time and place, the narration interrupted with ceremonial chants,
some of them reflecting antiwar themes, blending the "European
tradition of the novel with American-Indian storytelling" (MacShane
15).

98. Silman, Roberta. Beginning the World Again. New York: Viking,
     1990.

This novel examines the lives of the scientists and their wives at Los
Alamos, New Mexico during World War Two who were engaged
in a private war of their own to create the atomic bomb which
they believed would stop the threatening force of Adolph Hitler and
put an end to war.

Although the novel interweaves historical and fictional characters
involved in the Manhattan Project, it is the lives of the women, held
silently in the background of most accounts, which interests Silman
the most. Narrated from the perspective of the wife of one of the
physicists involved in the project reflecting back four decades later,
the novel attempts to humanize the special circumstances which
bonded these men and women together in a "voluntary prison,"
enclosed in barbed wire, isolated both physically and socially from the
rest of the country during the war.

The scientists characterized by Silman work under intense pressure,
driven by a certain "demonic genius" to bring to fruition the work of
scientists for the past three centuries to create what they term the
"gadget," an invention they hope will save the world from Hitlerism.
These scientists are continually energized by the knowledge that they
are "rearranging nature to create energy in ways that had never been
done before" (324).

When the historic moment arrives and the bomb is at last perfected,
the scientists return from the test site, not unlike combat veterans,
exhilarated with the victory of their discovery but sobered by the
ethical reality of the destructive power they have created weighing
heavily upon their consciences, a moral conflict to haunt them for a
lifetime:

They came back looking like men who have fought in battle.
No wounds or blood or even blackened faces or tattered clothes,
but like fatigued soldiers whose features are stamped forever
by combat. Some were jubilant and relieved; some looked
dazed with awe; others shell-shocked; still others grim and
pensive. (373)

The bleaker side of their mission is recorded by one physicist who writes with bitterness and some regret in his journal:

> Such a completely different kind of war out here, our secret war that has been fought in this New Mexico desert, our private war in which intelligence and precision matter in ways never before known, where things are not as chancy most of the time as on the battlefield, but at other times more chancy, and just as tense, just as scary. . . .

> This desert is the bleakest place on earth. . . . The sand and dust are those neutral buff and gray colors of deserts everywhere, and they are like a premonition of death—in our eyes, ears, mouths, noses, everywhere; our bodies have become repositories for this blowing heat and dust and grains of sand, nothing more. We are ghosts covered with it, learning to feel as little as possible so that our brains can work as quickly, as efficiently as possible, in isolation from our bodies.

> A fitting end to our labors, I sometimes think.

> Death's work in this land of death. (396)

The women who nurture, comfort, and support their engrossed and often alienated husbands and lovers in this novel represent that which is most real and lasting in this artificial environment where the scientists often feel more robotlike than human. These women also emotionally support one another out of the common need for understanding of their unique situation and isolated existence. For almost all of the women the desire to give birth becomes the most paramount mission in their lives as war wives:

> For having a child was the most positive thing a wife here at Los Alamos could do, a wife anywhere could do, I suppose. And maybe making a baby had everything to do with making a gadget. For when your husband is working on a weapon capable of unknown and perhaps unprecedented destruction, perhaps the only thing a woman can do to convince herself of a future is to have a child. A kind of balancing act, really. (233)

The narrator, who must live with the memory of the catastrophic bombing of Hiroshima and her husband's part in it, realizes in retrospect that to the idealistic scientists and their wives of Los Alamos, atomic power represented the magic ingredient that would change the world, the discovery that would "end the insanity that is war" and allow a rebirth of peace to follow. Forty years later she understands that a lasting commitment to peace is the only solution that can put an end to war on earth, a peace that demands "patience and superhuman strength and a tenacious vigilance that must never cease" of all of earth's inhabitants (414).

99. Stewart, Catherine Pomeroy. So Thick the Fog. New York: Charles Scribner's Sons, 1944.

So Thick the Fog documents the war experience of a Frenchwoman whose strength holds together her family of five children and sustains her own will to survive despite the obstacles they face under the oppressive and often inhumane rule of the Germans, whom the narrator describes as "less men than automatons." She explains: "They would not step out of their efficient groove to harm you, but they would crush with an impersonal cold-bloodedness any one who dared to cross their path. So we were to learn" (46).

Mademoiselle de Polnay narrates her story as if she "were whispering the nightmare to herself" (Green 13). For her family, life becomes a daily struggle to survive both physically and emotionally with meager resources under German authority. She watches in horror as a sentry clubs her young son over the head after German trucks have thoughtlessly trampled through the family's garden. She listens as an indifferent German official informs her that her husband is a prisoner of war (he later returns minus one arm and his sight). She simultaneously witnesses the birth of her first grandchild and death of her oldest daughter, too weak and malnourished from the lengthy ordeal of labor to live. While the delivery takes place on the second floor of their temporary home in the country, German soldiers wine and dine themselves below on the first floor, anticipating the hanging of the young woman giving birth who has been accused of murdering a young German commandant.

Through each tragic phase of war Mademoiselle de Polnay finds the momentum to press forward and keep her family united in a communal will to survive. In this she is symbolic of those French citizens whose spirit refused to break in spite of the physical ruin of their country, those whose spirit persisted even in the face of defeat (Green 13).

100. Traub, Barbara Fischman. The Matrushka Doll. New York: Richard Marek, 1979.

A matrushka doll is a series of dolls placed within a doll, each one progressively smaller, each a part of the others assembled together, yet separate unto itself. The wartime life of Lisa Engler, the female protagonist-Holocaust survivor of this novel, is much like the matrushka doll, each layer of her life revealing an identity that is separate yet part of the whole.

Born into a wealthy Transylvania family, Lisa grows up with all the amenities of life and an aspiration rare among her gender to study law. The advent of war changes the course of her life, as it did for so many European Jews, challenging her will and capability to survive the mentally and physically excruciating concentration camp experience at Auschwitz.

Traub's novel concentrates on the postwar homecoming of Holocaust survivors, such as Lisa, who imagine comfort and the warmth of acceptance awaiting them as they return home only to discover their homes have been destroyed and their once gentle neighbors are awkwardly distanced now, these people who allowed the Holocaust to happen without intervening or simply ignored its happening, as one concentration camp survivor explains:

> "The fact is *they* are not glad we are back. To the contrary. Our return merely points up their guilt. The fact is one half of the civilized world was exterminating us like vermin while the other half allowed it to happen. Or didn't know it was happening. I don't really know which is worse. Meanwhile, the survivors bleed, and I wonder if our bleeding can be stopped at all. . . . It's going to be hell, this our survival, that's for sure. But even if our wounds are permanent, we ourselves must stop the bleeding." (151)

"Where are the trumpets, the flowers?" Lisa cries in disappointment as she finally reaches her hometown and tries in vain to "force reality to match her dreams" (151). Lisa's readjustment is further hindered by recurring memories of the concentration camp experience that intervene unwillingly at any given moment—flashbacks of horror that persist relentlessly. One of the most devastating of these recalls a certain day early during Lisa's imprisonment when an "oldtimer" in the camp revealed to Lisa why she would not be reunited with her parents, as promised by the Germans:

> look idiot! she screams and grabs my head and turns it toward the big brick building with tall chimneys belching smoke.
>
> look idiot! that's where your mamma is, was. look at the chimneys, that's where she went out and up, up
>
> up
>
> up in the sky,
>
> your mamma and all the mammas. you idiot. now you know where your mamma is, was. so you'll stop pestering me with questions. idiot. (30)

Lisa's first postwar Yom Kippur celebration triggers memories of enforced fasting at Auschwitz, the daily challenge to endure starvation that prompted Lisa to create a Lord of Hunger and Lord of Death which governed her life in camp:

> Hunger was a driving force that made me fight death, perhaps against my will, a death i could or could not really fathom; still, a death that clung to me every instant, a ubiquitous presence that had become a familiar part of me, my own court: me. Death and hunger owned me. Whatever i did or whoever i

was, *then* and *there*, was the consequence of my obsequiousness to my two demanding, harsh, exquisitely cruel masters. (298)

On this Day of Atonement Lisa refuses to take more sin upon herself, daring to suggest to her fellow survivors: "It is God who must atone, not I," for allowing an atrocity such as the Holocaust to have happened (303).

As Lisa determines to move ahead with her life, she realizes, as many Holocaust survivors have, that survival is only the beginning of the Holocaust experience. Now she faces the creation of a new identity for herself, recognizing the war as but one layer of experience among many to eventually mold her life.

The narrative structure of The Matrushka Doll interweaves passages of historical texts explaining events of the World War Two period and flashbacks of Lisa's concentration camp experiences with the central narrative of Lisa's postwar homecoming. Thus, the present and past are co-mingled, underscoring the lasting impact of the Holocaust experience upon Jewish victims for whom survival assumed several layers of meaning and extended far beyond the declared end of the war.

SHORT FICTION

101. Adams, Alice. "1940: Fall." Prize Stories 1990: The O. Henry Awards. Ed. William Abrahams. New York: Doubleday, 1990. 196–212.

Alice Adams recalls herself during her teenage years as a young woman who was very similar to the adolescents characterized in this story who lived during World War Two but were "much more concerned with the next dance or the next fall of snow than with what might happen in Europe. However, in retrospect," she writes, "I see that we all to some degree felt that cloud, that heavy horrible menace, Hitler's Germany" (Biographies 410). The self-absorbed young characters in this narrative are contrasted with a politically active mother of one of the adolescents, who becomes one of the first Americans to speak out passionately against Hitler during a time when such outspokenness was unappreciated:

> Caroline's letters to the papers had to do with the coming war, with what Caroline saw as its clear necessity: Hitler must be stopped. The urgency of it possessed her, what Hitler was doing to the Jews, the horror of it always in her mind. And the smaller countries, systematically devastated. There in the isolationist Midwest she was excoriated as a warmonger (small, gentle, peaceable Caroline). Or worse, more than once—dirty toilet paper in the mail. (197)

As anti-Hitler sentiment grows within the country, American sympathy eventually moves in the direction of Caroline's. While Caroline remains tolerant of the differing priorities of her adolescent daughter and friends and their lack of concern about international politics, she remains politically active—and outspoken—even into her eighties where the story ends.

102. Ames, Candace Nosaka and Louann Nosaka. "Nasakenai." Fusion Too: A Japanese American Anthology. San Francisco: San Francisco State University, 1985. 57 – 62.

The tragedy of anti-Japanese prejudice which swept the United States after the Japanese bombing of Pearl Harbor and its impact on the lives of Japanese-Americans is illustrated in this short story, co-authored by Japanese-American writers. For Kyota and Kiyomi Yoshimasu and their family, the bombing of Pearl Harbor "was like an anguished scream, whose echoes will not die. Its reverberations haunted the lives of Kiyomi and Kyota, and filled them with worry" (57). Both husband and wife lose their menial positions as gardener and maid as Americans nationwide, in a sweeping "gesture of patriotism," dismiss their Japanese employees who become suddenly suspect as possibly dangerous and certainly not to be trusted. Although Kiyomi's firing comes like a "bad dream, a tragic nightmare like Pearl Harbor," made more confusing because she was once considered a beloved part of her employer's family, she mourns only briefly before plunging her hands into the soil and channeling her anger into the care of her garden. "There had been bad times," Kiyomi reassures herself, "but the family had never gone hungry and always survived. They would survive" (62). With a great sense of resolve and hope, Kiyomi remembers that spring always follows winter in nature's natural progression and life is renewed once more (62). This story illustrates the innate strength of Japanese-Americans in response to the emotional overreaction on the part of many Americans to anti-Japanese sentiment during World War Two.

103. Blue, Edna. "Nothing Overwhelms Giuseppe." Current Thinking and Writing. Series Two. Eds. Joseph M. Bachelor, Ralph L. Henry, and Rachel Salisbury. New York: Appleton-Century-Crofts, Inc., 1951. 107 – 111.

This narrative attests to the resilient strength of children, even during wartime. At nine years old, Giuseppe has lost his family and one leg to war, killed two German soldiers, lived in an orphanage as well as on the street, travelled to a foreign country alone, and learned to walk with an artificial leg. The young Italian's war experiences have made him tough beyond his years, yet he still retains his youthful enthusiasm for life. Children such as Giuseppe, the author writes, represent "the great reason to end wars forever" (110).

104. Boyle, Kay. "Army of Occupation." Fifty Stories. Garden City: Doubleday, 1980. 439 – 453.

This story probes the reactions and feelings of an American woman travelling alone by train through France to rejoin her journalist husband in Germany after eight months of separation. Surrounded by GIs hungry for the sight (and in some instances, the touch) of an American woman, even though French war brides are plentiful, the woman finds herself in an unenviable position of attention. One officer compares her to the women of France: "They don't make them like that over here. They don't know how" (450). Her presence evokes reactions ranging from protective to violent among the mostly drunken servicemen aboard. She remains calmly distant and self-assured, at least outwardly, until the men begin to fight for her attention, causing her to flee in search of more peaceful companionship in order to survive the remaining 13 hours of her journey. This story depicts the reactions of men deprived by war of association with women and illustrates the awkwardness of one woman caught by circumstance in a potentially dangerous situation among her own countrymen.

105. Boyle, Kay. "Canals of Mars." Fifty Stories. Garden City: Doubleday, 1980. 577 – 586.

In this O. Henry Memorial Award-winning prize story of 1943, Boyle traces the feelings of a war wife during the final, waning hours before her soldier-husband leaves for war. Despite their anguish at parting, this young soldier and his wife find comfort in knowing their grief is also shared by other couples separated by war. The wife, perhaps symbolic of many military wives, derives strength from the knowledge that she is not alone in her aloneness. She tells herself: "I'm not just one woman taking it alone. I'm a lot of women closing their teeth hard on what they're not going to let make any sound" (580). Her realization that "the individual struggle is part of a collective one" eases the agony of the inevitable departure of her husband to war (Spanier 157).

106. Boyle, Kay. "Defeat." Fifty Stories. Garden City: Doubleday, 1980. 294 – 304.

This O. Henry Memorial award-winning story for 1941 "presents the tragic defeat of spirit and principle that infected all of France after its fast capitulation to the Germans in 1940" (Spanier 154). Veterans and prisoners of war slowly trickling back to their homeland return dejectedly—"the men of that tragically unarmed and undirected force which had been the French army once but was no longer, returning to what orators might call reconstruction but which they knew could never be the same" (295). Many admit shame at their own lack of fortitude and inability to return home victorious. Boyle captures the mood of a country in this narrative that has been overwhelmed by a devastating sense of loss felt most dramatically by its returning veterans.

107. Boyle, Kay. "Effigy of War." Fifty Stories. Garden City: Doubleday, 1980. 246 – 253.

The overzealous nature of nationalism often heightened beyond reason during wartime and the accompanying prejudice that can result is illustrated in this short story. An Italian and a Dane living in France are violently beaten by a Greek recently granted French citizenship who resents these "foreigners" intruding on "his" country's soil who will not fight for France as all French citizens are required to do. "This country's not good enough for them, not good enough for either of them," he declares, as he sets out to drive them from the country where they are no longer welcome (252).

108. Boyle, Kay. "Hilaire and the Marechal Petard." Thirty Stories by Kay Boyle. New York: Simon and Schuster, 1946. 309 – 330.

This narrative depicts a time of extreme distrust among the citizenry of France following the despair of defeat by German forces in 1940. Suspicions of loyalty are strong while freedom of expression is suppressed under the new German occupation. An American woman relief worker cannot decide whether to interpret a French soldier's advances toward her as romantic or informational, and her young son is suspected of sedition for authoring a newspaper dedicated to telling the truth about the war. While she awaits news of her French husband serving in Syria, she must not only cope with the uncertainty of his safety (she has not heard from him in four months) but the repressive atmosphere reigning in his homeland as well where every action and word has now come under surveillance.

109. Boyle, Kay. "Let There Be Honour." Fifty Stories. Garden City: Doubleday, 1980. 305 – 328.

This narrative is a character sketch of "Honour Higgins," a Frenchwoman who risks her life operating an underground connection for escaping soldiers—a woman whose first name has become a magical password to freedom for many men. Some soldiers believe the story of Honour to be merely a legend. Others seek to discover for themselves if Honour is simply a phantom of imagination or a beautiful reality.

110. Boyle, Kay. "The Little Distance." Nothing Ever Breaks Except the Heart. Garden City: Doubleday, 1966. 157 – 178.

This moralistic narrative places minor conflicts of Americans in perspective against the larger dimension of war and calls for unity instead of division. The antagonism that has festered between two neighbors for years abruptly ceases when one of their sons becomes a war casualty. "Been fighting the wrong fight," one neighbor confesses to the other. "Now we're in it together. Damn them, damn them" (178). Their mutual anger can now be safely aimed outward at the Germans instead of inward at one another. Through the reconciliation of these neighbors, Boyle shows how war can dissolve individual differences when civilians realize the insignificance of their personal concerns compared to the larger conflict of war. Victory demands a peaceful homefront of citizenry willing to set aside their personal strife in a unified commitment to the war effort.

111. Boyle, Kay. "The Lost." Fifty Stories. Garden City: Doubleday, 1980. 514 – 534.

This story examines young victims of war left without families or home or identity. These displaced European orphans of war are neither civilians nor children who were adopted as GI mascots but left behind when American troops evacuated Europe. The conglomeration of Czeck, Italian, Polish, and Hungarian adolescent refugees—who recount experiences way beyond their years—speak with adopted regional American accents in typical GI slang. Considered luckiest among these orphans are those whose families are proven dead so they can immigrate to the United States where GIs have promised them homes. One 12-year-old Italian youth renounces his heritage, declaring to the Children's Center director: "I'm American. I wanna go home where my outfit's gone" (521). Another youth who claims to have spent more than two years in military service declares: "I saw action with three different outfits. I done everything that every son-of-a-bitch in the Army ever done" (525). Still another refugee desires to live with a black American buddy in Tennessee but learns that in the United States, the "color question" would prohibit their cohabitation.

This short story was originally refused by the New Yorker as somewhat unbelievable in detail. The rejection angered Boyle who promptly defended the tragic authenticity of her fictionalized account (Spanier 190). The young orphans of this story have experienced war before they have been given the chance to experience youth and have fallen prey to tragic unkept promises of American soldiers.

112. Boyle, Kay. "Major Engagement in Paris." Fifty Stories. Garden City: Doubleday, 1980. 239 – 246.

This short, satirical narrative features the same self-centered characters as the short story "War in Paris" and is similar in mission. While war rages around them, the American women portrayed in this story discuss the merits of toothpicks and the proper procedure for using these newfangled American inventions. Mrs. Hodges complains that during the "last war" the sirens were louder and seemed to have more "life" than those of this war and that the bomb cellars were certainly more comfortable. As this story and "War in Paris" illustrate well, Boyle exhibited little tolerance for those unconcerned and uninvolved with the war effort such as the women satirized in this story.

113. Boyle, Kay. "Men." Fifty Stories. Garden City: Doubleday, 1980. 275 – 288.

This story examines the psychological changes in prisoners of war
that can occur during their incarceration. As the story opens, a
road crew of prisoners for the French military encounter a young
woman—their first feminine sight in months. An Austrian prisoner
wins her sympathy and spends a few minutes in the hospitality of
her home before he must move on. She tries to reassure him
everything will "be all right" once France has won the war, but he
realizes something irretrievable has been lost during his captivity.
Awkwardly silent in her presence, he formulates unexpressed
thoughts which he wishes he could translate into words:

> He wanted to say: "Sometimes lying awake at night in camp
> among the others I scarcely believe in country or home or
> freedom or even in humanity anymore, that all this is a fool's
> dream, all less than nothing to us. It is something else that
> has perished for us, that thing you gave us by walking out of
> the door and coming across the yard to us," but he could not
> say it out. (287)

Boyle's story portrays the awkwardness of men who have been
segregated from women during war and examines the psychological
losses of prisoners of war that may never be regained.

114. Boyle, Kay. "Poor Monsieur Panalitus." New Yorker 20 Jan. 1940:
      19 – 22.

Boyle portrays the harshness of French prejudice against foreigners
during wartime in this portrait of pathetic Monsieur Panalitus who
fled his native country during a revolutionary period there and now
suffers social ostracism because he lacks a nationality at a time
when feelings of nationalism are so vehemently expressed in France.
Even though he volunteers for French military duty and holds an
official letter of rejection, he is the object of scorn for neighboring
peasants who have sacrificed every able-bodied Frenchman for the
war effort and show little respect for any man not in uniform.
Only the children continue to visit Monsieur Panalitus as he
cloisters himself away in his vacant hotel nursing his feelings of
shame and displacement. When a child accidentally drowns in his
pond, Panalitus is an immediate suspect for murder because he is an
outsider, not a French patriot. In this narrative Boyle characterizes
the helplessness of a man trapped by circumstance who must bear
the loneliness of rejection because he is without a country.

115. Boyle, Kay. "Their Name is Macaroni." Fifty Stories. Garden City:
      Doubleday, 1980. 339 – 348.

This narrative documents the prejudice against Italians prevalent
among the French during and after the war. "Their name is
macaroni and their blood is water" becomes the prevailing attitude
toward anyone of Italian descent. Even an Italian who now claims
France as his homeland spits in the face of a dead Italian soldier,
sneering, "Fascist. Alive or dead, that's what he is. Alive or dead, I

hate him. Fascist" (347). This story, together with other war fiction written by Boyle, illustrates the heightened dissension caused by war that overexaggerates feelings of nationalism and breeds unwarranted antagonism.

116.   Boyle, Kay. "They Weren't Going to Die." Fifty Stories. Garden City: Doubleday, 1980. 288 – 294.

Boyle indicts French bigotry and elitism in this story of Senegalese colonials imported to France to fight in a war unrelated to them. With childlike innocence and a sense of playfulness, the Senegalese regard their duty with a sense of invincibility and a certain levity. When they are gunned down by approaching Germans while tending the garden of a baron, the Africans are depicted as "foolish looking and rather giddy even in death, lying among the strawberry flowers and potato plants" (294). Neither the conquering Germans nor the conquered French regard the death of the Senegalese with concern or remorse as the soldiers are given a sniper's burial amidst the potato plants and strawberry flowers.

117.   Boyle, Kay. "This They Took With Them." Fifty Stories. Garden City: Doubleday, 1980. 328 – 339.

"This They Took With Them" reaffirms Boyle's often questionable faith in the integrity of individuals strained by the horrific experience of war. As thousands of citizens make a mass exodus from Paris in 1940, an ambulance catches fire. Only two of the marchers stop to remain for the night with the ambulance's wounded until help arrives. This unlikely combination of a Mexican diplomat and Parisian schoolteacher hold little in common beyond their motivation to help and the "accumulation of unalterable experience which made each of them what he was. This they carried with them, and no matter how irrelevant it might seem now, they could not put it down" (329). Boyle enters the thoughts of the schoolteacher to explain her decision to stay with the wounded soldiers: "There are men with the breath of life in them who can teach the rest of us to breathe; there are men with the breath of life in them, we can learn strength from them" (337). With their humanitarian gesture, the French woman and Mexican share a special bond for one night emanating from their mutual concern for the fate of these wounded, who have been largely ignored by the masses of citizens absorbed in their own self interests as they flee from the war.

118.   Boyle, Kay. "War in Paris." New Yorker. 26 Nov. 1938: 18 – 20.

This short story satirizes the triteness of upper middle class Americans living in Paris whose self-centered interests supercede their minimal concern for the war about to enclose upon them. One woman's major concern, as the German invasion approaches, is the safety of her 17-year-old cat, Major Ainslee. "No one his age," she declares, "ought to be asked to sit in a fifth-floor flat and wait for the bombs to fall on him" (19). Hitler and Mussolini's maneuvers are dismissed as "mischief" to this woman who is obviously oblivious to the gravity of the coming crisis.

119. Boyle, Kay. "Winter Night." Fifty Stories. Garden City: Doubleday, 1980. 596 – 606.

A comparison of two tragic mother-daughter relationships during war is drawn in this moralistic story. While her father is away at war, Felicia is continually left home at night with nameless "sitting parents" when her mother socializes after work. Felicia reminds one of her sitters of another young girl she once met in a concentration camp. This young girl too was separated from her mother, only their separation became a permanent one. As the sitter describes the life of the young girl to Felicia and answers her many questions, Felicia is introduced to the grim realities of war someone her own age has experienced. During their incarceration the young girl's mother never returned, the sitter reveals to Felicia, and the fate of the children in the camp remains a mystery. "They must be asleep now, all of them," the sitter tries to convince herself as much as Felicia. "They must be quietly asleep somewhere, and not crying all night because they are hungry and because they are cold" (606).

For the night, this sitter becomes a mother to Felicia, just as she became the mother of the child in the concentration camp—both of them abandoned children of war in need of love and nurturing. "By juxtaposing the cases of the two little girls left alone by their mothers and cared for by a stranger," Sandra Spanier writes in Kay Boyle: Artist and Activist "she shows that the failure of love is a tragic loss on an individual as well as on a social and political scale" (158).

120. Breuer, Bessie. "Bury Your Own Dead." O. Henry Memorial Award Prize Stories of 1945. Ed. Herschel Brickell. Garden City: Doubleday, 1945. 61 – 74.

"Bury Your Own Dead" examines the ways men and women cope with the grief of war. A soldier whose brother is reported missing in action attempts to share his bereavement with a WAC and bury his sorrow in a one-night stand with her. But the WAC, who has recently lost a brother during the war, refuses both the soldier's emotional and sexual advances, convinced that he must "bury his own dead" as she has. Although she is tempted to give in to his needs, she resists, feeling a combination of "grief and love and desolation," knowing that to comply with this soldier's invitation would merely prolong his acceptance of reality and might cause a regression in her own gradual acceptance of her brother's death, although later she berates herself for appearing to be "cruel and unfeeling and beastly" (74). The woman characterized by Breuer in this story has created a facade of indifference for emotional protection. By refusing to allow herself to demonstrate emotions, she has learned that the expression of feelings is an emotional handicap for women during wartime.

121. Breuer, Bessie. "Home is a Place." It's a Woman's World: A Collection of Stories from Harper's Bazaar. New York: McGraw-Hill, 1944. 142 – 151.

A newly widowed war wife begins to develop her own identity in this narrative which won an O. Henry Memorial Award prize as one of the best short stories published during 1944. Prior to her husband's death, Georgiana was always somebody's wife, never her own self. "Had I ever been Georgiana Cushing?" she asks herself in retrospect. "I had never been Georgiana Cushing. I had always been Georgiana, wife of—" (145). As a widow, no longer part of a couple, she feels she is a "bitter, useless creature" in the eyes of society. All the world seems set for two. Once Georgiana escapes from the smothering sympathy of well-meaning friends, however, she begins to sense her own independence apart from her husband's memory and returns home with a newfound confidence in her ability to build a future for herself. Although war causes the death of her husband, the loss of his life also offers Georgiana the opportunity to establish her own identity as more than "somebody's wife" for the first time.

122. Brownrigg, Leslie. "Man Gehorcht." Prize College Stories, 1963. Eds. Whit and Hallie Burnett. Random House: New York, 1963. 45 – 58.

Winner of the 1963 Story magazine prize for outstanding fiction by young writers, this narrative written by a pre-medical student at Barnard College, explores the conflicting feelings of a young French woman toward the "enemy." Left alone in a North African village when her officer-father heads to the front in Europe, the narrator becomes intrigued with a young German intelligence officer stationed in the village whose political ideals are as fluid as hers at this formative point in his life and whose interests are similar to her own. "We made poor enemies," she confesses (50). His interest in her, however, soon wanes when he receives orders for a new intelligence mission and requests that she direct him through a nearby mountain pass. Driven by a feeling recognized later as love, the narrator guides the German to his destination, only to bear the heavy guilt of betrayal against her country afterwards. She dreams of being tried in a court by the very men whose deaths she has caused with her treason:

> One by one the soldiers file into the courtroom to accuse me and to witness my guilt. In their testimony they tell their names and the love stories that ended with their deaths, their aspirations, the countless events and scenes recorded nowhere except in the bodies I destroyed. (56)

Realizing the gravity of her crime and her personal responsibility as a French citizen and patriot "to obey the dictates of my conscience despite my feelings," the narrator enlists the aid of Arab villagers to help her shoot the twelve Germans as they return through the mountain pass, burying them in a mass, unmarked grave. Brownrigg's portrayal of this young woman realistically portrays her conflict between human emotion and allegiance to homeland as she looks beyond the identity of "enemy" to discover an individual who is strikingly like herself and even worthy of loving.

123. Buck, Pearl S. "Begin to Live." Fourteen Stories by Pearl S. Buck. New York: John Day Company, 1961. 132 – 150.

"Begin to Live" describes the awkward transition of a one-armed World War Two veteran from military service to civilian life when he returns home hopeful he can "forget those two years, rip them out of his life, burn them up and scatter the ashes" but discovers his military indoctrination and persistent memories of war difficult to erase while he can find no adequate expression for his confused feelings (132).

Even though he arrives home to a receptive family, guaranteed job, and faithful fiancee, Tim has forgotten how to live in a civilian world without military orders to structure his life. And there are so many memories of the war clouding his vision. He feels frightened, unprepared, indecisive. He longs to share his experiences and feelings with someone but he can think of no way to verbalize the complexity or intensity of his encounter with war.

It is Tim's usually distant father, a veteran himself, who recognizes the same symptoms in his son as he brought home following his service during World War One: "The greatest problem that war leaves in a man," he explains to his son, "is how to recapture reality. That's because war is unreal. . . . You lose the habit of feeling, in war" (146 – 147). The best advice he can offer his son is to "just begin. Begin to work, begin to love. It doesn't matter how you feel. You begin to act, and then after a while—maybe a long while—feeling comes. And then things grow real again" (148).

124. Buck, Pearl S. "The Courtyards of Peace." The Good Deed and Other Stories of Asia, Past and Present. New York: John Day Company, 1969. 7 – 67.

In this fanciful story, an American pilot makes an emergency crash landing in a remote part of China isolated from the war. There he meets an American woman whose parents were killed during an earlier war. Ai-Lan has been raised in a lavish and peaceful estate by her adopted Chinese father who forbids the word "war" to be spoken in his presence. Walt marries Ai-Lan and begins a life of bliss and harmony in the peaceful solitude of this paradise. But he soon tires of the perfection of his new life and grows restless to know the outcome of the war and fate of the soldiers with whom he fought; he longs to fly over the mountain into the unknown again and become a part of the war effort once more. "I have had my feet on the ground too long," he confesses (58). But his protected wife clings to the security of her upbringing and refuses to venture forth. Soon the silence of the house "which had until now been so warm and kind about them, now seemed a wall. He longed for noise and human talk and the bantering of the soldiers he had known" (62). It is Ai-Lan's wise father who senses the emotional distance growing between his daughter and son-in-law and offers his wise advice, even as he gives up his daughter to an uncertain future:

> "You, my son must now make your own peace. I can feel the center of turmoil in you. Peace is something which a man makes for himself or he does not have it. In this house I have made my own peace. But it is not peace for you nor for the woman you have married who has become part of you. . . . I see it clearly. You must return to your own generation to find your peace." (64)

Although uncertain of what their fate will be, Walt and Ai-Lan take flight over the mountains in search of their own peace. As Walt leaves this Chinese paradise, he wonders if Adam really minded leaving Eden and renames his new bride Eve.

125. Buck, Pearl S. "The Enemy." The Best American Short Stories of 1943. Ed. Herschel Brickell. Garden City: Doubleday, 1943. 107 – 126.

This story takes war as a far away, nebulous entity and draws it closer as an individual conflict when a Japanese doctor and his wife come face to face with "the enemy." Although he feels nothing but animosity and revulsion for Americans, Dr. Sadao can neither abandon the wounded prisoner of war he and his wife discover washed ashore nor relinquish him as a prisoner of war, knowing he will be put to death. Despite the danger to their own lives for harboring an enemy in their household, Dr. Sadao and his wife take this risk until the American is well enough to escape by himself once more. An enemy is easily despised from a distance, the Japanese physician learns, but when that enemy becomes humanized on an individual level, the doctor's dedication to healing supercedes his antipathy. The story ends as Dr. Sadao contemplates his own inconsistency: "I wonder why I could not kill him?" (126).

126. Buck, Pearl S. "The Golden Bowl." East and West. Boston: G. K. Hall, 1975. 69 – 174.

The discrimination Japanese living in the United States during World War Two experienced as well as the persecution felt by Americans who continued to treat Japanese-Americans as human beings during the war are frankly revealed in this story. Forced to leave Japan as the war begins, James Briony reluctantly leaves the gentle people and culture that have been an endearing part of his life as a missionary for two decades. "Japan had stolen something from him, something Americans that he must regain again. Where would he find it?" he wonders (89 – 90).

The general consensus of American thought toward the war effort seems to be: "We've got to win this war, and there's only one way to win it. You've got to hate these Japs and hate 'em hard enough to kill 'em" (130). Briony's continued hospitality toward socially ostracized Japanese living in the United States combined with his refusal to propagandize against "the enemy" over American radio stations results in a brief period of imprisonment for a man whose patriotism has become suspect. But Briony continues to defend his stance, maintaining that "the necessity is not to hate the people of Japan. It is to be sure that what we fight for is the right" (131). Buck's narrative illustrates anti-Japanese prejudice at its most vehement among many Americans compared to the lonely convictions of a man who has intimately known the people behind the mask of "the enemy" and cannot bring himself to hate them, even at the insistence of his own country.

127. Buck, Pearl S. "Letter Home." The Good Deed and Other Stories of Asia, Past and Present. New York: John Day Company, 1969. 69 – 87.

This story describes a typical day for an American GI stationed in China during which he tries to find a home for a war orphan he has voluntarily adopted, disrupts a scene of domestic violence perpetrated by an angry husband whose wife has failed to produce a son, and rushes a wounded friend to medical assistance when his airplane malfunctions. At day's end the soldier tries in vain to verbalize these events in a letter home. "It had been a day like any other—there were life and death every day" (86). This soldier, undoubtedly symbolic of many soldiers, realizes his experiences in this strange, faraway land and his accompanying emotions are much too complex to condense in a simple letter. War has added an extraordinary dimension to his life that he now realizes only those who have experienced the same sensations at war can ever begin to understand.

128. Chidester, Ann. "When War Came." When Mother Was a Girl: Stories She Read Then. Ed. Frances Ullmann DeArmand. New York: Funk and Wagnalls, 1964. 105 –114.

A young woman's first confusing and unsettling encounter with war at the age of 16 is related in this narrative. The narrator searches for a definition of war and attempts to assimilate this new concept into her expanding realm of consciousness and experience. With the action of the war so far away and intangible, however, it is difficult for an adolescent with so many other competing concerns to comprehend its reality. The only tangible evidences of war she observes are gas rationing and defense stamps. "How do you go about a war when you've never seen one except in the movies?" she wonders (109). When military service claims the life of one of her classmates, however, war becomes real for the first time, ushering her into an adult world beyond the protected realm of childhood innocence.

129. Conway, Tina Marie. "World War II Picture." The Luxury of Tears. Ed. Susan Marie Greenburg. Little Rock: August House, 1989. 61 – 71.

This story records the impressions of an adult daughter witnessing the death of her mother while her mother's youth is forever preserved in an intimate photograph the daughter discovers her mother once mailed to her husband during the war. Passages in the narrative alternate between descriptions of the gradual demise of the narrator's mother who dies of cancer at the age of 57 and her earlier vibrancy, captured in a semi-nude photograph taken she she was 19 and carried by her husband for the next 36 years until her death.

The story is ultimately a tribute to a mother by her daughter who draws from the war memories of both her parents to piece together in her mind a lasting impression of a young woman who was a passionate, faithful, war wife and a devoted mother as well.

130. Coons, Joan. "The Christmas Gift: A Memory of Stalingrad." A Christmas Treasury. Ed. Jack Newcombe. New York: Viking, 1982. 84 – 90.

A young child's whimsical change of mind inadvertently saves her father's life when German spies plot to kill the great Russian pilot in this Christmas war story. A spy offers Nadia a candle normally forbidden in this remote region of Russia where peasants are attempting to conceal their hiding place. The spy convinces Nadia to burn the candle in the window of her shack on Christmas Eve after her father's return, assuring her, "A blessed candle on Christmas Eve lights the Christ Child to the door. No harm can come then . . . not even from the Germans" (87). But young Nadia decides instead to place the candle in the shack where her grandmother's dead body lies stiff with cold among others now deceased awaiting a less dangerous time for cremation. This is the shack the Germans target to explode, voluntarily sacrificing their own lives as they die convinced they have killed Russia's greatest aviator with their heroic act. As the facts of the incident are pieced together, Nadia explains the decision which ironically saved her father's life: "Grandmother was so worried that the Christ wouldn't find her soul when there were so many. I thought my father wouldn't mind if I put the candle in her shack instead of his" (90). Coons' story illustrates that children are not immune to the war experience; even their personal choices can result in life or death during war.

131. Durban, Pam. "Notes Toward an Understanding." All Set About with Fever Trees and Other Stories. Boston: David R. Godine, 1985. 149 – 172.

In this narrative a young pacifist daughter attempts to understand her World War Two veteran-father for whom war has become an integral part of his identity, a part of him that refuses to admit weakness, a part of him that sees life as a continual test of strength. She writes:

> Sometimes I think that in Papa the war is an old river, patiently working its way through rocky land, finding new channels when old ones are blocked. That it comes on, magnificent, grim, irresistible as the sight of Pickett's men making their charge, wave after wave, tide after tide, so many thrown against so many guns that the miracle is that anyone survives. But what is carried forward on that tide? What would he have us remember? This is as much as I can say— my father loves lost causes, ordeals, the great fighters, people who cling to the sides of mountains, rope gone, fingers loosening. He loves the hopeless cases, people who wrestle with God and go down, looking Him straight in the eye. I know that he loves both victory and defeat since both must be met with strength and courage. And I know that if he could, he would give us the great thing that he knows—how he came home alive. (161 – 162)

This story illustrates how attitudes toward war change from generation to generation. Durban's narrative also demonstrates how war can become an unalterable part of a veteran's self-perception and his impressions of the world around him.

132. Dworzan, Helene L. "The Almighty Power." New Voices 2: American Writing Today. Ed. Don M. Wolfe. New York: Hendricks House, Inc., 1955. 66 – 78.

This despairingly accurate narrative of the Nazi hunt for Jewish victims contrasts the coping mechanisms a Jewish couple in hiding for more than two years uses to endure the psychological strain of their ever-increasing fears and uncertain future. While Anna grows firmer in her religious conviction that an "almighty power" will surely spare their lives and may any day now strike every Nazi with a mortal disease that will paralyze them and rot their insides, David grows more cynical, convinced he will be long dead by the time their day of freedom arrives. Perhaps God even invented the Nazis as a cruel and sadistic trick that unexpectedly grew more powerful than even He anticipated, David imagines:

> But God sat up there, blindly dictating laws that no one obeyed, and playing like a trusting child with a huge kaleidoscope made of moons and stars. And when He got tired of playing, He picked a big louse from between His sweaty dirty toes and in a madman's nightmare, He wrought the NAZI. And the Nazi grew bigger and stronger than God Himself, and laughed at His dishevelled hair and His old magic tricks. Maybe the German was the new real powerful God. (71 – 72)

When the inevitable pounding at the door of their hiding place encloses upon Anna and David one night, it is David who emerges as the stronger of the two, calling forth reserves of energy and the will to survive while he remains calmly self-controlled in spite of the German soldiers' harshness toward them. In contrast, Anna flies into an uncontrollable rage that suggests she has come close to the brink of insanity—she who was so positively assured that both of them would see freedom together. All of her visions are shattered in a moment as she senses her fate and now feels betrayed that the almighty power has failed to hear her pleas.

133. Ehrlich, Gretel. "Champ's Roan Colt." Drinking Dry Clouds. Santa Barbara: Capra Press, 1991. 119 – 123.

This story enters the thoughts and feelings of a veteran who returns from war to his Wyoming ranch wounded and scared for his future. "All I've ever wanted to do is ranch—ranch and get laid," Champ admits, but unable to walk without his cane, which he refers to as "his goddamned wooden third leg," he faces the possibility that he may not be capable of performing the multitude of physically demanding chores required of ranchers. Scared at his own glaring incompetence, "scared of this everlasting limp," Champ returns from the war to face the possiblity that his physical limitations may prevent him from pursuing his chosen profession.

134. Ehrlich, Gretel. "Henry." Drinking Dry Clouds. Santa Barbara: Capra Press, 1991. 117.

This brief passage, a shortened version of "Madeleine's Day" narrated from Henry's perspective, enters the mind of a prisoner of war who has returned home to Wyoming after internment in a Japanese prison camp. Henry resents civilians for staring at him as if he were an oddity. "I'm tired of being the freak show," he confides. "In prison no one looked. We were all the same. . . . We could go forever, sleeping in the sun, sleeping in the snow, year around, who would care?" (117). He resents his wife for sleeping on the couch, as if his readjustment problems are "catching." He resents his own skeleton of a body for its inability to digest the hearty meals he once consumed before the war. Henry's "imprisonment," he begins to understand, is far from over; postwar readjustment is just another phase of a continuing war for him.

135. Ehrlich, Gretel. "Kai and Bobby." Drinking Dry Clouds. Santa Barbara: Capra Press, 1991. 31 – 48.

This narrative relates the experiences of two Japanese-Americans living in the United States whose lives are dramatically altered by the events of World War Two. Kai and his family respond to the American command given by President Franklin Roosevelt in 1942, "All Japs Must Go," joining 10,000 Japanese-Americans interned at Heart Mountain Relocation Camp, located on a barren plain in a remote area of Wyoming (39). Kai expresses his feelings of alienation and frustration in a letter to his Chinese lover, confessing:

> "Can you imagine how I feel? I don't even know myself. A little while ago a wave of loneliness came over me like nothing

I've felt before. . . . In fact, I don't know where we are. They
could be taking us to hell, for all I know. So I keep trying to
think of this ridiculous lapse in the democratic process as an
adventure. Maybe that's just being naive." (38)

Another Japanese-American characterized in this narrative
voluntarily gives himself up to authorities at Heart Mountain,
although the ranch hands where he has worked as a cook for the past
twenty years have offered to protect his identity because they value
his friendship as well as his services. One rancher assures Bobby of
his equal standing on the ranch despite the anti-Japanese sentiment
growing in the United States:

"You and I've been on this outfit a long time and I figure we're
just about the same man. We both come away from home
when we was kids and we know how to live high on the hog
and how to survive too. . . . And we're both gettin' old. And
under this is just an ol' boneyard, ain't it? Just a bunch of
bones and once they're scattered on the ground who will know
which is mine and which is yours and which is the coyotes?"
(44)

But Bobby, motivated by guilt or fear or ethnic loyalty, secretly leaves
the ranch and voluntarily enters Heart Mountain, trading a life of
security on the ranch where he has been respected as an equal for the
dehumanizing existence of a prisoner with little hope for happiness
to look forward to and a very uncertain future.

136.   Ehrlich, Gretel. "Kai's Mother." Drinking Dry Clouds. Santa
Barbara: Capra Press, 1991. 111 – 115.

"Kai's Mother" relates the experience and explores the feelings of an
aging Japanese woman who realizes as the war ends and she is
freed from imprisonment in a relocation camp that the burden of her
family's future rests in her own hands. With her son now serving in
the Army, her husband unable to believe that the Japanese have lost
the war and fantasizing he is going home to Japan, her family's
home, business, and possessions sold when they were ordered to
resettle in a relocation camp, and tales of American hatred of the
Japanese continuing, she has little left with which to build a new
foundation. Yet there is optimism and strength in her resolve to
begin anew rebuilding a life during the era of peace to come.

137.   Ehrlich, Gretel. "Madeleine's Day." Drinking Dry Clouds. Santa
Barbara: Capra Press, 1991. 95 – 103.

This story records the reactions and celebrates the strength of a war
wife whose husbands returns from imprisonment in a Japanese
prison camp "a living skeleton" of a man with both physical and
emotional problems that render him a stranger for many weeks
given to sudden outbursts of grief, hoarding of food, and inability to
interact socially. With patience and acceptance on Madeleine's part

the disrupted marriage gradually becomes whole again as she places faith in the fact that "in the natural geography of a marriage, love goes all over the place and the vows suspend disbelief until two people hook up again or go their separate ways" (98). It is Madeleine's efforts that keep the marriage from dissolving through Henry's difficult readjustment period as she offers her strength and compassion for him to lean upon until he is capable of trusting his own abilities once again.

138.   Ehrlich, Gretel. "Ted's Night." Drinking Dry Clouds. Santa Barbara: Capra Press, 1991. 154 – 160.

The veteran who narrates this story has come home from the war alive but is slowly losing his sanity. His thoughts are disjointed and confused, interspersed with painful reminders of his experience at war as a military doctor who was wounded while he was practicing medicine aboard a ship hit by a kamikaze pilot. "It's not like a stabbing pain," he attempts to describe the sensations in his head that indicate his fragile and unpredictable mental condition, "but a dull planetary roar, then sloshing as if ocean water had been poured into both ears" (156). War has left Ted with a physical wound that has healed but a mental scar that may never fade.

139.   Fisher, Dorothy Canfield. "Americans Must Be Told." Four-Square. New York: Harcourt, Brace and Company, 1949. 227 – 236.

In this narrative Fisher comments on Americans' lack of interest and inability to face the truth concerning the atrocities of war occurring in Europe. A Norwegian who has lived under the oppression of German domination visits the United States, imploring a longtime immigrant friend to circulate the truth of the war among Americans, lest Germany spread its empire across the Atlantic. "You must tell people about it," he commands Sigrid Hancock. "Americans must know. Nobody really tells them. They're like people working nice and quiet in their vegetable gardens, while somebody back of the house is putting poison into their well" (229). But when Sigrid tries to communicate with American friends, she is thwarted in her attempts by their disinterest and disbelief. A brutal war experience of her childhood remains secretly embedded in her memory, unshared with even her husband and children because Sigrid realizes they are among the protected Americans who have never experienced warfare on their own soil and are emotionally incapable of understanding its particular horror. Yet she also realizes that Americans "will not be safe if they are not warned." To prevent war, one must first be exposed to its horrors. Sigrid reaches the conclusion that the only way she can ever hope to enlighten Americans—so safe, so protected from the gruesomeness of war—is to offer a softened, euphemistic version of reality with the hopes of a gradual acceptance and awareness.

140.   Fisher, Dorothy Canfield. "The Knot-Hole." A Harvest of Stories. New York: Harcourt, Brace and Company, 1927. 309 – 335.

This short story, which placed second among the O. Henry Memorial award-winning short fiction for 1943, depicts the experiences and emotions of French prisoners of war, both soldiers and civilians. The narrative describes a representative French family separated by war in 1940. The wife, son, and infant daughter, whom the soldier-father never sees before she dies of starvation, are incarcerated in a small schoolhouse that houses more than 500 men, women, and children who must endure the strain of attempting to live cooperatively under such crowded conditions.

The story, too, examines the equally abhorrent, dehumanizing living conditions experienced by the father of the family, who is imprisoned in a German work camp. At one point he is among several prisoners hoarded onto a boxcar for several days, their destination unknown, where "every hour was exactly like the one which preceded it. In that windowless prison how could anything happen to make one hour, one minute, one day different from another?" he asks (326). The prisoners' only connection with the outside world is a tiny knothole one discovers no larger than the size of a man's thumb through which the prisoners glimpse their French homeland for the first time in years with uncertainty they will ever survive to return to it.

141.   Fisher, M. K. F. "The Unswept Emptiness." Sister Age. New York: Alfred A. Knopf, 1983. 48 – 58.

Fisher examines the feelings of emptiness and frustrations of overwhelming domestic responsibility experienced by a homefront war wife in this narrative. The visit of a travelling salesman—the "wax-man"—after a five-year interlude of war causes this wife and mother to reassess the substance of her life for the past half-decade, which seems despairingly inconsequential in retrospect: "two new children and the coming puppies, . . . the undusted floors and the unpolished nails and the unwashed heads of sweet babygirlhair" (58). Although she reassures herself that her husband's return from war will relieve the monotony of her routine and lighten the burden of domestic responsibility she has borne alone, the sudden wail of one of her daughters is a painful reminder of the "unswept emptiness" that has characterized her life as a confined and lonely homefront wife and mother.

142.   Geller, Ruth. "Her Date with the Rich Kid." Pictures From the Past. Buffalo: Impress Press, 1980. 157 – 167.

In this story Sally Goldstein develops a more perceptive awareness of her Jewish ancestral past through the coincidental juxtaposition of a disastrous date and a television documentary on German concentration camps her grandfather watches. While awaiting her date "with the rich kid," she hears the narrator's voice detailing the atrocities committed against Jews who were forced into a dehumanizing struggle for survival during the Holocaust. The documentary examines the terrible efficiency with which the Nazis ended thousands of Jewish lives and even profited from their extermination. The narrator explains:

"The extermination camps became a new Nazi industry where saleable commodities such as gold fillings and hair were removed from the corpses prior to cremation. Fatty acids were salvaged as an ingredient for inexpensive soap, and after cremation the ashes were used as fertilizer. From death itself the Nazis had found a way to profit, and the stench of burning flesh filled the countryside." (159)

At dinner with her date and his parents, Sally listens as her date discusses the similarity of the quail meat they are attempting to consume to human flesh. The prison camp experience of her ancestors is suddenly given tangible reality and painful clarity in Sally's mind:

In an instant she understood why she, unlike her classmates, had no great-aunts or second cousins or third cousins twice removed; the lack of family was not a matter of chance but a matter of design. It was an understanding as central as her bones, and as lasting, but one that she could flesh with fantasy and denial. (166)

Through the combination of these seemingly unrelated events, this young woman becomes a committed vegetarian and a more enlightened individual concerning the war experience of her Jewish forefathers and the potential inhumanity of mankind in general.

143. Gellhorn, Martha. "The Exile." The Honeyed Peace. Freeport, NY: Books for Libraries Press, 1953. 43 – 57.

The tragic plight of a German who immigrates to the United States during World War Two to escape Nazi rule yet cannot fit into American culture is sensitively narrated in this short fiction. At age 55, Heinrich Fleddermann—"neither a Jew nor a Communist nor even a Pacifist"—leaves his native homeland because he cannot stand the oppression, brutality, and distortion of truth and history that has transformed Germany under Nazi domination. But Heinrich fares little better in the Kansas City home of his American cousin where he is an obviously unwanted misfit. Heinrich finally concludes: "I am an exile, I am a man who belongs nowhere, and I have grown old without noticing it, but now it is too late" (56). His character is symbolic of many war victims who are left without a country when they flee their homelands invaded by war but discover they cannot integrate comfortably into any other culture.

144. Gellhorn, Martha. "The German." The Honeyed Peace. Freeport, NY: Books for Libraries Press, 1953. 177 – 179.

This brief sketch contrasts attitudes toward war between a German businessman living in Havana and the Cuban natives when they learn that the Germans have attacked Paris. The people of Havana "seemed lost now and hurt beyond healing. One could not feel that the French, any more than the Cubans, would be people to start a war" (177 – 178). But the businessman views war as an economic enterprise to be celebrated—a clash in perspective which ultimately culminates in violence between the Cubans and himself.

145. Gellhorn, Martha. "Good Will To Men." The Heart of Another. New York: Charles Scribner's Sons, 1941. 186 – 267.

This narrative documents the search of an American journalist for a fellow anti-Nazi German writer imprisoned in an French concentration camp at the beginning of the war. Despite the numerous roadblocks to her search, she perseveres because Max's "being in jail was as if he were a hostage for me and the people like me who could believe what we wanted, unpunished" (198). Having survived a previous war together with Max, she "had a closeness to him I would not have with other people. I did not want to wake in the night, in my house in a distant warm country, and think I had left Max where he was without speaking for him," she confides (198). The narrator also recognizes the imprisonment of this journalist could happen to any war correspondent, irrespective of gender or political allegiance:

> It would happen to all of us, sooner or later. Maybe it had already happened to me. Maybe that was why I was carefully turning my mind away from Finland and thinking of Max instead. I could not believe in anything except individuals any more. As long as I cared about Max, I kept some sort of confidence in the future. You wouldn't care whether a man lived or died, if there was going to be nothing to live for and no place worth living in. (227)

With World War Two only three months old, this journalist faces the uncertainty of her own future in the midst of an unpredictable war while she continues the search for a prisoner whom she realizes could very well have been herself.

146. Gellhorn, Martha. "The Honeyed Peace." The Honeyed Peace. Freeport, NY: Books for Libraries Press, 1953. 13 – 41.

War disrupts the long-time friendship of two women in this narrative when one is suddenly widowed and the other flees the country rather than attempt to cope with the bereavement of her friend. Although Anne has disapproved of Evangeline's passionate preoccupation with Renaud for the past 18 years, she travels to Paris following the war to offer financial and emotional support to Evangeline when her husband is imprisoned as a French collaborator. But when news arrives that Renaud has killed himself in prison—perhaps because he thought he would be shot or knew "there wouldn't be much future for him in France"—Anne catches the next plane for Berlin, where she is stationed as a volunteer, rather than face the widowed

Evangeline who has, in her own way, died as well. "There isn't any point to her without Renaud," a mutual friend points out. "She hasn't anything to be or do" (39).

Berlin, a city "bombed flat and full of soldiers," now appears appealingly familiar to Anne with its canteen full of "khaki men" to whom she can be comfortably "flirtatious and motherly according to need" and assume a role that is predictable and familiar once more rather than face the awkward situation of consoling a friend who has been devastated by war's loss.

147. Gellhorn, Martha. "In the Highlands." The Weather in Africa. New York: Dodd, Mead and Company, 1978. 77 – 199.

Gellhorn portrays the life of a World War Two prisoner of war trying to reestablish a life for himself in postwar Kenya in this narrative. When Ian Paynter buys an isolated farm in the African highlands, he retreats from memories of the war which claimed his immediate family as he shuns society in general. "I won't be lonely," he insists to the owner of the farm he purchases. "If you'd spent five years in a room with nine other men, and shared one and quarter acres inside barbed wire with three hundred men, you'd see that being alone in a lot of space is my idea of heaven. I don't want people. I don't know how to talk to them any more, I kind of gave it up in those five years" (82).

Ian later enters a disastrous marriage that remains unconsummated to a self-centered, lonely British woman whose proposal of marriage ruins one of his few friendships. Grace's memories of war are painful as well. In Ian she places faith that the pilot fiancee she fabricated out of loneliness will come true. But marriage guarantees nothing, she learns. Even after Grace takes steps to improve her homely appearance, Ian fails to notice, disappointing her and proving that he can never meet the expectations that only her imaginary pilot can fulfill:

> Her pilot would have told her he had to fall in love all over again with a bewitching new woman. Her pilot would have noticed each small detail, from the pearls in her ears to the high-heeled sandals, and kissed her saying she looked her true irresistible self. Ian was blind, deaf and dumb. She burned with anger against the cold unnatural man who cared for nothing and noticed nothing except his farm. (145)

Neither of these social misfits is able to meet one anothers' emotional needs, complicated by the circumstances of war. It is through the land and people of Africa that Ian discovers a purpose for living and the means to diminish his distressing memories of loss remaining from the war. The "true heroine" of this story, claims Victoria Glendinning in a review published in The New York Times Book Review, is "Africa itself, in particular the beautiful and derelict farm with which Ian, a lonely, war-scarred English bachelor, falls in love" (9).

148. Gellhorn, Martha. "Portrait of a Lady." The Heart of Another. New York: Charles Scribner's Sons, 1941. 50 – 122.

"Portrait of a Lady" traces the changes in an American journalist's feelings toward war when her journalistic distance dissolves and emotions take over. Covering her first war, rich and spoiled Mrs. Maynard arrives in Finland more concerned with the cold temperature and her own appearance than the ongoing war. That objective distance from the war fades abruptly when she becomes enamored with a Finnish aviator who dies during a flight mission. The tragic nature of war suddenly becomes a personal reality, no longer safely distanced. "I have lost everything I wanted, senselessly, cruelly, uselessly, without a reason," she mourns. "And there was this nearness now, this terrible nearness, it was close to you all the time, it could happen to any one, it could happen to you" (121).

Gellhorn's portrayal of the whimsical and self-centered Mrs. Maynard is effectively contrasted with the characterization of the young Finnish pilot, Lahit, who claims to love above all else his airplane, his country, and the men in his squadron and who vocally scorns journalists such as Mrs. Maynard who write about war as if it were a ski-jumping contest instead of a human tragedy. With Lahit's untimely death, however, war becomes a personal tragedy for the once emotionally detached American writer.

149. Gellhorn, Martha. "Till Death Us Do Part." Two By Two. New York: Simon and Schuster, 1958. 171 – 246.

A characterization of a talented combat photographer killed by a sniper during the prime of his career, "Till Death Us Do Part" examines one man's relationship with war. After ten years of photographing war all over the world, Bara vows to "give the whole thing up. Personally, I will retire," he announces. "And take photographs of beautiful girls with bosoms. If I never see some ugly men in khaki again, it will be a pleasure" (177). Through his numerous encounters with war, Bara becomes cynical toward human nature. At war, he acknowledges, "men were permanently engaged in losing what they loved, and destroying what others loved, and there was no help for this, it was the nature of man and the real shape of history" (243).

Although he may detest war—and what it symbolizes about mankind—Bara is also equally attracted to war, at least the variation of war observed from the photographer-spectator's angle. He thrives on the intensity and diversity the war experience offers and allows himself to set down no permanent roots which may stifle his freedom. In response to the pleading of one of his lovers to take marriage vows, Bara explains his own ephemeral nature: "Bara did not plan and worry, Bara lived in the moment; if he wanted to marry, he would do it as he did everything else, like diving joyfully off the top of a building" (216). "Till Death Us Do Part" examines not only what attracts men to war but what attracts women to men of war in relationships which often end tragically for women who long for more security than men who play the game of war are willing to give.

150. Gellhorn, Martha. "Week End at Grimsby." The Honeyed Peace. Freeport, NY: Books for Libraries Press, 1953. 59 – 88.

This story explores the inner thoughts and emotions of a woman attempting to regain control of her life after the war's end. Lily accepts an invitation to spend a weekend with wartime friends now living in a small English village, but the joy of renewed friendship is overshadowed by rekindled memories that only accentuate the pain of loss of friends and lovers killed in combat. Lily's veteran-friends predict only a few years of peace will pass before the British will attack the Russians. Men cannot live with peace for very long, one veteran explains. For men "make wars because that is what men like, they make a war so they get some excitement first before they die; or they only live and die, that is nothing much" (71). But Lily confesses she would rather move to a deserted island in the Dead Sea rather than live through another pointless war and have to cope with the inevitable aftermath of haunting ghosts in her life.

Feeling isolated from the new life these friends have carved for themselves, Lily realizes that her life has come to an impasse since the war ended; she has not moved forward with her life while she continues to grieve the loss of a beloved soldier. "How did you pick up the habit of living, once you had lost it?" she wonders. "How did you live with yourself after you had guessed for the first time, with disbelief and certainty, with horror, that you were a coward?" (88).

Inspired by the example of her friends, Lily resolves during her long train ride back to London from Grimsby to sever the cord binding her to past memories of war and look to the future as she gradually concludes: "There is no one to remember for, or no one to remember with; everyone must forget. The dead are dead, there is nothing to be done" (88). Life goes on, whether in war or peace, and the ghosts of the past deserve a permanent burial.

151. Gilchrist, Ellen. "The Time Capsule." Light Can Be Both Wave and Particle: A Book of Stories. Boston: Little, Brown and Company, 1990. 14 – 25.

This inquiring story presents a pre-adolescent's youthful curiosity and emerging perceptions of such concepts as time, womanhood, death, and war. As news from the Pacific front worsens, Rhoda decides that life is not permanent and it is time to build a time capsule as an artifact symbolic of her generation. Burying her capsule containing a movie star's picture, a string of beads, three pennies, and an empty perfume bottle, she offers future generations "a pretty good idea of what Seymour, Indiana was like in nineteen forty four" (19). Questions about war inevitably lead to questions about death, which Rhoda imagines as the worst of all possible experiences, probably very similar to her tonsillectomy last year. But Rhoda rises above her fears of death to accept the everyday challenges of civilians during war. When her military father announces the family will have to move once again, Rhoda regards the chore of packing as her patriotic duty. In this narrative the realistic and philosophical aspects of life and war are blended in the vision of an emerging adolescent.

152. Gilchrist, Ellen. "The Tree Fort." Light Can Be Both Wave and Particle. Boston: Little, Brown and Company, 1990. 3 – 13.

While World War Two rages in Europe, another war on a smaller scale takes place in the backyard of the eight-year-old narrator whose older brother builds a fort from discarded Christmas trees and suffers the loss of an eye during "combat," while she suffers from gender exclusion as the little sister who doesn't belong in the all-male regiment. She uses her own imaginative powers to rise above her disappointment, however, declaring "as soon as the war was over I was going to be a movie star. . . . For now, I was pure energy, clear light, morally neutral, soft and violent and almost perfect" (12 – 13). The vision of war as a children's game—sometimes fanciful, sometimes violent—is portrayed through the eyes of a young female who learns at an early age that war often excludes those of the female gender.

153. Gilchrist, Ellen. "Victory Over Japan." Victory Over Japan: A Book of Stories. Boston: Little, Brown and Company, 1984. 77 – 87.

A young girl's perceptions of a distant war and varied homefront experiences while growing up are intermingled in this story. The domestic "tragedy" of a classmate who suffers from a squirrel bite looms larger in Rhoda's mind than the international crisis that seems so remote from Seymour, Indiana. With the defeat of the Germans, and "only the Japs to go," the third-grade narrator joins her school's newspaper-magazine drive for the "war effort" during which she is introduced to, and terrified by, her first pictures of naked women lurking in the pages of magazines found in someone's musty basement. News of the approaching American victory in Japan evokes an ambivalent reaction in Rhoda who experiences a certain comfort in the expectation of victory but fears the return of her sometimes abusive and now safely distant father:

> Now the radio was bringing important news to Seymour, Indiana. Strange, confused, hush-hush news that said we had a bomb bigger than any bomb ever made and we had already dropped it on Japan and half of Japan was sinking into the sea. Now the Japs had to surrender. Now they couldn't come to Indiana and stick bamboo up our fingernails. Now it would be all over and my father would come home. . . .

Well, maybe it would take a while for him to get home. First
they had to finish off Japan. First they had to sink the other
half into the sea. I curled up in my soft old eiderdown
comforter. I was feeling great. We had dropped the biggest
bomb in the world on Japan and there were plenty more where
that one came from. (86 – 87)

In this short story Gilchrist characterizes war from a child's
perspective, her perceptions colored by her own self-absorption and
the other equally compelling forces influencing her young life.

154. Goldstein, Rebecca. "The Legacy of Raizel Kaidish: A Story."
America and I: Short Stories by American Jewish Women Writers.
Ed. Joyce Antler. Boston: Beacon Press, 1990. 281 – 289.

A Holocaust survivor's obsession with the moral education of her
child gradually distances her daughter in this story until finally
Raizel's resentment of her mother dissolves into hate. The narrator
explains how she was named after Raizel Kaidish, the "heroine of
block eight," who died in the gas chambers of Buchenwald after an
informer reported that Raizel planned to trade places with a sick
friend whose name had been placed on the death list in hopes that
both of them might survive. It is only at the end of the story, when
Raizel's mother is on her deathbed, that Raizel learns the dark truth
that her own mother was the informer who was rewarded with the
prisoner's coveted kitchen job.

Raizel's mother develops a stringent moral philosophy which she
imposes upon her young daughter, based upon rigid absolutes of
right and wrong and an uncompromising belief in the inseparable
nature of logic and ethics. Even suffering can be analyzed logically,
she teaches her daughter. During adolescence Raizel begins to
resent her "extensive moral training," sometimes fantasizing,
although with a sense of guilt, that she is part of another family
"with parents who were frivolous and happy and had no numbers
burned into their arms" (285).

It is when Raizel gives birth to her own child that her resentment
darkens and solidifies into hate. For whatever reason a mother bears
a child, she learns through the experience of motherhood, "the ends
of which one bore the child lose themselves in the knowledge of the
child itself" (286). But Raizel's mother was never able to immerse
herself in the sheer joy of her child and lose sight of her own
reason for giving birth, leaving something vitally missing in her
relationship with her daughter. Raizel now realizes that as she grew
up she "knew what no child should ever know: that my mother had
had me for some definite reason and that she would always see me in
terms of this reason. I sensed this in my mother, and I hated her for
it" (296). Only when Raizel's mother confesses her Holocaust
secret does her daughter begin to understand the underlying guilt
that is the source of her mother's moralistic view of life and obsession
with such a rigid philosophy. But by then it is too late. Raizel has

adopted her own positivist philosophy, deliberately contradictory to her mother's, and has severed whatever emotional ties may have once existed between them.

155. Greenberg, Joanne. "Elizabeth Baird." Prize Stories 1990: The O. Henry Awards. New York: Doubleday, 1990. 179 – 195.

The author combines autobiographical and historical elements in this O. Henry Memorial Award-winning narrative concerning an American nurse's imprisonment by the Japanese during the war. Greenberg explains the origin of the plot:

> I was a girl during World War II and remember much of the ambience of those times. Long ago I had been told about life in a prison camp in the Pacific. These were all unconnected and I never had a conscious plan to gather this combination of experience and hearsay or to form something from its unpromising scraps. It was when I began to think about my character—an odd, elfin little girl who had a slight brain lesion—that I found them there, waiting. (Biographies 416)

The female protagonist of Greenberg's narrative is incarcerated with other American nurses in a prison camp in the Philippines. During her internment Elizabeth Baird discovers that her slight neurological disabilities, a continual source of castigation and ostracism at home, are interpreted by the enemy as "Japanese feminine modesty" and become a key factor to her survival. Ironically, it is only during war that Elizabeth experiences approval of her individuality in an enemy culture with differing standards of femininity. Even though this acceptance aids her survival, it costs Elizabeth in terms of increased social rejection by fellow prisoners who are envious of her special privileges.

When Elizabeth returns to her hometown, she discovers that during her captivity the New South has emerged, her hometown made prosperous by the industries of war. Lauded for the first time in her life as a heroine of war but uncomfortable with her newfound glory, Elizabeth is painfully aware "with a wry feeling almost like a laughter from the deepest places in herself, that such acceptance and praise would never come again unless, of course, she visited the land of the enemy" (195). Elizabeth is a heroine without a homeland, for her experiences in captivity have set her apart from society, and the Southern homefront she left behind has been radically altered by war industries into a thriving metropolis that is hardly reminiscent of the home she recalls. Elizabeth's "acceptance" bears a hypocritical falseness, for she realizes it is not herself who is admired but a romanticized image of a prison camp survivor.

156. Hahn, Emily. "The Baby-Amah." 55 Short Stories From the New Yorker. London: Victor Gollancz Ltd., 1949. 422 – 431.

This story, set in Hong Kong after its surrender to the Japanese, describes the separation of wives and children from their incarcerated prisoner-of-war husbands. The only contact these women are allowed with their husbands consists of a monthly postcard of no more than 50 words, weekly parcels, and a glimpse across the barbed-wire encampment once a week. Some wives fear to attempt the Monday walks, for a breach of the strict rules of conduct imposed by the Japanese could easily result in their being shot instantly. But the narrator, risking her own life and that of her child during their last walk by the prison camp before they depart Hong Kong, allows her young daughter to wave to her father and shout goodbye, shattering the silence of the camp and boldly testing the humanitarianism of the outwardly dispassionate Japanese guards. In this story Hahn examines yet another facet of the war experience for women who attempt to preserve a sense of family unity with their estranged husbands, employing all of their ingenuity—and occasionally their audacity—to traverse the "barbed wire."

157. Hall, Martha Lacy. "Lucky Lafe." Music Lesson. Chicago: University of Illinois Press, 1984. 30 – 38.

Renowned for her "Mississippi storytelling" talents, Hall narrates this short story through the voice of a World War Two veteran who recalls the experience of his best friend at war, an experience that has been replayed over and over and savored by the small town southerners who never seem to tire of Lafe's infamous war legend. "I tell you, if I was a writer, I'd put it all down," the narrator explains. "Not just because it's a great story, but because of the way Lafe tells it. He ain't overdramatic, just cool, and he talks for his mother and Joel and the fellows at the pool hall just like he was in a play. Only it's not just a tale. It's all true" (30).

While serving in the Pacific, the legend begins, Lafe's ship is bombed by a Japanese kamikaze pilot. Although Lafe is unharmed, he is reported among those missing in action and is subsequently grieved by his hometown and family as dead. A month later Lafe shocks everyone as he arrives home without a wound. Lucky Lafe.

But war does not stop there for Lafe. His younger brother dies fighting in the Korean War, and his own son serves in Vietnam. "Ain't that the way with life?" the narrator observes. "It never ends with one story—or one war" (38). As Lafe's story ends both he and the narrator express the hope that the American tradition of war will not be passed on to Lafe's young grandson, although both sense that inevitability. In the southern tradition of storytelling, Hall depicts the male tradition of sharing war stories yet ends her narrative in a nontraditional manner with veterans expressing their hope that future generations will not have a reason to create more American war legends.

158. Hashimoto, Sharon. "When the World Winds Down." Echoes from Gold Mountain (1978): 50 – 55.

A Japanese-American watchmaker begins to relinquish the past and accept the death of his brother at war in this study of sorrow and growth. Intrigued with the intricacies of timepieces, Fred Fujita glories in the manipulation of their insides. "Here, with the pieces spread out before him, he could answer all questions. It was a beautiful world" (52). In his private world Fred becomes a controller of time who can leap forward into the future or reach back into the past at will. But continually reliving the past, he eventually learns, will not change the course of time or allow his younger brother, who enlisted in the war effort against Fred's will and died in combat at age 17, to live again. His brother's senseless death at such a young age can only be accepted through the healing grace of time and acknowledgement that the past can only be altered in the fantasy world of the watchmaker.

159. Johnson, Josephine. "The Rented Room." It's a Woman's World: A Collection of Stories from Harper's Bazaar. Ed. Mary Louise Aswell. New York: McGraw-Hill, 1944. 117 – 141.

"The Rented Room" focuses on the loneliness of a transient military wife who lives in a series of rented rooms but longs to plant roots and develop a sense of home and stability for her family, a dream denied by the continuation of war. As she expects her second child, Elizabeth feels her life contracting rather than expanding in a direction of uncertainty:

> Life was boxes inside of boxes, life an onion, a hive within a hive. First the space of stars, the cold, the bitter stratosphere; and then the circle of oxygen and mountains surrounding a world of war and blood and insanity; and in that world Mrs. McNary's red brick bandbox full of rooms, and in the rooms herself and Martin, and in herself pain and another child— and in that child . . . ? (119)

To escape from the constant demands of her young son and confinement of her life in impersonal rental room after rental room, Elizabeth fantasizes a "place of peace" of her own, a combination of idealized childhood memory and fabricated dreams that sustain her sanity through the monotony of each day. Johnson's portrayal of war life for women such as Elizabeth is despairingly realistic in its representation of the feelings of aloneness and insecurity of a war wife left without a sense of home or direction as she waits for the war to end and her life to begin once more.

160. Kalpakian, Laura. "Wine Women and Song." Dark Continent and Other Stories. New York: Viking, 1989. 35 – 86.

Kalpakian explores the effect of war on identity in this narrative focusing on a rather ordinary war wife who carves a new existence for herself and her two daughters while her husband is at war, and refuses to relinquish her newfound independence once he returns, even though her refusal ends their marriage. When Wesley returns from the war, he expects his wife to give up her job and move from her temporary San Diego home back to the small town in Idaho where he grew up because it offers the security of a job and family ties. But Shirley, who detests the conservative blandness of Wesley's hometown, has tasted independence and the divergence of lifestyles and opinions offered by a more cosmopolitan city—values that have become too precious to lose. Although she felt abandoned and rather hopeless when Wesley voluntarily joined the war effort, Shirley carves a new identity of self-assured competence for herself while he is gone that includes a change of name, residence, and perspective on the world. While the returning Wesley desires to erase the past four years and resume their married life where war intervened, Shirley realizes she is neither capable of being nor willing to try to become the person she gratefully left behind when her husband left for war.

161. Kornblatt, Joyce Reiser. "Flo." Breaking Bread. New York: E. P. Dutton, 1987. 61 – 93.

"Flo" is a narrative characterization of Fela Skolnik Teplitsky, a Polish immigrant, who survives Auschwitz and becomes a model of adoration for the young American narrator of this story who describes Fela's special strength: "She is a dozen women, a town's worth, an entire generation of daughters scattered over the world like crumbs from History's sweaty hand" (64).

Germany's invasion of Poland interrupts Fela's ambition to pursue a medical career, surrounding her life and family with bricks and barbed wire, diminishing her world—as well as that of all other Polish Jews—into "one tiny corner of Warsaw, the rest of the planet breaking off and disappearing into space, for all the connection the Jews of Poland have to this earth anymore" (72).

Although Fela (given an Americanized version of her Polish name— "Flo") reveals her experiences to her younger, curious friend in anecdotal bits and pieces, shaping and reshaping the dramas of her past so as not to forget them, she stops short of the morbid truth of her concentration camp experience—"the point in the world's history where conventional narrative no longer suffices, where language falters, defers to the silence in which a new alphabet struggles to form itself under the bone pits, under the eyeglass mounds. Hieroglyphs multiply in the ash-fed earth" (72 – 73). This experience is left to the young narrator to imagine for herself and investigate, which she pursues "with a compulsion some might call morbid" (72). In her worst moments of fantasy she imagines Fela's sister, Rachel, taken as a commandant's whore and Fela assigned as a carpenter crew member who builds scaffolding for the camp's daily hangings. Perhaps both sisters served as guinea pigs for scientific experiments and were subject to injected bacteria and induced fevers. At best the narrator visualizes the two sisters sustaining each other in a mutual effort to survive:

> Perhaps the sisters found some way to keep each other alive, developed between them certain rituals—a particular handclasp upon arriving and at night, before they fell into the few hours of stupor still named sleep; a secret word whispered into the other's ear, as lovers murmur the syllables only they two understand, as mothers sing to their babies the song that lulls no other child into dream; a daily exchange of food, morsel for morsel, crumb for crumb, a drop of water placed by each upon the other's tongue.
>
> A touch, a word, the semblance of food. With such small gifts we sustain ourselves, the receiving no more crucial than the offering. (74)

Fela remains a misfit in her adopted country as she shuns American materialism and experiences a continuing sense of incompleteness separated from her Polish sister by an impermeable Iron Curtain. When news of her sister's death arrives, there is nothing left for Fela in this land of "windowless shopping malls, their acres of cars like petrified cattle in cement fields" (92). She heads away from suburban U.S.A. to the rural countryside where "the land reclaims itself" and the sky "opens an unbroken span to her" (92). With nothing remaining to remind her of the old world, she "sets out on the long, trek, Fela Skolnik Teplitsky, my lost teacher, a refugee in the middle of nowhere, a grief-borne woman going home" (93).

This characterization is both a celebration of strength and individuality and a tragic commentary as well of a woman ultimately lost without a family or country where she can feel a sense of belonging.

162. Marshall, Paule. "The War." Brown Girl, Brownstones. 1959. New York: Avon, 1970. 56 – 155.

In this chapter of Marshall's coming of age novel, a poor black family's domestic war waged in Brooklyn parallels the ongoing world war. For Selina, the reality of the war so distant only becomes believable when her own adolescent body undergoes the drastic changes of sexual maturation:

> For a long time she did not really believe in the war, even with the air-raid drills in school, and Chauncey Street occasionally plunged in blackness, and Fulton Street chastened by the brown-out. Not until later that winter when the war seemed to reach out and claim her. For her body was in sudden upheaval—her dark blood flowing as it flowed in the war, the pain at each shudder of her womb as sharp as the thrust of a bayonet. (57)

Selina suffers the confusions of many adolescents, compounded by the "bitter, protracted struggle between her mother and father" which "haunts Selina's formative years, and is the most dramatic element in this novel" (Pinckney 26). The stormy relationship between her parents ends when Selina's mother arranges for the arrest and deportation of Dreighton on the basis of his illegal entry into the United States.

Although Silla's war with her husband may be over, she must now confront her own daughter as a formidable opponent as strong willed as herself and as rebellious as her father who has witnessed her mother's betrayal of her favored parent and now seeks retaliation. "The War" ends in a "climactic battle" between mother and daughter during which Selina spits the most derogatory name imaginable in her mother's face—"Hitler." As Silla's mother reacts in disbelief, "You's saying I's the worse person in the world?" Marshall reminds us again that "the war within this family has taken place in the context of a larger world war" (Christian 97). Even as the world war ends on the same day the family learns of Deighton's apparent suicide, the domestic war within this family continues as Selina, "who sees herself only as her father's daughter, becomes the angry one and takes on the responsibility of avenging the betrayal of his dreams" (Christian 98).

163. Miller, Heather Ross. "Stasia and Marek." A Spiritual Divorce and Other Stories. Winston-Salem: John F. Blair, 1974. 93 – 110.

In this narrative Miller weaves together short sketches narrated by two Jewish war orphans living in the United States who attempt to establish a sense of identity and morality out of the confused instability of their turbulent childhood. Because Stasia is too young to remember her mother, her brother draws pictures of maternal figures on the expansive walls of his grandmother's decaying house, motherly shapes with no faces which Stasia clings to out of unfulfilled need and begs: "Sing! Sing to me!" Marek's memory of his parents is more concrete, if still blurred, ending abruptly with their arrest and departure to separate and unknown fates. If war deprives these children of a sense of identity and security, it also presents them with an equally confused sense of morality. Although they are witness to repeated senseless and unjust acts of inhumanity, they retain a resilient, youthful optimism toward life, as expressed by Marek: "We do not entirely trust anyone, but we are still living. Surely, that is a kind of a moral, a kind of good sign" (110).

164. Miller, Heather Ross. "War Games." A Spiritual Divorce and Other Stories. Winston-Salem: John F. Blair, 1974. 39 – 50.

The realities of war are co-mingled with a young boy's imaginary war games in this short story. Daniel's father dies in the North African campaign. In Daniel's imagination, however, the war continues as he accepts the role vacated by his father. The death of Daniel's father necessitates his living in an old house with cousins and aunts and rats that scamper in the attic above during blackouts, as if they are running races. In his imagination, Daniel declares war on the rats, gunning them down. An imaginary war drawn with crayons on paper at school assumes a realistic dimension, however, when Daniel attacks an obnoxious classmate for throwing his aviator's helmet into a tree. But Daniel also learns that the hunter can unexpectedly become the hunted during war, when a tiger escapes from a travelling circus and selects him as a convenient victim. Since his father's death, both the mundane and extraordinary events in eight-year-old Daniel's life seem to revolve around the concept of war as he attempts to sort reality from fantasy and gradually assimilate his father's death at war.

165. Moore, Ruth. "The Soldier Shows His Medal." The Best Maine Stories: The Marvelous Mystery. Eds. Sanford Phippen, Charles Waugh, and Martin Greenberg. Augusta: Lance Tapley, 1986. 287 – 293.

A 20-year-old private home on leave from service in the Pacific longs to show his medal for valor to his rural Maine neighbors in this story but realizes they would frown upon such an act as ostentatious and self-serving. A middle-aged woman who once caught young Joey Hinckley stealing apples from the family orchard now forgives his breach of conduct, long since replaced by the maturity imposed on young men by war, and promises to spread the news of his heroism in a secondhand manner more acceptable to this tradition-bound community.

166. Morris, Edita. "Heart of Marzipan." The Best American Short Stories of 1944. Ed. Martha Foley. Boston: Houghton Mifflin, 1944. 280 – 284.

The greatest crime ever committed by war, Morris proposes in this award-winning story, is "putting out the laughter of children." "Heart of Marzipan" examines the secret kept by war children—"hungry and thin and scared—who share a common experience of victimization so huge it made us all belong together" (284). Cold boys and girls stick their fingers in their mouths seeking warmth. Young girls grow up believing they will never bear children because they have subsisted on a diet of turnips and eels during four seemingly endless years of war. Children steal other children's food rations in hungry desperation. A birthday cake made with real sugar is welcomed as an almost incredulous treat in a world of blackouts and bombings and the fears of children who live during wartime.

167. Mueller, Marnie. "Changes." Home to Stay: Asian American Women's Fiction. Ed. Sylvia Watanbe and Carol Bruchac. Greenfield Center, NY: Greenfield Review Press, 1990. 34 – 47.

The first Caucasian to be born in the Tule Lake Japanese Relocation Center in California during World War Two, Mueller remembers her father as a conscientious objector who volunteered to work in the relocation camps but met with such "virulent racism" against his Japanese ethnicity that he was persuaded "there were circumstances in which he would take up arms" (34). The memory of her father perhaps formed the basis of characterization for the male protagonist of "Changes" who is depicted as a fiercely nationalistic and proud Japanese farmer trying valiantly to retain his dignity and cultural heritage despite Americans' insensitive treatment toward the Japanese and the gradual Americanization of his wife and son.

Sitting on the steps of the tarpaper barracks he calls "this shit hole of a prison," Toru Horokawa recounts the changes in his life "that turned his heart raw in their newness," including his loss of home, country, land, and cultural identity. But most devastating of all to Horokawa is his son's decision to enlist in the American military to fight against the Japanese, an act which denounces his father's longtime allegiance to Japan and establishes his own with the United States. "You kill my ancestors," Horokawa rages at his son, striking him for the first time in his son's 18 years, provoking the wrath of his usually gentle wife in defense of her son. Too proud to weep, Horokawa dreams of more contented times before war robbed him of his freedom and simple lifestyle, before war alienated him from his devoted wife and only son.

168. Mueller, Marnie. "What Would You Have Done?" Unholy Alliances. Ed. Louise Rafkin. San Francisco: Cleis Press, 1988. 59 – 63.

The Jewish woman who narrates his story and her Nazi-descended husband gain a closer sense of intimacy after they view a movie concerning the activities of the White Rose, a war resistance group active in Europe during World War Two. In the past Andreas has defended his father's party affiliation as a necessity for his family's protection and security and has refused to answer his wife's confrontive questions. Following the film, however, Andreas is moved to confess to his wife that he once wrote a poem about the White Rose while he was a university student in which he imagined himself as one of the resistance members. This revelation assures his wife of his unspoken ambivalence he holds toward his father's beliefs and his own private alliance with the cause of peace.

169. Newman, Leslea. "Flashback." A Letter to Harvey Milk: Short Stories by Leslea Newman. Ithaca, NY: Firebrand Books, 1988. 129 – 146.

The lasting imprint of the Holocaust upon successive generations is vividly illustrated in this story which also emphasizes the strength of women who bond together for survival. Obsessed with the Holocaust since she first read The Diary of Anne Frank at the age of 11, Sharon Weinstein immerses herself in the diaries of concentration camp survivors "with an insatiable appetite," always wondering how they lived through such horror and where they derived their strength:

> While the books answered some of Sharon's questions, they raised a whole crop of others. Would she herself have survived? Would she had had the will to go on, after seeing her

> parents, her neighbors, her friends, all burnt to a crisp in
> Hitler's incinerators? Would she have had the stamina to
> work ten hours a day, standing outside in the freezing cold
> with nothing but rags on her feet? Would she have been able to
> ˙stomach being raped by German soldiers, and would she have
> given them special favors for an extra crust of bread? It was
> too awful to think about, but think about it she did, for Sharon
> didn't believe it could ever happen again, could never happen
> here, as her friends would tell her. Sharon yearned to know
> the answers to these questions, and at the same time she hoped
> she would never have to find out. (131)

During a hair cutting session Sharon experiences a sensation of deja
vu so overwhelming in intensity she doubles over in a catatonic state,
vividly imagining what it must have been like for the Jewish women
imprisoned in concentration camps who were unsuspectingly herded
into the gas chambers for haircuts before they were gassed, their
hair saved to stuff mattresses. Other signs of anti-Semitism in
American society combined with this vivid flashback convince
Sharon that another Holocaust, this time on American soil, is
imminent. She hides away in her apartment in a state of paranoid
fear for her life and that of all American Jews, terrified to even
answer the door.

After several weeks of hibernation, Sharon receives an invitation to a
party from a Jewish friend. Her feelings of paranoia are overcome by
an aching loneliness and longing for companionship. She resolves to
risk her life by daring to leave her apartment and join her friends,
becoming a woman of the Holocaust who, like those who preceded
her, would "lay down their lives for each other, just to show there
was still a little bit of humanity left in the world." Sharon becomes
one of a number of women who were inspired to survive the
Holocaust experience by their "desire to tell the world what was
happening so that it could never happen again. To name their
suffering. To validate it. So it could be witnessed by a world deeply
invested in denial" (143).

Although born 20 years after the end of World War Two, Sharon
allows her intense interest in the Holocaust to grow into an
exaggerated fear that another anti-Semitic movement may be
underway. But her understanding of women's experiences of the
Holocaust also reassures Sharon of the strength of those survivors
who extend emotional support to one another and will themselves to
endure, lest their experience be forgotten.

170. Newman, Leslea. "A Letter to Harvey Milk." <u>A Letter to Harvey
Milk: Short Stories by Leslea Newman</u>. Ithaca, NY: Firebrand
Books, 1988. Boston: Beacon Press, 1990. 32–47.

The elderly Jewish widower who narrates this moving story enrolls
in a writing class to "pass the time" but through writing, begins an
introspective digging into his past that proves to be both therapeutic

and painful. As he records random thoughts in his writing notebook, the narrator rediscovers memories in his family history of "hunger and more hunger, suffering and more suffering." In response to an assignment to write a story entitled "What I Never Told Anyone," he recounts a Holocaust tragedy once confided to him by a longtime friend whose homosexual relationship, discovered by concentration camp guards, resulted in the torture and eventual death of his best friend. The night Izzie revealed this tragic and intimate chapter of his life, the narrator recalls, he held his sobbing friend all night long in comfort and empathic acceptance. After completing this writing assignment, however, the narrator realizes he can no longer continue the class because the intense introspection he has undergone has evoked too many painful memories of loss. "I'm too old for this crazy writing," he concludes. "I remember too much, the pen is like a knife twisting in my heart" (47).

171. Oppersdorff, Rosamond. "I Was Too Ignorant." Wave Me Goodbye: Stories of the Second World War. Ed. Anne Boston. New York: Viking, 1989. 9 – 16.

This narrative documents the experience of a woman with no prior nursing experience who learns to overcome her fear and revulsion to the sight of blood to help aid the wounded in a Brittany military camp. "I do not think that I was either heroic or brave," she writes of the experience. "On the contrary, I was a coward and wanted to run. But I couldn't run. Fright is based on ignorance. I hope no one will ever be caught in such ignorance as I was" (9). Each day's account of the narrator's activities shows her diminishing fears and increasing confidence until finally she is performing the duties of a trained military nurse as waves of wounded men continue to fill the beds of the hospital ward. A year later the narrator still recalls the vivid memory of her experience, her mind still full of images of all the "queer mutilated shapes which I know by heart, but which frightened me so much at first," shapes which soon became familiar sights to a woman who shed her ignorance and fear without hesitation to meet the needs demanded by war (16).

172. Orgel, Irene. "Fish and Chips." The Odd Tales of Irene Orgel. New York: Eakins Press, 1966. 55 – 61.

Traditions hold strong, even in the midst of chaos and destruction, as evidenced in this short story, set in London during the German Blitz. Despite the obvious danger to her life, Mrs. Phipps refuses to give up her fish-and-chips shop, taking her trade underground during the Blitz with as few alterations as possible. Mrs. Phipps continues to serve her customers as before with a stubborn refusal to alter her lifestyle simply because a war has intervened (58).

One morning at daybreak following a night of heavy bombing activity, Mrs. Phipps emerges from an underground shelter with other Londoners who discover before their eyes "an unfamiliar world. Against a raging sky, still red with fire, they could not find their homes. They felt as the dead might feel, awakened after centuries on judgment day, to see the changes which had befallen familiar locations" (60). While sifting through the bombing debris, Mrs. Phipps discovers her cat has survived the bombing unscathed and now ecstatically caresses her ankles as if they "were like two survivors on a bare planet" (60). In the ruins of her shop, she discovers her gas stove, standing quite unharmed as a symbol of endurance and the continuance of life's patterns despite the destructive forces of war. At the request of a neighbor, she begins to brew a cup of tea as her cat sits perched on a fallen chimney pot, washing himself fastidiously in the warm sunshine. The character of Mrs. Phipps is representative of those who refuse to allow the forces of war to interrupt their routines or change their lifestyles but simply persevere with a tenacious commitment to tradition and survival.

173. Osterman, Marjorie. "Fraulein." New Voices 2: American Writing Today. Ed. Don M. Wolfe. New York: Hendricks House, Inc., 1955. 294 – 305.

This characterization of a German governess in postwar America illustrates how the anti-Semitism so pervasive in Germany during World War Two did not necessarily fade with the end of the war. The fraulein in Osterman's story bitterly resents working for an American-Jewish family more prosperous than her own family left in postwar Germany. All of the fraulein's repressed hatred seems aimed at the daughter of the Jewish family who becomes her emotional scapegoat, locked in a darkened closet as her first lesson in obedience and perhaps her first biting taste of the pain of anti-Semitic prejudice. The governess predicts that unless stopped, Jewish-Americans will take over the American economy as Jews attempted in Germany, and Americans will suffer while the rest of the world will learn to hate them, as they did the Germans. The fraulein's preciseness, emotional detachment, intolerance, and rigid authoritarianism personify the respect for control and order usually associated with the Nazi mentality that carried anti-Semitism to the most extreme degree of inhumanity during the war.

174. Ozick, Cynthia. "from Trust." Buying Time. Ed. Scott Walker. Saint Paul: Graywolf Press, 1985. 183 – 204.

In this chapter from the novel Trust, the unnamed adolescent narrator accompanies her mother to Europe at the end of the war, her mother intending to introduce her daughter to the wealth of culture and civilization there—"all spectacle, domination, energy, and honor"—in contrast to the United States, "all bare and blank by comparison" (202). But what her young daughter observes instead are the images of war that have ravaged this continent and its people in a land that still smells of death and abounds with corpses, even though the armistice is three months past. The "education" the narrator gleans from her visit to the countries of Europe reveals mankind's capacity for inhumanity and unwarranted prejudice.

175. Ozick, Cynthia. "Rosa." The Shawl. New York: Alfred A. Knopf, 1989. 11 – 70.

This sequel to "The Shawl," which won first-place among the O. Henry Memorial Award-winning short stories of 1984, skips forward in time from World War Two to the mid-1970s, from Germany to Miami, where Rosa Lublin lives as a reclusive, self-proclaimed "madwoman and scavenger," with her loathing mistrust of the human race and self-absorbed grief over the murder of her 15-month-old daughter by Nazi concentration camp guards during the war. Surrounded by aging retirees, Rosa finds little consolation in the opportunities that exist for companionship, preferring to believe that southern Florida is populated by elderly people similar to herself who have been robbed of living: "It seemed to Rosa Lublin that the whole peninsula of Florida was weighted down with regret. Everyone had left behind a real life. Here they had nothing. They were all scarecrows, blown about under the murdering sunball with empty rib cages" (16).

If Rosa's prized shawl symbolizes a life-giving force in "The Shawl" in this narrative it exhibits the magical quality of sustaining her infant daughter's image in Rosa's memory so tangibly she is convinced she can still smell "the holy fragrance of the lost babe" in its fibers (31). Magda's image assumes a divine quality as the shawl is transformed into a holy relic which Rosa worships, practicing her own form of idolatry (Prose 39). Rosa drafts letters to her daughter as if she were still alive, entering that world of fantasy she has created as the only desirable existence for herself where memories are given concrete form and maternal bonding is made possible once again.

Although written in a different narrative style, "Rosa" shares a similarity to "The Shawl" in its illustration of how the war experience of one woman becomes a continuous presence that weighs heavily on her caustic perspective of life and her refusal to experience what life may offer beyond the boundaries of unrelenting memory.

176. Ozick, Cynthia. "The Shawl." The Shawl. New York: Alfred A. Knopf, 1989. 3 – 10.

Winner of both the O. Henry Memorial and Best American Short Story of the Year awards, "The Shawl" describes with swift and stark realism the futility of a mother's attempt to nurture and sustain the life of her infant daughter while they are imprisoned in the Nazi concentration camp. Aware that her daughter would be killed if discovered, Rosa Lublin conceals baby Magda in the folds of a shawl which assumes magical qualities, providing protection from the danger of discovery as well as nourishment for the suckling infant long after Rosa's milk supply has run dry from malnutrition: "The shawl was Magda's own baby, her pet, her little sister. She tangled herself up in it and sucked on one of the corners when she wanted to be very still" (6).

Ultimately the shawl which supports life also denies life to Magda when her older cousin steals the shawl for warmth, revealing the mute baby's hiding place. Rosa witnesses a scene as graphically brutal as any observed by a combat soldier during war. A concentration camp guard heaves her daughter's tiny body against a wall while Rosa stands horrified, watching her daughter's "feathered round head and her pencil legs and balloonish belly and zigzag arms splashed against the fence. . . " (10).

The shawl once again sustains life as Rosa rejects the voices within urging her to try to protect her daughter, knowing that such a move would only forfeit her own life as well. Instead, she stuffs her own mouth with the fibers of the shawl "until she was swallowing up the wolf's screech and tasting the cinnamon and almond depth of Magda's saliva; and Rosa drank Magda's shawl until it dried" (10).

The idea for writing "The Shawl" originated from a sentence Ozick read in William Shirer's Rise and Fall of the Third Reich that described babies being thrown against electric fences. ". . . I guess that image stayed with me," Ozick remarked during a New York Times interview (Heron 39). Although Ozick wrote both "The Shawl" and its sequel, "Rosa," in 1977, it was four years later before she considered trying to publish "The Shawl." She put away both stories for awhile after writing them, she explained, because she feared that by fictionalizing the Holocaust, she might be corrupting history, as she believes fiction sometimes does (Heron 39).

177. Parker, Dorothy. "The Lovely Leave." The Viking Portable Library: Dorothy Parker. New York: Viking Press, 1944. 21 – 40.

"The Lovely Leave" compares a war wife's fantasized anticipation of her husband's furlough with the actual awkwardness of their reunion. As Mimi prepares for her husband's leave, she assumes the responsibility to insure that this visit, unlike his last, will be idyllic. But such romanticized notions fall apart when Steve arrives home, his original leave greatly abbreviated. The pressure felt by both Steve and Mimi to avoid conflict inevitably breeds friction, with this leave ending as disastrously as the last.

As Dorothy Sauber explains in her "Historical Context/Literary Content: Women Write About War and Women," the husband of Mimi's fantasies "is a man from the past" who no longer exists (66). Steve has become the ideal soldier who has efficiently eliminated the need for romance from his life in order to do his job effectively. While he has successfully separated himself from women in order to concentrate on his assigned tasks, he has forfeited those very traits that previously made him a loving husband. A few hours' leave does not provide sufficient enough time for him to begin the transition from soldier to husband. Thus Steve remains detached from his wife and distracted by the concerns of military decorum that have recently dominated his life.

For Mimi, however, "war has meant isolation and loneliness and the sacrifice of her romance to war" (Sauber 67). While Steve's life has expanded during his military service, hers has contracted in an unfulfilled introversion of solitariness. "You see," she attempts to explain her feelings of loss to him, "you have a whole new life—I have half an old one. Your life is so far away from mine, I don't see how they're ever going to come back together" (88). Mimi confesses she envies his comradeship with fellow soldiers and the importance of his mission:

> "I know it's hard for you. But it's never lonely, that's all I mean. You have companionships no—no wife can ever give you. I suppose it's the sense of hurry, maybe, the consciousness of living on borrowed time, the—the knowledge of what you're all going into together that makes the comradeship of men in war so firm, so fast" (90).

Steve's "lovely leave" bears no loveliness and only creates additional frustration for his war wife who realizes that she has, at least temporarily, lost her husband both physically and emotionally to the institution of war which excludes women and often alienates them from their soldier-husbands.

178. Petry, Ann. "In Darkness and Confusion." Cross Section 1947. Ed. Edwin Seaver. New York: Simon and Schuster, 1947. 98 – 128.

Racism and war combine as themes in this story of a black mother and father who seek violent revenge on the white community for what they perceive as the injustice of the American military system reaped upon their innocent son.

Pink and William both desire their son to have a better quality of life than their own simplistic lifestyle. And Sam has shown promise with outstanding grades and demonstrated basketball skill. Both parents worry apprehensively when he decides to enter the Army, especially when they learn he has been stationed in Georgia, a state reputedly full of "nigger haters."

When his letters home cease to arrive, Sam's parents' worst fears are confirmed. William learns that his son has been court martialed for shooting an MP who reportedly shot Sam first "because he wouldn't go to the nigger end of one bus." Sam has been sentenced to 20 years of hard labor for his crime. William's normally passive approach to life turns militant as he follows his wife on a violent looting spree through the streets of New York City in what develops into a personal war of destructive retaliation aimed at all the white "sons of bitches" who have robbed their son of the dreams they cherished for him.

179. Porter, Katherine Anne. "The Leaning Tower." The Leaning Tower and Other Stories. New York: Harcourt, Brace and Company, 1944. 149 – 246.

This narrative captures the "horror and corruption of the rising tide of Nazism" through the perspective of a young American artist living in Berlin during 1931 (Mooney 35). In the story Porter's "awareness of history complements her sense of disaster; both elements, however, register themselves only in the consciousness of the individual round whom her story centers, and never in any direct author's comment" (Mooney 37). Within the atmosphere of Berlin and in the attitudes of German citizens as well, Charles Upton senses an unrest that he perceives as a continuation of the ancient ritual of battle that has colored history since ancient times:

> And even at the moment, like the first symptoms of some fatal sickness, there stirred in him a most awful premonition of disaster, and his thoughts, blurred with drink and strangeness and the sound of half-understood tongues and the climate of remembered wrongs and hatreds, revolved dimly around vague remembered tales of Napoleon and Genghis Khan and Attila the Hun and all the Caesars and Alexander the Great and the dim Pharoahs and lost Babylon. He felt helpless, undefended. . . (234).

The turbulence that Charles senses brooding in Germany is not an individual one but a collective unrest that is "insidious, pervasive, and indefinite," a "social and political, rather than individual, evil, capable of destroying an entire society" (Mooney 36). The possibility that the destruction of another civilization caused by social and political enmity may be pending is symbolized by the fragile, plastic leaning tower which Charles accidentally shatters. Throughout the story Porter describes the "hostile elements" of society that often result in war—nationalistic pride, inflation, class disparity, greed, racial hatred (Unrue 118). Through her writing she succeeds in illuminating "nothing less than the huge and public disasters of her time, their mysterious and terrible nature rendered clear and meaningful by the poetry of her prose and through the medium of Charles Upton's consciousness" (Mooney 38).

180. Ravin, Bernice Lewis. "Cabin Class to Pubjanice." <u>A Good Deal: Selected Short Stories from The Massachusetts Review</u>. Eds. Mary Heath and Fred Miller Robinson. Amherst: University of Massachusetts Press, 1988. 112 – 122.

This story records the impressions of a Jewish-American woman toward war and her European cultural heritage. Unaware that war is about to break out in Europe in 1938, the 15-year-old narrator's family travels to visit the Polish shtetl of the father's youth. She compares her father's triumphant superiority of spirit when he returns to his humble homeland as a symbol of American success with her own revulsion at being "taken from a comfortable two-family house ghetto in Boston to Pubjanice, a tiny Polish village where the bedbugs had long ago claimed as theirs the only lodging house available to passers through" and her snobbery among cousins whose "Europeen ways" seem primitive and unrefined (115). The narrator's observations of growing anti-Semitism spreading across Europe foreshadow the Holocaust to come, which will eventually obliterate the entire Jewish population of Pubjanice.

181. Roberson, Sadie L. "The Nationality." Killers of the Dream. New York: Carlton Press, 1963. 60 – 85.

The German invasion of France strips a renowned opera singer of her career, her wealth, and most of her family in this short narrative. Lisa and her younger sister, who hides among the bodies of dead soldiers until she is discovered, are the only survivors remaining of a family of seven after the war ends. The war witnessed by this women is characterized by Roberson as a "war in the raw" that has been stripped of its "beautiful tailored uniform, minus the proud, stiff, and erect back of a handsome soldier of battle. The uniform was blood-spattered now," she writes, "and covered with dried mud where the soldier had fallen in battle never to rise again" (61). The "face of war" described by Roberson is "the cruel, ugly face, glaring and jeering at you as you walked amid the shambles of junk piled everywhere" (60). It is a war in which the betrayed dare not trust anyone anymore:

> Friend had sold friend down the river for a piece of bread. A husband had betrayed his family to escape the fierce brutality of a prison camp. Mother had been separated from child, neither knowing if the other were dead or alive. Each wondered if they would ever see the other again once the war were over. (60)

Although the two sisters immigrate safely to the United States, Lisa never regains her musical fame and enters the last years of her life as a lonely woman, impoverished by war and isolated from her European homeland.

182. Roosevelt, Eleanor. "Christmas." A Christmas Treasury. New York: Viking, 1982. 382 – 389.

This narrative presents three differing perspectives of war and the observance of Christmas during wartime in 1940. To the young European girl from whose perspective most of the story is told, war is a strange, unknown force that clothes her father in a strange uniform and carries him away, never to return again, causing financial hardship and near starvation for her mother and herself. The advent of Christmas offers her the opportunity to ask the Christ Child to bring her father back home again. To her mother the war is a reminder of the sacrifice of her husband and loss of closeness with her daughter as now she must continually work so that the two of them will not starve. For her Christmas is a time of renewed hope for peace to come and a future life of less hardships. To a visiting stranger who professes no faith in the Christ Child, war is symbolic of the "luxury of power" and domination over others gained through greed and personal ambition at the expense of others' suffering. The feelings of each of these characters seem intensified by the significance of the season and unnatural circumstances of life occasioned by war.

183.   Sandor, Marjorie. "The Gittel." America and I: Short Stories by American Jewish Women Writers. Ed. Joyce Antler. Boston: Beacon Press, 1990. 266 – 280.

A Jewish woman's refusal to live outside of her own fantasized dreamlike world of innocence results in tragedy in this narrative when she returns to her German birthplace with three of her children, unaware of the anti-Semitic storm that has swept Europe since she has lived in the United States. The narrator's grandmother, who is the central character of the story, inherits a tragic family tradition of living in a fantasy world of her own design, oblivious to the world outside. To Gittel, returning home to Germany brings to mind sentimental images of "magic shows and lace curtains and hot potato kugel." Even when she gazes out the train window and her eyes rest upon the "new red and black flags" flying over Berlin and a fellow passenger aboard gasps at the sound of her last name, Gittel refuses to acknowledge the changes that have made her homeland a deathtrap for all Jews. Instead, like her ancestors of the past cursed with the same character flaw, she walks out of her "haze of dreams" into the waiting "arms of the current executioner"—the Nazi exterminators.

184.   Sargent, Pamela. "Gather Blue Roses." The Best of Pamela Sargent. Ed. Martin H. Greenberg. Chicago: Academy Chicago Publishers, 1987. 1 – 7.

The suffering of Holocaust survivors' children is given recognition in this short narrative. The narrator of this story not only recalls suffering the pain of anti-Semitic ridicule from other children as she was growing up but also remembers vicariously sharing the lingering pain of her mother's death camp memories and feeling the sting of rejection each time her mother felt the need to break away from her family and seek solitude for short periods of time.

The narrator's mother confides to her father that the Holocaust experience will probably be more difficult for her daughter than it has been for herself. All the guilt, the shame, the fears, and misery borne by Holocaust survivors have been passed on to another generation, many of whom, such as this daughter, did not experience the Holocaust directly but have accepted the emotional burden of the experience as a natural part of their Jewish identity.

185.   Sinclair, Jo. "The Brothers." Cross Section 1947. Ed. Edwin Seaver. New York: Simon and Schuster, 1947. 352 – 360.

The younger brother of an American corporal becomes an unintentional scapegoat for his military brother's anger and frustration in this short story. To put an end to a growing pattern of juvenile delinquency developing in Lenny, his school principal requests that Ben, who has become Lenny's idolized war hero, publicly reprimand his younger brother. "Spank him before his class," the principal suggests. "Before those boys to whom he has boasted about you. Wearing the uniform of which he is so proud" (356). Ben reluctantly submits to her request, convincing himself that the humiliation of a public spanking is preferable to the prospect of Lenny serving time in a juvenile detention home. But as he begins to administer the dreaded punishment, Ben is suddenly overcome with a barrage of past images of his own unhappy childhood, during which he frequently endured spankings and anti-Polish gibes, and the violence of war still vividly fresh in his mind. As Ben's blows to his brother's body grow stronger in intensity, Ben forgets he is striking his own brother as he mentally strikes out at all the unfortunate circumstances of his life beyond his control to change.

186.   Sinclair, Jo. "Second Blood: A Rosh Hashonoh Story." America and I: Short Stories by American Jewish Women Writers. Ed. Joyce Antler. Boston: Beacon Press, 1990. 134 – 141.

The Holocaust sufferings of European Jews remind a non-orthodox American Jewish of his cultural identity and inspire him to make a personal sacrifice in this short narrative.

Dave feels assured he is doing his patriotic duty as an American citizen by conserving, rationing scarce resources, and rigging up a blackout room for his family in the basement of their home. But as he watches an enlightening newscast documenting the treatment of Jews in occupied European countries, David realizes that his allegiance as an American during this war is not enough; he must also honor his Jewish heritage. The sight of a Jewish woman shown on a televised newscast who bears a striking resemblance to his mother, "her eyes stern, trapped, accusing—and unafraid," a woman who has been denied the right to worship on the eve of a Jewish holiday, reminds Dave that not only does he have obligations as an American, but as a Jewish-American as well. On the next Jewish holiday—Rosh Hashonoh—Dave makes his second contribution of blood to the Red Cross, feeling a sense of sacrifice and renewed Judaic bonding as he joins "a never-ending march of shining glass flasks full of blood across the world" (139).

187.   Stuart, Alison. "Sunday Liberty." O. Henry Memorial Award Prize Stories of 1944. Ed. Herschel Brickell. Garden City: Doubleday, Doran and Company, Inc., 1944. 205 – 213.

Differing attitudes among men and women toward war are contrasted in this award-winning short story. Two landlocked sailors spend Sunday afternoon on the seashore with their lovers, anxiously awaiting their orders overseas. "I'm sick to hell of this duty," Ernie admits. "I want to get out in a fleet, in a convoy—anything. Hell, how I'd like to get into that fight!" (207). His friend agrees. Moments later a young soldier, wearing a facial expression similar to a stray dog, jumps overboard and tries unsuccessfully to resist rescue efforts in an attempt to take his own life so that he will not be forced to take others. While one of the women sympathizes with the soldiers' reluctance to kill, Ernie feels his anger rising and the blood rushing to his face, as he confesses: "He don't want to, but I do. . . . I'd like to kill that little yellow soldier. Wearin' the uniform of the United States, an' talkin' yellow like that. That little yellow bastard" (213). This story illustrates how divergent views toward war can transcend gender differences as these men take decidedly different stances toward the anticipation of combat duty.

188. Willis, Connie. "Fire Watch." Fire Watch. New York: Bluejay Books, 1985. 2–45.

In this fantasy, a history student time travels back and forth from the twenty-first century to the World War Two period during the German Blitz of 1940 where he serves his practicum protecting St. Paul's Church in London. While living in a crypt with a fellow volunteer the narrator suspects is a Communist spy, Bartholomew serves long hours on "fire watch," guarding the safety of the roof of the church from sporadic bombings.

By the end of his three-month practicum when Bartholomew takes his graduate exams, he has realized through his harrowing experience with war that it is people who are history, not "bloody numbers." People are "back there in the past with nobody to save them," he laments. "They can't see their hands in front of their faces and there are bombs falling down on them and you tell me they aren't important? You call that being a historian?" (40 – 41). Contrary to the objective distance the university's history department has tried to instill in students, Bartholomew has developed a more humanitarian approach to historical scholarship and learned that some things can last forever, if saved and cherished in memory.

189. Yamamoto, Hisaye. "The Legend of Miss Sasagawara." Seventeen Syllables and Other Stories. Latham, NY: Women of Color Press, 1988. 20 – 33.

"The Legend of Miss Sasagawara" is a characterization of a nonconforming Japanese-American woman whose eccentricities isolate her from the other internment camp residents during World War Two. Miss Sasagawara refuses to socialize, preferring to remain an isolated enigma to the other camp residents who derive most of their impressions of her through rumors that circulate through the camp and observations of her occasionally bizarre behaviors. The narrator of the story loses contact with Miss Sasagawara when she leaves for college, only to experience a "thrill of recognition" later when she discovers a poem published in a small poetry magazine written by Miss Sasagawara, applauded as "the first published poem of a Japanese-American woman." In the words of the poem the narrator recognizes another dimension of Miss Sasagawara's character which she kept hidden from public view while they lived in the camp. Miss Sasagawara's poetry reflects the character of an individual attempting to achieve Nirvana, "the saintly state of moral purity and universal wisdom," a devotion which misguided others might interpret as a "sort of madness."

190. Yarbro, Chelsea Quinn. "Renewal." Shadows 5. Ed. Charles L. Grant. Garden City: Doubleday, 1982. 127 – 182.

In this tale of what editor Charles L. Grant terms "dark fantasy," a World War Two journalist who suffers fatal injuries when he is thrown from an overturned jeep during an ambush learns that he is a vampire who has been given a renewal of life. Under the guidance of a fellow vampire who has lived more than 3000 years, James learns that if he protects his nervous system, the most vulnerable part of a vampire, takes certain precautions peculiar to his "breed," and trusts only those sympathetic with his fate, he could live indefinitely despite the fact that war has robbed him of his first life as a human being.

191. Yolen, Jane. "Names." Tales of Wonder. New York: Schocken Books, 1983. 253 – 258.

This tragic narrative illustrates the continuing influence of the Holocaust experience on successive generations. An adolescent Jewish daughter absorbs the obsessive ritual of her mother's mourning Jewish Holocaust victims and sacrifices herself at age 13 in what she perceives to be an act of daughterly devotion.

Even before Rachel was born, she heard her mother's continuous recitation of names of Holocaust victims listed in alphabetical order—"Abrahms, Berliner, Brodsky, Dannenberg, Fischer . . ." (253). During childhood she memorized the names "as another child would a nursery rhyme" (256). As her mother's number was burned into the flesh of her arm—"a permanent journal entry"—so her recital of names became "an epic poem, a ballad of alphabetics, an incantation." The names of Holocaust victims were imprinted in the memories of young children such as Rachel by parents who insisted their offspring become "little speaking candles" to testify to their parents' victimization. "If you do not remember, we never lived," warned the adults. "If you do not remember, we never died" (254).

But simply memorizing the names and repeatedly listening to the Holocaust stories behind each name is not enough. Rachel realizes she must do more to please her mother—to make her smile. At age thirteen, "it seemed that, all at once, she knew what to do. Her mother's duty had been the Word. Rachel's was to be the Word Made Flesh" (256). And so she gradually starves herself, taking her last breath as she mutters the names of her mother's sacred incantation.

Yolen's short but powerful story—the narrative interrupted intermittently with lists of Holocaust victims' names—illustrates how the burden of the war experience is often inevitably passed on to, even imposed upon, succeeding generations of children who often feel an obligation to suffer as well, as the protagonist of this story evidences.

LITERARY CRITICISM AND BIBLIOGRAPHIC SOURCES

Abrahams, William. Introduction. Prize Stories 1981: The O. Henry Awards. Garden City: Doubleday and Company, 1981. 9 – 11.

Aichinger, Peter. The American Soldier in Fiction, 1880-1963: A History of Attitudes Toward Warfare and the Military Establishment. Ames: Iowa State University Press, 1975.

Angress, Ruth K. Afterword. An Estate of Memory. By Ilona Karmel. 1969. New York: The Feminist Press, 1986. 445 – 457.

"The Art of Fiction XCV: Cynthia Ozick." Paris Review 102 (1987): 154 – 190.

Balakian, Nona. "Two Cards at a Time." Rev. of 1939, by Kay Boyle. The New York Times Book Review 15 Feb. 1948: 22.

Beidler, Peter G. Rev. of Ceremony, by Leslie Marmon Silko. American Indian Quarterly 3 (1978): 357 – 358.

Berger, Alan L. Crisis and Covenant: The Holocaust in American Jewish Fiction. New York: State University of New York Press, 1985.

Bilik, Dorothy Seidman. "Fiction of the Holocaust." Handbook of American-Jewish Literature: An Analytical Guide to Topics, Themes, and Sources. Ed. Lewis Fried. Westport, CT: Greenwood Press, 1988. 415 – 440.

"Biographies and Some Accounts by the Authors." Prize Stories 1990: The O. Henry Awards. Ed. William Abrahams. New York: Doubleday, 1990. 410 – 423.

Blackman, Murray. A Guide to Jewish Themes in American Fiction: 1940 – 1980. Metuchen, NJ: Scarecrow Press, 1981.

Blake, Patricia. "In Extreme Cases." Rev. of The Honeyed Peace, by Martha Gellhorn. The New York Times Book Review 30 Aug. 1953: 4.

"Bloody Ballet." Rev. of Dragon Seed, by Pearl S. Buck. Time 26 Jan. 1942: 80 – 81.

Boatwright, Taliaferro. "A Novel of the Atom Bomb." Rev. of Command the Morning, by Pearl S. Buck. The New York Herald Tribune Weekly Book Review 3 May 1959: 4.

Braunstein, Bennell. "Smoke of War and Cigarettes." Rev. of Wine of Astonishment, by Martha Gellhorn. The New York Herald Tribune Weekly Book Review 3 Oct. 1948: 10.

Cantor, Aviva. The Jewish Woman 1900 – 1985: A Bibliography. Fresh Meadows, NY: Biblio Press, 1987.

Cargas, Harry James. The Holocaust: An Annotated Bibliography. 2nd ed. Chicago: American Library Association, 1985.

Cheung, King-Kok, and Stan Yogi, eds. Asian American Literature, An Annotated Bibliography. New York: The Modern Language Association, 1988.

Christian, Barbara. Black Women Novelists: The Development of a Tradition, 1982 – 1976. Westport: Greenwood Press, 1980.

Cook, Alexander. Rev. of The Baders of Jacob Street, by Henia Karmel-Wolfe. America 17 Oct. 1970: 294.

Cooperman, Stanley. World War I and the American Novel. Baltimore: Johns Hopkins Press, 1968.

Davidson, Edith T. A. "War and Love." Rev. of Gone to Soldiers, by Marge Piercy. Belles Lettres Mar/Apr 1988: 10.

Doyle, Paul A. Pearl S. Buck. Boston: Twayne Publishers, 1980.

Ehrlich, Gretel. Author's Note. Heart Mountain. New York: Viking Press, 1988. xv – xvi.

Ezrahi, Sidra DeKoven. By Words Alone: The Holocaust in Literature. Chicago: University of Chicago Press, 1980.

Farber, Marjorie. "Symbolic Heroine." Rev. of Liana, by Martha Gellhorn. The New York Times Book Review 16 Jan. 1944: 4.

Fleisher, Leonard. Rev. of The Baders of Jacob Street, by Henia Karmel-Wolfe and Kindergarten, by Elzbieta Ettinger. Saturday Review 23 May 1970: 50.

Gellhorn, Martha. Afterword. Liana. By Gellhorn. 1944. London: Virago Press, 1987. 253 – 255.

Gellhorn, Martha. Afterword. Point of No Return. By Gellhorn. 1948. New York: New American Library, 1989. 326 – 332.

Glendinning, Victoria. "Colonials." Rev. of The Weather in Africa, by Martha Gellhorn. The New York Times Book Review 30 March 1980: 9.

Graeber, Laurel. Rev. of Safe Houses, by Lynne Alexander. The New York Times Book Review 22 Dec. 1985: 18.

Green, Anne. "The Armistice Without a Peace." Rev. of So Thick the Fog, by Catherine Pomeroy Stewart. The New York Times Book Review 27 Aug. 1944: 13.

Green, Myles. "Taut, Tender, Tough." Rev. of Point of No Return, by Martha Gellhorn. The New York Times Book Review 17 Oct. 1948: 44.

Hanna, Archibald. A Mirror for the Nation: An Annotated Bibliography of American Social Fiction, 1901 – 1950. New York: Garland, 1985.

Hapke, Laura. "WWII Novels." Rev. of A Stricken Field, by Martha Gellhorn. Belles Lettres. Mar/Apr 1987: 9.

Hauser, Marianne. "Noise of Guns." Rev. of The Heart of Another, by Martha Gellhorn. The New York Times Book Review 2 Nov. 1941: 20.

Hauser, Marianne. "What Comes With Defeat." Rev. of Primer for Combat, by Kay Boyle. The New York Times Book Review 8 Nov. 1942: 6.

Havighurst, Walter. "Avalanche in the Haute-Savoie." Rev. of 1939, by Kay Boyle. Saturday Review 28 Feb. 1948: 12.

Havighurst, Walter. "Public War and Private Consciousness." Rev. of Wine of Astonishment, by Martha Gellhorn. Saturday Review 9 Oct. 1948: 36.

Heinemann, Marlene E. Gender and Destiny: Women Writers and the Holocaust. Westport, CT: Greenwood Press, 1986.

Heron, Kim. "'I Required a Dawning.'" The New York Times Book Review 10 Sept. 1989: 39.

Hoffman, Eva. "Growing Pains." Rev. of Rumors of Peace, by Ella Leffland. Saturday Review 1 Sept. 1979: 45 – 46.

Hongo, Garrett. "Love Beyond the Fences." Rev. of Heart Mountain, by Gretel Ehrlich. The New York Times Book Review 6 Dec. 1988: 37.

Houston, James D. "Growing up with wartime headlines and gossip." Rev. of Rumors of Peace, by Ella Leffland. Christian Science Monitor 13 Aug. 1979: B3.

Hudson, Richard. "Bomb-scarred Love." Rev. of The Seeds of Hiroshima, by Edita Morris. Saturday Review 21 May 1966: 34.

Janeway, Elizabeth. Rev. of An Estate of Memory, by Ilona Karmel-Wolfe. The New York Times Book Review 21 Sept. 1969: 1.

Lowin, Joseph. Cynthia Ozick. Boston: Twayne Publishers, 1988.

MacShane, Frank. "American Indians, Peruvian Jews." Rev. of Ceremony, by Leslie Marmon Silko. The New York Times Book Review 12 June 1977: 15.

McCormack, Lorraine E. "Travail, Opium Unique." Rev. of Liana, by Martha Gellhorn. Belles Lettres Fall 1988: 21.

Mooney, Harry J. The Fiction and Criticism of Katherine Anne Porter. Pittsburgh: University of Pittsburgh Press, 1957.

Nelms, Elizabeth D. and Ben F. Nelms. Rev. of Marek and Lisa, by Ilona Karmel-Wolfe. English Journal Feb. 1985: 102.

Nelson, Keith L. The Impact of War on American Life: The Twentieth Century Experience. New York: Holt, Rinehart and Winston, Inc., 1971.

"Nerve War in the Caribbean." Rev. of Liana, by Martha Gellhorn. Time 7 Feb. 1944: 100 – 102.

Novak, William. "Jewish history larger than life." Rev. of Anya by Susan Fromberg Schaeffer. The New York Times Book Review 20 Oct. 1974: 36.

Overton, Jeanne K. Pearl Buck: Bibliography and Criticism. Boston: Simmons College, 1942.

Palmer, C. B. "Battle of Burma." Rev. of The Promise, by Pearl S. Buck. The New York Times Book Review 31 Oct. 1943: 6.

Penner, Jonathan. "All's Fair in Love and Physics." Rev. of Beginning the World Again, by Roberta Silman. The New York Times Book Review 4 Nov. 1990: 29.

Piercy, Marge. "Of Arms and the Woman." Harper's Magazine June 1987: 30 – 31.

Pinckney, Darryl. "Roots." Rev. of Brown Girl, Brownstones, by Paule Marshall. The New York Review of Books 28 Apr. 1983: 26 – 29.

Prose, Francine. "Idolatry in Miami." Rev. of The Shawl, by Cynthia Ozick. The New York Times Book Review 10 Sept. 1989: 1.

Reed, John. Rev. of Kindergarten, by Elzbieta Ettinger. The New York Times Book Review 8 Feb. 1970: 32.

Reed, John. Rev. of The Baders of Jacob Street, by Karmel Henia-Wolfe. The New York Times Book Review 27 Sept. 1970: 47.

Reuben, Elaine. "Novel of Power." Rev. of Anya, by Susan Fromberg Schaeffer. New Republic 18 Jan. 1975: 30 – 31.

Rev. of Primer for Combat, by Kay Boyle. The Atlantic Monthly Dec. 1942: 152.

Rolf, Robert. "The Short Stories of Hisaye Yamamoto, Japanese-American Writer." Bulletin of Fukuoka University of Education 31.1 (1982): 71 – 86.

Rosen, Norma. "The Holocaust and the American-Jewish Novelist." Midstream Oct. 1974: 54 – 62.

Rosenstein, Harriet. "The Ferocity of Adolescence." Rev. of Rumors of Peace, by Ella Leffland. Ms. August 1979: 40 – 41.

Rowan, Diana. "Southwestern novelist celebrates Indian ways." Rev. of Ceremony, by Leslie Marmon Silko. Christian Science Monitor 24 Aug. 1977: 19.

Sauber, Dorothy. "Historical Context/ Literary Content: Women Write About War and Women." Thesis. Hamline University, 1988.

Sayre, Nora. Rev. of Touching Evil, by Norma Rosen. The New York Times Book Review 14 Sept. 1969: 29.

Schweik, Susan M. "A Word No Man Can Say for Us: American Women Writers and the Second World War." Thesis. Yale University, 1984.

Spanier, Sandra Whipple. Kay Boyle: Artist and Activist. Carbondale: Southern Illinois University Press, 1986.

Steinberg, Sybil. Rev. of Safe Houses, by Lynne Alexander. Publishers Weekly 6 Sept. 1985: 56.

Stevenson, David L. "Daughter's Reprieve." Rev. of Trust, by Cynthia Ozick. The New York Times Book Review 27 July 1966: 29.

Strouse, Jean. "A House Divided." Rev. of The House on Prague Street, by Hana Demetz. Newsweek 8 Sept. 1980: 77 – 78.

Sullivan, Richard. "Science and the Bomb." Rev. of Command the Morning, by Pearl S. Buck. The New York Times Book Review 3 May 1959: 29.

Szonyi, David M., ed. The Holocaust: An Annotated Bibliography and Resource Guide. New York: KTAV Publishing House for the National Jewish Resource Center, 1985.

Thurman, Judith. "Unchanged by Suffering?" Rev. of Anya, by Susan Fromberg Schaeffer. Ms. Mar. 1975: 46 – 47.

Tilghman, Christopher. "A Man Who Barked and Chased Cars." Rev. of <u>Drinking Dry Clouds</u>, by Gretel Ehrlich. <u>The New York Times Book Review</u> 26 May 1991: 6.

Uehling, Edward M. "Tails, You Lose: Kay Boyle's War Fiction." <u>Twentieth Century Literature</u> 34 (1988): 375 – 383.

Ulrich, Mabel S. "Growing Pains." Rev. of <u>No Longer Fugitive</u>, by Ann Chidester. <u>Saturday Review</u> 23 Oct. 1943: 19.

Unrue, Darlene Harbour. <u>Understanding Katherine Anne Porter</u>. Columbia: University of South Carolina Press, 1988.

Wallace, Margaret. "In Search of Destiny." Rev. of <u>No Longer Fugitive</u>, by Ann Chidester. <u>The New York Times Book Review</u> 10 Oct. 1943: 20.

Willms, Dean. Rev. of <u>Heart Mountain</u>, by Gretel Ehrlich. <u>Library Journal</u> 1 Oct. 1988: 100.

Wolitzer, Hilma. "Woman at War." Rev. of <u>Gone to Soldiers</u>, by Marge Piercy. <u>The New York Times Book Review</u> 10 May 1987: 11.

"A woman writer treads on male turf." <u>U.S. News and World Report</u> 18 May 1987: 74.

Woods, Katherine. "Pearl Buck's New and Exceptional Novel of China." Rev. of <u>Dragon Seed</u>, by Pearl S. Buck. <u>The New York Times Book Review</u> 25 Jan. 1942: 3.

3

Vietnam War

INTRODUCTION

Even though more than two decades have passed since American military involvement ceased in Vietnam, the war continues to impress itself upon our collective vision, begging for reconciliation and definition. As the literary canon emerging from this war experience continues to evolve, women writers have made a significant contribution with their distinctive literary interpretations of this still difficult-to-define war experience. In his American Literature and the Experience of Vietnam, Philip Beidler suggests that Vietnam War writers are sculptors of a kind who give shape to an experience otherwise devoid of meaning:

> It would become the task of the Vietnam writer to create a landscape that never was, one might say—a landscape of consciousness where it might be possible to accommodate experience remembered within a new kind of imaginative cartography endowing it with large configurings of value and signification. In this way, what facts that could be found might still be made to mean, as they had never done by themselves, through the shaping and ultimately the transforming power of art. (16)

Portions of this chapter were originally published in the following journals: "Visions of the Vietnam War in Women's Short Fiction Experience" Vietnam Generation (special issue entitled "Gender and the War: Men, Women and Vietnam,") Vol. 1, Nos. 3-4, Fall, 1989; "Women Novelist-Sculptors of the Vietnam War Experience" Hurricane Alice: A Feminist Quarterly Vol.7, No. 3 Fall, 1990; "Variations on Vietnam: Women's Innovative Interpretations of the Vietnam War Experience" Extrapolation Vol. 32, No. 2, Summer, 1991; and "Creating a Landscape That Never Was: Women's Fictional Interpretations of the Vietnam War Experience" Midwest Quarterly (forthcoming).

Writers who have accepted this task have collectively creating a landscape that is varied and inquisitive about the nature of men and women and their relationship to this divisive, controversial war. Contemporary writers of both genders have adopted an expanded vision of war, interpreting the Vietnam War as a "story of universal victimization" that has extended far beyond the borders of one war-torn country and encompassed victims of both genders, soldiers and civilians alike (Elshtain 218). Vietnam War literature takes a hard and critical look at what war does to the individual and what psychological toll the war experience takes upon the mind and spirit of both soldiers and civilians, regardless of gender. Male and female victims of the Vietnam War experience share a common bond of victimization that has left indelible scars and unanswerable questions as its legacy.

Vietnam War literature authored by women reflects the turbulence that characterized this period in American history and the controversy that surrounded this war. American involvement in this war could not be rationalized by writers as it was during World War One and World War Two. The antiwar sentiment that pervades this literature is obviously stronger than that written by women during previous wars. During the Vietnam War era the burgeoning feminist movement in the United States also empowered women with the self-assuredness to question aspects of the patriarchal system they opposed, including war as a way of asserting power and resolving conflict, a trend also apparent in this literature.

Only a minority of women writers have attempted to simulate the war experience from a male perspective. Their novels and short stories offer insight into the combat experience as well as the tedious and often painful postwar readjustment for many veterans who were welcomed home from a divisive, bitter war with hostility and rejection. In this literature Vietnam War soldiers are consistently portrayed as victims engaged in an increasingly unjustifiable war whose potential deaths seemed to have little significance to their country beyond the daily "body count." For those who did return, their abrupt reentry to a country bitterly divided over the war promised significant readjustment problems. Novelist Susan Schaeffer documents a Vietnam War grunt's experiences in her epic Buffalo Afternoon. To write the novel she interviewed 15 veterans during a two-year period. Reviewing the novel for Publishers Weekly, Sybil Steinberg finds Schaeffer "as convincing as any of our Vietnam novelists so far in depicting the ways men become brutalized by carnage, and sometimes immobilized by pity" (75). Corinne Brown, Joyce Carol Oates, Bobbie Ann Mason, and Ellen Wilbur offer sympathetic insight into the lives of Vietnam War veterans who might be classified as M.I.L.—Missing in Life—because their war wounds are so extensive they can never hope to regain independence or lead normal lives again.

Two former Vietnam War nurses have fictionalized their encounters with war in novels that read very similarly to factual memoirs and oral histories published by Vietnam War nurses since the war's end. The nurse-protagonists characterized in Elizabeth Ann Scarborough's The Healer's War and Patricia Walsh's Forever Sad the Hearts both volunteer for Vietnam War service as idealistic, caring young women responding to a youthful president's summons to "ask what you can do for your country," but soon become disillusioned, cynical questioners of the war, trapped in a hopeless cycle of suffering wrought by the devastation of war perpetrated by their own country.

The majority of women authors of the Vietnam War experience have written novels and short stories in the tradition of realism. These women write from a homefront perspective focusing on the sociological effect of war on the significant others in the lives of combat soldiers and returning veterans. In their nurturing, caring roles as nurses, mothers, wives, lovers, and sisters, these women are often the forgotten victims of war whose suffering is more internal and less visible than the male veteran's although equally painful and valid. The nurse-protagonist in Elizabeth Ann Scarborough's The Healer's War who returns from Vietnam feeling like an alienated misfit in her own country is a victim of war. The sister in Jayne Anne Phillips' Machine Dreams who drifts in a surrealistic world of childhood fantasies in a desperate attempt to keep her brother's image alive after she learns of his classification as Missing in Action somewhere in a Vietnamese jungle is a victim of war. The war wives in Maxine Kumin's "These Gifts" and Bobbie Ann Mason's "Big Bertha Stories" who can no longer relate with their veteran-husbands too become victims of war. The Indian mother in Leslie Silko's "Lullaby" is a tragic victim who sacrifices her son to a white man's war she neither condones nor understands.

Many of the characters in these novels and short stories are fictionalized versions of the estimated 900,000 Vietnam War wives and partners, 1,098,000 children, and 4.7 million extended family members who are or will eventually become victims of the Vietnam War as a result of their close relationship with veterans who have exhibited Post-Traumatic Stress Disorder symptoms (Matsakis xiii). This fiction documents the pervasive repercussions of a psychologically devastating war on veterans and their closest relationships and validates the victimization of those who may not have experienced direct combat but have nevertheless undergone a special kind of suffering. The emotional baggage brought home by many of these veterans has been shared by many women who unknowingly donned "frilly nightgown smiles" and "snuggled next to walking time bombs" when their husbands and lovers returned (Matsakis xii). The devastating impact of this war on marriages and intimate relationships is evident in the novels and short stories authored by women.

The sons and daughters of soldiers and veterans touched by the war experience through their veteran-fathers are also recognized as indirect victims of war in this fiction. The daughter of a Vietnam War casualty in Bobbie Ann Mason's In Country in search of the father she has never known and an understanding of the complex morality of war (if indeed there is one) is a victim of war one generation removed. The six-year-old son of a paralyzed veteran who has developed an irrational fear of any man who can walk in Linsey Abrams' "Secrets Men Keep" is too one of war's victims.

A minority of women writers of the Vietnam War experience have departed from the realistic tradition in form, content, and perspective in pursuit of an experimental approach more closely representative of their individual perceptions of war. Non-traditional literary representation may be the closest interpretation possible for these women to reflect a war where absolutes appear to be missing and reality remains so obscure. Innovation offers these writers the freedom to examine war from all possible points on the literary spectrum—even the postmodern extreme. Searching beyond the limited boundaries of realism, innovative women writers utilize their unqualified license to explore war in varied directions and experiment with their interpretations of war in novel ways. Jayne Anne Phillips uses a variety of narrative devices in the loosely structured Machine Dreams to give voice to all four family members who narrate the novel. Joan Didion's Democracy is narrated in a fragmented, staccato style that reminds readers "of the rapid cross-cutting that Hollywood, a Didion haunt, has imposed on modern narrative" and leaves deliberate gaps for readers to fill with their own imaginations (Hitchens 1018). Didion and Kay Boyle both show innovation in their writings as they interrupt the narrative process with informal conversations about the writing process and their own fictional strategies. In The Healer's War Elizabeth Ann Scarborough inserts a section of pure fantasy into a novel otherwise convincingly autobiographical in tone. Emily Prager innovates by merging the comic and ironic modes in a satirical and cerebrally humorous combination in her bizarre short story "The Lincoln-Pruitt Anti-Rape Device," representing a radical feminist point of view of the war.

Some literary critics of the Vietnam War canon believe that science fiction and fantasy are the best modes of representation of this illusory war, as expressed by editors Jeanne Van Buren Dann and Jack Dann in their introduction to the short story collection In the Field of Fire: "The Vietnam War was so psychologically cyclonic and horrific in its effect on individuals that perhaps the dark personal 'truth' of their experience can best be reflected through the devises of metaphor and fantasy" (14). In his review of the short story collection In the Field of Fire, David Bradley makes the claim that "Vietnam *was* science fiction" (26). He explains:

> The landscape was alien. . . . The people were alien-seeming—and certainly we, with our cold beer and napalm and helicopters, must have seemed to the Vietnamese to be an invading horde of bug-eyed monsters. . . . The place seemed like an alternate universe, where all the sanity, rationality, logic just seemed to not work. (26)

Critic Ihab Hassan, who analyzes postwar science fiction in Contemporary American Literature, proposes that science fiction offers the capability to explore "both the creative and destructive potentials of current experience," thus making it a logical choice for the representation of war. Karen Joy Fowler, Susan Casper, and Ursula Le Guin innovate using the science fiction genre for their interpretations of the war while Kate Wilhelm writes what she terms "speculative fiction" to predict what atrocities can occur even on our own country's soil when Americans fail to question authority and act as directed without thought.

Women have differing motives for writing about war. The nurses who served in Vietnam who have fictionalized their experiences may have discovered writing to be an emotional catharsis and written out of a need felt to document their individual versions of war, now seasoned by time and distance. When Bobbie Ann Mason began writing In Country she did not intend to write a novel about the effects of war on a family. "I started out with the family," she said during an interview, "and then I probed around and discovered what their problems were. It was as though the war came out of someplace where it had been hiding" (Conarroe 7). Susan Schaeffer's initial interest in the Vietnam War stemmed from an incident she witnessed during the late 1960s. A teaching assistant lecturing to a class of Vietnam War veterans, she remembers, "backed herself as far away from the class as she could, right up on the chalk tray," obviously petrified of them, while the veterans, equally frightened, crowded together at the other end of the classroom. It was later when she learned that a friend of many years had fought in Vietnam that she realized "there was this huge area of experience that I was completely ignorant of" (Proffitt 7). Her research into this experience eventually evolved into Buffalo Afternoon.

These fictional interpretations may also represent a method of self-definition for writers of the Vietnam generation, who seek through literary expression of shared experience and emotion to examine how this war has shaped their lives and helped to define their existence. The search for war thus becomes a search for self. In her introduction to the short story "Letters From Home," Karen Joy Fowler explains: "I do think those of us around my own age were defined by Vietnam in ways those much older and much younger will never understand. Which leave us only each other to turn to for understanding" (70).

These writings are too an attempt by writers to give whatever shape and substance is possible to such an elusive war that continues to mystify and horrify those who encountered the unreality of Vietnam and have attempted to translate that experience into literary expression. Writing about the Vietnam War experience may also be a way for writers to further reconcile this war, not to bury or forget the trauma of the experience, but to find a protective place in the collective unconscious of American society where its significance can be kept in perspective and continue to influence vision and direction.

Women fiction writers of the Vietnam War experience have created a literature that is both realistic and innovative, often changing and unpredictable. It is a literature that is morally ambiguous and subtle in intent, characterized by its openness for interpretation and speculation.   It is a literature full of understatement and irony that often questions more than answers. The landscape of this literature is still in transition as the genre continues to mature with the contributions of both men and women continuing to give shape to the Vietnam War experience through literature.

NOVELS

192. Brown, Corinne. Body Shop: Recuperating From Vietnam. New York: Stein and Day, 1973.

Body Shop examines the existence (or lack of existence) of wounded Vietnam veterans whose lives were saved by rapid evacuation and modern medical technology during the war, but whose resulting handicaps are so severe they can never regain normalcy. These are the veterans classified by the nurse-protagonist in Patricia Walsh's Forever Sad the Hearts as M.I.L.—Missing in Life. Often grossly disfigured, with charts that read like a "medical index of the war," these men are described by Brown as "faces mostly, then trunks, then stumps—pink folded in material, not really like skin or bone—or casts" (26). Although a few of these veterans may escape imprisonment in the Letterman General Hospital in San Francisco and test their ability to reintegrate into post-Vietnam America, most will remain imprisoned in the "body shop" for an unknown duration of time with only the camaraderie of shared loss and past memories of war to relive again and again with others equally Missing in Life.

Brown allows several veterans to recall their own life histories in the novel, lives which inevitably climax in the heat of combat when an unexpected crisis precipitates their stunning moment of loss. These veterans bring the battlefield back to the body shop, for although many of them voice strong antiwar sentiments and criticize the senselessness of continued American involvement in Southeast Asia, the war remains their strongest tie with one another. Among each other they candidly share their feelings about killing, dying, beginning their "second lives" as handicapped veterans, people's reactions to their deformities, and the often taken-for-granted aspects of normal life they miss most as veterans Missing in Life. The body shop becomes an intricate network of men who have been shunned by an indifferent American citizenry, hidden from public view, and offered generous monetary compensations for their losses but who have been rejected as human beings. Through one another these veterans build a caring support group of their own to counter their exclusion from the outside world.

193. Didion, Joan. Democracy. New York: Simon and Schuster, 1984.

The internal drama of this novel of romance and murder is "set against the historicity of the Vietnam War," beginning with the fall of Saigon in March of 1975 and ending the following year in the final stages of the war (Ching 180). Within this time span the narrative moves back and forth between 1952 and 1975 but "succeeds in creating the illusion of simultaneity," which adds to the elusiveness of the novel and its "sense of disorder" for readers, Stuart Ching writes in "'A Hard Story to Tell': The Vietnam War in Joan Didion's Democracy." While the novel's characters fall apart in their private domestic world, the "external historical world" simultaneously collapses (Ching 184). The situation in South Vietnam, emphasized in Part Three of the novel, is portrayed as "one of growing hysteria and confusion, and the collapse of the moral center heightens this rapid disintegration" (Ching 185). The author does not attempt to pass judgment on the war in her novel, Mark Royden Winchell writes in Joan Didion. Instead, he writes, "what she gives us in the fall of Saigon is another vivid image of things falling apart, of a culture vexed to nightmare. But it is an image untainted by tendentious political moralizing" (130). Didion "observes, reveals, and records, but she does not explain," Ching states. "Nor does she provide an answer to the questions raised by the Vietnam War" (186). In his review Francis Marnell characterizes Democracy as a novel that laments the loss of connection among Americans prevalent during the war period. He writes of Didion:

> Her Democracy shows us a nation that maintains only fragile ties with its history and institutions and with the rest of the world, and which is governed by persons hypersensitive to the media and oblivious of everyday reality. Present-day American society, as Miss Didion sees it, does not distinguish very well, even on a working basis, between such basic categories as friend and foe, right and wrong, and Americans are disoriented by this incoherence. (52)

The unconventional, elusive structure of Didion's novel consists of fragments (termed "fitful glimpses" by the author) loosely woven together. Intentional gaps leave readers with the prerogative to fill the voids with their own imaginative details. Didion's authorial voice intercedes repeatedly, even confessing at the beginning of the novel that "This is a hard story to tell" (15). At the end of the novel there is another confession to be made: "It has not been the novel I set out to write," Didion admits, "nor am I exactly the person who set out to write it. Nor have I experienced the rush of narrative inevitability that usually propels a novel toward its end, the momentum that sets in as events overtake their shadows and the cards all fall in on one another and the options decrease to zero" (232). In this novel of a turbulent period in world history the options remain open: "Anything could happen," she concludes (233).

194. Mason, Bobbie Ann. In Country. New York: Harper and Row, 1985.

Bobbie Ann Mason examines the effect of war's lingering aftermath passed on to yet another generation of Americans in this novel. Sam Hughes was barely conceived when her young father became a casualty of the Vietnam War. Now, as she graduates from high school, "a war which ended when she was but a child is at the center of her life" (Stewart 166). In her essay "Sex Combat and the Female in In Country," Katherine Kinney explains that for Sam the Vietnam War is "like the blank piece of paper she actually receives in lieu of a diploma—until she can fill in the imaginative space occupied by her father and the war, her education will remain incomplete" (40).

Sam longs to discover the father she has never known and understand the war that most Americans, even her own mother, seem to want to repress and forget. Sam's probing for answers to the morality of war, and the Vietnam War in particular, becomes a continued quest that leaves people uncomfortably bewildered while Sam remains perplexed in frustration because no one seems to want to hear her questions, much less answer them. She expresses such morally complex concerns as: "If you go to war, a bad war, and you believe you're doing the right thing, is it your own fault if you get killed? If the war is wrong, then do you deserve to die for believing the wrong thing?" (71). Sam wonders if the ritual of battle has become an inevitable part of American history for the males of each generation who feel compelled to prove their masculinity and vent their aggressive drives in heroic combat. She questions a society that seems too dependent upon such brutality for fulfillment and even entertainment. Has war indeed become man's "basic profession?" she wonders. "I don't get it. If there wasn't a war for fifty years and two whole generations didn't have to fight, do you mean there should have been a war for them? Is that why we have wars—so guys won't miss out?" (87).

Sam also begins to mistrust a country that seems to have so little compassion for Vietnam War veterans such as her Uncle Emmett who returned from the war to a hostile and indifferent country, ashamed of its first loss and weary of overexposure to the prolonged "television war." Emmett and the circle of his veteran friends introduced in the novel "form a microcosm of Vietnam veterans' feelings, complaints, and problems regarding reintegration into civilian society, and the symptoms and behavioral signs typical of these problems pervade the text," Matthew C. Stewart writes in his essay "Realism, Verisimilitude, and the Depiction of Vietnam Veterans in In Country (167). He continues: "As a social domument In Country is worthy of attention because of its comprehensive representation of troubled Vietnam Veterans" (167). Some of these veterans returned from Vietnam with permanent physical disabilities. For others, the losses extended much deeper. "There's something wrong with me," cries Emmett. "I'm damaged. It's like something in the center of my heart is gone and I can't get it back" (225). Sam defends veterans who were abused by their country during the war and have been misunderstood afterwards:

> Nobody understands the vets. They're different. People expect them to behave like everybody else, but they can't. If the Russians sprayed Agent Orange over here, it would be chemical warfare for sure, but the United States poisoned its own soldiers. I can't imagine why you'd defend a country that would do that. (87)

Hunting for clues to her father's war experience, Sam searches through his war diary and letters. In an attempt to simulate his experience more closely, she heads for a nearby swamp armed with C-rations (Dorritos, pork and beans, and granola bars) and her sleeping bag, imagining "Charlie" behind every bush. Sam's trek to the swamp," Kinney writes, "is both a running away from and a running toward her knowledge of her father, of war, and of herself" (46). "By reenacting a soldier's experience," he explains," she paradoxically hopes that by trespassing directly on the male domain of combat she will discover that she is different from her father and by extension all men" (Kinney 46). For Sam has had to confront the uncomfortable truth, while reading her father's letters, that her youthful father had the same casual and dispassionate attitude toward the Vietnamese that was pervasive among dehumanized American soldiers who served during the war.

Sam's crusade to answer the persistent questions of war culminates in a pilgrimage to the Vietnam Veterans Memorial in Washington, D.C. where she not only touches her father's name but discovers her own named engraved on The Wall as well—Sam A. Hughes. As she touches the name of the soldier that matches her own she experiences an epiphany, realizing that she too is a part of this continuing war—she who refuses to stop questioning, she who refuses to let the Vietnam War silently sink beneath the surface of a seemingly apathetic country. As Sam stands before The Wall she experiences a feeling "so strong, it is like a tornado moving in her, something massive and overpowering." Sam comes to realize that she is "just beginning to understand" the Vietnam War through what will be a lengthy and very gradual process. In this "final image" of the novel set at The Wall, writes reviewer Joyce Kornblatt, "In Country incarnates the horror and the grief that Vietnam has willed us all and the catharsis each of us requires" (7).

In his essay "The Literature Born of Vietnam," Stephen McCabe explains how Mason's novel brings the war back to American soil:

> Sam's questions are our nation's questions. Unlike the fiction from previous wars, In Country correctly places the conflict not on the battlefield but in the hearts and minds of the American people. . . . In Country makes a statement about Vietnam by showing the reader the lasting effect of war on those who never saw a battlefield. The war itself is only one aspect of the larger effect of the Vietnam experience continues to have on the American people. . . . Vietnam will never be wholly understood. What can be understood, though, is the very human emotion and reasoning that makes us understand life by looking to art. (31)

Through the perspective of a sensitive young woman coming of age, grasping for identity and maturity, In Country illustrates the long-term effects of war, even upon generations once removed from actual experience, and questions both the morality of war in general, and the Vietnam War in particular, while it challenges the validity of American male fascination with the game of war.

195. Phillips, Jayne Anne. <u>Machine Dreams</u>. New York: Pocket, 1984.

<u>Machine Dreams</u> is an innovative compendium of letters, journal
entries, flashbacks, personal narratives, and flows of stream of
consciousness from alternating perspectives of four West Virginia
family members. The novel's only real continuity derives from the
motifs of dreams and machines that loosely bond the narrative
together. <u>Machine Dreams</u> follows the Hampsons through two
wars, concentrating on the Vietnam War, as the family tries
unsuccessfully to solve its own internal conflicts as well as those
imposed externally by war. As their parents' marriage dissolves,
Billy and Danner grow closer, attempting to keep whatever family
unity still survives intact. Their childhood fantasies revolve around
stalking the imaginary enemy in the forest, flying the pretend jet
into enemy territory, fantasizing what phantoms might appear if
they dared to open their father's World War Two army trunk that
frequently entices them to the family attic. This war play may be
fanciful and intriguing during childhood but assumes sinister
proportions in the hands of adults who wage lethal warfare.

When Billy becomes a college dropout, the lottery machine
determines his destination to Vietnam where he rebuilds his own
sense of morality and country based upon the peculiar ethics of war.
In a letter home to Danner he confides: "These guys are the only
country I know of and they're what I'm defending—I'm not stupid
enough to think my country is over here" (291). The war has an eerie,
dreamlike quality of its own, a horrified version of Billy and Danner's
innocent childhood play. Hunting VCs, Billy writes, is "like cowboys
and Indians, except the Indians are ghosts and they can't lose
because nothing kills them" (290).

The telegram announcing Billy's reclassification as Missing in
Action represents the final disintegration of the Hampson family's
tenuous ties. While Billy's mother floats in a dream world of past
memories of her son and cannot face the present, his sister becomes
an embittered, isolated victim of war who continually relives their
childhood fantasies in a desperate but futile attempt to keep Billy's
image alive. In her own way, Danner is as "missing in action" in
this country as her brother is in Vietnam (Bradley 17).

The novel's sustained, hazy, dreamlike tone of magical but ominous
fantasy gives readers the sensation of floating through its lyrical and
often sensual prose. The interaction of the four family members'
voices during various stages of their lives in the narrative offer
divergent views of war and its effect upon those who serve and those
who wait. The possibility of war seems always hovering, like an
overcast summer day that may suddenly give way to torrential rains
and clamorous thunder at any moment. <u>Machine Dreams</u>, writes
Susan Wolf, "captures the way the war seemed to shatter all the
given values, rendering all the customary things unstable" (258). She
describes the novel as a "meditation on loss, the unresolvable loss
of unfulfilled lives, of a family amputated by a loss that cannot be

named" (259). Village Voice reviewer Geoffrey Stokes classifies Machine Dreams "among the wisest of a generation's attempts to grapple with a war that maimed us all in a stunning surprise" (17).

196. Scarborough, Elizabeth Ann. The Healer's War. New York: Doubleday, 1988.

Based upon Elizabeth Ann Scarborough's experience as a Vietnam War nurse, The Healer's War is an innovative blend of fiction based upon fact, and fiction that dissolves into pure fantasy as it narrates the odyssey of an idealistic young Midwestern woman awakened to the horrors of warfare and victimized as a forgotten Vietnam War veteran.

From the first round of incoming mortar fire whizzing by her head after she's been assured hospitals are non-combat zones, Kitty McCully quickly loses sight of her romanticized, John Wayne vision of war in Part One of the novel entitled "The Hospital." Her heroic notions of war are replaced by the reality—or lack of reality—of the war in Vietnam: Kitty has to inform an amputee that his knee couldn't possibly hurt because it no longer exists. "Home" becomes a humid, mildew-infested hootch the size of a closet. Frazzled medical teams with inadequate supplies work around the clock in a never-ending battle against death that most often ends in despair. Maimed civilians and napalmed children—the silent sufferers of war—fill civilian hospitals wards to capacity. GIs assume that most nurses who volunteer for Vietnam tours are either lesbians or whores and treat them accordingly. Life assumes a schizophrenic dimension:

> While we were on duty, we were responsible for the lives and deaths of our patients, calming their fears and administering treatments that could cure or kill them. Off duty, we were treated as a sort of cross between a high-ranking general who deserved to be scrounged for, taken around, and generally given special treatment, and a whore. (34)

For Kitty, all the values once entrusted to her generation seem shattered by the tragedy of American involvement in Vietnam:

> Most of us in Nam were the children of the last war that was ever supposed to be fought anywhere in the world. All of the baby boys were promised that they would grow up and become successful and all of the baby girls were promised that someday their princes would come. Then along came the goddamn government and bingo, it sent the princes off to battle communism and issued them the right to hate anyone not in their unit. Then it sent them home in body bags, or with their handsome faces melted or blown away, their bodies prematurely aged with disease or terrible wounds, and their idealistic souls turned into sewers. (76)

Part Three of the novel, "Coming Home," reads like the typical script of a returning Vietnam War veteran—the anticipation of returning to the "World," the lack of decompression and transition back into civilian life by the military, the shock of the comparative triviality of American society, the loneliness of incompatibility, and finally, the alluring temptation of steak knives in the bathroom as the final escape. "From being someone with special power," Kitty laments, "I had become someone who was another body, in the way, who had spent a year of her life doing something that was not to be mentioned in polite conversation" (229).

"The Jungle," Part Two of The Healer's War, is as unrealistic as the first and third sections are realistic. When the stressful reality of war nursing brings Kitty close to a psychological breakdown, Scarborough allows pure fantasy to intervene as she sends her protagonist on a hallucinatory trek through the jungles of Vietnam with an amulet as her only protection, empowering Kitty to see brilliant auras that reflect individuals' changing emotional states.

The innovative perspective in this section allows Scarborough to project both inside and outside views of the war, from both male and female viewpoints. When Kitty becomes an unwilling participant of war, she discerns she must adopt the non-traditional role of soldier as well as her accustomed role of nurturer of the wounded if she is to survive her first encounter with the enemy. To interpret the fantasy of her imaginary adventure, the narrator assumes the roles of multiple personae, offering various impressions of the conflict as it progressively grows more absurd. The mosaic composite of war offered in this part of the novel is an amalgam of fantasy, romanticism, postmodern commentary, and impressionism created as an alternative to the realism that controls the narrative in the beginning and ending sections. Kitty's hallucinatory adventure may serve to save her sanity by offering a respite from the intensity of nursing during an emotionally exhausting war, but the experience also serves as an introduction to the insanity of war presented in the guise of fantasy. The Healer's War thus innovates with elements of realism and postmodernism, blending fantasy with reality to assemble a multi-faceted interpretation of one woman's encounter with war.

197. Schaeffer, Susan Fromberg. Buffalo Afternoon. New York: Alfred A. Knopf, 1989.

Susan Fromberg Schaeffer is among a minority of women writers who have recreated the war experience from a male perspective. To write her epic narrative, Schaeffer interviewed 15 Vietnam War veterans during a two-year period (Proffitt 7). Pete Bravado may represent a composite of these veterans' lives and oral histories of the war. Born into a blue-collar, Italian-American family with an abusive father, Pete graduates from an unhappy childhood to reform school and on to the Army where at 17 he hopes for a break in the unfortunate monotony of his life: "The story never changed. It's not here. Join the army and see the world. People respected soldiers. The army taught you how to take care of yourself. The army could teach him a trade. Maybe Vietnam was the change he needed" (87).

Once Bravado reaches Vietnam, Schaeffer takes readers on what reviewer Nicholas Proffitt describes as a "Dantesque tour of a green hell" (7). "It's all here," Proffitt declares. "The hardship of grunt life in the bush; the night thoughts and emotions of men reduced to an animal state by fear and exhaustion, no longer concerned with right and wrong; all the horror and banality of war" (7). In one scene American GIs play soccer with severed heads of Vietnamese soldiers. In another equally disturbing scene soldiers drop their military payment certificates into a circulating pot, the collection to be awarded to the grunt who "wastes" an unpopular sergeant reportedly "not into survival." In a less violent but equally moving part of the novel, one GI dreams of having "a glass of chocolate milk in one hand and a glass of white milk in the other and his head in a bowl of Oreo cookies" while surrounding soldiers fantasize their own dreamlike versions of home, feeling "like people blown farther and farther from shore, only beginning to realize, as they lost sight of land, that land was what they wanted" (164).

The haunting images of brutal carnage in Vietnam are followed by Bravado's return to an unstable family life and a society that has remained detached from the very war that has been the center of his life for so many months. Bravado slips into the classic Post-Traumatic Stress Disorder pattern of many veterans, and his postwar attitude toward the nature of man and war assumes a bitter, cynical tone:

> Everyone wants to know: what started it? How did the war begin? Let's find out so we won't do it again. But it began with the explosion that started the solar system. It began with violence and it will end in violence. Because even if I'm not sure where it began, I know where it will end. After the last bomb goes off, after the earth's surface is a crust of ash, after the only living things are the cockroaches and the leeches, after the oily black wind stops circling the ash-covered earth, after all that's left of the earth's surface is sand and black earth and giant anthills and giant ants, somewhere, somehow, a human being is going to crawl out of his hole, and in his hand, he's going to be carrying a gun. He's going to be carrying a gun and it's going to be loaded and he's going to know how to use it and the whole thing will start all over again. (19)

Pete undergoes a tedious and painful recovery from the war, with the support of identifying veterans who find solace in the fact that, at least for now, their country is at peace. In Vietnamese terms, it's a "buffalo afternoon." "We're going to make it," Pete assures a fellow veteran. "It's the peaceful time. It's time to wander the fields and bring it all back home" (535).

Not as fully developed and less effective in the novel is the voice of a young Vietnamese woman who symbolizes the rural simplicity and resilience of the Vietnamese culture, devastated but never defeated by the continual invasion of enemy forces throughout history. Li's character is an intermittent reminder of the human side of the Vietnamese culture disrupted and threatened by American invasion. In a Belles Lettres interview, Schaeffer explained the Vietnamese narrator's role as necessary to "give the novel a wider context than it would have had if she had included only United States servicemen" and to "underscore her belief that Vietnam was more than a war" (9).

198.   Walsh, Patricia L. Forever Sad the Hearts. New York: Avon, 1982.

The highly autobiographical Forever Sad the Hearts is based upon Walsh's service as a nurse anesthetist in a Da Nang civilian hospital. Like many Vietnam War nurses, the protagonist of this novel responds to a youthful president's contagious spirit and volunteers for a tour in Vietnam. Kate's idealistic zeal is quickly undermined by the realities she witnesses: Vietnamese women picking lice from their hair and biting them to check overpopulation; displaced Vietnamese men setting up their homes in temporary toilets set up by Americans; Vietnamese children infested with worms; Vietnamese peasants fertilizing their gardens with human feces; and a constant stream of civilian casualties infiltrating the hospital.

After her first day nursing in Vietnam, Kate returns to her prison-like room with blood-encrusted hands to discover she has no running water. Later that night, as an unanticipated rebellion against foreign food and water grips her body from both ends, she curses a toilet that flushes—as if in defiance—only occasionally. It only takes a few months of working 18-hour days with grossly inadequate medical supplies for Kate to conclude that she is part of an illogical, adversary trap of healer versus injurer, that she has been sent to Vietnam to cure the suffering of another country— suffering that has been imposed by her own country. An American soldier questions the paradox of his and Kate's respective roles: "You mean we shoot 'em and you fix 'em up?" he asks. "You're over here risking your life to save people I'm risking my life to shoot?" (109)

Kate witnesses first hand another of the ironies of the Vietnam War. Due to rapid evacuation and modern medical technology, more lives of wounded soldiers were saved in Vietnam than during previous wars, but many of these soldiers would never again be able to lead normal lives. In Kate's mind, this war created a new category of veterans—the M.I.L.s:

> There seemed to be numbers and labels for everyone—K.I.A.s, M.I.A.s, wounded in action, enemy killed. But this war needed a new category, a name for those who could be saved by rapid evacuation and modern technology but could never return to a normal life. The ones who would spend the rest of

their days lying in deteriorating Veterans' Hospitals, hidden away in dark corners because of their grotesqueness, or sent home to hide within the shelter of their families from a society that did not wish to be reminded of this unpopular war. They were the Viet Nam M.I.L.s Missing in Life. (119)

As Kate becomes a short-timer, counting the days left in her tour, she begins to have nightmares of trying to hide charred bodies in her apartment back in the "world." Although desperate to leave Vietnam, she feels guilty for leaving so much yet to be accomplished behind: "How could I go home and work in a modern antiseptic institution with the cries of napalm victims interrupting my every thought?" (376). Kate leaves Vietnam prematurely with injuries sustained during the Tet Offensive (Even nurses were not immune to incoming rounds; Kate spends many a night under the dubious protection of her mattress cover). Bereft of youthful innocence, her initial caring has been reduced to numbing by the contradiction of her part in the war: "I felt my humanity draining from me like the sweat that trickled down my extremities," she confesses. "The fluids could easily be replaced, but how did you restore a soul that was steadily becoming dehydrated?" (104)

The experiences and accompanying emotions of Kate in this novel closely parallel the oral histories and personal narratives of Vietnam War nurses who eventually emerged from their closet of silence and have spoken and written about their once repressed, unwelcomed experiences during the war. Written much like a factual memoir, Forever Sad the Hearts is described by a Washington Post Book World review as a "moving and explicit look at a little known side of a well-known war" (12).

SHORT FICTION

199. Abrams, Linsey. "Secrets Men Keep." Mademoiselle Aug. 1985: 144 – 146+.

At six years old, Jeffrey has undergone counseling for two years in an attempt to cope with his father's Vietnam War injury. Jeffrey develops an irrational fear of all men who can walk, originating from his father's paralysis, and tries to counteract his own fear that he will "get caught like Daddy was" by creating an introverted fantasy world where he believes if he remains as "silent as an Indian" and avoids contact with adult males, no one will ever be able to "deaden his legs" (283). This story illustrates how fears related to war can become disproportionate and very inhibiting in the mind of a sensitive child.

200. Agee, Jonis. "Clinton's War Story." Sweet Eyes. New York: Crown Publishers, Inc., 1991. 186 – 193.

In this novel excerpt, the narrator tells a story within a story of a local Iowan who was sent to Vietnam and assigned to work in an intelligence unit as an interrogator of Viet Cong prisoners. Although Clinton was sheltered from the dangers of combat during most of his tour of duty and survived without so much as a hangnail during his two years of service, he witnesses the death of his senior officer during an air attack shortly before he is scheduled to leave Vietnam.   The experience is so devastating it eventually drives Clinton out of military service and toward insanity before death mercifully ends his misery.

201.   Alberts, Laurie. "Veterans." Love Stories/Love Poems. Eds. Joe Bellamy and Roger Weingarten. San Diego: Fiction International, 1982. 56 – 64.

The unnamed narrator of "Veterans" feels an intense jealousy toward the "other woman" who lingers in her lover's mind, representing a history he has experienced that she, as a woman, has been denied. The ugly, battle-scarred, mysterious other woman in his life is Vietnam. The narrator comes to realize that she and Stefan are hopelessly out of accord. While she has been too overzealous in her attempts to penetrate his barrier of silence and experience the war vicariously, Stefan has internalized his war wounds and refused to express whatever anger or guilt or sense of loss he feels. "I don't have answers for you," he replies to her continual questions about the war in an effort to protect his past (57). Clues in the story such as his violent/pacifist tendencies (he cries at the thousands of toads squashed by cars on the road each spring, but hurls dishes across the kitchen in an angry rage), his inability to express his feelings, his abrupt emotional swings, and his preparation for the inevitable nuclear disaster (a sailboat and a rifle), suggest that Vietnam is still an existing, if not an interfering wedge of influence in his life. The attraction between the two lovers eventually dissolves, the narrator admitting to herself, "I have no time for Stefan. For him there is no time" (64). This story offers perceptive insight into the frustration of a woman, longing to penetrate the forbidden territory of the male domain of war and touch the most enigmatic and well-guarded part of her lover's psyche, and a veteran who needs the intimacy of a relationship but refuses to let anyone break down the wall he has carefully erected around his war experience.

202.   Bambara, Toni Cade. "The Sea Birds Are Still Alive." The Sea Birds Are Still Alive: Collected Stories. New York: Random House, 1977. 71 – 93.

This story examines the aftermath of the Vietnam War on refugees coping with the chaos of uncertainty and changes wrought by revolution in their country. One Vietnamese woman aboard the refugee boat, where much of the story's development takes place, relives the torture she endured as a prisoner during the war:

> At the precinct bunker, they'd stuffed hoses up her nose and pumped salty water, fish brine, water from the district's sewer till her belly swelled up, bloated to near bursting. Then they beat her with the poles, sticks, rods of bamboo, some iron till she vomited, nearly drowning. She told them nothing. (91)

While recalling this tragic memory, she also remembers the words of the elders passed on from generation to generation who taught her as a child that revolution is the "chance to amend past crimes, to change to be human" (92). A refugee farmer, whose sovereignty after the war is dissolved like the near-worthless currency he carries strapped to his belly, ponders his uncertain future:

> What was to become of him now that his seed was scattered in the winds? Who would manage the land, keep up the line, the traditions? . . . . His wife was far too old to further family. He wondered if indeed he should find a new wife and start again. (87)

A hill woman sewing straw mats to keep herself fed and clothed stabs herself with her needle "cruelly to fix her mind on the work at hand. To substitute for the pain she felt hopeless to deal with, with a pain she could understand" (75). An orphaned barrow boy making a living on the streets of a Vietnamese city in turmoil longs for the companionship and security of home and family no longer possible in this postwar crisis.

The picture of postwar Vietnam depicted by Bambara is a society based upon chaos, upheaval, uncertainty, and instability. Yet the Vietnamese people she describes are a resilient, industrious, courageous, and proud people, determined to resume their lives, determined to survive despite the wars that have plagued their tiny country for centuries.

203. Boyle, Kay. "You don't have to be a member of the congregation." Little Victories Big Defeats. Ed. Georgess McHargue. New York: Delcorte Press, 1974. 11 – 18.

Although Kay Boyle authored many traditional, modernist short stories during the World War Two period, this story departs from her earlier pattern of obvious didacticism with a subtler moral message conveyed in an innovative, metafictional fashion. Boyle, who assumes the role of author-narrator, begins the story in a totally unconventional manner with a direct confession to the reader which expresses her difficulty in writing this particular story: "For a long time I didn't know how to begin this story, or how I'd manage to keep it going if ever I got the opening sentence down" (11). She discloses the plot summary and climax to readers in the second sentence and discovers the beginning of the story at its end where she admits relief that at last she has found the catalyst to begin her story. Several times through the progress of the narrative—a simple plot detailing a Saigon professor's hunger strike in an American church during the Vietnam War and the narrator's attempts to elicit public awareness of his plight—Boyle intrudes with informal, confessional dialogues addressed as much to herself as to her readers. This innovative approach to storytelling allows readers to witness Boyle the writer as well as Boyle the antiwar protest sympathizer. These separate but compatible roles permit her to make a convincing but not overbearing moral statement about the war through the persona of a lieutenant who comes to confess to the Vietnamese hunger striker: "I wanted to say I've told them I won't fight in Vietnam"—a moral choice Boyle would certainly approve (18).

204.   Bradley, Jane. "What Happened to Wendell?" Power Lines and Other Stories. Fayetteville: University of Arkansas Press, 1989. 13 – 24.

A disturbed Vietnam War veteran blows himself away with a shotgun in this story while his memory persists in haunting the sister of his former fiancee. Wendell represents the veteran who has lost both self control and self respect, who resorts to the violent ways of war as the only method he knows to escape rejection.

While engaged to Lavita, Wendell describes his war experience in Vietnam to the sisters "as if it had all been a movie," the narrator remembers:

> He could say things like dead babies and naked women half-buried in the mud, and he wouldn't flinch. He told how he saw a friend blown to bits right beside him. He had heard a blast, hit the ground, and when he looked up, he saw a leg go flying through the air. "To tell it slows it down, but it happened so fast," he said. "it took one second, and he was gone." After he told each story, he would lean back on the couch and say, "Nam was hell. Pure hell." (15)

Distrustful of everyone, Wendell drives away Lavita with his intense jealousy and begins to deteriorate both physically and emotionally, unable to control his violent eruptions, ultimately aimed inward upon himself. In a review of Power Lines and Other Stories published in The New York Times Book Review, Mark Childress discusses the use of violence in Bradley's writing and finds that the originality of her short story writing "lies in bringing that violence to the surface with her strong, precise prose. The loaded gun and the clenched fist have ceased to be remarkable in the lives of her characters," he writes (38).

205.   Casper, Susan. "Covenant With a Dragon." In the Field of Fire. Eds. Jeanne Van Buren Dann and Jack Dann. New York: Tom Doherty Associates, 1987. 305 – 324.

The Vietnam War veteran in this science fiction story is trapped between two cultures and his emotional commitments to both his wartime and postwar families. Although Richard establishes an

American family of his own following the war, he continues to fantasize about the woman he loved in Vietnam 14 years ago and the daughter he fathered, whom he has always assumed died with her mother during the war. When he meets an orphan refugee his daughter's age and sees his own reflection in her face, he realizes this may be his daughter and recognizes that his Vietnamese ties have an equally strong claim on his devotion and sense of responsibility. "It's a terrible thing for a child to be without a father," he concludes as he goes to claim the young woman he believes to be his daughter (322). It is equally difficult for a father to live without his daughter, he realizes, even one he has never known. Torn between his American wife's blatant prejudice against the Vietnamese people and her unpredictable reaction to his wartime liaison and his desire to know and nurture his Vietnamese daughter, Richard becomes enmeshed in a conflict so stressful he begins to experience hallucinatory visions of fighting dragons that, although violent and disturbing, nevertheless help guide him toward a resolution. This story portrays the emotional burden of the veteran whose allegiances are torn between his wartime and postwar relationships. The realization that these relationships—strained by cultural barriers and biases—may not be able to coexist peacefully presents the veteran with difficult choices.

206. Cherry, Kelly. "War and Peace." Georgia Review 44.1 – 2. (1990): 33 – 47.

The psychological adjustments of two victims of trauma—one who served in Vietnam and one who was sexually abused by her father—are contrasted and eventually integrated in this narrative of a search for individual peace. The narrator, whose experience dominates most of the narrative, joins a therapy support group, gaining emotional strength through mutually shared feelings and the incentive for introspection offered by a supportive network of mutual survivors of incest. The Vietnam War veteran, employed as a night custodian for the Vet Center where the therapy group meets, comes to gradually absorb the trauma of his war experience through the repetition of continued viewing of films of the war which offer him the security of knowing that, through the camera's eye, he has witnessed the totality of the combat experience; nothing has been "overlooked." After the narrator and veteran view one of the films together, she fantasizes a variation of the film of her own creation in which the two of them blissfully picnic in a grassy rice field while the sounds of war continue to burst like fireworks in the background. In this setting, she chooses to share with the veteran the most important personal discovery she has made during therapy: "If we are ever going to make peace with ourselves," she confides, "we have to do it in the midst of the war that is always going on all around us" (47).

207. Cook-Lynn, Elizabeth. "Going Home." The Power of Horses and Other Stories. New York: Arcade Publishing, 1990. 79 – 89.

The Indian veteran who dominates this narrative returns to American soil from Saigon in 1969 to renew the ongoing war in his own homeland —the white man versus red man conflict that has been ongoing for many years. What was once Sioux territory in South Dakota has been invaded by white Americans who disregard the rights of Indians to their own land. Like so many Vietnam War veterans, Young Nephew returns to the United States abruptly with no readjustment period and no welcome home. But while the homecoming of many veterans meant the end of their involvement in the war and the beginning of their readjustment to a peaceful life once more, for Young Nephew the return home from Southeast Asia only means the continuation of another war as he is expected to resume his active participation in the protection of the Sioux Indians against the white man who continues to infringe upon their rights and property.

208. Doubiago, Sharon. "Vets." The Book of Seeing With One's Own Eyes. St. Paul: Graywolf Press, 1988. 283 – 335.

"Vets" is the concluding story among a group of connected short stories in this collection that chronicle the coming of age of a drifting writer during the 1960s and 1970s, representative of many members of her generation who sought identity and values outside of themselves, grasping ephemeral trends instead of searching within, and invariably failed in their search. "Vets" takes place in Utah logging country where former Vietnam War helicopter pilots operate the same kind of choppers they navigated in Vietnam while they work on a seismic project by day, frequent local bars by night, and pursue women for short-term pleasure. Against the backdrop of rock and roll music of the era, Doubiago captures the confused impermanence and instability of values of a generation grappling with the aftermath of Vietnam and its resurgent memories that continue to cloud perceptions of what is real and lasting in life. One vet fondly recalls a former co-pilot— "the war's first hero—who flew his last mission over Nam naked. Said he wouldn't wear his uniform to do the shit. Said he couldn't do that to the American flag" (297). Another veteran describes a recurring flashback nightmare that continually awakens him:

> I'm looking from the chopper right into the eyes of a Vietnamese guy on the ground. Guess I killed him. I don't know for sure. I can hear so vividly the sound of it. It's weird. Like I'm right there low in the chopper and he's right there on the ground. He's looking right into my eyes. A moment out of a million frozen just like that. (329)

Belles Lettres reviewer Patricia Schwartz assesses The Book of Seeing With One's Own Eyes as a "difficult, demanding, unsettling, yet essential work, a woman's answer to the male war novel (especially of Vietnam). Women on the home front sustain heavy fire and high casualty rates every day" (18).

209.   Erdrich, Louise. "A Bridge" and "The Red Convertible." Love
        Medicine. New York: Holt, Rinehart and Winston, 1984. 130 – 142
        and 142 –154.

Erdrich uses a variety of narrators in Love Medicine, each relating a
facet of the American Indian experience in their own voices.   These
two chapters focus on Henry, a returning Vietnam War veteran who
served nine months of combat before he spent six months in captivity
of the North Vietnamese Army. Adrift only three weeks later in "A
Bridge" he meets a 15-year-old runaway in Fargo, North Dakota who
is equally outcast. The two spend one night together, but Henry's
drunken attempts at lovemaking become violent and domineering,
the aggressor subduing his victim whose fear only serves to
motivates him more. The next morning as she accidentally touches
Henry in his sleep, he awakens screaming but instead of attacking
his would-be assailant, he weeps at his own pathetic predicament,
his once powerful image dissolving in despair.

"The Red Convertible" is narrated by Henry's younger brother who
finds his brother an incomprehensible stranger once he returns from
Vietnam.   Lyman describes his veteran-brother's change of
character since the war:

> When he came home, though, Henry was very different, and
> I'll say this: the change was no good. You could hardly expect
> him to change for the better, I know. But he was quiet, so
> quiet, and never comfortable sitting still anywhere but always
> up and moving around. I thought back to times we'd sat still
> for whole afternoons, never moving a muscle, just shifting our
> weight along the ground, talking to whoever sat with us,
> watching things. He'd always had a joke, then, too, and now
> you couldn't get him to laugh, or when he did it was more the
> sound of a man choking, a sound that stopped up the throats of
> other people around him. They got to leaving him alone most
> of the time, and I didn't blame them. It was a fact: Henry was
> jumpy and mean. (147 –148)

Alternating between silence and violence in his erratic approach to
life, Henry eventually ends his life in violence as he drives into a
raging river stream, fulfilling the stereotype of both a "crazy Indian"
and a crazed Vietnam veteran.   In her writing Erdrich vividly
depicts the dilemma of the veteran who is a double outcast
representing both an unpopular war and an equally shunned
minority ethnic group of American society.

210.   Fowler, Karen Joy. "The Lake Was Full of Artificial Things." Isaac
        Asimov Science Fiction Magazine Oct. 1985: 125 – 135.

Written in the science fiction genre, this story examines the profound
guilt of a former lover of a Vietnam War casualty who terminated
her relationship with him during the war because she opposed
his involvement. Miranda has since never reached an inner

reconciliation for the responsibility she assumed for Daniel's death. Through intense therapy and hypnosis Daniel is reborn in Miranda's mind. As they continue their former relationship and attempt to resolve lingering conflicts through this psychotherapy, Miranda insists, "The war's over now." But Daniel counters: "Wars never end. . . . Do you imagine for one minute that it's over for me?" (130).

Most irreconcilable to Miranda is Daniel's confession that he killed a six-year-old Vietnamese boy. As she relives the moment during therapy, Miranda witnesses the murder, powerless to intervene and change the past:

> Miranda had never imagined a war could be so quiet. Then she heard the chopper. And she heard Daniel. He was screaming. He stood right next to her, beside a pile of sandbags, his rifle stretched out before him. A small, delicately featured child was just walking into Miranda's view, his arms held behind him. All Miranda had to do was lift her hand. (135)

To Daniel's plea for forgiveness, she responds with the question: "Was it a crime of cowardice or of cruelty? I'm told you can be forgiven the one, but not the other" (135).

Using fantasy and psychotherapy techniques, this innovative story explores the feelings of those who never participated directly in the war but nevertheless must confront unresolved emotional pain and guilt that lingers from the war. The fantasy elements of this story allow Miranda to explore her past and face the painful realities of war.

211. Fowler, Karen Joy. "Letters From Home." In the Field of Fire. Eds. Jeanne Van Buren Dann and Jack Dann. New York: Tom Doherty Associates, 1987. 71 – 89.

The structure of this story is actually an extended letter addressed to a soldier who went to Vietnam not because he supported the war but because he believed he might "have some impact from within" to end the conflict. The narrator never learns his fate, for the soldier never writes to her from Vietnam, as promised. In her continued letter to him, she juxtaposes her own life's story of war resistance with what she fantasizes his life must have been like during and after the war. But her imaginings remain only conjecture, and it continues to disconcert her—even fifteen years later as the story is written—that she has never learned his or any other veteran's personal version of the war. The truth, if it is to be found, keeps eluding her.

The 35-year-old wife and mother narrator of this story is symbolic of many of the Vietnam generation still groping for meaning and context of this ambiguous war in their lives. The narrator defends the members of her generation who did not experience combat against the imagined accusations of her fantasized veteran that civilians somehow "escaped" the trauma of war. She explains: "Some of us were killed. (And the numbers are irrelevant.) Some of us went to Canada and to Sweden. And some of us had a great time. But it wasn't a clean escape, really, for any of us" (88).

In the introduction to her story Fowler explains the influence of the war upon the lives of those of her generation: "I do think those of us around my own age were defined by Vietnam in ways those much older and much younger will never understand. Which leaves us only each other to turn to for understanding" (70). This extended letter represents this Vietnam generation author's "gesture of reconciliation" written in an innovative style that reflects the disillusionment of many who may not have fought during the Vietnam War but were deeply affected by their encounter with war.

212. Geller, Ruth. "Pat's Friend Norm." Pictures From the Past. Buffalo: Impress, 1978. 187 – 194.

This narrative describes a veteran's sudden fears and uncertainties when he discovers the Vietnam War is not entirely part of his past history, as he once imagined. A victim of Agent Orange defoliation, Norm discovers he is becoming bald and his skin is turning red and scaly. He becomes apprehensive of what might happen to his life next. "When I got back from Nam in one piece, I thought, man, I lucked out. But now I'm not so sure," he confides to a friend. "I'm thirty-one years old, man. I got a wife and kid, and another one on the way. I just bought a goddamned house. I did my time in Nam. I been working steady at that plant for eight years. If it's some shit I been breathing, who knows what'll happen to me next" (193). Mental reminders of the war come in unexpected places as well. Norm's son buys a new cereal supposed to taste like chocolate chip cookies, reminding Norm of a box of cookies a friend once shipped to him in Vietnam. "The cookies were packed so badly that they arrived in crumbs, but he forgave her immediately and ate the stale cookies with milk, like cereal" (189). Geller's story illustrates the point that war never really ends for veterans who are sometimes jolted by surprising reminders of their experiences at unexpected moments.

213. Gordon, Elizabeth. "On the Other Side of the War: A Story." Home to Stay: Asian American Women's Fiction. Ed. Sylvia Watanbe and Carol Bruchac. Greenfield Center, NY: Greenfield Review Press, 1990. 49 – 51.

This five-part narrative, written by a Vietnamese-American author born in Saigon but raised in Tennessee, fictionalizes her early immigration to the United States and the adjustment of her mixed-heritage family to American society.

No one was prepared for her birth, the narrator writes. Her American veteran-father always expected to marry a wholesome hometown girl whose father was a garage mechanic, like his own father. "There'd been no Nguyen Ngoc Huong from Saigon in his crystal ball" (49). Neither had her Vietnamese mother dreamed "she'd live in an aluminum house on wheels" overlooking a cow pasture. Both of her parents had significant adjustments to make.

One vignette describes a family photograph that appears typically American—except that something seems "not quite right" about the family. Is it the "incomparable blackness" of the mother's hair? "Or maybe it has something to do with the baby's eyes which, though blue, are shaped exactly like the woman's: round at the center, narrow at the corners, and heavy-lidded. What are eyes like that doing among frame houses and a shiny Chevrolet?" (51).

Another segment of the narrative describes Elizabeth's awkwardness when she tries to fill out school forms. Just how should she classify her race? The form includes no blank to check to accurately describe her ethnic origin. Finally her father advises his daughter to simply place an "H" in the blank to represent the human race. "I didn't understand what that meant, back then," the author confides. "But it sounded like a good race to me" (51).

These short episodes of life give insight into the awkwardness of a Vietnam War bride attempting to adapt to American culture and the confusion of identity experienced by Amerasian children conceived during the war.

214.   Grau, Shirley Ann. "Homecoming." The Wind Shifting West. New York: Alfred A. Knopf, 1973: 41 – 54.

In this short story a mother attempts to fabricate a relationship that never existed between her daughter and a Vietnam War casualty so that she can relive her own tragic, historical drama when her own husband was killed during an earlier war. The story examines the conflict between the daughter's honest feelings—that Harold was only a casual date, a "poor bastard" whom she pitied more than admired, not worth the effort of mourning—and the hypocritical displays of emotion expected of Susan by her mother and neighbors who assume she will play the role of the bereaved widow following his death.

The telegram announcing Harold's death becomes an excuse for a social gathering of Susan's neighbors during which members of the World War Two generation relive their individual moments of glory during a war remembered as far more honorable than Vietnam. One of the World War Two veterans speaks of war as a need for those of his gender: "Always seemed to me like men have got to have their war. I had to have mine twenty-five years ago. When you're in it maybe it's different, but you got to go. Once you hear about it, you got to go to it" (523). But Susan, born of a different generation and attitude toward war, dares to disagree: "That doesn't make any sense to me," she replies. "None" (523). Instead of assuming her father and Harold died as heroes, she even considers the idea that maybe they weren't brave after all; maybe "they just got caught." Or maybe Harold pulled the "trigger against his own head in fear" (523). Gray's story illustrates how attitudes toward war can dramatically change during the span of a generation, from romantic heroism to anti-heroic realism, and how these differences can create familial conflicts even among non-participants who endorse disparate attitudes toward war.

215. Harrington, Joyce. "A Letter to Amy." The Year's Best Mystery and Suspense Stories 1986. Ed. Edward D. Hoch. New York: Walker and Company, 1986. 83 – 101.

The Vietnam War veteran misfit personified in this story, doing time for murdering his lover and daughter in a jealous rage, writes letters to his daughter from prison as if she were still alive and tucks them under his mattress with hundreds of others, all stamped and addressed, as his collection grows. He reflects upon his postwar life as a series of disappointments of a would-be hero who expected admiration and acceptance from his hometown upon his return from the war but encounters apathy and hostility instead, even from his own family. Lashing back with violence and rage, he loses his job and distances himself from those who are most important in his life before he takes the ultimate step in estrangement, turning his violence inward upon himself. This story analyzes a veteran who anticipated a smooth readjustment back into civilian life after the war but encounters obstacles wherever he turns, a veteran who brings home the violence of war and resorts to it as his only defense against society's rejection.

216. Inness-Brown, Elizabeth. "Release, Surrender." The Pushcart Prize, VII: Best of the Small Presses. Ed. Bill Henderson. Wainscott, NY: Pushcart Press, 1983. 150 – 158.

This narrative juxtaposes the experiences of a GI who becomes enmeshed in the violence and insensitivity of the military system during war while his girlfriend left waiting on the homefront withdraws into silence. During his military indoctrination, the "body and the mind become equally firm, equally impenetrable, equally calloused" (152). He is trained only to think of the enemy, for if he allows thoughts of "the girl" to enter his mind, he might endanger his own life by momentarily forgetting the enemy. On the homefront the GI's girlfriend retreats into a world of her own, refusing to eat. In one contrasting passage, her concerned parents attempt to force food into her mouth as they did while she was an infant while in faraway Vietnam GIs feed rice to Vietnamese prisoners who are near starvation while they callously stand by to watch as the Vietnamese die from the ingestion of food:

> When the rice is cooked, the GIs give it to them in sticky clumps, and at first they eat quickly. Then they begin to vomit, their stomachs having shrunk to the size of walnuts. But the GIs train their guns on them and the old men, the women pick up what they have vomited and eat it again, and feed it to the

> children, hoping to save them, and then the GIs give them
> more, more, and they begin to cry as they eat, their tiny faces
> twisted with pain. They vomit, and eat, and eat more. When
> the rice is gone, the GIs sit down and watch the people die,
> their yellow eyes rolling back into their skulls. (156)

Another contrasting image ends the narrative. While the GI's thirst
for lust and violence ends tragically in a Vietnamese whorehouse,
the mother of his child on the other side of the world begins to
reawaken with the experience of childbirth as the cycle of life makes
another complete turn.

217.   Kalpakian, Laura. "Veteran's Day." Stand One. Eds. Michael
       Blackburn, Jon Silkin, and Lorna Tracy. London: Victor Gollancz,
       1984. 9 – 30.

The protagonist of this story is one of the most disturbed and violent
veterans characterized in these women's short stories. As a juvenile
delinquent, Walter Sutton is "sentenced" to Vietnam by a judge who
is hopeful the military training "would still make a man of him,"
but his sister-narrator recalls that the "Army spits him back like he
was a slug we'd tried to slip in a juke box" (20). Once he returns from
the war, Walter fits into nothing. "Not his clothes. Not the house.
Not the family" (20). During meals he clutches a sandal brought
home from the war, although he can't remember exactly why he
promised to save it. Walter suffers from paranoid delusions that the
government is "putting chemicals everywhere so they can putrefy our
brains and we'll obey them and not have a single thought of our own.
They're controlling us just like they controlled all those boys who
went to Vietnam" (24). To protect innocent American citizens from
this conspiracy, he begins to distribute long nozzled gas masks when
he is not serving time for terrorism or theft in the State Loony Bin.

"Veteran's Day" points to the fallacy of using the military for
rehabilitation, for in Walter's case, his military experience in
Vietnam only intensifies his psychological problems. The story also
illustrates how sisters of veterans can become indirect victims of war
as a result of their close association. While the sister in this
story rationalizes her brother's bizarre fantasies and defends his
irrational fears, she develops the same paranoia and post-Vietnam
dementia that plague her brother. Although she did not fight in the
war, she has allowed herself to become an accomplice in Walter's
private war against governmental authority, a war in which both
of them will ultimately be losers. Watching the late-night television
news, the narrator slips into one of Walter's masks and relishes a
moment of calm serenity and temporary relief from her growing
paranoia: "It's real quiet inside that gas mask. I can hear myself
breathe and I know if I wear it enough they'll never get me" (30).

218.   Kaplan, Johanna. "Dragon Lady." Writing Under Fire: Stories of
       the Vietnam War. Eds. Jerome Klinkowitz and John Somer. New
       York: Dell, 1978. 22 – 34.

While Vietnamese women fought in the official armed forces of their country during the Vietnam War, women snipers also fought in the unofficial armies, as this story illustrates. Kaplan begins the story with a journalistic report of the arrest of a "dragon lady" that could easily have been an actual account:

> SAIGON (AP)--Police indicated today a woman arrested in connection with the shooting of a Nationalist Chinese officer may be the Dragon Lady who has been gunning down people from the back of a motorcycle.
>
> The National police director, Brig. Gen. Nguyen Ngoc Loan, said Miss Phung Ngoc Anh, a 24-year-old Vietnamese of Chinese descent, was arrested carrying a .45 caliber pistol which ballistics tests show was used to fill five persons, including two Americans. Loan said the woman admitted three of the shootings. (22)

Switching to the narrative mode, Kaplan examines the ancestry and motives of this woman for murder, concluding, "If her heart is remote, she'd be the last one to know it. Fleet as a fawn, she shoots with both hands" (34)

219. Kornblatt, Joyce Reiser. "Susan." Breaking Bread. New York: E. P. Dutton, 1987. 143 – 172.

"Susan" is the portrayal of two women co-workers, one of them a 19-year-old Vietnam War wife, who are groping to find their identity and individuality during the late 1960s. Susan's reaction to the war and racial strife dividing the country is to create her own reality through mind-altering drugs that produce the illusion of security that fantasies are indeed a possibility. Earth, she imagines, is "just one silly little planet and if we don't like the way things are turning out, we can just go somewhere else! Right? We can start all over again, right?" (149).

Susan and her equally young soldier-husband, she tells the narrator, plan to become famous artists living in a cliffhouse overlooking the Pacific Ocean after "the war," the words pronounced "as if there were a place with precisely that name, as if all the battles ever fought and all the bombs dropped and all the civilians buried in the huge pits that pocked the earth were located in one tiny spot on the planet" (164). John's pictures mailed home from Vietnam depict a young man grown old during only a few months of combat, "his boyish features toughened, his open grin turned into a smile tight and covert, his soft eyes glassy-hard" while his wife seems to grow "younger and younger each day in his absence." Susan replaces the void her husband has left in her life with a dependence on drugs that leads to a fatal overdose when John's status is changed to Missing in Action and further denial of reality becomes impossible (165). This narrative illustrates one woman's self-destructive attempt to cope with the repercussions of war and possible widowhood even before she has firmly established her own identity in life.

220.   Kristen, Marti. "With the Guard." Trace Spring 1966: 72 – 75.

Narrated from the viewpoint of a World War Two veteran who returns to revisit the Texas camp where he trained for infantry service in the South Pacific, this story clearly illustrates the difference in attitude toward war between a veteran sobered from his experience in combat and a youthful military policeman anxious to test his newly acquired military skills. The older veteran tries unsuccessfully to temper the younger soldier's romantic perception of war: "A war is a pretty grim thing," he warns. "Especially for the individuals fighting it. A friend of mine had his knees shot up by machine-gun fire. He doesn't walk much these days. Another bled to death in the grass because no one could get to him" (74). But the young MP seems unmoved by the veteran's explicit descriptions of warfare: "Men get their guts blown out, their testicles turned to bloody paste, their brains spattered over walls" (74). As if he doesn't really hear (or want to hear), the MP keeps insisting, "We're going to whip them (the Commies) this time" (74). It is as if the thrill of anticipated victory in Southeast Asia overshadows whatever grimness might be anticipated in war. Kristen's short narrative contrasts attitudes toward war between those who have seen combat and those who eagerly await the experience, as yet untempered by reality.

221.   Kumin, Maxine. "The Missing Person." The Best American Short Stories 1979. Ed. Joyce Carol Oates. Boston: Houghton Mifflin, 1979. 234 – 242.

The disappearance of both her son in Vietnam several years ago and her husband on a busy city street one night evokes a surprising source of strength in Ellie, the protagonist of this short story. "The Missing Person" is the story of one woman's moment of crisis when she is presented with the choice of either acting decisively or succumbing to stress, not altogether unlike the psychological demands placed upon a soldier in combat. Although portrayed as dependent and fragile, Ellie discovers an inner fortitude that surfaces spontaneously and allows her to respond rationally when her husband suddenly vanishes. The crisis also allows her to finally admit to herself that her only son Missing in Action in Vietnam for several years is dead. It is as if enduring the mental pain of her son's disappearance in Vietnam has provided her with a reservoir of emotional strength to draw upon during crucial situations.

222.   Kumin, Maxine. "These Gifts." Why Can't We Live Together Like Civilized Human Beings? New York: Viking, 1975. 75 – 84.

The youthful marriage of high school lovers does not survive the changes each partner undergoes during the war in this story. While Neddy is fighting a half of a world away, Sheila is formulating her identity as an individual. Neddy returns, "a daring boy the war reduced to a dreamlike state," so passive at times he reminds his wife of a turtle in winter hibernation (83). Sheila emerges as the stronger of the two, a woman who would rather face life alone than cope with her husband's postwar estrangement and withdrawal. This story depicts the consequences of a relationship severed by the experience of war, one partner continuing to grow and self-actualize, the other frozen in time, more of a parasite than a companion. Like many estranged veteran husbands, Neddy is left alone to confront his inability to adjust to life after Vietnam.

223.   Lee, Evelyn and Gloria Oberst. "My Mother's Purple Dress." Making Waves: An Anthology of Writings By and About Asian American Women. Ed. Asian Women United of California. Boston: Beacon Press, 1989. 99 – 115.

These women writers intersperse current psychiatric evaluation reports of a mental patient with flashbacks of war ten years ago to document the multiple psychological repercussions of one woman's encounter with war in this narrative. A Chinese woman whose family immigrated to Vietnam, Huu Tien Ly and her relatives are swept involuntarily into the tumult of war in Saigon. Her father, who attempts to sustain his terrified family with the wise maxim— "Today we pay with tears for tomorrow's joys"—is crushed by a collapsing hotel while hunting for his daughter. Huu Tien Ly's brother (who never realizes his ambition to soar and fly—"like one of his kites"—in an American Army helicopter) is senselessly shot in the throat before her eyes by an American soldier who, as an afterthought, realizes he has shot "only an unarmed boy." Her mother dies in a refugee camp where two volunteer doctors attempt to care for 3,000 people and antibiotics are scarce. To Huu Tien Ly, who has witnessed death, rape, and war in the first two decades of her life, it seems that tomorrow's joys her father envisioned "would never come. There was only today's pain" (110).

When Huu Tien Ly arrives alone in the United States, she faces yet another survival test in a foreign land where she knows only a few Vietnamese relatives. The accumulation of her war experiences and feelings of alienation living in a strange country are manifest in bizarre behaviors that indicate psychological trauma and possible mental illness. Easily agitated and verbally abusive, she is admitted to a psychiatric ward after she threatens to kill her sister with a kitchen knife during an argument. Huu Tien Ly also builds such an irrational distaste for anything colored purple (her mother's dying wish was to be buried in her best loved dress, which was purple), she threatens to destroy anything of that color.

It is through careful therapy and recognition of her "unwanted feelings" that Huu Tien Ly is able to understand the roots of her anger, fear, and feelings of guilt and unworthiness as she begins the slow process of recovery from "the scars of war and the pain of mental illness" in anticipation that "now will begin the time of joy"

(115). Huu Tien Ly is representative of Asian-American women whose loss of home and family to war and subsequent aloneness result in significant psychological disorders requiring extensive therapy and the gradual healing that comes with time in order to make peace with their past and reestablish a postwar life of their own.

224. Le Guin, Ursula K. The Word for World is Forest. Again, Dangerous Visions. Ed. Harlan Ellison. Garden City: Doubleday, 1972. 28 – 118.

This novella, set during a future century, depicts the destruction of another planet very similar in terrain to the country of Vietnam and the disruption of the Athshean planet's peaceful inhabitants by invading American troops. Although Vietnam is never mentioned specifically by Le Guin, the parallels between the war on the planet Athshe and Vietnam are obvious. The invading Americans are led by a captain who regards the Athsheans as subhuman and expresses his belief that "the only time a man is really and entirely a man is when he's just had a woman or just killed another man" (81). American soldiers are supplied with drugs and prostitutes for recreation. Numerous land mines and underground tunnels mar the landscape, helicopters continuously comb the sky, and monstrous, oversized weaponry shipped to the planet from Earth prove as worthless for fighting on the Athshean terrain as they did in the jungles of Vietnam a century before. The most obvious parallels, however, are the defoliation and ecological rape of the lush Athshe landscape and the violation of its peaceful inhabitants. Writing in the science fiction genre, Le Guin launches a fictional protest against the war, prophetic in its pessimistic prediction for the ecological future of planet Earth and its future generations.

The Word for World is Forest, originally titled The Little Green Men, was written in 1968 while Le Guin was living in London for a year with no opportunity to publicly protest war as she had done so actively in the United States. With no outlet for her increasing frustration, she turned to writing. "And 1968 was a bitter year for those who opposed the war," she explains:

> The lies and hypocrisies redoubled; so did the killing. Moreover, it was becoming clear that the ethic which approved the defoliation of forests and grainlands and the murder of noncombatants in the name of "peace" was only a corollary of the ethic which permits the despoliation of natural resources for private profit or the GNP, and the murder of the creatures of the Earth in the name of "man." The victory of the ethic of exploitation, in all societies, seemed as inevitable as it was disastrous.
>
> It was from such pressures, internalized, that this story resulted: forced out, in a sense, against my conscious resistance. I have said elsewhere that I never wrote a

story more easily, fluently, surely—and with less pleasure.
(151 – 152)

225. Lowell, Susan. "David." Southern Review 7 (1971): 254 – 264.

"David" is the story of a wistful relationship that never has the
chance to mature because the narrator convinces herself her would-
be lover will never return from his tour in Vietnam. A drifter who
enlists in the Marines, David "is Hamlet and Huckleberry Finn
and Lucifer flaming on his way to hell," she concludes, envisioning
him on a self-created, tragic mission of demonic futility (255). "I am
in love with David in a temporal way," she admits, "and he is going to
die. The end is inescapable" (254). Lowell constructs the emotional
defense of a woman who finds it safer to resist beginning a
relationship than to allow herself to become involved and then have to
live with the uncertainty of a lover's return from Vietnam.

Lowell's characterization of the narrator, Susan, is an effective
contrast to many of the youths during John F. Kennedy's Camelot
years who were reared on romanticized images of warfare, who
envisioned their country (and themselves) as invincible, only to
become severely disillusioned at the total lack of romantic adventure
and proliferation of death and destruction awaiting them in
Vietnam. Susan portrays the opposite end of that idealistic spectrum
in her cynical view of the war and the probable fate of many young
men sent to fight in Vietnam.

226. Mason, Bobbie Ann. "Big Bertha Stories." Unwinding the
Vietnam War. Ed. Reese Williams. Seattle: Real Comet Press,
1987. 121 – 134.

The Vietnam War veteran featured in this story is obsessed with
reliving his war experience, his vision narrowed by a combination of
regretful hindsight that Americans didn't employ the power of more
Big Bertha machines to win the war and his overbearing guilt for the
part he played in the destruction of the Vietnamese landscape and its
gentle people. Donald's wife becomes convinced he must be having
an affair with another woman, "someone that large in his mind."
And indeed there is another woman who dominates his attention—
her name is Vietnam.

Despite Jeannette's attempts to understand the complexity of
Donald's psychological dilemma, hampered by her impatience and
frequent intolerance ("Wasn't Vietnam a long time ago?" she
continually reminds him), Jeannette slips comfortably into the
single parent role when Donald admits himself to a Veterans
Administration hospital for an undetermined length of stay. The
realization that she has thought of Donald as husband, father, and
provider (and found him equally deficient in all three roles), but
never really thought of him as an individual, never attempted to look
deep inside of him—comes too late. Not only has her marriage
disintegrated, but her dreams as well have become disquieting

nightmares of the same haunting variety that continually disturbed Donald's sleep before their separation. Involuntarily, Jeannette has become another noncombat victim of the Vietnam War experience, and her marriage yet another casualty.

This story too illustrates how even the occasional presence of a troubled father can have detrimental effects upon an impressionable young child. Every time Rodney's part-time father appears, he is caught between the urge to run and hug his father's knees or hide in the closet (he does both). While his father is at home, Rodney draws disturbingly violent pictures illustrating the "Big Bertha" stories his father narrates. It is only when his father commits himself for treatment that Rodney's pictures assume a more peaceful imagery.

227.   Miner, Valerie.   "In the Company of Long-Distance Peace Marchers." Movement. Trumansburg, NY: Crossing Press, 1982. 24 – 31.

In this excerpt from the novel Movement, Miner recreates the feelings of a woman living in Canada in protest of American involvement in the Vietnam War who marches in what is reported to be "the last peace march" before the peace treaty is signed. Susan marches, not out of desire, but perhaps "out of faith in ceremony, in proclamation of principle" (24). She marches because antiwar demonstrations have become a part of her identity—even a habit. But there is a sameness to this march—"just like the last march and the one before that" (30 – 31). In the midst of all of these protesters who obviously feel similarly to Susan, she experiences "an odd loneliness," a feeling of lethargy and ineffectiveness of cause. For, as she "pretends to serve in the last peace march," she remembers that "in the faraway land of power" President Nixon is preparing his million dollar inaugural ball, while simultaneously, "in the faraway land of bombings," Indochinese women are watching their children "ripped to shreds" (31). Miner captures the feelings of cynical futility of this young woman, perhaps symbolic of many of her generation, who goes through the motions of protest, even as she doubts the value of one more peace march against the continuation of war.

228.   Miner, Valerie. "Uneasy Borders." Reweaving the Web of Life: Feminism and Nonviolence. Ed. Pam McCallister. Philadelphia: New Society Publishers, 1982. 336 – 346.

"Uneasy Borders," a narrative extracted from the novel Movement, illustrates the political naivete and youthful idealism of two young Americans moving to Canada during 1970 to resist the draft and protest the war in Indochina. As the Berkeley couple approaches Canada, which Susan has visualized in her mind as a "huge National Park," their main concern is whether or not border guards will permit them to immigrate to "the land of the possible." The political climate in Canada is never considered by either, but taken for granted as peaceful. But while American involvement in Southeast Asia has escalated, an internal war has begun within

Canadian borders. On the same day that Susan and Guy pass border inspection with relief, Canadian Prime Minister Trudeau enacts a decree of martial law across Canada to quell the mounting internal strife dividing his own country.

Susan is symbolic of many "pre-feminist" women who were sensitive about the issues of the Vietnam War but not as perceptive about conflicts erupting on the homefront. "Both Susan and Gary are naive about Canada and the cultural imperialism they carried with them across the border," Miner writes in the introduction to the story. "Clearly their pacifism and their politics face a lot of tests ahead" (336). Susan is also representative of many women who fled to Canada to protest American involvement during the war. "There were just as many women as men who did this, but they always get overlooked," Miner explains.

229.   Oates, Joyce Carol. "Out of Place." The Seduction and Other Stories. Los Angeles: Black Sparrow, 1975. 154 – 164.

Narrated from the viewpoint of a veteran paralyzed and grossly disfigured by his experience at war, so tormented by flashbacks he is unsure of his own name (although he is certain he is not the same individual who served in Vietnam), this story portrays the pathos of a veteran who realizes his painful appearance and vacillating mental clarity, coupled with his identification as one who served in an uncelebrated war, render him "out of place." This permanently disabled veteran accepts without protest his estrangement from a family that strains to be too superficially positive in his presence and his displacement in a society that is so blatantly obvious in its rejection of the Vietnam War veteran.

230.   Phillips, Jayne Anne. "November and December: Billy, 1969." Soldiers and Civilians: Americans at War and at Home. Ed. Tom Jenks. New York: Bantam, 1986. 126 – 154.

In this excerpt from the novel Machine Dreams, set during the last two months of 1969, Billy Hampson celebrates his nineteenth birthday and sets his fate for Vietnam. Unmotivated by college, he withdraws and allows the lottery machine to determine his destination:

> It was a joke, really. His birthday—today—written on a white plastic ball and bounced around in a machine. Exactly whose hand would touch the machine? Sometimes Billy dreamed about the lottery, a close-up interior view: hundreds of days of white balls tumbling in a black sphere, silent and very slow, moving as though in accordance with physical laws. A galaxy of identical white planets. No sun. Cold, charged planets, simple, symmetrical, named with months and numbers. (128 – 129)

Billy's older sister borrows the money to send him north to Canada, warning him against military service: "One way or the other, they're going to fuck you up. Look if you're standing on a railroad track and a locomotive is coming slower, very fast, don't you step off the track? Don't you get the hell out of the way?" (144). But Billy opts to "go with the numbers." Although he admittedly knows nothing about politics—or the Vietnam War—he trusts in his luck. "The best way to be lucky is to take what comes and not be a coward," he assures Danner. "I'm going to go. It's in the cards" (145). Billy is representative of many 19-year-olds during the Vietnam War era, caught between adolescence and adulthood, who didn't know where they belonged, and thus became pawns in a misguided military scheme that eventually cost them their lives.

231. Prager, Emily. "The Lincoln-Pruitt Anti-Rape Device." A Visit From the Footbinder. New York: Simon and Schuster, 1982. 130 – 180.

This macabre postmodern feminist satire proposes a radical solution to end the Vietnam War. As the failure of American troops in Vietnam is acknowledged, female troops of former prostitutes programmed as emasculators eager to wield their vaginal wrenches with a degree of viciousness no male ever envisioned are dispatched to Vietnam to test their experimental weaponry against the Vietcong. These women go armed with ingenious, if sadistic, vaginal inserts guaranteed to inflict instant death on seduced Viet Cong soldiers. As these women assume the role of warring aggressors, the act of creation reverses itself to become an equally passionate act of destruction. This story is a sustained lampoon, countering the absurdity of war with an equally absurd solution. Writing from a radical feminist point of view, Prager employs both the comic and ironic modes of fiction in a combination that examines war in a cerebrally humorous light. Her story leaves a lingering, satirical bite with its commentary on war, sex, and gender equality.

232. Rascoe, Judith. "Soldier, Soldier." Yours, and Mine. Boston: Little, Brown, 1969. 164 – 179.

Contrary to many short stories which point to the Vietnam War experience as the cause of the breakdown of many relationships, in this story a soldier's experience in Vietnam is what attracts war resister Nola to him. One of the few young men in their community who returns from Vietnam, Nicholas becomes an object of curiosity. Has he changed? Is he corrupted? Is he a homosexual? People looked upon these returning veterans as if they had no pasts:

> One assumed, if anything, that their whole lives had been aimed at their presence in Vietnam; spent, like bullets, denuded (where was the cartridge case? or were they the cartridge cases?) they rebounded into college, objects of curiosity among the undergraduates. Inscrutable because so rudely transparent, like shop windows. (167 – 168).

Nola finds this veteran's mysterious mannerisms and unpredictable intentions both exotic and intriguing. She is eager to vicariously experience the realities of war denied to most women because of their gender. "What's it like to hold a rifle?" she wonders. Nicholas' undisclosed experiences in Vietnam form the basis of Nola's attraction to him and her willingness to begin a relationship with uncertain direction.

233.   Ritchie, Mary. "Hunt and Destroy." New American Review 6 (1969): 64 – 68.

Ritchie is among a minority of women short story writers who examine the war experience from a male point of view. "Hunt and Destroy" is a character sketch of a Marine who craves leadership as much as his patrol willingly delegates him this unwanted responsibility. "He was brave and so they let him do things first— jump first, be point on patrol, be first into villages. They did this because otherwise, he very soon became inattentive and wasn't much use" (64). Jimmy feels especially powerful when he steals a Vietnamese prisoner's snake which intimidates everyone except him. Later, he shoots an enemy soldier more intent upon watching an advancing cobra than protecting himself against Jimmy's approach. This story evaluates the characteristics that place one soldier above another in rank and offers an accurate depiction of the nature of guerilla warfare.

234.   Silko, Leslie. "Lullaby." The Best American Short Stories 1975. Ed. Martha Foley. Boston: Houghton Mifflin, 1975. 254 – 262.

In this story an aging Navajo mother wraps herself in her youngest son's Army blanket—all that she has left of him—and huddles against the cold with memories of her three children, all taken away by white men in khaki uniforms whose language she could not comprehend. Two children were separated from her during their childhood with infectious diseases, while Jimmy was shipped to Vietnam where he disappeared with his helicopter. This story presents a tragic example of a mother's American Indian stoicism, a defense built gradually in response to learned helplessness. The Vietnam War claims yet another son from a mother who has sacrificed her third and last remaining child to a white man's cause she neither understands nor condones.

235.   Stanton, Maura. "Oz." The Country I Come From. Minneapolis: Milkweed Editions, 1988. 25 – 35.

Stanton draws a symbolic comparison between a Midwestern family seeking safety against the imminent danger of an approaching tornado, and the inevitable departure of one son for the equally turbulent war in Vietnam. The physical and emotional closeness of the family members huddled together in their basement shelter (not unlike the World War Two bomb shelters remembered by the mother) makes the unspoken absence of the recently drafted son awkwardly prominent in their minds. The recorded sensations of the sister-narrator, who leaves the safety of the basement to hunt for the family's missing cat and witnesses the full fury of the storm, resemble the impressions that might be expected from a sensitive soldier experiencing his first vivid and terrifying impressions of war. "I felt dizzy, as if I had been spinning and spinning," describes the narrator. "This must be like the future, I thought. Your past did not blow away. It was you who blew away. You looked out the window and everything was different" (35).

236. Taylor, Diane. "The Skull." Masques III: All-New Worlds of Horror and the Supernatural. Ed. J. N. Williamson. New York: St. Martin's Press, 1989. 169 – 179.

This story originated from the author's chance encounter with a Vietnam War veteran, who unexpectedly "pulled up his T-shirt to show me scars from Viet Nam" after he stopped to ask for a match. Aware that his internal scars were "much deeper and much uglier," Taylor was motivated to write this narrative.

The 14-year-old adolescent who narrates the story attempts to establish a father-daughter bond with her estranged veteran-father whom she has never really known. But the presence of a skull of a Viet Cong soldier her father killed during the war that sits perched in a place of honor above the fireplace in his remote cabin as a trophy of war provokes nightmares during the first night of her visit that ruin the intimacy they attempt to share. As she returns to her mother, her father disappears from her life, becoming yet another veteran who lives in isolation and cannot connect with the outside world, not even with his own daughter.

237. Taylor, Pat Ellis. "A Call From Brotherland." Afoot in a Field of Men. New York: Atlantic Monthly Press, 1988. 107 – 112.

Narrated from the viewpoint of a sister who dreams that her veteran-brother commits murder, this is a story of a nightmare come true of a veteran trying to readjust to civilian life who is pushed too far until he erupts in violence.

Returning from Vietnam, Okie joins the California Motorcycle Black-Leather Brotherhood of Veterans and Dropouts. He stays with this gang until "the Vietnam wounds of his brain were completely fried, cauterized with alcohol and acid, visions of chain-beatings, blood in the alleys, hot steel, friends dead of heroin overdoses in muggy LA tenement-motels overlaying the old Vietnam wounds with hot red layers of new skin" (108). When he begins to hallucinate that he sees the "devil licking at the sound in his brain that had never healedright, making hell itself spew out in visions of friends left to maggots in the shag carpets of living rooms like piles of half-eaten junk food and women with blow torches for hands," he turns himself into the Veterans Administration for electroshock therapy, but the VA offers him money and drugs instead (108). Okie later heads to Oklahoma to stay with friends, where he becomes a popular guy who is generous with his disability check and three Valiums a day provided by the VA. But when Thieving John and Okie both show up at an all-night party and John threatens to steal Okie's motorcycle, the stress becomes too intense and Okie reacts without self-control. In her narrative, Taylor characterizes a veteran in need of therapy and transition treatment before he can begin to adjust to postwar life, who is unfortunately "put on the streets again" by an indifferent Veterans Administration before he is able to control his irrational impulses and propensity for violence.

238. Taylor, Pat Ellis. "Descent into Brotherland." Afoot in a Field of Men. New York: Atlantic Monthly Press, 1988. 99 – 106.

This narrative describes the environment typical of Veterans Administration hospitals and the impersonal attitude of "Mr. Bandaids-For-The-Millions-While-Top-Brass-Plan-The-Bombs-And-Clean-Their-Fingernails" psychiatrists who are assigned to evaluate readjusting veterans. Okie joins a sea of "would-have-been-beautiful-well-made men" who have "come to the hospital from that place called War," their minds and bodies "war broken," their will to live uncertain, their perspective on life definitely distorted. The sister-narrator of this story who accompanies her veteran-brother to the hospital is overwhelmed by a sense of frustrated helplessness as she observes the bizarre aberrations of behavior manifested by the veteran patients treated there. She witnesses the detached, almost indifferent attitude of the psychiatric staff members and criticizes their reliance upon a heavily drug-oriented therapy as an obviously ineffectual approach for the healing of these veterans' mental and physical postwar problems.

239. Thacker, Julia. "A Civil Campaign." New Directions in Prose and Poetry 44. Ed. J. Laughlin. New York: New Directions, 1982. 83 – 88.

The female protagonist in this short story must cope with one of the most difficult psychological problems faced by female partners of veterans—the potential impotence of her once passionate veteran lover—yet she emerges as a strong character whose assertiveness reassures a realistic possibility for an enduring relationship.

As wheelchair-bound Gus becomes more withdrawn and reclusive with his war wounds, Leah becomes more disgruntled and impatient with his "hollow" existence. Their relationship assumes an awkward, polite distance, becoming bland and stagnant. In a passionate confrontation that shatters the distance separating them and nearly climaxes in violence, Gus takes his first decisive action since his homecoming. Leah humbles herself in deference to his unexpected assertiveness, and their relationship begins to assume balance and vitality once more.

This story depicts in detail the veteran who returns from Vietnam but withdraws from society where he can hide his incontinence and accept his potential impotence in solitary security. It is also a character study of a woman assertive enough to risk challenging her lover's dormancy rather than allow him to vegetate in self pity or abandon him to confront his condition alone. "A Civil Campaign" is a study of the delicate equilibrium of the sexual battlefield, upset by the experiences of one partner on a strange and distant military battlefield.

240. Vaughn, Stephanie. "Kid MacArthur." Prize Stories 1986: The O. Henry Awards. Ed. William Abrahams. Garden City: Doubleday, 1986. 226 – 244.

The brother-sister relationship in this short story is strengthened by the Vietnam War which he fights and she protests. Once the war ends, MacArthur's sister becomes the only family member who can relate with her brother's isolationism, vegetarianism, and laissez faire attitude toward the future. She becomes the sole intermediary between her brother, who has chosen to live a solitary existence in a rural farmhouse, and his estranged parents, bitterly disappointed that MacArthur has rejected the military career they envisioned for him, even as he was named at birth. Although MacArthur's life seems defined by negatives—"no jobs, no college, no telephone, no meat"—he seems content in his self-imposed exile. His sister accepts his lifestyle and peculiarities (he once gives her the ear of a dead Vietnamese soldier which she tucks under the front car seat) without judgment, continuing to remain his one assured link with the outside world. Although their methods of expression may differ, this brother and sister both rebel against their military upbringing and its corresponding set of rigid values. The Vietnam War experience draws them closer as siblings who share a common rejection of their family's regimented, hawkish traditions and lack of tolerance for individual differences.

241. Wilbur, Ellen. "Wind and Birds and Human Voices." Wind and Birds and Human Voices and Other Stories. New York: New American Library, 1984. 5 – 34.

Written from the viewpoint of a veteran-psychiatrist patient of more than 30 years, this story offers a frightening picture of the permanent mental anguish and sense of utter alienation that result from the intensity of a veteran's war experience. Although extensive drug therapy has wiped out years of his memory, "as if they had been bombed into oblivion," this veteran remembers that as he became more seriously mentally ill, he "saw all life with a clarity and distance which shattered innocence, with the loneliness of a voyeur who feels the shame of his detachment as if it were the greatest sin of all" (15). "I was twenty," he remembers, "and I saw the world with the detachment and nostalgia of a dying man" (14).

Every summer an imaginary army invades the narrator's mental landscape, destroying whatever stability he might have regained during its absence. Studying his own madness "with the coldness of a scientist who prides himself on his detachment," he tries to analyze the motives for these recurring visits. But only one purpose remains clear: "the army's purpose was the purpose of all armies; to demoralize and to defeat the enemy, which was me" (19). He befriends another longtime veteran-patient and experiences an unexpected sense of belonging and need fulfilled only to be emotionally shattered later when he realizes that Henry Baron is but a phantom, a symptom of his own continuing madness. He wonders bitterly if the army "had made the Baron up just so that they could take him away from me" (33).

Wilbur's story is a poignant, sensitive portrayal of a veteran's loss of control over his own mental stability and his intense isolation from the world of normalcy. This veteran has created his own reality, a reality that continues to be dominated by the horrifying entrapment of war and the insanity perpetuated by his prolonged isolation from the "real world," not unlike the nightmarish alienation of the combat soldier trudging terrified through the dense jungles of Southeast Asia.

242. Wilhelm, Kate. "The Village." The Infinity Box. New York: Harper and Row, 1975. 277 – 287.

This short piece of speculative fiction simulates a reenactment of the 1969 My Lai Massacre which killed 347 Vietnamese civilians, most of them women and children. This time American troops are ordered to murder en masse unsuspecting small-town Southerners trapped "when the wrong village and the wrong war meet" (Introduction 12). The structure of the plot oscillates back and forth between perspectives, abruptly switching from the complacency of the village citizens carrying on their daily ritualistic routines—garden club meetings, shopping sprees, gossip exchanges—as if defiant of the inevitable, to the assertive search-and-clear maneuver of American troops approaching the village with orders to "clean out." While Mildred Carey argues with the local grocer over the price of tomatoes, one of the soldiers en route to the village expresses his indifference to the task ahead: "One fucken village is just like the others" (277). In a similar style to the one Shirley Jackson used three decades earlier to write "The Lottery," this story manifests a foreboding sense of doom that climaxes in imagined atrocity. "The Village" stands as a potent reminder of the tragic consequences of unchecked aggression and the dehumanization of the American military system. In his essay "The Vietnam War as American SF and Fantasy," H. Bruce Franklin writes that "Wilhelm's fantasy of a time-space zone where America and Vietnam merge poignantly expresses a growing consciousness that America's war against Vietnam was coming home" (349).

243. Yates, Ethel. "Seeds of Time." Alabama Prize Stories 1970. Ed. O. B. Emerson. Huntsville: Strode, 1970. 263 – 273.

At age 17, Harry Hartley longs to escape the confines of small-town Southern living to play the Marine Corps game glamorized by a visiting recruiter. "Harry is anxious to prove that he is a man. He is the seed of time to come. He intensely wants to be a man today! And to him the fastest, simplest, and surest way is to join the Marines!" (263). Harry's father wishes he could pacify his son's temporary infatuation by buying the Marines "as if it were a game of Monopoly. A game that Harry could play and when tired of it put in the closet with the other toys. But being a Marine is no game" (267).

In Vietnam Harry "captures the height of manhood" when he proves his confidence under intense pressure, but his tour of glory is cut short prematurely when part of his butt is blown away by a land mine and "left to rot on the field in Vietnam" (272). At age 18, Henry has been an Indian warrior on the warpath but is now a cripple. "His crutches are kept as close as his companion rifle was in combat" (273). This story contrasts the idealized version of warfare as a game often presented by the military to impressionable adolescent recruits with the reality of combat that abruptly humbles young heroes who are suddenly awakened to the realization of their own vulnerability and the true nature of the game in which they are engaged.

LITERARY CRITICISM AND BIBLIOGRAPHIC SOURCES

Beidler, Philip. American Literature and the Experience of Vietnam. Athens: University of Georgia Press, 1982.

"Belles Lettres Interview." Belles Lettres. May/June 1988: 9.

Boston, Anne. "With the vets in Hopewell." Rev. of In Country, by Bobbie Ann Mason. Times Literary Supplement. 18 April 1968: 416.

Bradley, Christie. What Happen on the Inside: Women Write About Vietnam. ERIC, 1988, ED 296 340.

Bradley, David. "War in an Alternate Universe." Rev. of In the Field of Fire. Eds. Jeanne Van Buren Dann and Jack Dann. The New York Times Book Review 3 May 1987: 25.

Bucknall, Barbara. Ursula K. Le Guin. New York: Frederick Ungar, 1981.

Butler, Deborah A. American Women Writers on Vietnam: Unheard Voices: A Selected Annotated Bibliography. New York: Garland, 1990.

Childress, Mark. "People in Pain." Rev. of Power Lines and Other Stories, by Jane Bradley. The New York Times Book Review 24 Sept. 1989: 38.

Ching, Stuart. "'A Hard Story to Tell': The Vietnam War in Joan Didion's Democracy." Fourteen Landing Zones: Approaches to Vietnam War Literature. Ed. Philip K. Jason: Iowa City: University of Iowa Press, 1991. 180 – 188.

Clifton, Merritt, ed. Those Who Were There. Paradise, CA: Dustbooks, 1984.

Conarroe, Joel. "Winning Her Father's War." Rev. of In Country, by Bobbie Ann Mason. The New York Times Book Review 15 Sept. 1985: 7.

Dann, Jeanne Van Buren and Jack Dann, eds. Introduction. In the Field of Fire. New York: Tom Doherty Associates, 1987. 9-14.

Elshtain, Jean Bethke. Women and War. New York: Basic Books, 1987.

Fowler, Karen Joy. Introduction. "Letters From Home." In the Field of Fire. Eds. Jeanne Van Buren Dann and Jack Dann. New York: Tom Doherty Associates, 1987. 70.

Franklin, H. Bruce. "The Vietnam War as American SF and Fantasy." Science-Fiction Studies 17 (1990): 341 - 357.

Hassan, Ihab. Contemporary American Literature: 1945 – 1972. New York: Frederick Ungar, 1973.

Kinney, Katherine. "'Humping the Boonies': Sex Combat, and the Female in In Country." Fourteen Landing Zones: Approaches to Vietnam War Literature. Ed. Philip K. Jason: Iowa City: University of Iowa Press, 1991. 38 – 48.

Kornblatt, Joyce Reiser. "Kentucky Characters." Belles Lettres. Sept./Oct. 1985: 7.

Le Guin, Ursula K. "Introduction to The World for World Is Forest." The Language of the Night. Essays on Fantasy and Science Fiction. Ed. Susan Wood. New York: G. P. Putnam's Sons, 1979. 149 – 154.

Marnell, Francis. "The Hawaii Connection." Rev. of Democracy, by Joan Didion. National Review 21 Sept. 1984: 52 – 53.

Matsakis, Aphrodite. Introduction. Vietnam Wives. By Matsakis. Kensington: Woodbine House, 1988. xi – xvi.

McCabe, Stephen. "The Literature Born of Vietnam." The Humanist Mar./Apr. 1986: 30 – 31.

"New in Paperback." Rev. of Forever Sad the Hearts, by Patricia Walsh. Washington Post Book World 3 July 1982: 12.

Newman, John. Vietnam War Literature: An Annotated Bibliography of Imaginative Works About Americans Fighting in Vietnam. Metuchen: Scarecrow Press, 1988.

Portales, Marco. "People with Holes in Their Lives." Rev. of Love Medicine, by Louise Erdrich. The New York Times Book Review 23 Dec. 1984: 6.

Proffitt, Nicholas. "Pete Bravado's War and Peace." Rev. of Buffalo Afternoon, by Susan Schaeffer. The New York Times Book Review 21 May 1989: 7.

Schwartz, Patricia Roth. "Patchwork, Piecework, Bedtime Stories, and Gossip." Rev. of The Book of Seeing With One's Own Eyes, by Sharon Doubiago. Belles Lettres Spring 1989: 18.

Spanier, Sandra. Kay Boyle. Carbondale: Southern Illinois University Press, 1986.

Spivack, Charlotte. Ursula K. Le Guin: Boston: Twayne Publishers, 1984.

Steinberg, Sybil. Rev. of Buffalo Afternoon, by Susan Schaeffer. Publishers Weekly 10 Mar. 1989: 75.

Stewart, Matthew C. "Realism, Verisimilitude, and the Depiction of Vietnam Veterans in In Country." Fourteen Landing Zones: Approaches to Vietnam War Literature. Ed. Philip K. Jason: Iowa City: University of Iowa Press, 1991. 166 – 179.

Stokes, Geoffrey. "Jayne Anne Phillips Wises Up." Rev. of Machine Dreams, by Jayne Anne Phillips. Village Voice Literary Supplement June 1984: 17.

Tal, Kali. "Feminist Criticism and the Literature of the Vietnam Combat Veteran." Vietnam Generation 1.3 – 4 (1989): 190 – 201.

Tyler, Anne. "The Wounds of War." Rev. of Machine Dreams, by Jayne Anne Phillips. The New York Times Book Review 1 July 1984: 3.

Wilhelm, Kate. "Introduction." The Infinity Box. New York: Harper and Row, 1975.

Winchell, Mark Royden. Joan Didion. Boston: Twayne, 1989.

Wittman, Sandra M. Writing About Vietnam: A Bibliography of the Literature of the Vietnam Conflict. Boston: G. K. Hall, 1989.

Wolf, Susan. "Women and Vietnam: Remembering in the 80s." Unwinding the Vietnam War. Ed. Reese Williams. Seattle: Real Comet Press, 1987. 243 – 261.

4

Nuclear War

INTRODUCTION

Twentieth century inhabitants of earth share a unique experience unknown to our ancestors of past centuries. Through continued scientific inquiry and advanced technology, we have created nuclear weaponry that has the capacity to destroy all forms of life on this planet. Imaginative literature, which originally predicted the destructive capability of nuclear weapons long before they were invented, allows us to "explore and cope with this overwhelming fact" of our capability for self-destruction (Franklin 11).

If the origin of nuclear weapons stems from early twentieth century science fiction literature, this fiction must also be given credit for acting as a deterrent in the prevention of nuclear war. From the safe distance that fiction allows, this literature allows us to vividly imagine what devastation might result from the irresponsible misuse of our overly sophisticated nuclear weaponry.

Nuclear war differs from earlier, more conventional warfare in significant ways that in turn affects its representation in fiction, as Paul Brians details in Nuclear Holocausts: Atomic War in Fiction, 1895 – 1984. First of all, Brians points out, if a nuclear war were to occur, it would last for a much shorter period of time than conventional wars of this century. Anti-nuclear activist Helen Caldicott visualizes a holocaust that would be swift and lethal:

> Erupting with great suddenness, a nuclear war would probably be over within hours. Several hundred to several thousand nuclear bombs would explode over civilian and military targets in the United States. . . . Each weapon's powerful shock wave would be accompanied by a searing fireball with a surface temperature greater than the sun's that would set firestorms raging over millions of acres. . . . The fires would sear the earth, consuming most plant and wild life. (232)

In her novel <u>The Last Day: A Novel of the Day After Tomorrow</u> Helen McCloy (as Helen Clarkson) predicts that human life on earth will end within six days following the explosion of a nuclear bomb. Carol Amen visualizes a gradual but thorough eradication of life on this planet within days of the initial nuclear explosion in "Testament."

Additionally, many of the features associated with conventional warfare would become irrelevant in the event of a nuclear disaster. There would be no "noble sacrifice" of soldiers in defense of country and loved ones at home, no reenstatement of a draft system, and no civilian support of the war effort. "Indeed," Brians explains, during nuclear war "the distinction between civilian and military is largely erased except that the military personnel most directly engaged in conducting the war are the most sheltered, and innocent civilians the most likely casualties" (2).

Unlike conventional warfare, nuclear war exists paradoxically as its own prevention—deterrence. During nuclear war the enemy must be convinced that adversary nations are willing to fight a war which may be self-destructive to themselves. "The more unthinkable the war becomes," writes Brians, "the more we must think about it. Unlike in other wars, the enemy must be well informed of our plans and resources, for a secret deterrent is no deterrent at all" (2 – 3).

The threat of nuclear war promises no benefits for either gender as does conventional warfare. In her essay "Women and War" Janna Thompson points out that for men modern wars have been "a means of defining masculinity and confirming their superiority over women" (67). For women, these wars have "sometimes provided opportunities for independence and entry into public life." But nuclear war, she writes, "threatens to subvert all political and personal ends; to destroy the political organizations that are irrational enough to use war as a means, and to make all equations between war and manhood ludicrous" (67).

Authors of nuclear war fiction "lack many of the resources of traditional war narratives," for they explore a literary genre that has more in common with the literature of catastrophes than the literature of war. But neither are these writers bound by tradition or committed to realism. Their imaginations are given free rein to probe into the unknown future, to explore the unthinkable, to interpret the worst of our nightmares given life through literature. Thus, these writers have developed their own conventions to create a war literature distinctive in style and approach (Brians 3).

Most nuclear war writers take one of two approaches to the interpretation of nuclear war. While some writers describe the war itself and its immediate consequences, others set their writings in the future and examine the state of a post-nuclear world. The majority of writers offer post-holocaust versions of nuclear war that are varied but decidedly bleak. Only a few envision the actuality of a nuclear holocaust happening. To directly confront the threatened end of life on earth is too disturbing for most writers; to read such an account "is too much like staring into one's own grave" (Brians 83). In her antiwar writings, Helen Caldicott stresses the dangers inherent in our lack of initiative to confront the possibility of nuclear disaster:

> Is it not remarkable how we manage to live our lives in apparent normality, while, at every moment, human civilization and the existence of all forms of life on our planet are threatened with sudden annihilation? We seem to accept this situation calmly, as if it were to be expected. Clearly, nuclear warfare presents us with the specter of a disaster so terrible that many of us would simply prefer not to think about it. But soothing our anxiety by ignoring the constant danger of annihilation will not lessen that danger. On the contrary, such an approach improves the chances that eventually our worst fears will be realized. (233 – 234)

Among the writings included in this chapter, only Helen McCloy's (as Helen Clarkson) The Long Day: A Novel of the Day After Tomorrow and Carol Amen's "Testament" are set during an imagined nuclear war, and only McCloy dares to envision the awesome and terrifying sight of a nuclear explosion. Both of these narratives present women as emotionally strong survivors who accept the inevitability of their deaths gracefully. While the narrator (and perhaps last survivor on earth) of The Long Day: A Novel of the Day After Tomorrow dies bearing the guilt of her generation for carelessly breaking the chain of life on earth, the narrator of "Testament" assures those who may discover her journal that most of earth's inhabitants were inherently caring and peaceful people. "If only we could have lived as well as we have died," she regrets (82).

The landscape of post-nuclear earth envisioned in these novels and short stories is invariably bleak and barren. Margaret St. Clair offers one of the most dismal among these futuristic visions in "The Hole in the Moon." Surviving Americans live in a vast junkyard where resources are scarce and foraging for food is a necessity for survival. Women are infected with a plague that makes them hideous in appearance and is lethal to males, if transmitted. An equally grim vision of the earth more than eight million years after nuclear war obliterates all life on the planet is presented in Caroline Janice Cherryh's (as C. J. Cherryh) "Pots." In her narrative the only signs of life on earth are just beginning to appear in the form of simple lichens and protozoans, evidence that a new evolutionary cycle is just beginning to emerge in this "sere, rust-brown world."

Other writers depict a landscape that is so depleted of resources it can support only a few inhabitants left on earth whose lives have been reduced to a primitive subsistence. In the few communities remaining on earth all energies of survivors are concentrated on day-to-day survival, and individual differences are set aside in favor of the common good. The knowledge that life may cease at any time provides a strong incentive for tolerance and cooperation as illustrated in Diana L. Paxson's "The Phoenix Garden" and Susan B. Weston's Children of the Light. Weston implies that although such a harsh existence may be difficult in contrast to the casual lifestyle enjoyed by many contemporary Americans, the survival experience evokes some of the finer character traits to be found in the human race. The characters in her novel excel in their cooperation, tolerance, and mutual acceptance of one another.

The post-nuclear societies envisioned in Joan Vinge's "Phoenix in the Ashes" and Leigh Brackett's The Long Tomorrow are rigidly fundamental and conservative in nature. Order and restraint of freedom are regarded as the only solutions which may save a world on the edge of collapse. Set in the twenty-first century, The Long Tomorrow visualizes a country where rural simplicity experiences a rebirth and the growth of cities is carefully controlled. Technology is frowned upon as destructive, advanced learning is discouraged, research is prohibited, and inventions are outlawed. All books published prior to the Destruction are burned by the New Mennonites who now rule with a controlling hand. Joan Vinge describes a restrictive post-nuclear community in "Phoenix in the Ashes" where individual freedom is no longer recognized as a human right. Catherine L. Moore even condones the use of atomic warfare in "Tomorrow and Tomorrow" to put an end to a world government that has become so restrictive in its zeal to maintain peace on earth that it has banned all forms of research, including medical. Revolutionaries who conspire to break that power are convinced that atomic warfare is a minor price to pay for their freedom, hopeful that a select group of postwar survivors "will inherit a renewed and purified Earth" (Bartter, "Nuclear Holocaust as Urban Renewal" 153).

Women often suffer a severe loss of equality in the post-nuclear societies visualized by these writers. In Joan Vinge's "Phoenix in the Ashes" women are valued solely as servants to men, given little individual choice and no educational rights, and are required to veil their faces in public. The males in Suzy McKee Charnas' Walk to the End of the World blame women for the "Wasting" that has devastated the earth and consequently enslave them as punishment. The only hope for liberation for these women is an unlikely escape into the unknown wilderness beyond the imprisoning walls of Holdfast.

Pamela Sargent offers a contrasting view of a future society that is vehemently anti-male in The Shore of Women. While the women in this novel reside in exclusively female cities, men are forced to lead a primitive existence in the surrounding wilderness and are valued only for their sperm donations which support the continuation of life through artificial insemination.

A common element in this body of literature is the emphasized necessity for human reproduction to insure the continuation of life on earth. Whether accomplished through sexual intercourse (usually without the motivation of love), artificial insemination, parthenogenesis, or cloning, reproduction is a primary concern to the few survivors who inherit the responsibility to repopulate the earth. In Susan B. Weston's Children of the Light the act of procreation based upon love has disappeared from American life. The government dispatches a "Federal Man" to impregnate the few surviving females during their fertile periods to insure the continued reproduction of the species. Alice Eleanor Jones focuses on the plight of a woman in "Created He Them" who endures a stifling, loveless marriage in order to continue to reproduce offspring because she is one of the few women left on earth who is still able to bear normal children. The characters in Diana L. Paxson's "The Phoenix Garden" view the act of making love with ambivalent frustration, torn between the urge to "make something beautiful in the midst of this hell" and the knowledge that if they reproduce themselves they run a high risk of giving birth to defective children. The women in Pamela Sargent's The Shore of Women produce offspring through artificial insemination while the Riding Women of the Plains in Suzy McKee Charnas' Motherlines reproduce parthenogenetically with young stallions.

In her essay "Apart to the End?" Barbara L. Baer stresses the differences in "focus" between men and women who write of nuclear war. "Men have had a relationship with weapons over the centuries that women have not," she writes. "Even when a male author's aim is to evoke the horror of war, the history and technology of its weaponry still fascinate him, often occupying a central point in his narrative" (167). Women, in contrast, de-emphasize weaponry and descriptions of war in their writings, interpreting the possibility of a nuclear holocaust primarily in terms of survivors. (167). Baer elaborates:

> Whatever the reason, women novelists, unburdened by the need to question *Why?*, are freer to ask the concrete question, *What?* What can we do now that this thing has happened? How can we live and make life as bearable as possible for the survivors, the children? Children, in fiction as in life, are the truly innocent. Their suffering is unbearable to us. They are also our posterity. If they die, so in a sense do we. We project ourselves in them. We hope to live on through them. (169)

As is true of other war writings authored by women throughout this century, nuclear war fiction literature written by women frequently emphasizes the individual encounters of fictionalized women characters with war. Carol Amen's "Testament" is written in the form of a journal which records the thoughts and reactions of a woman who witnesses the gradual disappearance of life on earth, including her own, resulting from nuclear radiation. Her journal entries portray a woman who is terrified but strong, furious but calm, resigned but determined as she buries two children and awaits her own death and that of her last remaining child, strengthened by her determination to leave a written testament of her personal encounter with war. In "Survivor" Katherine V. Forrest enters the thoughts of a nuclear war survivor whose life expectancy is estimated at only a few days and captures the self-assurance with which she gratefully accepts the gift of death. In a more positive but equally fatalistic illustration of post-nuclear life, Carol Emshwiller follows a family on a rare visit to the seashore in "Day at the Beach" where they experience a brief interlude of peaceful calm from the strains of survival which now characterize their tenuous lives. In a world where neighbor can no longer trust neighbor and the resources that sustain life are dwindling rapidly, Myra and Ben feel as primal as Adam and Eve sitting on the beach alone, enchanted by the rhythmic certainty of the ocean's movements in a world full of uncertainty. Mary Gordon takes the global threat of nuclear disaster and reduces it to a very personal level in "The Imagination of Disaster." The female protagonist in this narrative forces herself to imagine what a nuclear disaster would be like and how she would react to protect her family, yet she admits that such a horrific vision lies beyond even the most vivid of imaginations. The heroine of Suzy McKee Charnas' Motherlines escapes the confines of a male-dominated settlement where women are enslaved and discovers beyond the prison walls a world free of males where women are allowed to live a peaceful existence of freedom.

These women writers are often critical of contemporary American society, which they consider far too dependent upon war for conflict resolution. Future archaeologists exploring earth centuries into the future in Grace Shinell's "Atlantis Discovered: Meet the Skyscraper People of the Burning West" conclude that warfare was a way of life among earth's inhabitants who were "over-achievers of self-destruction" and destroyed themselves with environmental pollution and continual warfare. Mary Arkley Carter is equally critical of contemporary society in The Minutes of the Night. Her novel predicts how Americans might react to a nuclear holocaust, and the imagined portrayal is not flattering. The panic-stricken civilians in her novel react to crisis with irrational hysteria, violence, and greed, and prove incapable of accepting their own powerlessness and unable to confront their own individual weaknesses. Whereas Susan B. Weston's The Children of the Light suggests that nuclear war can bring out the best character traits among survivors, Carter's novel reminds us that such a crisis may also call forth the worst. In her spoof on the British upperclasses, Evelyn E. Smith's "The Last of the Spode" satirizes those who refuse to part with the amenities of life just because a nuclear disaster happens to be at hand. Kate Wilhelm enters the conscience of an engineer who assists in launching the "Bomb" but is troubled with the moral implications of his role as an accomplice in the act.

Since nuclear war fiction is predictive, it is natural that much of this literature have been written in the science fiction genre. These women's visualizations of nuclear war reach far into the future beyond the limitations of realism to a literary dimension where imagination has no boundaries. The protagonist of Susan B. Weston's Children of the Light literally steps out of present time and enters the future tense where nuclear war has already occurred. One of Alice Hastings Sheldon's (as James Tiptree, Jr.) survivors in "The Man Who Walked Home" becomes a victim of time travel trapped in a future time period, while the last survivor on earth depicted in Sheldon's "Her Smoke Rose Up Forever" is sentenced to repeatedly relive painful memories of lost hopes and dreams in a self-perpetuating psychological hell on earth.

While these writings confront the end of life on earth with fatalistic certainty and express regret over the powerlessness of earth's inhabitants to prevent the demise of civilization because of their propensity to wage war, there are occasional evidences of hope for the future expressed in this literature. In many of these post-nuclear novels and short stories, cities—symbolic of the evils of technology, corruption, and depersonalization—have been destroyed and, life is renewed in the pristine environment of the wilderness where survivors are given a second chance to begin a simpler, more self-sufficient lifestyle as pioneers of a new frontier (Bartter, "Nuclear Holocaust as Urban Renewal" 149). In Kate Wilhelm's Where Late the Sweet Bird Sings, a rebirth of human life takes place in the wilderness, offering hope that the human species will survive, despite the proliferation of clones existing on earth, because survival in such a primitive environment requires individual creativity that is lacking in clones. Although post-nuclear life on earth consists solely of the lowest forms of planets and animals in Caroline Janice Cherryh's (as C. J. Cherryh) futuristic "Pots," the lichens and protozoans offer optimistic proof that a new evolutionary cycle is beginning that may, perhaps millions of years into the future, result in homo sapiens walking the earth once again. The reunion of males and females foreshadowed in Pamela Sargent's The Shore of Women may insure the continuation of the human race. The collective cooperation of survivors in Diana L. Paxson's "The Phoenix Garden" and Susan B. Weston's Children of the Light offers optimism that life may be prolonged despite nuclear disaster. And the commitment of nuclear war survivors in Margaret St. Clair's "Quis Custodiet . . . .?" to become careful custodians of planet earth tenders hope that there may be a future existence for them and their descendants.

Regardless of their individual approaches, these women writers project readers into the future and force us to consider our own capacity for self-destruction realized only through the technological advances made during this century. Their post-nuclear visions of life in the future are consistently bleak for the human race, especially for women. The writings of these women question the validity of war, criticize our propensity for war, and caution us to stop and consider the consequences of a nuclear war before it is too late, before we must ask ourselves in horrifying regret, as the protagonist of Kate Wilhelm's "Countdown" does in retrospect, "My God, what have we done?" (178)

NOVELS

244. Brackett, Leigh. The Long Tomorrow. Garden City: Doubleday, 1955.

Brackett depicts a post-Destruction society in this novel that has reverted to agrarian simplicity and rigid fundamentalism. The New Mennonites of the twenty-first century, once a minority regarded as "quaint and queer," now dominate American society. From generation to generation these New Mennonites pass on their version of the Destruction—an atomic bombing which destroyed American cities now considered symbolic of frivolous luxuries and destructive technology. This war, ordered by the Lord, has heralded a rebirth of rural self-sufficiency throughout the country. The 13th Amendment now restricts the growth of rural communities so that cities have disappeared, although there are rumors that one city has survived somewhere in the West. Advanced learning is discouraged; curiosity is suspect. Books published prior to the Destruction have been burned, and any "artifact" such as a radio that may be discovered is regarded as a "tool of Satan" to be destroyed (Arbur 8). Anyone who dares to question the beliefs of the New Mennonites is promptly stoned to death in the old tradition.

The male protagonist of The Long Tomorrow is cursed with a questioning mind and appetite for exploration that is misplaced in such a restrictive society. Determined to break away from the stifling atmosphere of his home environment and narrow vision of his father, Len Colter heads westward to locate the only city rumored to still exist in the country. There he discovers Barterstown does exist but is a closely guarded, underground complex housing the country's only surviving atomic reactor. Barterstown has become a community of scientists "obsessed by their quest for control over nuclear power" who are, in their own way, as rigidly dogmatic as the anti-progress Mennonites Len has always known (Arbur 8). Len's pilgrimage to uncover the secrets of Barterstown represents a quest for individuality, truth and knowledge made all the more desirable because they have been suppressed in this post-Destruction age.

245. Carter, Mary Arkley. The Minutes of the Night. Boston: Little, Brown and Company, 1965.

The Minutes of the Night is a study of human character under stress, a hypothesized prediction of how Americans might react to the imminent threat of a nuclear war. "The time of this novel is the future," Carter writes in the novel's preface, "but it might equally well be the present or the past, whenever fear gains the ascendancy over reason. . ." (2). The setting is Sequoia, California, reputed to be the "safest town in the U.S.A." Overnight, the sighting of a possible warhead satellite launched by military revolutionaries in China turns this once peaceful community into a chaotic center of hysterical Americans fleeing larger population centers in search of safety. Carter depicts these panic-stricken Americans, reacting to crisis with irrational hysteria, violence, and greed, as incapable of accepting their own powerlessness and unable to confront their own individual weaknesses. While many Americans resort to looting and ransacking businesses in a frenzy of uncontrollable panic, others flock to churches in overflowing numbers in pursuit of urgent religious blessing and the assurance of salvation to soothe the anguish of their helplessness. The spirit of cooperation and mutual support necessary to survive a nuclear crisis appears to be missing in most Americans, if Carter's portrayal is accurate.

The Minutes of the Night is an examination of the predicted reactions of typical Americans to the threat of a worldwide holocaust. Although the fictionalized crisis in this novel is eventually averted, the characters are left to confront their often overblown fears, their insecurities, and the darker side of themselves that has emerged during this near disaster.

246. Charnas, Suzy McKee. Motherlines. New York: Berkley Books, 1978.

As Charnas was writing Walk to the End of the World, she explains in "Dear Frontiers: Letters from Women Fantasy and Science Fiction Writers," the story "yielded a female character so strong that she demanded and obtained a book for herself and a story for herself" (67). This sequel became Motherlines.

Set in the same bleak futuristic world as Walk to the End of the World, this novel follows Alldera, a fem who escapes the confines of Holdfast, to the unknown Wild country where she discovers two surviving groups of women—the Riding Women of the Plains, who can reproduce parthenogenetically by mating with young stallions, and the Free Fems who, like herself, have escaped Holdfast and hope to eventually liberate all fems from the victimization of men. Alldera leaves a repressive society where women have been blamed for the destruction of civilization and are regarded as lesser beings than slaves by the ruling males. She enters a utopia free of males where women live their primitive existence peacefully without masters or recrimination for the exercise of personal freedom. Alldera, writes Frances Bartkowski in Feminist Utopias, "travels not through time as do other utopian guests or dreamers, but between histories and identities" (96). During the first part of her life, she was a femmish slave in Holdfast; by the end of this novel she has spent twelve years among the women of the Grasslands. Motherlines responds to Walk to the End of the World "as a set of consolations offered by the discovery of a new community where the struggle (for Alldera) is to enter rather than to find a way to leave" (Bartkowski 83).

247. Charnas, Suzy McKee. Walk to the End of the World. New York: Ballantine Books, 1974.

"The predicted cataclysm, the Wasting, has come and—it seems—gone: pollution, exhaustion and inevitable wars among swollen, impoverished populations have devastated the world, leaving it to the wild weeds" (3). So writes Charnas as she begins her novel with a description of the future state of the earth. In her bleak and vehemently anti-female futuristic vision of society, women have been blamed for the fall of civilization and are held in contemptible bondage as a sub-human caste by men who feel responsible to guard against a reprisal by the cunning "fems". These pathologically dominant males maintain a perverted social order in which narcotics and homosexuality have been institutionalized and little encouragement is offered to advance toward a more civilized existence. Women are imprisoned in guarded compounds and forced to perform heavy labor tasks. Life, such as it is, is contained in a coastal settlement called Holdfast where seaweed and hemp are primary among the limited resources still left on earth. The only hope for freedom from this enslavement for the women of Holdfast is escape to the unknown Wild territory outside its borders.

In Science Fiction: The Best 100 Novels, David Pringle refers to Walk to the End of the World as a "savage novel, not only in the angry, political sense, but in terms of the uncompromising quality of unfettered imagination which Charnas displays" (163). As this novel was written during a "fractious time" for feminists during the early 1970s, writes Frances Bartkowski in Feminist Utopias, the society envisioned by Charnas "is an imaginary future fashioned by men as backlash to the feminism and radical politics of the late twentieth century" (82).

248. Le Guin, Ursula K. The Dispossessed: An Ambiguous Utopia. New York: Avon, 1974.

This post-holocaust novel is set sometime in the distant future when nuclear war has almost obliterated life on planet Earth. Whereas once the planet was populated by nine billion inhabitants, only a half billion (along with millions of little pieces of plastic that refuse to disintegrate) live there now. One survivor describes the state of the earth and how it came to be: "My world, my Earth, is a ruin. A planet spoiled by the human species. We multiplied and gobbled and fought until there was nothing left, and then we died. We controlled neither appetite for violence; we did not adapt. We destroyed ourselves. But we destroyed the world first" (279).

Human life has spread to the planet Urras and its moon, Anarres, but a climate of cold war tension has developed between the two very dissimilar societies. The powerful, capitalistic Urras is very similar to pre-holocaust Earth, "an exaggerated version of modern America," with its abundant resources, propensity for war, inequality among the sexes, and extremes of wealth and poverty (Wood 4). Anarres has been settled by a group of idealists who deserted the capitalistic Urras to found an ideal anarchy on its moon. Survival on the barren environment of Anarres requires the cooperation of its inhabitants, who lead a primitive but humane existence free of crime, war, governmental control, and oppression, with no need for the institutions of marriage or property ownership. But even this utopian vision is not ideal. Urras is a society "at war with itself and with its own contradictions" (Hamilton-Paterson 704). The inhabitants of Urras prove they are capable of creating an invisible system of power and privilege, even though their socialist society is supposedly apolitical, leaving readers to conclude "there is no universal prescription for Utopia" or ideal existence (Jonas 49).

Readers view both of these worlds through the dual vision of a physicist who explores the benefits and drawbacks of each society. "The overall result is a richly textured quest: an honest and ever shifting series of paradises Lost and Paradises–to–be–Regained unified by an intense awareness of bestial and angelic human urges" (Sargent 374). In her novel Le Guin combines elements of classical, nineteenth century utopian fiction with modern utopian literature and science fiction "to present an exciting and complex re-evaluation of the utopian hero and the quest for utopia" (Sargent 373).

249. McCloy, Helen Worrell Clarkson (as Helen Clarkson). The Last Day: A Novel of the Day After Tomorrow. New York: Dodd, Mead, and Company, 1959.

The Last Day is narrated from the viewpoint of a woman who may be the last surviving human on planet earth following a nuclear holocaust. Covering six days, the novel recounts the horror of those who witness the nuclear explosion and the uncertainty which grips all the survivors in a small New England coast community as they lose all contact with the outside world and realize their provisions for survival are limited. The author details the communal efforts of survivors to band together and prolong life as long as possible in the hopeless face of disaster. Each day radiation takes it toll on more and more victims until at last, by the sixth day, only the narrator is left to die alone, bearing the guilt of her species for breaking the chain of life with their own self-destruction. She regrets her generation's self-centered suicidal wish come true:

> We were the first to forget that life is not an absolute possession but an entailed estate that each generation holds in trust for the generations to come. We had not considered our ancestors or our descendants. We had considered only ourselves and we had squandered a patrimony that was not ours to squander. We were the first who had said to life: *Hold! Stop! We've had enough. We don't want any more. Our problems are insoluble. We'd rather die than live with them.* (175)

In realistic detail McCloy depicts the awesome and terrifying scene of a nuclear explosion taking place on the horizon:

> It was then that we saw it—far across the dunes, on the horizon—the vast, idiot glare, more blinding than the sun itself. The whole world woke to light and color and even shadow. The sand was dazzling white, then red as hellfire in that sudden, monstrous, man-made day that came without dawn and fled without dusk.
>
> It did not fade at once. It was vast in terms of time, as well as space. It fired the sky from horizon to zenith and hung there ponderously—a flash in slow motion that broke the familiar limits of all normal dimensions. It was as if the mouth of hell had opened and we had seen a vision of eternal fires. (44)

For the first few days following the nuclear explosion the narrator shares the cautious optimism of her husband and neighbors who hope that if they can make contact with another community, they may be able to secure necessary life-sustaining provisions. Even if their own generation has made a grave mistake, these survivors nurture the hope that their children "would rebuild the world, a world where no one would ever make war again. They could never forget what had happened this time. There would be mutants to remind them in each generation" (123). But as their radios continually fail to produce any evidence that life exists beyond their limited borders and radiation fatalities multiply with each passing day, the narrator loses faith in any future for the human race. "We could not go forward and there was no way back," she writes on the fifth day after the explosion. "The past had always been inaccessible except in memories or dreams. Now the future was inaccessible, too, except in dreams. There was only now—a now that had become a prison" (148).

In her characterizations, McCloy compares different survivors' reactions to the stress of disaster, the instinct to survive, and the knowledge that their own impending deaths are inevitable. Her novel also documents the procedures followed for protection against the radiation from a nuclear war as well as the symptoms of illness resulting from radioactive fallout, which inevitably result in death.

250. McIntyre, Vonda N. The Exile Waiting. Garden City: Nelson Doubleday, 1975.

In this novel centuries have passed since the Final War transformed Earth into an uninhabitable radioactive desert where life can only thrive underground. Survivors live in a vast cavern called the Center constructed in natural caves. In this closed society where minimal contact is maintained with the environment above ground and technology is limited, a few survivors dominate many, their vision narrowed by the protective isolationism of the Center. Everything beyond the borders of the shelter is considered potentially threatening so that it is difficult to distinguish between true dangers and those born of paranoia. Birth defects among children are common and the mutants which abound are banished to the deepest underground tunnels where they are kept a safe distance from the rest of this society which demonstrates little tolerance for divergence.

251. Moore, Catherine L. Judgment Night. 1943. New York: Dell Books, 1979.

Judgment Night, considered the most fatalistic of all of Moore's battery of science fiction, probes the question of personal ethics during warfare and their consequences for the human race. The narrative depicts war in a highly technological empire, threatened by an invasion from without and a conspiracy from within among its own citizenry. Decidedly antiwar, the novel contrasts short-term militant attitudes toward war with more reasoned pacifist attitudes which consider the long-term effects of warfare on the survival of the human race.

War in this futuristic empire has become so advanced that weaponry has been invented which will trace and attack the enemy on an individual level at the whim of his assailant. Moore explains the new invention:

> With every other comparable weapon, its operator has to sight and fire while the enemy is exposed to view. With the new one, a man may be killed not only at any distance, but at any time, once its sight has been fixed upon him. A quasi-photograph of the victim's brain pattern is snapped, and he is doomed from

that moment, though you may not choose to pull the trigger for many days. Then, irrevocably, the weapon remains focused upon him, figuratively speaking, until it is discharged. He will be unable to travel far enough to escape it, and no hiding place can save him. (57)

The creation of such weaponry is both progressive and regressive. Instead of continuing the pattern of "bigger and bigger weapons with greater range and scope," this invention reverses the direction and brings war back to an individual level. But weaponry of this nature, Moore points out, also tenders the possibility of man and machine becoming an inseparable entity during war, threatening man's capability for rational thinking and compassion.

Originally published in 1943 at the height of World War Two, the fatalism pervasive in Judgment Night, "the sense that civilization is sliding down into darkness and that the human race may well be finished, reflects the reality of the period as in a mirror" (Mathews 17).

252. Norton, Alice Mary (as Andre Norton). Star Man's Son. New York: Fawcett Crest, 1952.

Set three centuries after the nuclear holocaust, this novel pictures earth's survivors regressing to a primitive state of Amerindian tribalism. Star Men inhabit the mountains while Plainsmen rove in tribes and men driven to the South by earthquakes and volcanoes constitute a third primitive segment of society. Most feared by these survivors are the Beast Things, grotesque mutants that have resulted from atomic radiation. The protagonist of the novel, a mutant and an outcast from the Star Men tribe, embarks on a quest of his own to explore the cities of the "Old Ones" and the remnants of pre-holocaust civilization. There he observes the wreckage of the machines of war and "white bones mixed with the rust and the debris driven in by years of wind and storm"—all that remains of the holocaust:

> He had a queer distaste for approaching the dead machines more closely, no desire to touch any of the bits of rusted metal. Here and there he saw one of the atom-powered vehicles, seeming almost intact. But they were dead too. All of it was dead, in a horrible way. He experienced a vague feeling of contamination from just walking beside the wreckage. (30)

Eventually the survivors make an alliance of peace among themselves against the Beast Things with the realization that to survive will require a mutual commitment to peace and cooperation. They must not make the mistakes of the "Old Ones," who failed to see each other as integral parts of one body and resorted to war to reconcile their differences, almost destroying the earth. These survivors must carefully put the body back together again and respect each section as part of the whole, as one explains:

"If the body grows together again it must be because each part, knowing its own worth and taking pride in it, recognizes also the worth of the other two. And color of skin, or eyes, or the customs of a man's tribe must mean no more to strangers when meeting than the dust they wash from their hands before they take meat. We must come to one another free of such dust—or it will rise to blind our eyes and what the Old Ones started will continue to live for ever and ever to poison the earth." (102)

If they can live in peace, these survivors envision one day exploring space, an opportunity their forefathers abandoned "when his madness fell upon him and he reached again for slaying weapons" (222). "We who were meant to roam the stars," one survivor suggests hopefully, "go now on foot upon a ravaged earth. But above us those other worlds still hang, and still they beckon. And so is the promise still given. If we make not the mistakes of the Old Ones then shall we know in time more than the winds of this earth and the trails of this earth" (222).

253.   Sargent, Pamela. The Shore of Women. New York: Crown Publishers, 1986.

From the ruins of the old world, devastated by atomic warfare, the women in this novel create their own society where they reside in exclusively female cities while men lead a primitive existence in the surrounding wilderness. "Here," writes Jacqueline Pearce in "Feminist Utopian Vision and Social Change," "women have become associated with the city and rationality, while men are associated with uncontrolled nature" (54). Women control all science and technology and carefully guard their superior position, lest males regain power and once again attempt to destroy the earth. A historian of the Rebirth, who narrates much of the novel, explains:

Once, women had given men the power over life that women had held since the beginning of human history; so we have all been taught. Men had used their power for evil, and the world had been devastated and poisoned in ancient times by the weapons men had controlled. (95)

As the earth begins to heal from the devastation of war, women emerge as the superior sex, shunning the procreation of children as an act of love as a luxury no longer affordable in their society. The continuation of the race is assured by the donated sperm of submissive males used for artificial insemination.

One woman, exiled from the protective walls of the city, dares to trust her own innate biological urges against the learned prejudices she has been taught in a female-dominated culture all of her life and determine for herself whether male-female relationships can survive once more in this post-Destruction age.

The Shore of Women is narrated in three voices—Birana, the outcast, Arvil, her eventual mate, and Laissa, the omniscient historian. As the novel closes, Laissa's words foretell a change in this rigidly post-feminist society which may result in the reuniting of males and females and thus insure survival of the human species:

> I do not want to destroy what we have built. We saved Earth and came to know our true power. Our daughters grow up unscarred by the wounds that marked the lives of women in ancient times; we must never go back to what once exited. Yet we have made this life for ourselves at the cost of the lives of those outside. To be free, we have enslaved them. . . .
>
> We were forced to choose this pattern once because our survival was at stake. I believe it may be at stake once more. We may stagnate, as life does when it holds to a pattern that is no longer needed, which can keep it from growing and becoming something more. It may be time for us and for those outside to begin to reshape ourselves and become another kind of being. (468 – 469)

Although the women in this novel have built a new world from atomic ruins which may have many of the elements of a feminist utopia, they have in effect created a dystopia with their exclusion of men, as Pearce explains:

> Sargent shows that women are just as capable as men of creating a society that violently oppresses what it fears. The women of the cities have stereotyped all men as violent, irrational and uncaring. This novel reminds us that true human liberation must free both women and men from the constraints of cultural perceptions so that both may rediscover the spectrum of human potential and connection to nature. (54)

254. Weston, Susan B. Children of the Light. New York: St. Martin's Press, 1985.

The post-nuclear holocaust American society in this novel is revealed through the perception of a 19-year-old Jeremy Towers whose solitary canoe trip in the Great Lakes region turns into a harrowing nightmare as he steps out of his present "Time of Light" into a future time period where nuclear war has reduced the American population to 12 million survivors who are striving to insure that the human race continues. Theirs is a primitive agricultural existence where daily tasks leave little time or energy for any pursuits beyond the basics of survival, as Jeremy describes:

> It would have been like camping out—fetch the water, gather the fuel, make a fire, cook the food, heat the water to wash the dishes—except that all these activities took place in the context of a suburban neighborhood. It was as if a power failure had

struck a community that went on living for years in the daily expectation that the power would resume tomorrow. (29)

The act of procreation based upon love has long since died. A "Federal Man" representing the government impregnates the few surviving females during their fertile periods to insure the continued increase of population. But even within these constraints, the primitive subsistence of these survivors has evoked some of the finer character traits to be found in the human race. "Their culture is marked by cooperation, tolerance, and mutual acceptance, even of the disfigured and retarded, even of bizarre, confused, bewildered Jeremy" (Easton, Rev. of Children 183). As Jeremy gradually adjusts to this radically altered lifestyle, he emerges as a leader among these resilient, hopeful survivors with his attempts to advance civilization through remembered technology of the "Time of Light" from whence he came. The experience also helps Jeremy reach an understanding of his own insignificance in relation to the collective whole of society:

> Every one of those twelve million lives was important, individually; yes, but no single one mattered as long as the collective whole survived. People were like cells in a single complex organic community, each cell thinking itself the center of the world, and capable of mourning only the loss of other, specific cells. It was a terrible failure of the mind, this mental ladder that it climbed from the specific, where emotion was possible, to the abstract, where one sat indifferent on the edge of the universe. (190 – 191)

In this novel, Weston has combined the coming of age of a young man with the wrenching horror of nuclear holocaust, writing with a "vigorous prose that rises to moments of lyricism without strain and that always suggests more than it says" (Jonas, "Science Fiction" 23).

255. Wilhelm, Kate. Where Late the Sweet Birds Sang. New York: Harper and Row, 1976.

The end of civilization, assured by war, radiation, pollution, disease, and famine, is saved from complete extinction in this futuristic novel. As human fertility wanes, an enterprising Virginian family isolates themselves while they develop the technology to insure the continuation of the human race through cloning. But the new strain of beings created, many of them identical, "which may be the last remnant of human beings on earth," shares a fatal flaw—they lack both individualism and creativity. Bred in a laboratory to perform certain tasks, similar to ants in an ant colony, they excel in efficiency but not individuality and lack the necessary skills to survive in the wilderness that is left of earth.

In this brave new world, however, a few human survivors refuse to give up their identity. One naturally conceived male founds his own colony in hopes of precipitating a rebirth of humanity. Returning twenty years later he learns the human race has not been extinguished but is beginning to thrive once more. "The fan of possibilities had almost closed, but was opening once more, and each new child widened its spread. More than that couldn't be asked" (250). The most reassuring evidence of the continuation of mankind he observes upon his return are the children—all of whom are distinctly different. In The Way to Ground Zero, Martha Bartter interprets Wilhelm's novel as a warning that "no artificial substitute for humanity can inherit this earth" should we make our environment uninhabitable for human life (230).

SHORT FICTION

256. Alvarez, Julia. "Snow." Warnings: An Anthology on the Nuclear Peril. Eugene, OR: Northwest Review Books, 1984. 21 – 22.

A child's innocent introduction to American culture and the concept of war is presented sensitively in this short narrative. After her family moves to the United States in 1960, the South American immigrant who narrates the story begins to assimilate the English language through the recitation of such words such as "laundromat, corn flakes, subway, snow." When the Cuban Missile crisis begins, she is introduced to an entirely different vocabulary consisting of such words as "nuclear bomb, radioactive, half life"—and the fear of war. To illustrate what a nuclear explosion might look like, her teacher draws a picture of a mushroom on the blackboard and a "flurry of chalkmarks" illustrating the "dusty fallout that would kills us all" (21). During the first winter of the narrator's life in the United States when she observes white crystals falling from the sky, she shrieks, terrified that "the bomb" has been deployed. Her teacher assures her that the fine powder floating peacefully through the air is not the advent of war but snow, each flake different, "irreplaceable and beautiful" (22).

257. Amen, Carol. "The Last Testament." Ms. Aug. 1981: 72 – 82.

Written as a journal, which becomes the narrator's final "link to sanity, to civilization," this sensitive, intimate tragedy chronicles the thoughts and reactions of a woman to the knowledge that she and her family—as well as the rest of Americans—will eventually all die of nuclear radiation. Her husband is the family's first fatality, caught away from home on business in San Francisco, which vanished almost instantly when the bomb was dropped. "My rock," she writes of him. "I am raw. My insides ripped out without anesthetic" (73). Her children soon perceive their own limited lifespan when the leaves of a flowering plum tree turn to "papery tatters," hanging like "shrouds" from its limbs. "We're going to die, too, aren't we, Mom?" asks the narrator's oldest son (74).

As gas and food supplies dwindle and cemeteries overflow with casualties of the fallout, the writer of this journal experiences a closeness "to all poets, craftspeople, and workers who have ever tried to make a statement" of themselves. "Will anyone survive," she wonders, "to gaze at Michelangelo's creations, a Navajo rug, or my own scribblings?" (81). As evidence of the gradual extinction of all living things continues to grow, she drafts a final entry for those who may find her journal in the future and wonder about the nature of the inhabitants who preceded them : "If survivors come here. Want them to know something. We didn't act like animals. Most people were good. Helped. Tried. If only we could have lived as well as we have died. I wish—" (82)

In her narrative Amen reveals a woman's most inner thoughts and emotions during a critical time when the inhabitants of earth face the extinction of life, self-imposed by the lethal power of modern technology. Her journal entries reveal a woman who is terrified but strong, furious but calm, resigned but determined as she buries two children and awaits her own death and that of her last surviving child with graceful resignation to their fate and a determination to leave a written testament of her personal encounter with the tragic consequences of nuclear warfare.

258. Brady, Maureen. "Seneca Morning." The Question She Put To Herself. Freedom, CA: The Crossing Press, 1987. 89 – 101.

"Seneca Morning" records the experiences and corresponding emotions of a woman who joins a mass demonstration of women protesting against nuclear arms. As a statement of purpose for the news media, the narrator explains their mission:

> We are women who have blockaded the truck gate as a protest against the deployment of Cruise and Pershing II missiles to Europe. We are establishing, at this gate, the Women's Encampment for a Future of Peace and Justice, Number Two. We have spent the night here, and many useful dialogues have begun between us and some local residents, the state troopers, and even some M.P.'s. (100)

In the narrative Brady interweaves both the narrator's feelings of apprehension for the future of the planet which motivated her to march and protest (she carries a mental "vision of destruction" of what the earth may look like after the bomb—"charred and pocked and crusted with ash") with her strong sense of camaraderie among these protesting women, mainly lesbians, who share common antiwar feelings and similar sexual needs.

259. Cherryh, Caroline Janice (as C. J. Cherryh) "Pots." Afterwar. Ed. Janet Morris. New York: Baen Books, 1985. 214 – 250.

Eight and a quarter million years after the obliteration of life on earth, archaeologists from other worlds in this story carefully sift through the artifacts that have endured on this now "sere, rust-brown world." Although most of the materials of twentieth century construction have long since disintegrated, simple pieces of pottery have outlived the massive skyscrapers which scientists theorize may have lasted thousands of years intact but were eventually reduced to rubble. Life on earth has experienced a rebirth with the beginning of a new evolutionary cycle of prehistoric life that exists in the form of simple plant and animal life. "It's the weed, this little weed that gives one hope for this world," one archaeologist explains. "The little life, the things that fly and crawl—the lichens and the life on the flatlands" (224).

Over the centuries a mythology has evolved around the "peaceful Ancients" believed to have lived on earth, legends that have been an inspiration against war for these other-world inhabitants. Evidence discovered by this archaeological expedition, however, refutes the belief that earth's inhabitants were a peaceful population. The catastrophic destruction of life on earth, it strongly suggests, was self-inflicted and atomic in nature. "The statistics, the pots, the dry numbers," one archaeologist explains, "doom us to that answer. The question is answered. There were no descendants; there was no escape from the world" (236).

260. Emshwiller, Carol. "Day at the Beach." Beyond Armageddon: Twenty-One Sermons to the Dead. Eds. Walter M. Miller, Jr. and Martin H. Greenberg. New York: Donald I. Fine, Inc., 1985. 97 – 107.

Myra and her family experience a brief renewal of joy for life in this story by spending a day at the beach for the first time in four years since the Megawar so dramatically altered their lives. Completely bald, Myra and Ben live with their three-year-old retarded son in a society where electricity is an erratic and unpredictable luxury, food is a scarce commodity that precipitates daily violence among urban hunters attempting to protect their families from starvation, and gas is an even more precious resource. Neighbor cannot trust neighbor, the resources that sustain life are dwindling so rapidly. Driving ten miles to the beach is a dangerous enough risk for this family to warrant arming themselves with wrenches and hammers for protection against gas thieves, "weapons" which Ben is eventually forced to use to protect his family and limited gas supply.

Once at the seashore, the lure of the ocean seems to obliterate—if only temporarily—the memory of war and its repercussions for their heavily burdened lives:

> Then, at last, there was the sea, and it *was* exactly as it had always been, huge and sparkling and making a sound like . . . no, *drowning out* the noises of wars. Like the black sky with stars, or the cold and stolid moon, it dwarfed even what had happened. (102)

Alone on the beach, Myra and Ben experience a feeling as primal as if they were Adam and Eve: "You know there are people here and there in the houses," Myra explains, "but here, it's like we were the only ones, and here it doesn't even matter. Like Adam and Eve, we are, just you and me and our baby" (103).

In her narrative Emshwiller describes a family's brief interlude from the misery of the aftermath of nuclear war that renews marital bonds and a sense of contentment in spite of the war that has reduced the quality of their life to a daily challenge for survival.

261.   Erdrich, Louise. "Nuclear Detergent." Writing in a Nuclear Age. Ed. Jim Schley. Hanover, NH: University Press of New England, 1983. 175 – 183.

Erdrich proposes a rather ingenious solution to nuclear arms disarmament in this story which celebrates the success of a seemingly powerless woman for the antiwar cause. Jailed for trespassing on a missile site, the Reverend Blossom Treadle reveals to her cellmate how she unexpectedly discovered that the cleaning agent she and her husband peddle to financially support their ministry will reduce the complex internal mechanism of nuclear missiles, "turning their insides to mush." Interpreting their discovery as a sign of God's will for their mission in life, the couple travels around the United States "putting them intercontinental ballistic missiles smack out of commission," supporting their "ministry" with the distribution of this remarkable, multipurpose cleaning agent they have labelled W-O-W (Wonder of the World) (176).

262.   Forrest, Katherine V. "Survivor." Dreams and Swords. Tallahassee: Naiad Press, 1987. 101 – 105.

This narrative explores one woman's reaction to nuclear war and the inevitability of her own death. One of the few survivors of a nuclear holocaust, the protagonist of this short narrative is offered a lethal drug at the same time she discovers her body is covered with nitric acid burns and her life expectancy has been narrowed to only a few days. Rather than endure an extremely painful and inevitable death, the unnamed survivor accepts the gift of a cigarette and suicidal pill from a military officer as she lies calmly awaiting the peaceful approach of death.

263.   Gordon, Mary. "The Imagination of Disaster." Temporary Shelter. New York, NY: Random House, 1987. 19 – 22.

Mary Gordon takes the global threat of nuclear warfare and reduces it to a very personal level in this short story, narrated from the viewpoint of a wife and mother who attempts to imagine how she will react when nuclear disaster poisons the earth and threatens all of life on this planet.

Should she and her husband put aside pills so that they may commit suicide peacefully, holding hands, when the disaster strikes? Or should they, as he suggests, fight to survive in hopes that they may have a chance to be among the survivors, if there are any, of such a holocaust? Should she condition herself to more pain, learn better survival skills, rear her children less innocently of such a possibility? If such a disaster were to occur, would she be able to kill her best friend in order for her own children to have food?

Even though all human beings on earth, like our predecessors, must live with the knowledge of death, none of us has the capability to imagine "the poisoned earth abashed, empty of all we know," writes Gordon (22). Such a vision is beyond the limitations of our most vivid imaginations, even at their most expansive moment.

264. Haake, Katharine. "The Meaning of Their Names." Writing in a Nuclear Age. Ed. Jim Schley. Hanover, NH: University Press of New England, 1983. 47 – 61.

A young woman who loses a lover during the Vietnam War and consequently becomes a collector of names for nuclear disarmament petitions learns that the war has not left everyone with the same antiwar commitment she feels so strongly in this story. During her pilgrimage from Sacramento to Washington, D.C., Constance discovers that most people who sign her anti-nuclear petition do so because of their motivation for personal preservation, not out of concern for the continuance of the human race.

> In the end their motives were alike—for their own good. Constance wanted that their motives should be different. She wanted that they shouldn't have their weaknesses and prejudices, which showed so clearly in their eyes, in how they slung their bodies back against their seats. Where had they been when the other war was on? Why had they strayed so far from home? (56)

Although Constance recognizes she is but a "small person" with little power, she idealistically clings to the belief that the accumulation of names of many "small people" may result in a positive change for peace. "However small they might be, they might, by living just and proper lives, transcend the limitations of their size and move the greater people to recognize the meaning of their names" (56 – 57).

Also a collector of numbers, Constance records the number of deaths that have resulted from war for each country on earth, beginning with the fatality count during the Vietnam War, continuing into the 1980s with the death toll worldwide exceeding ten million. But the threat of nuclear war produces numbers beyond Constance's imagination. "For that kind of number was unimaginable. That kind of number was not to be written or fathomed. That kind of number sent her reeling—eventually off to Washington, D.C., armed with her petitions and her faith" (58).

"If all people dream of peace," she wonders, "why are things the way they are?" (56). But all people do not dream of peace, she soon learns. Despite the lingering aftermath of the Vietnam War and increasing possibility of nuclear exchange, Constance encounters Americans once she arrives in the nation's capital who are unwilling to sign a petition to make a commitment against war.

265. Jones, Alice Eleanor. "Created He Them." Fantasy and Science Fiction June 1955: 29 – 37.

This narrative is a portrait of a woman trapped in a "desolate, dying, bombed-out world, with its creeping wastelands and its freakish seasons," where even the basic necessities of survival are scarce, and an equally stifling marriage with an intolerant, self-centered husband. Even though Ann Crothers' existence is miserable—her only real joy was once her children who were taken away at the age of three, as are all children in this postwar society, to be raised in a communal Center—she feels compelled to continue to live because she is one of the few women left on earth who is still able to bear normal children. "We hate each other," she frankly confesses to her husband, "but we breed true" (37). "We have to live," she tells him. "Till we are all called in, or our children, or our children's children. Till there is nowhere else to go" (37). Jones portrays a post-holocaust woman who endures her own unhappiness for the sake of the survival of the human race threatened by nuclear war.

266. MacLean, Katherine. "Games." Operation Future. Ed. Groff Conklin. New York: Permabooks, 1955. 301 – 310.

MacLean applies parapsychology to the concept of war in this unusual short story which juxtaposes a young boy's fantasy of war play with his duel identity as a pacifist-scientist, imprisoned when he refuses to reveal his biochemical research findings because he fears they might be applied to warfare. Ronnie involuntarily moves back and forth between identities, attempting in childlike confusion and adult wisdom to reconcile the two competing forces in his mind. Ronnie has been given the psychic gift of entry into the scientist's mind and the ability to draw from its rich contents, as one would draw words from a dictionary, as he matures and learns to differentiate between the childhood fantasy of war games and the destructive reality of war often realized only during adulthood.

267. MacLean, Katherine. "Interbalance." Fantasy and Science Fiction Oct. 1960: 63 – 69.

Contrasting attitudes toward the continuation of post-nuclear life are explored in this narrative set in South America. While the young native girl in the story grows up with the belief that the key to survival is prolific breeding and a belief in the spiritual power of Interbalance, an American scientist searches for the key to immunity to radiation "to save the race" in his secret laboratory. Although his research is aimed at supporting life, the scientist ostracizes himself and his son from the neighboring "degenerating savages" and is quite willing to shoot those who would disagree with his narrow, autocratic vision of life. Could he be affected by radiation sickness or is old age contributing to his demented perception of life? "Interbalance" intervenes to save "civilization" from his "advanced learning" before he has an opportunity to complete his research or blow away the native population.

268. Moore, Catherine L. (with Henry Kuttner as Lewis Padgett). "Beggars in Velvet." Mutant. New York: Gnome Press, 1953. 113 – 164.

This narrative envisions the United States in the twenty-first century, following the 1950 atomic Blowup, as a nation of decentralized atomic power (each village has its own protective cache) and greatly reduced population. Exposure to radiation has caused mutations in a minority of Americans called Baldies, who have telepathic power. While most mutants have accepted their minority status as "beggars in velvet," realizing their telepathic power is a menace as well as "the greatest privilege any race on Earth has ever known," a particular strain of paranoid Baldies advocate war against humans in order to gain their rightful superiority. A three-way conflict thus threatens the peaceful coexistence among humans, the peaceful Baldies, and the aggressive, paranoid Baldies. When a pogrom threatens the safety of one small community, its inhabitants destroy their own village and retreat underground to begin an experimental community "benevolently" controlled by telepaths who plan to reduce humans to a minority status and attempt to discover how those species left on earth can coexist in peace.

269. Moore, Catherine L. (with Henry Kuttner as Lawrence O'Donnell). "Clash By Night." Astounding Science-Fiction March 1943: 9 – 39.

This futuristic narrative reflects back 900 years to the twenty-fifth century and examines the civilization that has evolved on the planet Venus. All that remains of earth at this time is a star "since atomic power had been unleashed there two centuries ago. The scourge had spread like flame, melting continents and leveling mountains" (11). Before the destruction of earth, there were few unexplored frontiers left, but on Venus such territories still abound. Below ground the undersea culture of the Keeps maintains a highly specialized, scientific, social culture devoted to cultural progress. Above ground a primitive, warlike culture reigns led by bands of Free Companies, "harsh, gallant, indomitable," who serve the "god of battles"(10). As doomed as Tyrannosaurus Rex was once destined for extinction on earth, this society of warriors, whose propensity toward war heralds their eventual obliteration, serves as an evolutionary step in the eventual eradication of warfare on Venus, their legends becoming infamous in the pages of interplanetary literature.

270. Moore, Catherine L. (with Henry Kuttner as Lawrence O'Donnell). "Fury." <u>Astounding Science-Fiction</u>. May 1947: 6 – 49 and June 1947: 103 – 162 and July 1947: 105 – 145.

This lengthy short story is set in the twenty-seventh century, six hundred years since the destruction of earth. As man invades the alien land of Venus, where the ecology is similar to earth, he discovers the planet is still in the Jurassic period, an era long since passed on earth before the evolution of man began. He discovers his weapons are "either too weak or too potent" and will not help him conquer or survive. "He could destroy utterly, or he could wound lightly, but he could not live on the surface of Venus. He was faced with an antagonist no man had ever known, because the equivalent had perished from earth before marsupials changed to true mammals. He faced fury" (7). The science that destroyed earth but made interplanetary travel possible can also build artificial environments under the ocean. On this alien planet, man returns "to the sea from which he sprang. The race had returned to the racial womb" (7). A few mutants whose body compositions were altered by atomics can anticipate a life expectancy on Venus of more than seven hundred years.

271. Moore, Catherine L. (with Henry Kuttner as Lewis Padgett) "Humpty Dumpty." <u>Mutant</u>. New York: Gnome Press, 1953. 166 – 209.

In this narrative the atomic Blowup results in the formation of a sub-species of bald mutants with telepathic powers whose lives are endangered by the hatred of the majority humans who fear their superior intellectual power. The Baldies work to perfect two inventions which may insure their self-preservation—an Inductor, which can induce telepathic power in non-telepaths, and Operation Apocalypse, the release of a virus which could destroy all non-telepathic humans. A pacifist strain of Baldies favor the use of Operation Apocalypse only as a last resort as self-defense in the event of a pogrom to eradicate their species, while a paranoid strain of mutants favors the release of the virus to exterminate the human race and claim their rightful status as the superior race.

As the Inductor reaches the final stages of production and undergoes testing, the Baldies discover that only young children whose minds are still open and whose superegos have not get been formed, who have not yet built defensive walls of fear and mistrust to protect themselves, can become telepaths. The story ends as the Baldies offer their discovery for acceptance or rejection to the humans, whose decision will determine if the mutants and human can live in peace or will wage war once more.

272. Moore, Catherine L. (with Henry Kuttner as Lewis Padgett) "The Lion and the Unicorn." <u>Mutant</u>. New York: Gnome Press, 1953. 73 – 112.

A race of bald mutants emerges on earth after the atomic Blowup, a minority divided into two opposing factions. Baldies who believe gradual assimilation into the human strain is the best way to insure peaceful coexistence, differ in their position from those paranoid mutants who advocate a widespread pogrom to wipe out the humans and pave the way for the birth of a "Baldy civilization, complete and perfect." The more peaceful Baldies use their telepathic powers with discretion, lest the demonstration of their superior intellectual skills alienate them from the humans who might retaliate in fear and annihilate the entire species. The predicament of his species is characterized metaphorically by one Baldy: "We're in the position of a unicorn in a herd of horses. We daren't use our horn to defend ourselves. We've got to pretend to be horses" (98). Living on "borrowed time," their one hope for survival and freedom to practice their telepathy openly without discrimination or fear of reprisal is to create a civilization on another planet.

In this story a Baldy who has lived among the primitive, nomadic Hedgehounds since he was adopted as an infant learns that he is not human and must make the difficult choice between the identity of his birth and that of his upbringing.

273. Moore, Catherine L. (with Henry Kuttner as Lewis Padgett). "The Piper's Son." Mutant. New York: Gnome Press, 1953. 3 – 34.

Hard radiation left after the atomic Blowup produces a race of bald mutants on earth who are blessed with telepathic powers but cursed with the necessity to suppress this unique intellectual trait in order to insure self-preservation. For to employ their full telepathic powers might intimidate and offend the majority humans, who might then retaliate out of fear and distrust. "We're really buying safety for our species by foregoing certain individual advantages," one Baldy explains. "Hostages to destiny—and destiny spares us. But we get paid too, in a way. In the coinage of future benefits—negative benefits, really, for we ask only to be spared and accepted—and so we have to deny ourselves a lot of present, positive benefits. An appeasement to fate" (27).

In this story one of the mutants whose son shows antisocial tendencies by the age of eight worries his father that he may not develop the compliant behavior necessary for acceptance as a mutant minority. Reluctantly the father uses his telepathic power to begin "reconditioning" his son's thoughts into more socially acceptable channels so that hopefully he will find acceptance as a member of a minority in a world dominated by humans.

274. Moore, Catherine L. (with Henry Kuttner as Lewis Padgett). "Three Blind Mice." Mutant. New York: Gnome Press, 1953. 35 – 72.

The effects of atomic radiation have created a race of telepathic mutants called Baldies on earth, most of whom have accepted their minority status and have peacefully blended their lives with non-telepathic humans in hopes of gradual and complete acceptance of their differences. But one group of psychotically paranoid mutants remembers all too clearly the lynchings of mutants in past days and considers themselves to be "homo superior." These paranoids threaten the preservation of all Baldies with their plan to subjugate the human race by creating an atmosphere of "ultimate social chaos" which they hope will upset the "smoothly running machine" organized by humans and allow a swift overthrow of power. The more peaceful Baldies fear such a radical move may prove suicidal for the entire race of mutants. For if the humans detected such a strategy, they would surely annihilate all mutants. The ensuing conflict pits the more peaceful Baldies, willing to accept gradual social change, with more militant mutants who view their race as a "helpless minority" of "gods pretending to be human because it'll please humans," anxious to take their rightful place as the dominant race on earth (64).

275. Moore, Catherine L. (with Henry Kuttner as Lewis Padgett). "Tomorrow and Tomorrow." Astounding Science-Fiction. Jan. 1947: 6 – 56 and Feb. 1947: 140 – 177.

Atomic warfare is regarded as an inevitable step in evolutionary progress for mankind in this long narrative. After an aborted World War Three threatens the survival of life on earth, a Global Peace Commission is established which has maintained peace for the past one hundred years, forbidding any technological research and prohibiting interplanetary travel. Its unlimited control and stifling effect on progress are questioned by those who envision a more progressive future for earth, even if destruction is a resulting byproduct. As variant possibilities of planet earth are explored, those who oppose the Global Peace Commission become convinced that atomic warfare is a minor price to pay for the investment of a better earth. The earth will not be totally destroyed by deployment of the bomb, they are assured by scientists, but improved by the stronger remnants of civilization which survive to rebuild the planet. In taking a "long step backward," earth's inhabitants will really be moving forward, perhaps toward a utopian society where research is supported, diseases are eradicated, and human beings enjoy a lifespan of 200 years.

276. Morris, Janet. "Hero's Welcome." Afterwar. New York: Baen Books, 1985. 14 – 25.

Nuclear war survivors retaliate against a veteran who pays for his involvement in nuclear war with his life in this short story. Post-nuclear America is depicted as sparsely populated with scarce resources, little communication, and no currency. A restaurant owner "barters" the virginity of his 16-year-old daughter to the veteran but ambushes him from behind shortly after orgasm. Just before he is murdered, the veteran describes nuclear war to the inquiring daughter as both the responsibility and suicide of everyone on earth. "Everyone fought in this one, honey," he confides to her.

"The whole world. And everybody died. On the spot. Some of us just don't know it yet" (25).

277. Oates, Joyce Carol. "Nuclear Holocaust." Raven's Wing. New York: E. P. Dutton, 1986. 244 – 246.

In this brief narrative the narrator conversing with a therapist reveals numerous psychological problems. Although the closest she has come to the idea of a nuclear holocaust is "a picture of a Japanese man whose shadow was baked into a wall when the atomic bomb went off," she prays that God will send "the bomb to punish us at last in Your mercy and bless us in the same instant, for ever and ever" so that she, along with all other sinners, can return safely to Him (245 – 246).

278. Paley, Grace. "Anxiety." Writing in a Nuclear Age. Ed. Jim Schley. Hanover, NH: University Press of New England, 1983. 191 – 195.

The concern of a woman for a younger generation of Americans who may experience the horror of a nuclear holocaust is expressed in this short narrative. The narrator of the story, leaning from her tenement window to talk to two young fathers and their children walking below, berates one of the fathers for impatiently admonishing his daughter, for she may very well be a member of the "last generation of humankind." "Son," the narrator warns, "I must tell you that mad men intend to destroy this beautifully made planet. That the imminent murder of our children by these men has got to become a terror and a sorrow to you. . ." (193). Overcome by an overwhelming surge of maternal protection for all children who will undoubtedly live with the threat of nuclear war during their fragile lifetime, the narrator entreats these young fathers to cherish every moment they possibly can with their children while there is still time.

279. Paxson, Diana L. "The Phoenix Garden." Afterwar. New York: Baen Books, 1985. 132 – 170.

Described in the introduction as a story of "survivalist reality" of that place where "metaphysics and reality meet," this story focuses on the radically changed lives of members of a small California community six months after nuclear war obliterates the San Francisco area and leaves unmeasurable amounts of radiation behind to haunt the war's survivors. These survivors plant gardens, arm themselves in self-defense, and cling tenaciously to one another for communal strength, uncertain how long they will endure in a post-nuclear world. Torn between the urge to "make something beautiful in the midst of this hell," and the knowledge that reproducing themselves may result in defective children, the characters in this story view the act of making love with ambivalent frustration. The miscarriage of a deformed fetus by one of the young women of the community is received as both a relief and a cause for mourning among the closely united survivors of Phoenix Creek who long to grasp onto some tangible proof that life will continue. Individual differences melt away in this community when these survivors are faced with their own mortality. Even a woman reputed to practice witchcraft is offered acceptance and her mystical relationship with the communal garden is allowed to flourish unquestioned in a world where so little seems to thrive. The evidence that this barren soil may again support life, brought forth by the hands of this woman, offers hope for the future as expressed from the viewpoint of one survivor:

> Maybe the tortured world outside these hills would one day overwhelm them, but if the life he felt in this garden could become a fertile seed underneath the ashes of the world, then there was hope. Surely it would be better to live with hope's illusion than to starve the spirit waiting for certainty. (169 – 170)

280. St. Clair, Margaret (as Idris Seabright). "The Hole in the Moon." Fantasy and Science Fiction February 1952: 122 – 126.

St. Clair depicts a post-nuclear future in this narrative where the moon has been marred by a lunar explosion and Americans live in junkyards, spending their days foraging for food. Women are infected with a plague—the "enemy's masterpiece"—which betrays itself "only in their pitted skins, their roughened voices, their cracked lips" (123). When this plague is transmitted to males, it results in a swift and unpleasant death. Males have become wary of intimate relationships yet are frustrated bitterly by their continued natural desire for women.

281. St. Clair, Margaret. "Quis Custodiet . . . .?" Startling Stories July 1948: 109 – 114.

Three hundred years after the dropping of the "big bombs"—which reduced the population of North America from 222,000,000 to 500,000—the flowering of a plant is regarded as a special miracle in this story. Two main factions are left on earth to determine its future. While the Formers are committed to rejuvenating and protecting life in all forms, the Blown-ups feel equally compelled to destroy all forms of life. When the Formers discover a Blown-up spy in their midst and see the opportunity to use him as an experiment which would sterilize all Blown-ups, one wise Former opposes such a strategy. "Without the Blown-ups," she points out, "we might forget" the threat of nuclear destruction and become too casual in the protection of earth's scarce resources. Looking back in time, she explains her concern:

> "There were thousands of human generations before the bombs, and none of them understood it the way we do. Long before the bombs our people chopped down the forests and left burned-over stumps where the trees used to stand. They plowed up the grasslands and made deserts out of them. They tore the heart out of the continents and sent it floating down in

the muddy water of the rivers to end at the bottom of the sea. The bombs just finished something that had been long ago begun.

Earth's done for. We destroyed it. But we won't always be on earth. Some day we will visit the other worlds. And then we'll have a chance, again, to be custodians." (114)

Realizing they are risking their own survival against the anti-life Blown-ups, the Formers allow the spy to escape in hopes that the continued presence of Blown-ups on earth will serve as a reminder that humans once failed as custodians of life and will continue to motivate the Formers to remain careful guardians of future life on earth.

282. Sheldon, Alice Hastings (as James Tiptree, Jr.). "Her Smoke Rose Up Forever." Final Stage: The Ultimate Science Fiction Anthology. Ed. Edward L. Ferman and Barry N. Malzberg. New York: Charterhouse, 1974. 253 – 278.

A nuclear holocaust leaves a lone survivor in this story who lives in a perpetual eternity of psychological pain, doomed to continually relive only the most painful memories of loss from his pre-Holocaust life, ranging from a broken heart suffered during adolescence to the more significant almost-won Nobel prize during adulthood:

What happened? He does not know, can never know which of the dooms or some other had finally overtaken them, nor when; only that he is registering eternity, not time, that all that lived here has been gone so long that even time is still. Gone, all gone; centuries or millennia gone, all gone to ashes under pulseless stars in the icy dark, gone forever. Saving him alone and his trivial pain. (271)

Everything that once lived on planet earth has died "excepting only that in himself which he would most desperately wish to be dead" (271). The earth is a barren plain of "endless, lifeless rubble under a cold black sky, in which he or some pattern of energies sense much more that distant presence: wreckage, machines, huge structures incomprehensibly operative, radiating dark force in the nightmare world. . . ," but the sole survivor is condemned to live eternally with his worst reminiscences as his only companion (268).

283. Sheldon, Alice Hastings (as James Tiptree, Jr.). "The Man Who Walked Home." Looking Ahead: The Vision of Science Fiction. Eds. Dick Allen and Lori Allen. New York: Harcourt Brace Jovanovich, 1975. 280 – 293.

The worldwide holocaust envisioned in this narrative, precipitated by an accidental explosion, ends the Age of Hardscience, alters the biosphere so that climatic cycles are ever-changing, leaves the earth defaced by craters, obliterates much of the world's population, and forces the earth's few survivors to regress to a primitive level of existence.

One of the few survivors of the explosion also becomes a victim of time travel, catapulted into the future where "our past is his future and our future is his past." He remains stranded in a future time period "of profound otherness," severed from his life on earth as he struggles across time and space to try to return home.

284. Shinell, Grace. "Atlantis Discovered: Meet the Skyscraper People of the Burning West." <u>Nuke-Rebuke: Writers & Artists Against Nuclear Energy & Weapons</u>. Ed. Morty Sklar. Iowa City: The Spirit That Moves Us Press, 1984. 114 – 133.

Written from a futuristic perspective, this narrative is presented as a sociological examination of humans living during the second millennium who destroyed themselves with environmental pollution and continual warfare. "We must conclude," the narrator writes, "that the Skyscraperans' most damning vice was over-achieving. They were such selfish producers that in the final analysis they were over-achievers of self-destruction" (126).

Historical analysis of this civilization indicates warfare "was a way of life" which existed without benefit of rules or guidelines. This warring civilization showed a preference for red fire as a weapon, and during the "war to end all wars" fires "raged uncontrollably over the earth in all-consuming holocausts from which only a few sacral isles escaped" (115).

Among the artifacts of this civilization that were preserved and have been illustrated by the author at the end of the story is a cannon which she has labeled a "Southern Genitalia Monument (uncircumcized)."

285. Smith, Evelyn E. "The Last of the Spode." <u>Fantasy and Science Fiction</u> June 1953: 123 – 126.

In this science fiction satire on British aristocracy, set in post-holocaust Great Britain, the last surviving members of the British upper class continue to argue linguistics and look down their noses at Americans while nibbling on scones and sipping tea. The "most ghastly" horror they confront is the realization they may run out of tea while awaiting the danger of radiation to subside during the next fifty years.

Smith explains her motivation for writing "The Last of the Spode" in the story's introduction: "The British are so fond of writing science fiction in the American idiom that I felt it only courteous for an American (me) to write one with a British flavour," she writes (123).

286. Vinge, Joan D. "Phoenix in the Ashes." <u>Millennial Women</u>. Ed. Virginia Kidd. New York: Delcorte Press, 1978. 66 – 123.

Set in the post-holocaust period where war has devastated the landscape of North America so that it now resembles the barrenness of the moon, this narrative depicts life as existing only in small, scattered communities.

A Brazilian prospector scanning the ruins of Los Angeles basin area for mining resources develops amnesia after his helicopter crashes near one of the country's few surviving communities. Cristovao meets a woman who has been cast out of her community as a pariah because she dared to love a man her father disapproved. In Amanda's community, rigid fundamentalism rules and women are valued only as servants to men. They must cover their faces with veils and are considered unworthy of even being taught how to write. As mutual outcasts, Amanda and Cristovao are able to develop their own reality and separate peace apart from a society where individuality is longer recognized.

287. Wilhelm, Kate. "Countdown." Countdown to Midnight: Twelve Great Stories About Nuclear War. Ed. H. Bruce Franklin. New York: Daw Books, 1984. 166 – 179.

First published in 1968, this story monitors the thoughts of an engineer who assists in launching a missile into space which houses the "Bomb" even as he questions the morality of the decision in his own conscience. Ken would like to accept the simple rationalization of a fellow engineer that if *they* (the Russians) rendezvoused in space ten days ago and have remained silent then we must anticipate the worst and act accordingly. He'd rather his conscience not be burdened by the moral implications of this gigantic "beast of burden" with such destructive force. He keeps reassuring himself that his wife and infant daughter will welcome him home without reproach for his role in the offensive. Despite his best efforts to build a psychological defense, Ken feels compelled to ask himself the question which others with equally troubled consciences will also undoubtedly ask, perhaps all too late: "My God, what have we done?" (178).

288. Willis, Connie. "A Letter from the Clearys." Fire Watch. New York: Bluejay Books, 1985. 115 – 128.

Evidence that a nuclear war has taken place is confirmed in this narrative when a Colorado family receives a letter two years after it was mailed by friends in Chicago who were supposed to visit but never appeared. The narrator's father theorizes what crisis may have intervened to prevent their trip:

> "I would imagine they were close enough to Chicago to have been vaporized when the bombs hit. If they were, they were lucky. Because there aren't any mountains like ours around Chicago. So they got caught in the fire storm or they died of flash burns or radiation sickness or else some looter shot them. . . . I have a theory about what happened the summer

before last. I don't think the Russians started it or the United
States either. I think it was some little terrorist group
somewhere or maybe just one person. I don't think they had
any idea what would happen when they dropped their bomb. I
think they were just so hurt and angry and frightened by
the way things were that they just lashed out. With a bomb."
(124 – 125)

Evidence also exists that the deadly aftermath of the war is
spreading, even into the safety of the Colorado mountains. Weather
patterns are changing, gardens are becoming less productive, looting
is on the increase, and paranoia is running rampant. The letter that
the narrator discovers confirms the unspoken suspicions of this
family that their lives will be tragically shortened by the
repercussions of nuclear war.

LITERARY CRITICISM

Andreadis, Athena. "Expanding to Embrace the Universe." Belles
Lettres Spring 1989: 3.

Arbur, Rosemarie. "Leigh Brackett: No 'Longer Goodbye' is Good
Enough." The Feminine Eye: Science Fiction and the Women Who Write
It. Ed. Tom Staicar. New York: Frederick Ungar, 1982. 1 – 13.

Baer, Barbara L. "Apart to the end?" Commonweal 22 March 1985:
167 – 170.

Barron, Neil, ed. Anatomy of Wonder: A Critical Guide to Science
Fiction. 3rd ed. New York: R. R. Bowker, 1987.

Bartkowski, Frances. Feminist Utopias. Lincoln: University of
Nebraska Press, 1989.

Bartter, Martha A. "The Hand that Rocks the Cradle." Extrapolation
30.3 (1989): 255 – 266.

Bartter, Martha A. "Nuclear Holocaust as Urban Renewal."
Science-Fiction Studies 13 (1986): 148 – 158.

Bartter, Martha A. "Science Fiction: The Roots of 'Star Wars.'"
USA Today May 1990: 52 – 54.

Bartter, Martha A. The Way to Ground Zero: The Atomic Bomb in
American Science Fiction. Westport, CT: Greenwood Press, 1988.

Brians, Paul. Nuclear Holocausts: Atomic War in Fiction, 1895-
1984. Kent, OH: Kent State University Press, 1987.

Caldicott, Helen. Untitled. My Country is the Whole World: An Anthology of Women's Work on Peace and War. Ed. Cambridge Women's Peace Collective. Boston: Pandora Press, 1984. 232 – 234.

Cooper, Susan. "New high for sci-fi." Rev. of The Dispossessed, by Ursula K. Le Guin. Christian Science Monitor 26 June 1974: F4.

Curley, Thomas. "No Place to Hide." Rev. of The Minutes of the Night, by Mary Arkley Carter. The New York Times Book Review 12 Sept. 1965: 46.

"Dear Frontiers: Letters from Women Fantasy and Science Fiction Writers." Frontiers 2.3 (1977): 62 – 78.

Easton, Tom. Rev. of Children of the Light, by Susan B. Weston. Analog Science Fiction-Science Fact. Oct. 1986: 183.

Easton, Tom. Rev. of The Shore of Women, by Pamela Sargent. Analog Science Fiction-Science Fact. Aug. 1988: 139 – 140.

Franklin, H. Bruce. "Nuclear War and Science Fiction." Countdown to Midnight: Twelve Great Stories About Nuclear War. Ed. H. Bruce Franklin. New York: Daw Books, 1984.

Frisch, Adam J. "Toward New Sexual Identities: James Tiptree, Jr." The Feminine Eye: Science Fiction and the Women Who Write It. Ed. Tom Staicar. New York: Frederick Ungar, 1982. 48 – 59.

Hamilton-Paterson, James. "Allegorical imperatives." Rev. of The Dispossessed, by Ursula K. Le Guin. Times Literary Supplement 20 June 1975: 704.

Jonas, Gerald. "Of Things to Come." Rev. of The Dispossessed, by Ursula K. Le Guin. The New York Times Book Review 26 Oct. 1975: 48 – 49.

Jonas, Gerald. Rev. of The Shore of Women, by Pamela Sargent. The New York Times Book Review 18 Jan. 1987: 33.

Jonas, Gerald. "Science Fiction." Rev. of Children of the Light, by Susan B. Weston. The New York Times Book Review 9 Mar. 1986: 23.

Magill, Frank N., ed. Survey of Science Fiction Literature. Vol. 2 Englewood Cliffs: Salem Press, 1979. 5 vols.

Mathews, Patricia. "C. L. Moore's Classic Science Fiction." The Feminine Eye: Science Fiction and the Women Who Write It. Ed. Tom Staicar. New York: Frederick Ungar, 1982. 14 – 24.

Newman, John and Michael Unsworth. Future War Novels: An Annotated Bibliography of Works in English Published Since 1946. Phoenix: Oryx Press, 1984.

Parish, Margaret. "Science Fiction." English Journal Feb. 1978: 117 – 119.

Pearce, Jacqueline. "Feminist Utopian Vision and Social Change." Alternatives 16.3 (1989) 50 – 54.

Pringle, David. Science Fiction: The 100 Best Novels. New York: Carroll and Graf, 1985.

Rosen, Michael. "Fems and fillies." Rev. of Walk to the End of the World and Motherlines, by Suzy McKee Charnas. Times Literary Supplement 7 Nov. 1980: 1264.

Sargent, Lyman Tower. Epilogue. America as Utopia. Ed. Kenneth M. Roemer. New York: Burt Franklin and Company, 1981. 373 – 374.

Thompson, Janna. "Women and War." Women's Studies International Forum. 14.1 – 2 (1991): 63 – 75.

Trenfield, Karen. "Feminist SF: Reality or Fantasy: a review of recent sf by women." Hecate 4.1 (1978): 99 – 108.

Wood, Michael. "Coffee Break for Sisyphus." Rev. of The Dispossessed, by Ursula K. Le Guin. The New York Review of Books 2 Oct. 1975: 3.

Yoke, Carl. "From Alienation to Personal Triumph: The Science Fiction of Joan D. Vinge." The Feminine Eye: Science Fiction and the Women Who Write It. Ed. Tom Staicar. New York: Frederick Ungar, 1982. 103 – 130.

5

War and Peace

INTRODUCTION

The novels and short fictions written by American women included in this chapter include diverse interpretations of war and peace that are not specific to World War One, World War Two, the Vietnam War, or nuclear war as well as writings which encompass more than one of these wars. The chapter also includes narratives of foreign wars, Indian war narratives, and fictions which predict what futuristic wars may be like during coming centuries. Also contained in this chapter is utopian fiction written by American women who have visualized societies where war is absent and peace is a natural aspect of life.

Some American women authors of this century have written fictional interpretations of foreign wars which have been waged without American involvement. Foremost among these are Pearl S. Buck's novels and short stories which emphasize the effect of an almost constant state of war on the common people of China during the first half of the century. The writings of Agnes Smedley and Adet Lin (as Tan Yun) focus on individual Chinese women swept into the turmoil of war and revolution. Short stories written by Cecilia Manguerra Brainard and Linda Ty-Casper are set during revolutionary periods in the Philippines while Christina Glendenning's images of war are drawn from Central America, Diana Chow's are set in Southeast Asia, and Barbara Bedway's originate in the Middle East.

American war fiction necessarily includes Indian narratives which celebrate a distinctive culture and corresponding outlook on war. Anna Lee Walters honors a Pawnee warrior born into the wrong century in "Warriors" who clings to an outmoded reverence for beauty and individuality and passes these ideals on to his young niece before he dies as a dejected hobo in a society which no longer honors such ideals. Opal Lee Popkes visualizes an Indian family in "Zuma Chowt's Cave" continuing their primitive existence while hiding in a west coast cave. So isolated are they from white culture, these Indians are unaware that a world war is ongoing. Pamela Sargent depicts a young Indian woman in "The

Broken Hoop" who is unwilling to allow her imaginative powers to transport her to a more peaceful world free of white man's domination.

Women's varied relationships to war are emphasized in these writings. Denna Metzger contrasts male warrior and female pacifist attitudes in her innovative novella The Woman Who Slept With Men to Take the War Out of Them. Women make love with soldiers, according to her fiction, to reaffirm their commitment to life over death and to find unity, if only briefly, through that union. Laura Kalpakian characterizes an elderly mother in "The Battle of Manila" who endures the prolonged pain of the loss of her son to war while she wages her own battle for independence and mental stability threatened by the aging process. Another elderly woman portrayed in Mildred Clingerman's "Minister Without Portfolio" quite unexpectedly saves the earth from destruction by invading aliens with her convincing spiritual and pacifist beliefs. In one of the few stories set during the Korean War, a Korean-American prostitute in Pearl S. Buck's "Duet in Asia" is victimized by war and her misfortune of finding herself trapped between two cultures. While the woman warrior in Maxine Kong Kingston's "White Tigers" takes a brief respite from war to give birth to a son and then resumes fighting, the maternal desire to procreate proves stronger than the aggressive drive to continue military service for the protagonist in Rhondi Vilott's "Persephone."

Sally Gearhart offers an innovative vision of women as non-violent protectors of the environment against male aggression in "The Chipko." Katherine MacLean offers a similar view of ecological warfare waged by environmentalists to protect endangered wildlife in "Small War."

Women characters in Joanna Russ's futuristic "When It Changed" and Alice Hastings Sheldon's (as James Tiptree, Jr.) "Houston, Houston, Do you Read?" resist the infiltration of men into their peaceful all-female societies because they fear that allowing men to live with them might result in loss of sexual equality and the possible reintroduction of war. In contrast, Pamela Sargent visualizes alien females as warriors descending upon earth to conquer the human race in her short story "Shadows." Kit Reed depicts a different kind of war in "Songs of War" where women flee the domestic homefront in pursuit of sexual equality, but their revolution against males eventually dissolves for lack of unity.

A minority of women examine war from a male perspective, but seldom do they attempt to simulate the combat experience in their fictions. Cecilia Manguerra Brainard enters the thoughts of a soldier in "The Black Man in the Forest" who acknowledges during a contemplative moment the common humanity he shares with the dead soldier he has killed. Sara Vogan's "Scenes From the Homefront" contrasts the attitudes of three generations of American males toward war, the youngest of these refusing to fight in a war he considers unjust. Similarly, Deborah Moffatt also contrasts the attitudes of two generations of men with differing cultural identities toward war in "Willie's War." Helen Norris, Tillie Olsen, and Gladys Swan portray the painful readjustment process of disturbed veterans in their short fictions.

War's impact on children is illustrated in short stories written by Diana Chow and Rita-Elizabeth Harper. The horror of merciless assault is detailed through the eyes of a young victim in Diana Chow's "The Village" while the 13-year-old adolescent female in Harper's "Survivors" accepts responsibility far beyond her years for the welfare of her younger brothers and sisters caught in the chaos of postwar uncertainty. Zenna Henderson implies that adults might look to children for peaceful solutions in her short story "Subcommittee." It is the alien and human children in this story who are able to overlook superficial differences and communication barriers to find compatibility because they realize their similarities outweigh their obvious differences while their parents search in vain for a peaceful resolution to war.

Strong antiwar statements are made by these writers through the medium of fiction. Beulah Marie Dix's The Battle Months of George Daurella is a pacifist indictment of war which strips away the romanticized visions of war young men often have through the persona of a young "unheroic hero" who emerges from the experience of combat "bruised and scarred for life." The bizarre fairy tale of sorts written by Kathyrn Kramer entitled A Handbook For Visitors from Outer Space imagines a nebulous war created in the minds of Americans that is nowhere and everywhere at the same time and has no visible enemy except the definite, tangible signs of war's destructive force. In Dorothy Canfield Fisher's "Memorial Day" the corpses of soldiers buried in a cemetery attempt to communicate with young men still alive to warn them against the futility and senselessness of war. Although the futuristic women in Joan Slonczewski's A Door Into Ocean successfully employ non-violent resistance to prevent war when aggressive males invade their peaceful planet, Ursula K. Le Guin reminds us in The Eye of the Heron that non-violent resistance is not always an effective tool against violence and aggression perpetrated by war.

These writers are often critical of American attitudes toward war and the United States military in their novels and short stories. Kathryn Kramer satirizes the complacency of Americans in "Seeds of Conflict" who consider themselves immune to war, yet refuse to acknowledge the seeds of conflict that begin war on an individual level. Nancy Mackenroth's "To Sleep, Perchance to Dream" traces one of the causes of war to our fear of the unknown and inability to accept individual differences. In Catherine L. Moore's "The Fairy Chessmen" war is acknowledged as a natural state on earth while a prolonged period of peace is considered "psychologically unendurable." When Americans are temporarily left without an enemy, they look toward outer space to invent an enemy which must be lurking somewhere in the hostile universe. Alice H. Sheldon (as James Tiptree, Jr.) depicts a sensitive soldier in "Beam Us Home" who escapes the violence of earth by allowing his mind to ascend into outer space where he discovers a sanctuary of peace. In "Yanqui Doodle" Sheldon criticizes an American military that would resort to the misuse of drugs to control the thoughts of its military forces during war to insure compliance and victory. Invading aliens reject the human race as too violent and obviously uncivilized to be worth conquering in Dorothy De Courcy's "Rat Race." All of these writings express disappointment in Americans' propensity toward violence and acceptance of war as an expected part of contemporary life.

Two women writers combine the themes of race and war. Odella Phelps Wood focuses on the war for racial equality in the United States during the first half of the century, set within the framework of two world wars. Her novel High Ground demonstrates how war places all soldiers, regardless of race, on the same plane of experience while periods of peace often allow prior prejudices to resurface. Alice Childress' short stories envision peace as something more than the absence of war. Peace, as defined in her writing, requires the elimination of violence in our society and relies upon nonviolent resolution of racial inequities.

If women visualize war through literature, they also envision a world at peace. American women writing during the twentieth century, beginning with Charlotte Perkins Gilman in the second decade, have authored many fictionalized utopias which envision perfect or near perfect societies where war has been eliminated. While the word "utopia," coined in 1516 by Sir Thomas More, literally means "no place," the utopian concept recognizes an ideal state located somewhere within each of our minds. In her essay "Communities of Sisters: Utopian Fiction by U.S. Women, 1970 – 1980," Carol F. Kessler cautions against interpreting utopian writings "as literal blueprints for a future better world." "Rather," she writes, "we need realize they are 'experiences,' attempts at imagining positive possibilities in response to present needs. They are mind-looseners and mind-openers that ask us to realize the unlimited nature of human possibility" (81).

The visions of feminist utopian writers during the early part of the century were similar to those of women peace activists who resisted and protested against World War One. These women "envisioned ideal communities of harmony based on female attributes of nurturance and altruism" and were committed to the belief that "men and women could only co-exist harmoniously in a world order which promoted full equality for all" (Sauber 232). More recent utopian fiction still reflects these ideals. In her essay "Feminist Utopian Vision and Social Change," Jacqueline Pearce defines feminist utopian fiction as literature which "imagines what things might be like if the world were based on the values of felicity and interrelation rather than domination and hierarchy, and if 'masculine' and 'feminine' qualities were reunited" (50). "In the construction and content of their writing," she further explains, "feminist utopian authors attempt to express a mode of consciousness in which there is no artificial separation of personal, political, and metaphysical concerns" (50).

To this end the progressive citizens of Mary Alice White's imagined Prire in Land of the Possible: A Report of the First Visit to Prire vote against financial support of a strong defense budget, favoring instead the improvement of their quality of life with their tax resources. In Winnifred Harper Cooley's "A Dream of the Twenty-First Century" the future inhabitants of earth living at the beginning of the coming century have attained universal peace and have redirected their energies toward making the world more habitable both physically and morally. While some of these fictionalized utopias are exclusively female, others are populated by both sexes. All of them have in common a respect for human rights and the innate dignity of each individual, a belief in peaceful resolution of conflict, and a commitment to a respectful coexistence with the environment.

"Utopian vision" as exemplified in these writings, "calls us to strive for what we must believe is within our reach: a world better suited for the meeting of basic human needs and for the blossoming and nurturing of individual and communal selves" (Pearce 54).

Some contemporary writers have combined the genres of science fiction and utopian fiction in their writings, adding another dimension to the literary concept of utopia. While women who write science fiction have "humanised and feminised a genre mostly written by males for a male readership," those writers who have blended the genres of utopian fiction with science fiction have "expanded the horizons of utopia," as Nan Bowman Albinski explains in Women's Utopias in British and American Fiction. "Although not always earthbound, earlier works by women rarely included off-world societies, time and space travel, or aliens" as more contemporary utopian fictions often do, such as those authored by Ursula K. Le Guin, Joan Slonczewski, and Joanna Russ (162 – 163).

While most of these literary interpretations of war and peace are written in the tradition of realism, innovations too are present. Ursula K. Le Guin expands the possibilities of the novel form and utopian fiction simultaneously in Always Coming Home. Deena Metzger has experimented with the novella in her The Woman Who Slept With Men to Take the War Out of Them, writing her narrative in the form of a dramatic monologue. Kathryn Kramer's A Handbook for Visitors from Outer Space integrates the comic and tragic, ironic and satiric, and realistic and fantastic, the narrative moving in several directions at once to describe an illusory war that is nowhere and everywhere at the same time within the minds of Americans. Alice Childress has written her effective short stories in the form of informal conversations. Still other women such as Pamela Sargent, Margaret St. Clair, and Catherine L. Moore have chosen the freedom of the science fiction genre to express their futuristic interpretations of war.

NOVELS

289. Broner, Esther Masserman (as E. M. Broner). Weave of Women. New York: Bantam Books, 1978.

In this novel a diverse group of international women come together in Jerusalem to found a utopian commune where they can forge new identities and celebrate womanhood. "The house of Broner's women," writes Frances Bartkowski in Feminist Utopias, "is a place of warmth, passion, asylum, and retreat to which women come when need or ceremony require their presence" (116). From the United States, Poland, Germany, England, and Israel these powerless women, "rejected by cultures that have given them no history, no traditions, no power as women," come together to form their own peaceful community and create their own rituals and ceremonies which celebrate each phase of women's lives (Franks 34). An aura of feminist spirituality and shared history of "oppression, humiliation and self-degradation" as women sustains the group through the inevitable resistance they encounter with the outside world. The novel is the story not only of the commune itself, but of each of its 15 members, "their tales and lives woven together in marvelous combination of the mythical and the ordinary" (Weaver 119). In his review of A Weave of Women John Leonard refers to the structure of the loosely woven novel as a "kind of epic poem, a recapitulation of the rhythms of female consciousness. It is circular and sinuous and ceremonial . . . a myth of nurture" (C6).

290. Buck, Pearl S. The Living Reed. New York: John Day, 1963.

This novel traces the history of Korea through a noble Korean family from 1883, when the United States ratified a treaty of amity and commerce assuring that the United States would defend Korea should it be invaded, to the end of World War Two. The period covered by the novel is a tragic one of despair for Koreans when their small country "had to grapple with the cultural disruption produced by new Western ideas and simultaneously submit to the competitive encroachments of three big and greedy neighbors, Russia, Japan and China" (Durdin 40). Yet the Koreans, personified by the Kim family, are not to be defeated. Despite their continued oppression, they are like the shoots of the bamboo plant, from which the title of the novel is taken, which spring forth anew each year, like the "ever-present spirit of independence" which fortifies Koreans with an amazing resilience.

The Living Reed is a blending of textbook and novel with fictionalized characters set against a backdrop of authentic detail. In the historical note which prefaces the novel Buck notes that Korea was founded 4000 years ago by "a people in search of peace" (10). "Situated as we are, surrounded by three powerful nations, Russia, China and Japan," one of the early premiers explains to his people, "we can only saves ourselves from their greed by withdrawal from the world. We must become a hermit nation" (23). But Korea's history has not been a peaceful one and small though it may be, the rest of the world has not allowed it to withdraw in isolation. In the epilogue, Buck relates the role of the Korean War to the historical content of the novel, recognizing that American soldiers "climbed the rugged slopes of Korean mountains and fought in homesickness and desperate weariness for the sake of a people strange to them and for reasons they scarcely understood, even when they yielded up their lives" (478).

291. Buck, Pearl S. The Patriot. New York: John Day Company, 1939.

This novel covers the revolutionary movement in China during the late 1920s and the Sino-Japanese War, ongoing as the novel was written. The narrative focuses on an 18-year-old university student who joins the revolution full of youthful idealism but leaves China after he becomes disillusioned by the unfulfilled promises and betrayal of the Chinese people under the leadership of Chiang Kai-shek. The patriot emigrates to Japan but later returns as a soldier to defend his homeland against the invading Japanese, his idealism tempered by maturity and reality, aware that "it will be a long time before peace comes" and he can be reunited with his Japanese wife and children. And when peace finally does come, I-wan realizes "there may be no cities left. When peace comes there may be nothing left but the land. When peace comes—what? No one can answer. They can only fight on" (Woods 2).

A historical novel of political and social importance, The Patriot contrasts Chinese and Japanese cultures, including their respective attitudes toward war. Japanese women, I-wan's wife tells him, are expected to produce sons during times of war. They no longer belong to themselves, but to the country. "In times of war everyone belongs to the country," she explains (211).

In her review of the novel, Katherine Woods characterizes Buck's work as a "story of human beings, of human passions and frustrations and valor and patience and strength. It must have been written at white heat under stress of intense feeling," she writes. "Yet its intensity is not of bitterness and hate, but of insight and compassion" (2).

292. Buck, Pearl S. Sons. New York: John Day, 1932.

A sequel to The Good Earth, this novel chronicles the revolutionary period in China during the early twentieth century when the country was torn apart by factional war lords who provided irresponsible leadership and kept the peasant-dominated countryside in constant turmoil and fear. The novel follows the developing manhood of the sons of Wang Lung, protagonist of The Good Earth, none of whom choose to till the soil as he and his ancestors have done for thousands of years. In particular Buck focuses on Wang Lung's youngest son who chooses war as a way of life, his commanding figure earning him the nickname "Wang the Tiger." As he builds his army of men, Wang the Tiger develops his own identity and cries with pride:

> "These are my own men—sworn to follow me. My hour is come! God brothers! This is who I am! I am a man humble as yourselves. My father farmed the land and I am from the land. But there was a destiny for me beyond the tilling of the fields and I ran away when I was but a lad and I joined the soldiers of the revolution under the old general." (117)

Wang the Tiger's life is spent in search of progressively larger conquests and the attainment of power. When his appetite for conquest begins to wane with age, Wang the Tiger fathers a son, assuming that he too will attend the "school of war lords" and pursue a military career. But the grandson of Wang Lung returns to the earth instead, choosing the path of the farmer, as his grandfather once did, to his father's consternation. Thus the cycle of life is complete. "The rise and fall of the families is the rise and fall of the Chinese race. Out of the good earth they have come, to the good earth

they must return, or else disintegrate" (Jen 123). The role of war in
this centuries-old pattern of Chinese conflict is vividly illustrated in
this novel.

293.   Dix, Beulah Marie. The Battle Months of George Daurella. New
        York: Duffield and Company, 1916.

A pacifist indictment of war, this novel strips away the romanticized,
idealistic visions of war which often accompany young men such as
George Daurella as they eagerly anticipate the opportunity to prove
their valor in combat. Daurella, a "trained instrument" of several
years' attendance in a War School, enters war fully cognizant of the
death and suffering that he will undoubtedly encounter but equally
convinced of his own invincibility. Whatever reason might try to
warn him about the reality of war has been overshadowed by the
power of his emotions which have convincingly assured him "he was
confident, unreasoning, with primal young egoism, that death or
serious discomfort was not for Lieutenant Daurella. . . . He had no
doubt, on this day of sunshine, that in big things and in little Fate
was his very good friend" (29).

But the fates of war are not kind to Lieutenant Daurella, who
witnesses the brutal force of war in its cruelest state, shattering his
once cherished belief that as an officer he would somehow be "lifted
above the rest of humanity" (Daurella 213). War reduces all of
humanity, regardless of status or rank, to the same level of
vulnerability, and civilians are no less immune to its destructive
strength as they are often the victims of indiscriminate bombing and
mass slaughter.

War, Daurella concludes as he vows to fight no more, "unravels" the
advances civilization has made during the past 2,000 years. "We're
slipping back the road we've come with such hard labour," he
believes. "Wherever the war cloud darkens, it's turning us to devil.
Doesn't matter that we all set out for the best of reasons, and with the
best of purposes" (313).

Daurella emerges from his initial, sobering taste of war "bruised and
scarred for life, but at least alive," writes Dix in the epilogue to the
novel.   Because he represents no certain country, Daurella
represents all countries. "Is he a symbol, maybe, this unheroic hero
of ours" she asks rhetorically, "a symbol for the youth of a continent,
the young, strong, decent men, with heads full of the dreams that
should be reality for the next generation, stumbling pitifully into the
ditches that run with blood?" (320)

The Battle Months of George Daurella was written at the beginning
of World War One when most Americans were naively confident the
war would end shortly and triumphantly. Neither intended to be
realistic nor romantic, Dix describes her antiwar novel as a
"humoresque, a fantasy of war" written with the hopeful
assumption that "even as Alice discovered in the Looking-glass

Country, Truth is sometimes quickest met with when we turn our backs upon the truth" (319 – 320).

294. Gearhart, Sally Miller. The Wanderground. Watertown, MA: Persephone Press, 1979.

Set in a future postnuclear period, The Wanderground is a group of interconnected stories which envision the segregation of men, confined to the violent, repressive atmosphere of the city, and women, who take to the hills to create a "nurturing, healing, loving" community built on the concept of nonviolent sisterhood. "The novel pits this strong unified society of women, celebratory of female virtues and blessed by mother nature, against that of the men, who are essentially rapists, not only of women but of the earth itself" (Lefanu 68). In a non-threatening atmosphere beyond the confines of the city, women are given the freedom to refine individual skills and creativity. Each develops telepathic powers which become the preferred mode of communication.

In the opening story of the collection a fully-armed woman stranger arrives in the hills. Reluctantly, she sheds her armor and weapons at the request of the hill women, who will teach her she has no need for such apparatus in their peaceful community where women become one with their natural environment and live a truly organic existence in harmony with nature.

295. Gilman, Charlotte Perkins. 1915. Herland. New York: Pantheon Books, 1979.

Herland, first serialized in Gilman's newspaper, The Forerunner, in 1915, was rediscovered and published as a book 64 years later. The novel successfully "interweaves time and history and parallels the tasks of feminism and utopia: to seek out a past, to examine the present critically, to posit a future, and to tell a tale of and for that imagined future" (Bartkowski 24). In Herland Gilman envisions an all-female utopia built upon the philosophy of socialism and the tradition of motherhood. Her imagined utopia "transforms the private world of mother-child, isolated in the individual home, into a community of mothers and children in a socialized world," writes Ann J. Lane in the introduction to the reprinted version of Herland (xxiii). "It is a world in which humane social values have been achieved by women in the interest of us all" (xxiii). Dorothy Berkson describes Herland as "part feminist fantasy and part political document establishing a blueprint for a total restructuring of the dominant male society" in her essay "So We All Became Mothers" (107).

By "ironically turning patriarchy's assumptions around," Berkson contends, the women of Herland are able to achieve this harmonious, communal utopia because they have followed their own natural instinct to cooperate instead of adopting the natural inclination of men to live competitively. As the women of Herland age, they grow together harmoniously "not by competition, but by united action" (60). In such a culture where each individual is granted full humanity, war has no reason to exist:

> The tradition of men as guardians and protectors had quite died out. These stalwart virgins had no men to fear and therefore no need of protection. As to wild beasts—there were none in their sheltered land.

> The power of mother-love, that maternal instinct we so highly laud, was theirs of course, raised to its highest power; and a sister-love which, even while recognizing the actual relationship, we found it hard to credit. (57 – 58)

Herland is narrated by a male sociologist, one of three American explorers who discover this feminist utopia. It is through his memory that readers are introduced to the women of Herland and their community. The introduction of males into the culture of Herland establishes the novelist's intent not only as a critic of America's male-dominated society but also, more importantly, as a reformist with valid ideas for social change that stress the common humanity shared by both genders, not the differences which separate them. The reeducation of these men with the maternal and domestic values of Herland, Gilman believes, may save a decadent America from further disintegration (Berkson 108). If women are encouraged to be physically active and intellectually independent and allowed to play a primary role in the public sphere while men are taught to be less violent and more nurturing, then a restructuring of society may result in a world comprised of both new men and new women, sharing the best of their respective traits, where members of both genders might live at peace with themselves and one another.

296. Kayser, Martha. The Aerial Flight To The Realm of Peace. St. Louis: Lincoln Press and Publishing Company, 1922.

The narrator takes flight with a friend in a balloon destined for another planet in this novella. There they discover a utopia in which "order is the natural outcome of Universal Brotherhood," and the peaceful inhabitants of all races and colors are "governed entirely by the Divine Laws" (22). On this planet, so glaringly different from earth, "each nation and each individual realizes it is a part of a stupendous whole so dependent for its development and welfare" (49). In a land such as this where each individual is "trained to think exclusively constructive, harmonious thoughts" there are no enemies, and thus, no need for war. When given the choice to stay in this paradise or return to earth, the visitors agree they "Never! NEVER!! **NEVER!!!**" desire to return to earth again.

297. Kramer, Kathryn. A Handbook for Visitors from Outer Space. New York: Alfred A. Knopf, 1984.

Sensing the end of the world is near, Cyrus Quince's grandfather orders his grandson to write a handbook for visitors from outer space so that extraterrestrial beings, "consulting it would understand what had happened in the world to make it come to an end" (181). The result is this novel, a bizarre fairy tale of sorts, that weaves together seemingly disparate stories into an apocalyptic vision of the last days on earth.

This last of all wars, so ambiguous and enigmatic in nature that some even deny its existence, is perceived more through feeling than observation, the general mood of the American populace being one of "crossness, now and then superseded by a preternatural gaiety— a general ennui broken by brief riots of celebration" (9). A first (as well as last) of its kind, this war offers little tangibility for Americans to grasp hold of, no visible enemy for them to vent their hatred upon: It is nowhere; it is everywhere. "It's as if our generalized fears of impending destruction were given form" (Allen, Bruce 21).

By creating a war that is so unbelievably senseless, the novel illustrates the senselessness of war (Sternhell 10). The antiwar parable weaving its way through the narrative satirizes our seeming need for war, our thrill of living "on the verge," not knowing if our destructive risks will leave any tomorrow to experience or not. "Everything tastes so much better when one is listening for boots on the stairs," one soldier confesses (10). It is as if war has become a state of mind, and we are gradually and inevitably defeating ourselves while we are engaged in an addictive game that we have perfected all too well.

Only in the combined preface-afterword at the beginning of the novel, "The House at World's End," do we learn that earth's citizens were tragically naive about the war games they played, believing that life would continue ad infinitum through successive generations. By the time this idyllic vision was corrected by the reality of the coming Armageddon, it was too late. They began to realize they had been living a fairy tale with no happily ever after ending, after all.

In the preface-afterword of the novel Kramer explains that the final war, which offered so little tangible proof of itself, has obliterated all forms of life on earth. She writes: "Now it is over. The world is empty. . . " (4). But amidst the silence is the sense that life "might be taken up again at any moment" (3). The silence "contradicts nothing, and it seems possible that soon water will be heard running, or a voice calling a dog back in" (5). But if no human being arrives to break the silence and divulge the truth of what happened on earth, "there will be no choice but to believe that the end was known from the beginning, this quiet was planned"(4).

Integrating the comic and tragic, the ironic and satiric, the realistic and the fantastic, Kramer's handbook manages to move in several directions at once and blend several narratives together without loss of continuity. Most significantly of all, this novel asks us to reexamine our propensity to wage war, our presumptuous confidence in our infallibility, our unquestioned faith in a future for coming generations on Earth. If we fail to do this, perhaps we, like the typically American citizens of Kramer's fictitious Arborville, may begin to wake up to reality only to discover we have already slept too late.

298. Le Guin, Ursula K. Always Coming Home. New York: Harper and Row, 1985.

Always Coming Home is an innovative variation on the novel form which intersperses narrative with a variety of literary genres, including drama, song, and poetry. These writings form an "Archaeology of the Future," offering a thorough examination of a utopian culture set 500 years into the future. The peaceful Kesh depicted by Le Guin inhabit the northwestern coast of what is left of the United States after technology and pollution have taken their predictable toll. In the Valley of the Na this female-dominated, pastoral culture, where inhabitants are reared to value serenity and honor equality, coexists in harmony with the environment. Although tribal wars do occasionally take place, these conflicts are minor compared to the "technological megawars" of the twentieth century (Delany 56).

The main narrative thread which weaves through and unites the whole of the novel is narrated from the perspective of Stone Telling, a young woman who has experienced both the militaristic, male-dominated city culture and the peaceful, female-oriented culture of the Kesh. Between these narrative chapters Le Guin introduces the sociological observations of a cultural anthropologist who studies the Kesh culture in depth.

Lest the intent of her narrative be misplaced in the myriad of imaginative literature contained within the novel, at one point Le Guin makes clear her intent in writing this utopian novel to indict technological civilization and envision a more perfect life for those who may inherit the earth as we know it:

> This is a mere dream dreamed in a bad time, an Up Yours to the people who ride snowmobiles, make nuclear weapons, and run prison camps by a middle-aged housewife, a critique of civilisation possible only to the civilized, an affirmation pretending to be a rejection, a glass of milk for the soul ulcered by acid rain, a piece of pacifist jeanjacquerie, and a cannibal dance among the savages in the ungodly garden of the farthest West. (316)

Always Coming Home does not offer "a blueprint for a perfect society," writes Naomi Jacobs in "Beyond Stasis and Symmetry: Lessing, Le Guin, and the Remodeling of Utopia." The novel is "rather, a vision of an alternative, an other way of living, from which we may draw comfort, hope, and the will to change a world so much less lovely than the one we have helped to create in reading a book like this," she writes (43). In her essay "Women's Utopias: New Worlds, New Texts," Lee Cullen Khanna describes <u>Always Coming Home</u> as a "new text" in the utopian genre that "celebrates, with a corresponding richness of invention, the dynamic, fluid culture central to many feminist utopias" (132 – 133).

299. Le Guin, Ursula K. <u>The Eye of the Heron</u>. <u>Millenial Women</u>. Virginia Kidd. ed. New York: Delacorte Press, 1978. 124 – 302.

<u>The Eye of the Heron</u> contrasts two former earth cultures which colonize the planet Victoria sometime in the future. While the inhabitants of Victoria City develop a society based upon violence and domination, the people of Shantih (meaning "peace" in Hindu and Sanskrit), exiled from earth for their refusal to participate in war, build a peaceful existence in the rural countryside. When differences in ideology between the two groups intensify, the people of Shantih attempt to resolve their conflicts utilizing the techniques of nonviolent resistance demonstrated on earth by Mahatma Gandhi and Martin Luther King—negotiation, noncooperation, the issuance of ultimatums, and civil disobedience. At no time do they resort to violence. Le Guin's narrative is tragic, however, for the pacifist techniques of the people of Shantih prove inadequate to resist the violence imposed upon them. Instead of offering armed resistance, they secretly flee their homes in search of another "beginning place" in the wilderness where they may reestablish a life of peace.

Parallel to the social conflict of the novel, Le Guin develops the personal conflict of Luz Marina, born of aristocratic origin in Victoria City, who rebels against her family and society's values and joins the People of the Peace as they discover a new homeland. Le Guin's novel serves as a reminder that peaceful resistance is not always an effective stand against violence and aggression and may have tragic consequences for dedicated pacifists.

300. Le Guin, Ursula K. <u>The Lathe of Heaven</u>. New York: Charles Scribner's Sons, 1971.

This allegorical novel, set in Portland, Oregon near the year 2000, envisions a new parapsychological power called "effective" dreaming which can change the course of history, including war. Granted this questionable power is the protagonist, a survivor of a disastrous atomic explosion, whose "effective" dreams under stress materialize into history the following morning, often changing the past. Although his first dreams have only localized, minor consequences, in time his dreams expand beyond George's control, altering history and the world. A psychiatrist who discovers this bizarre phenomenon attempts to control George's dreams and thus further his own career, altering history to suit himself, but the results are not always what is anticipated. Hoping to create a peaceful resolution to for recurring wars in the Middle East, Dr. Haber plays an antiwar tape for George as he falls asleep. Instead, George dreams another variation of war, and Earth experiences its First Interstellar War with alien beings attacking the earth in one of his most vivid dreams. Apologizing to Haber, George explains how war has become a part of mankind's collective unconscious that is almost impossible to eradicate:

> ". . . I guess I can't or my subconscious can't, even imagine a warless world. The best it can do is substitute one kind of war for another. . . . Your own ideas are sane and rational, but this is my unconscious you're trying to use, not my rational mind. Maybe rationally I could conceive of the human species not trying to kill each other off by nations, in fact rationally it's easier to conceive of than the motives of war. But you're handling something outside reason. You're trying to reach progressive, humanitarian goals with a tool that isn't suited to the job. Who has humanitarian dreams? (86 – 87)

Le Guin develops The Lathe of Heaven as a "series of meetings between Orr and Haber, patient and therapist, dreamer and scientist, visionary and rationalist, critic and utopist" (Cummins 157). Through the character of Haber she satirizes the concept of a "planned utopia" with a psychiatrist who fantasizes himself as capable of remaking the world into such a utopia.

By speculating what might happen if dreams could change reality in this novel, Le Guin takes readers through at last ten world changes, including war, and blurs the boundaries which separate reality and dreams. But even such an ingenious idea as "effective dreaming" cannot guarantee an end to world problems such as war. Her novel illustrates that "We cannot stand outside the world and direct it but must be content to be part of the whole" (Prescott 106).

301. Lin, Adet (as Tan Yun). Flame from the Rock. New York: John Day, 1943.

This tragic novel of war love, written by a 20-year-old Chinese-American woman, is set during one of the Japanese invasions of modern China. The narrative centers on the relationship of two unlikely lovers—a nurse who is open, warm, and sensitive and a soldier who is emotionally reserved, distant, and hardened by the demands of war. Their first encounter, during which Wang Tsai's blood is transfused with Kuanpo's after she has been injured during a bombing, unites them in a physical bond which gradually develops into an emotional one as well. When they first meet Wang Tsai identifies himself only as a soldier:

> Wang Tsai had been so long a soldier that he could not even imagine what else he might have been. . . . He had been in the war such a long time and such a lot his whole mind and body were hardened to it. He knew about little else. He was proud and often unfriendly. The others regarded him as sullen. At

the front and in the rear he remained alone, loving his silence. He sulked and felt an intense longing for something. (45)

But Kuanpo helps Wang Tsai nurture the peaceful, affective side of life and takes pride in her ability to make him laugh. With his death at the front, however, Kuanpo is filled with emptiness and a longing to understand the cruel reality of fate:

> If there was truth anywhere, she thought—good hard truth— it was that Wang Tsai lived and died, and the remaining truth was her mortal memory of him, and the blood. And all that fierce passion must be forced back, squeezed into that little space, the heart, must be locked there in silence with a heavy lock. Its walls must imprison it forever (193).

Unable to conceive of a life without Wang Tsai, Kuanpo eventually loses her own will to live, becoming yet another victim who cannot survive the emotional loss of war.

302. Petesch, Natalie L. M. Duncan's Colony. Athens: Swallow Press, 1982.

The setting of this novel is the 1960s, a time of instability and war when many Americans explored the idea of communal living for varied reasons, as Petesch explains at the beginning of her novel:

> Those who were of an invincibly optimistic nature gathered together in agrarian or utopian communes reminiscent of the nineteenth century. Others, who believed that these crises and wars augured the end of civilization by nuclear warfare, gathered together for a brief season of love in colonies where they hoped to survive the destruction of the world. (2)

Duncan's Colony relates the story of a nearly year-long communal experimentation involving eight Americans ranging in age from 14 to nearly 80, including a Vietnam War veteran who refused to kill enemy soldiers during his tour, selected by the communal leader to live together because they are convinced that the end of life on earth perpetuated by war is near. The novel is narrated from the viewpoint of several members of Duncan's Colony, an isolated commune in the southwestern part of the United States where communication with the outside world, procreation, and infiltration of outsiders are all forbidden. The commune is doomed from the start by internal strife within its members who cannot achieve cooperation or harmony. "An experiment in survival should be challenging, courageous, a chronicle of serendipities," one member suggests. But Duncan's Colony does not live up to that expectation and disintegrates when the the principle upon which it was founded—the vision of an imminent apocalypse—does not materialize and its members are left to consider "what to do with a leftover life."

In his review of the novel, Brian Morton praises Petesch's ability "to give a sense of the variety of American pasts and an impression of what it was like, how it felt to be an American in 1965, how it felt to survive Cuba and Vietnam and keep sane enough to survive Richard Nixon" (1142).

303.   Piercy, Marge. Vida. New York: Harper and Row, 1979.

This novel examines the antiwar movement of the 1960s a decade later from a feminine viewpoint, "a viewpoint that deals with people and their relationships rather than ideas and ideals" (Hawes 675). The central character of Piercy's sixth novel, a radical political activist who was at the forefront of some of the more violent demonstrations of the antiwar movement, has gone underground since the movement dissipated. She now lives in a "strangely suspended world" among fugitives constantly on the move from one refuge to another, changing their identities as they go. Vida once believed "her actions might change history. Now everything she does is a matter of self-preservation" (Jackson 47). The novel recalls a militant time period when history was a "blur of chaotic events, with recognizable dangers, but with no definable point to it" (Walzer 39). Although Vida forms some intimate relationships and belongs to an underground Network of former activists, ultimately she is left alone "with only her own courage and her commitment to a cause that has lost its momentum" (Hawes 676). Judith B. Walzer describes Vida as "an adventuress, risking an unconventional acceptance of her own needs, a present-day Moll Flanders who fervently believes her goals are valid because they are hers" (40). An Atlantic review of the novel calls Vida "a compelling character, one whose personal problems are achingly familiar and whose political dilemma seems only an extreme example of the powerlessness that has overtaken us all in the past decade" (96).

304.   Piercy, Marge. Woman on the Edge of Time. New York: Alfred A. Knopf, 1976.

Piercy juxtaposes the present with the future, realism with science fiction, and a harsh assessment of present-day American society with visions of an idyllic utopia in Woman on the Edge of Time. The protagonist is a 37-year-old Chicana welfare recipient representing poor and powerless contemporary women, whose relatives commit her to a state mental institution—a Keseyesque nightmare of a place symbolizing "the cruelest side of a technological, power-hungry society" (Jefferson 94). Unsuccessful in her attempt to escape, Connie fights her way out of her powerlessness instead, using her psychic powers to connect with the future.

Piercy places her protagonist in an androgynous, non-industrialized community in Massachusetts in the year 2137. In contrast with the dehumanizing mental hospital, Connie discovers Mattapoisett to be "a society of communes in close touch with nature and respectful human dignity" reminiscent of the 1960s era in values and philosophy (Betsky 39). In Mattapoisett a "nurturing culture has replaced the old hierarchical, competitive culture" which entrapped many women such as Connie (Berkson 112). Traditional male qualities are conspicuous in members of both genders, while males as well as females "mother" children in a society which places great importance on the nurturance of its young. In this non-sexist community where humanism and individuality are prized, Connie discovers a vision of the future powerful enough to help her rise above the intolerable present, if only temporarily, and preserve what sanity she has left.

Although conflicts within Mattapoisett are rare, the community takes precautions to defend itself from outside aggressors, rotating defense duties among all citizens. Having learned the need to defend herself in Mattapoisett, Connie instigates her own war on the staff members of the mental institution who attempt to experiment with her mind. "Realizing that she will suffer in return," writes Lucy M. Freibert in "World Views in Utopian Novels by Women," Connie views "retaliation as something she can bear with dignity, knowing that she is counteracting the violence which the doctors, and society in general, have perpetrated against her very being" (56).

Piercy explains her intent in writing this novel in "Dear Frontiers: Letters from Women Fantasy and Science Fiction Writers." "With Woman on the Edge of Time," she writes, "I wanted very strongly to create a society not at all fantastic but one we can have it we fight for it, one almost attainable now, in which feminist values are the prevailing values. I wanted to imagine the people of a nonsexist society, one which socialized people to be cooperative, gentle, open, respectful of other living beings, in touch with their own various layers of mind and feeling" (64).

305. Slonczewski, Joan. A Door Into Ocean. New York: Arbor House, 1986.

This utopian vision, written by a Quaker, is set thousands of years in the future on the water-covered planet of Shora where "self-awareness and ecological awareness are so linked that the inhabitants refer to themselves as Sharers" (Jonas 22). A compassionate race of women who reproduce by parthenogenesis and shun technology in favor of enlightened knowledge inhabits this distant planet where a complex philosophical and ethical system has been developed based upon peaceful coexistence with one another and the environment.

In contrast to this idealistic world stands Valedon, an Earthlike planet dependent upon technology where the dominant occupations are trade and war and aggressive inhabitants aspire to wealth and power. When armed men from Valedon disrupt the peaceful isolation of Shora, threatening invasion of the satellite planet, the nonviolent Sharers must protect their planet's carefully balanced ecology without discarding their own commitment to non-violent resistance. In her <u>Women's Utopias in British and American Fiction</u> Nan Bowman Albinski writes that Slonczewski "persuasively argues the case for successful non-violent resistance" in her novel (165). She further analyzes the Sharers' "victory" and their source of strength:

> Despite the suffering that they must endure, and the temptation to use force themselves, thus becoming that which they despise, the women of <u>A Door into Ocean</u> hold fast to their principles. Their 'victory' over the brutal colonisers who would destroy their way of life is eclipsed by their victory over the temptation to use their own, and greater, powers: in this lies their strength, and, with this strength, they accept a man into their planet. (165)

In her <u>Belles Lettres</u> review of the novel, Ann Kottner states that in writing <u>A Door Into Ocean</u> Slonczewski has "balanced science and fiction in a way that brings credit to the genre. She is part Rachel Carson, part Ursula LeGuin," she writes (4).

306. Slonczewski, Joan. <u>Still Forms on Foxfield</u>. New York: Random House, 1980.

As the earth heads toward an inevitable nuclear war in the year 2002, Slonczewski envisions a group of Quakers fleeing to another planet where they can continue to practice their religious beliefs and live peacefully in this novel. Although the Foxfield environment is harsh, the less than 1,000 inhabitants thrive with each citizen having an equal voice in decisions made for the whole. A century later Foxfield citizens imagine Earth, through the recollections of their ancestors, as a planet of "giant cities and empty deserts. Exotic jungles and poisoned oceans. Monuments modern and ancient, beautiful and grotesque" (5). But after four generations of silence, a spaceship from earth arrives on Foxfield, claiming that the survivors of the nuclear holocaust which did occur on earth have created a high-tech utopia on the planet. But increased lifespans of earth's citizens necessitate new worlds to accommodate the expanding population. The Friends of Foxfield are faced with the infiltration of their peaceful planet by inhabitants of earth whose values may be very different from their own.

307. White, Mary Alice. <u>Land of the Possible: A Report of the First Visit to Prire</u>. New York: Warner Books, 1979.

White creates an alternative society in this novel where inhabitants live in harmony with the environment and one another. Poverty, pollution, hunger, noise, crime, litter, loneliness, thirst for power, greed, and violence do not exist in this utopia where the hectic pace of life characteristic of contemporary American society and its inherent stress have been replaced by a calmer, more relaxed lifestyle. This society has no need of a strong defense, for Prire has not engaged in war in more than 200 years. The citizens of Prire, given a very active voice in governmental affairs, decided two centuries ago that they could not afford both a strong defense budget and the quality of life they wanted. Their votes indicated that their quality of life was a higher priority than powerful weaponry. Although the citizens of Prire do not claim to have eliminated the "warring impulse" evident in human nature for the past 10,000 years, they do believe they have succeeded in tempering that impulse to be less destructive by offering healthy, competitive outlets as an alternative to military engagement.

308. Wood, Odella Phelps. High Ground. New York: Exposition Press, 1945.

Although the black protagonist of this novel works for equality of the races all of his life, it is only during wartime that he sees color barriers disintegrate among American soldiers united against a common enemy. In Part One of the novel, which focuses on Jim Clayton's experiences during World War One, war becomes a common leveler among men. All soldiers, regardless of race, experience hunger, loneliness, and fear as they face combat for the first time in the vast, majestic Argonne Forest, "a place for frightened children with the forms of men to hide in until they get a chance to run out and blast the life out of some more frightened child-men—and scurry back if they can" (28). Although he had imagined what the Front would be like, Jim finds himself unprepared for what he observes:

> All around him was a hellish flame-light as the huge guns spewed forth hot, rending, terrible death of whistling missives—soldiers were everywhere like so many flies—rising and falling, and shooting and gouging with their bayonets— the ground fairly ran with gore. The American columns were sweeping thunderously, gloriously onward about an eighth of a mile from where the truck stopped. But in their wake was left strewn on the sod, scores and scores of mangled, groaning bodies—some silent but still writhing in agonizing mutilation. (32)

Although the veterans of World War One return home as heroes, the class barriers erased by war are once more placed as dividers between the races. With bitterness many black veterans object to their lack of equality. "De white folks got all the good paying jobs; they got all de money," one observes (57). Jim shuns from such outspoken militancy, working for racial equality in a more subtle, positive manner as he gradually betters his status in life.

Part Two of the novel, set during the World War Two period, focuses on Jim's second wife, who voices strong antiwar sentiment and a cynical view of mankind at the inception of another war:

> "Is this why we were created? Nature does not destroy us fast enough, so we destroy each other, and face that great void

which some call otherwhere! We are like children groping in the dark—we shut out eyes and run to meet our fate—because we cannot go through the torture of waiting for our fate to catch up with us. Some call it bravery; others call it fear. But to us poor mortals that we are—fear and bravery are alike, and when some wretched creature who is too tired to fight any more takes what we call the easy way out and chooses to face the unknown rather than to endure the known, we call it cowardice! But who are cowards, those who live or those who choose to die?" (95)

Despite her hatred of war, Marantha supports the war effort on the homefront by working in a munitions factory, observing that once again "bigotry, class and race hatred" have been temporarily erased by war. Eventually she decides to return to her Southern homeland, realizing that the "war" for racial equality must be fought on Southern soil. "It doesn't require courage to live in a place where no fighting is necessary," she explains to her northern co-workers. "But it does require courage to live where you have to fight every inch of the way for your birthright" (192).

Wood examines a war within a war—the war for racial equality waged during the first half of the twentieth century, set within the framework of two world wars. Her novel illustrates how the war effort temporarily erases class distinctions, uniting all Americans against a common enemy. Once that threat is erased, however, former racial tensions resurface, leaving black veterans to wonder what did they gain by risking their lives for a white-dominated country that refuses to recognize them as equal citizens during peacetime.

SHORT FICTION

309. Bedway, Barbara. "Death and Lebanon." The Pushcart Prize, VII: Best of the Small Presses. Ed. Bill Henderson. Wainscott, NY: Pushcart Press, 1983. 118 – 128.

The 11-year-old narrator of this story describes the escape of her older sister and herself from Lebanon, where their father remains fighting a prolonged civil war in a country unsafe for children. Although the sisters have lived in freedom in the United States for two years as the narrative takes place, their thoughts and prayers are still dominated by concern for their native country and Lebanese citizens whose lives are continually endangered by the ongoing war.

310. Boyle, Kay. "The Loneliest Man in the U.S. Army." Fifty Stories. Garden City, NY: Doubleday, 1980. 587 – 596.

Boyle examines the loneliness of newly drafted soldiers awaiting orders overseas in this story. Although the men periodically award a palm to the loneliest man living on the base, any one of them could be given the dubious honor, for these men and their emotional needs have become lost among the masses of khaki-clothed men facing military duty during wartime.

311. Brainard, Cecilia Manguerra. "The Black Man in the Forest." Amerasia 12.1 (1985 – 1986): 101 – 105.

Set in the Philippines during 1901, this short story explores the relationship of a wounded Philippino general with a dead American soldier and the nature of compassion when the enemy is recognized as innately human during war. It is a black American soldier who wounds General Gregorio in the left thigh before the Philippino retaliates with a fatal wound to the chest. Gregorio's men are intrigued by the American soldier's size and color and wonder if he might be an "enchanted being," for most of the Americans they have encountered during war are "albinos with hair the color of corn kernels." This large soldier must have eaten all the food he wanted, they imagine with envy, their "mouths watering at the thought of real food," for they have "subsisted on roots and lizards, listened to children wailing, smelled the stench of blood for so long" (103).

Left alone with the corpse of the black man, "immobile like a beached whale," a "frozen expression of terror" still on his face, General Gregorio begins to scrutinize this enemy soldier as an individual for the first time:

> He most certainly had a mother who carried him in her womb, brought him into the world, and gave him a name. There was a woman Sara whom he remembered even as the bullet pierced his skull—and surely Sara called this man by name. The general became somber at these thoughts and he felt a longing to name this person. (104)

Realizing that if the black American had been a better marksman he could have been the casualty himself, Gregorio comes to realize with sorrow "saturating his being" that with no real family ties and no friends, no one would mourn his own death. Gregorio carefully cleans the body of the dead soldier and floats it downstream in a river before one of his soldiers who usually consumes the livers of dead American soldiers has the opportunity to molest his body. Gregorio offers the black soldier at least "this bit of dignity" before this brief interlude of enlightenment passes and the present intervenes, reminding Gregorio that unless his men can soon locate another regiment with provisions, they will perish for lack of the essentials of survival.

312. Buck, Pearl S. "A Certain Star." May Your Days Be Merry and Bright and Other Christmas Stories by Women. Ed. Susan Koppelman. Detroit: Wayne State University Press, 1988. 198 – 221.

In this short story an atomic scientist attempts to reestablish emotional bonds with his family grown distant over the past decade during his intense preoccupation with the creation of atomic power. Although the scientist admits that he shares his family's fear for the future—"a human fear of a future—hideous but possible—because of what he and his fellow scientists had done"—he rationalizes his involvement with atomic research as necessary for the protection of the world from "subhumans" such as Adolph Hitler. The father explains to his family:

> "I wish it could have begun differently—in peace instead of in war. I wish I could have lighted cities and made houses warm and perfected a fuel for wonderful machines that aren't even invented yet. . . . . But it couldn't begin that way, it seems First of all we had to stop a subhuman man from destroying the world. . . . The only thing I fear in life is the subhuman. I trust the energy in the atom—you can know it and learn to use it—it's predictable. And I trust a good man as I trust God. But the subhuman—no! He's the enemy—the only one we have. And he may live next door as well as across the sea. He might be alive in one of us—even in me!" (216)

As a scientist who knows intimately the power locked within the nucleus of each atom, a terrifying secret of potential destruction from which there is no escape, the father recognizes he is necessarily a lonely man carrying a great burden. He also realizes that as a father he has failed, for he has ignored the importance of human relationships in his life. He selects Christmas as a time to attempt to re-enter the lives of his wife and children to whom he has become a stranger during the past several years, admitting that despite the significance he places upon his research, "everything depends upon the human being."

According to the story's introductory notes, "A Certain Star" was first published in the December 22, 1957 issue of American Weekly and subsequently reprinted in 1,200 separate copies by the publisher, distributed in ten countries, and translated into seven languages. "A Certain Star," Buck explains, is a "plea for the development of peaceful uses of atomic energy, a reaffirmation of faith in a divine being, and a very human tale of a family's attempt to become whole again" (198).

313. Buck, Pearl S. "Dagger in the Dark." The Good Deed and Other Stories of Asia, Past and Present. New York: John Day Company, 1969. 89 – 103.

The impossibility of maintaining neutrality during war is illustrated graphically in this narrative. A Chinese physician who offers medical attention to both Japanese and Chinese soldiers during World War Two later refuses to flee his family's lifelong village and continues to treat both Nationalists and Communists fighting over governmental control of his country. Threatened by a Communist general who orders him to deny medical care to any more Nationalist soldiers, Liang Yu refuses: "When the Nationalists were in power," he explains, "I healed the Communists who were few and fearful. Now in turn I will heal these few frightened Nationalists. All men are alike to me, if they need my skills" (99).

For his commitment to offer medical aid irrespective of political allegiances, Liang Yu pays with his life. As his family flees for safety, two of this brothers studying medicine in the United States prepare to return to China to further his work and establish the medical-research center in honor of his family's name.

314. Buck, Pearl S. "Duet in Asia." The Good Deed and Other Stories of Asia, Past and Present. New York: John Day Company, 1969. 187 – 212.

In this story set during the Korean War, both men and women are victimized by the unnatural circumstances of war that thrust them into unwanted situations. Although Jim attempts to repress his sexual feelings in order to remain faithful to his American fiancee and concentrate his attention on his military duties, he loses his self-control in a near-violent eruption of passion for a Korean-American prostitute that culminates in sorrow for both. Miya is a victim of war, born of a Korean mother and American father, who is considered unpure in her own country but knows no ways to meet potential American mates other than through prostitution, a practice which seems to evoke the most undesirable qualities in men. In "Duet in Asia" Buck offers a sobering depiction of how war affects sexual relationships while she also explores the feelings of men and women coping with their individual emotional struggles and the intrusion of war into their lives at the same time.

315. Buck, Pearl S. "Father Andrea." Asia Aug. 1929: 626 – 629.

"Father Andrea" is a characterization of an Italian Catholic priest whose identity changes from that of a philosophical and benevolent priest to a suspect foreigner when the Communist revolution in China during the 1920s begins. A peaceful, reverent man with a "soft, mystic soul," Father Andreas preaches that no man is free and attempts to help Chinese students bear the burden of oppression. "No man is free—we are not free of one another—we can never be free of God," he insists (626). But when the revolution begins one of his former students, symbolic of many young revolutionists, rejects all that Father Andrea has taught, declaring, "In the revolution there is no God and there is no duty. We are all free, and we preach a gospel of freedom for every one" (628). Gradually, the Chinese who once respected his wisdom and were nurtured by his kindness withdraw from Father Andrea until he is forced to cloister himself away for his own safety. When an army of revolutionists arrives at his doorstep, Father Andrea is defenselessly murdered by the young revolutionists who have labelled him, as they have all foreigners, an "Imperialist and capitalist," even though the priest has no idea of the meaning of those words or the strategy of the revolution. As he dies, Father Andrea hears the revolutionists vow to set everyone free although their brand of freedom does not extend to those such as he who may be innocent in motive but are pronounced guilty by association. Father Andrea is symbolic of many victims of war who attempt to remain separatists but are often swept into conflict against their will and targeted as "the enemy."

316. Buck, Pearl S. "The New Road." Asia May 1930: 358 – 361.

The impact of the Chinese revolution of the 1920s on successive generations is contrasted in this short story. Lu Chen, who has tended the cauldrons of his family's water shop all of his life, resists the inevitable approach of a new road, symbolic of the coming revolution, to slice a 60-foot wide strip through the center of the city and demolish his family's business of the past six decades. Although he prices the worth of his shop at $10,000 and vows he will accept no less for the loss, he is forced along with the other merchants along the path of the new road to sacrifice his business for the revolution he neither wants nor understands. Under the "new republic," he is assured there will be pipes to carry hot water for everyone and thus, no need for water shops such as his. With no trade and little pride left, Lu Chen quickly becomes aged and sullen. "His eyes, which had always been narrow and watchful and snapping, grew dull and hidden behind the veil of dimness that belongs to old people" (369). Lu Chen's son, however, welcomes the revolution that offers him a construction job on the new road, promising a greater income than Lu Chen has ever imagined.

As father, son, and grandson survey the newly finished road, it is pride that Lu Chen's son feels while his father is overcome with fear. "It—looks as if a mighty storm had swept through the city," Lu Chen observes, his lips trembling (370). Lu Chen comes to accept the fact that his son cares for the road as much as he once cared for his own water shop and the inevitability that his grandson will grow up taking the new road for granted. But Lu Chen ponders the future soberly, wondering where this revolution—symbolized by this massive slate of concrete cutting through their lives—will lead.

317. Buck, Pearl S. "The Revolutionist." Asia Sept. 1928: 685 – 689. Reprinted as "Wang Lung" in The First Wife and Other Stories by Pearl S. Buck. London: Methuen and Company, 1956. 153 – 175.

A simple farmer with little knowledge of politics, lured by the promise of riches to transform his meager lifestyle, is swept into the violent surge of the Communist revolution in this short story. Weary with the injustice of his condition—with only six acres and a three-room, mud-plastered hut to look forward to as an inheritance—Wang Lung swallows the vision offered by revolutionists of a better life to follow. One revolutionist predicts that the "time of prosperity" is near, promising Wang Lung:

"The rich will become poor and the poor will become rich. . . .
In all republics it is so. In America all men live in palaces,
and only the rich are compelled to work. As soon as emperors
are put away and the Revolution comes, these things happen.
That is why my hair is cut off. It is to show that my spirit is
free. I am a revolutionist. I and the other revolutionists will
save the nation and uplift the poor and oppressed." (686)

Wang Lung is both attracted to the promises of the revolutionists,
having convinced himself he is worthy is such overdue wealth, and
repelled by the violence accompanying the movement (accused
revolutionists are beheaded as a warning for would-be traitors). But
Wang Lung's curiosity and bitterness against his fate as a lowly
peasant win out as he decides to join of hoard of volatile revolutionists
plundering a foreigners' home, snarling like wild dogs as they hunt
for riches. Wang Lung discovers himself "possessed of a greed so
great that it left room for nothing else in his mind" as he seizes first
one treasure and then drops it for another in childish fickleness
(755). When the rioting subsides and Wang Lung is about to leave the
ransacked mansion, he witnesses the sight of the bereaved family
whose home and privacy has been violated. Suddenly confused over
his intentions, Wang Lung realizes the minimal value of his plunder
in comparison to their grief.

318. Buck, Pearl S. "Singing—to Her Death." Asia Aug. 1930: 580 – 583.
Reprinted as "The Communist" in The First Wife and Other Stories
by Pearl S. Buck. London: Methuen and Company, 1956. 176 – 186.

This narrative searches the thoughts and emotions of an unidentified
Chinese woman—perhaps symbolic of many Chinese—shortly before
she faces death at the hands of Revolutionists eager to rid their
wartorn country of Communist sympathizers. This young woman
embraces the passion and spirit of the Communist Revolution as an
opportunity to break the shackles of tradition and start anew.
Believing that "everything was to be changed, everything destroyed,
everything marvelously rebuilt," she forsakes her parental loyalty
("The Revolution is my father and my mother," she declares) and
rejects the neighbor's son to whom she has been betrothed all of her
life ("I am married to—to the Revolution," she confesses). The
morning of her death the sight of the young and beautiful comrade
marching to her death is shocking to many who witness her singing
as she goes, her natural fears strengthened by the knowledge that
she is dying as a free citizen.

319. Casper, Linda Ty "Cogon Full of Quail." Solidarity (1986) 74 – 80.

Revolution in the Philippines infiltrates the lives of common people
as it tears apart family allegiances and bonds between friends in this
story. A young man is forced to choose between his own safety and
the life of a boyhood companion who has joined the insurgents when
he witnesses ammunition being stolen from a barn he has been
assigned to guard. An elderly man, who might have been his

grandfather, is tortured as he is strung by his feet into a deep well for his part in transporting food and supplies to the insurgents. Witnesses to his needless death become involuntary participants in the scramble for military power that has spread throughout the country, leaving no one untouched.

320. Cherryh, Caroline Janice (as C. J. Cherryh). "Cassandra." Hugo Winners Ed. Isaac Asimov. Vol. 4. Garden City: Doubleday, 1985. 488 – 495.

The prophesy of war is fulfilled in this fantasy in which a woman with a past history of mental illness predicts the inevitable destruction of life and property to come with the advent of war yet keeps her prediction secret, for who would believe a "crazy" woman with a history of mental instability? When the bombing she foresees does occur, Alis finds contentment as one of the survivors among the ghost-buildings and fiery ruins. She faces the future with an odd sense of relief, for she has already dreamed the worst of all possible nightmares and it has come true. Life can only improve from now on: "One could live in ruins," she concludes, "only so the fires were gone. And the ghosts were all in the past, invisible" (495).

321. Childress, Alice. "Interestin' and Amusin.'" Like One of the Family: Conversations from a Domestic's Life. Boston: Beacon Press, 1956. 159 – 161.

One of 62 imaginary conversations between a black domestic and her friend which comprise this novel in celebration of black women who are "no less dignified for having spent time on their knees," this sketch offers Mildred's interpretation of the concepts of war and peace. Mildred relates to Marge how she was asked to tell the difference between war and peace by rich, white folks while she was serving at a cocktail party where "wonderful" and "amusin" were the most popular words afloat. At first the partygoers laughed at Mildred's simplistic statement: "I'm against war and if most of the people feel like that there'll be peace" (160). But as she continued her treatise on war, she tells Marge, the amused reactions she saw at first on the white faces gradually faded away:

> "I do not want to see you folks washed in oil and fire. . . . No, and I don't want to see your bodies stacked like kindlin' wood. . . . I don't want to see mothers and fathers screamin' in the streets. . . . I don't want to see blood flowin' like the Mississippi. . . . I don't want to see folks shakin' and tremblin' and runnin' and hidin' . . . but I *do* want to see the KINGDOM COME on *earth* as it is in Heaven and I do not think that bombs and blood and salty tears is a *Heavenly* condition." (160 – 161)

Finally, the room became pensively silent, Mildred recalls, as she offered her concluding remark to the white audience: "When there is true peace we'll have different notions about what is *amusin'* because *mankind* will be *wonderful* " (61).

322. Childress, Alice. "Merry Christmas, Marge!" <u>Like One of the</u>
      <u>Family: Conversations from a Domestic's Life</u>. Boston: Beacon
      Press, 1956. 151 – 153.

One of 62 imaginary conversations between a black domestic and her
friend which comprise this novel in celebration of black women who
are "no less dignified for having spent time on their knees," this brief
sketch ponders the meaning of the word "peace," a word so often
heard "blarin' out of every store front" at Christmastime but seldom
analyzed. To Mildred, peace is more than the absence of war, more
than "no mother mournin' for their soldier sons."   Peace, as
visualized by Mildred, means the absence of violence and racial
segregation, the elimination of such words as "lynch," "murder," and
"kill" from the dictionary, and the resolution of racial inequities
which draw artificial lines of conflict between blacks and whites. "If
I could ride a subway or a bus and not see any signs pleadin' with
folks to be 'tolerant' . . . regardless of what I am . . . I know that
would be peace 'cause then there would be no need for them signs,"
Mildred declares (152). If she could visit a school and see a black
teacher teaching white children, Mildred tells her friend, she would
sing out, "Peace it's truly wonderful!" (153).

323. Chow, Diana. "The Village." <u>An Asian American Anthology</u>. Eds.
      Chris Planas, Kevin Yuen, Elaine Becker, and La Schele Neal.
      Berkeley: University of California, 1980. 27 – 30.

In this intense and gruesomely realistic narrative of war a young
girl hidden between the walls of her home witnesses the slow and
torturous deaths of her mother and father by invading soldiers before
she faces her own equally horrifying death by the same invading
"demons" who kill everyone in her village. Watching through a crack
in the wall, praying for her mother to "please die fast," the narrator
observes:

> Her momma died slowly, she died in parts; her gentle face, her
> feelings, her voice, her eyes—those deep, loving pools
> becoming shallow walls of hate—then playfully poked, then
> plucked by filthy demon knives. Before she died, each part of
> her was tormented, was cut off—stripped of pride, of love, of
> life.
>
> She watched her momma. She watched her daddy. It was
> easy to see him, his face—he was hanging in the tree by his
> neck.   She saw his face as he died watching momma,
> watching the demons perform hideous acts serving devils'
> passions. They had put him up, so he could see, as he hanged.
> She hoped daddy died first, it was hard to tell—his eyes were
> still staring at the demons on her momma. He took a long
> time to die . . . but not as long as momma. (27)

She discovers parts of her baby sister in the rubble of disaster left
behind by the invaders and runs through the darkness of night

"trying to escape the laughter of the demons, the tearing screams, the moans of the dead" (28 – 29). But the demons return, blissfully raping and violating the body of the sole survivor of their hideous raid before one rams a grenade into her dead body and removes the key.

It is the aggressors of this story who become the victims of their own ruthless war play, however, as their overcrowded jeep overturns when the drunken driver is suddenly overcome by the haunting image of the face of the young girl whose body they have just "stripped, spread, used, chopped" and loses control of the vehicle. As the jeep explodes, and the body pieces of the celebrating soldiers are launched into the night sky, there is a "song of bloody, violent victory, of death and destruction, vibrating in the air" (30).

Chow's disturbing narrative illustrates that the inhumanity of war honors no boundaries, disregarding age and innocence. But the horror of war can also reverse itself in surprise attacks on the mental defenses of those who cannot forget the haunting images of war's suffering victims.

324. Clingerman, Mildred. "Minister Without Portfolio." Invaders of Earth. Ed. Groff Conklin. New York: Vanguard, 1952. 215 – 222.

An elderly woman unknowingly and quite innocently saves the earth from war with her traditional ethics and pacifist beliefs in this science fiction narrative. When Ida Chriswell meets uniformed soldiers while she is birdwatching in an open field, it never occurs to her that the men she befriends are actually aliens from another planet investigating conditions on earth for potential attack. Ida's sincerely expressed beliefs in God, the dignity of man, and possibility of peaceful coexistence convince the extraterrestrials that the world may be worth saving, after all. Headlines of major newspapers the next day read: "Unknown Woman Saves World Say Men from Space." "ONE SANE HUMAN FOUND ON EARTH. TOTAL DESTRUCTION OF WORLD AVERTED" (221). But Ida is as oblivious to the connection between the media reports and her "adventure" of the previous day as she is to the green skin of the soldiers' children evident in the pictures she proudly presents to her own grandchildren, who react to such oddity with fear and revulsion.

325. Coldsmith, Sherry. "Caruso." When the Music's Over. Ed. Lewis Shiner. New York: Bantam Books, 1991. 270 – 274.

In the vignettes which comprise this narrative, four characters of a future century make individual attempts to establish peace in a world where war and violence have almost obliterated the meaning of the word. Whether in ink, in sand, or in blood, each of these characters succeeds in writing the word "peace" as a symbolic statement of self and ideology and the recognition that alternatives to war still exist, even in the midst of violence.

326. Cooley, Winnifred Harper. "A Dream of the Twenty-First Century."
      Daring to Dream. Ed. Carol Farley Kessler. Boston: Pandora, 1984.
      205 – 211.

As the twentieth century unfolds, the narrator of this story dreams
she has skipped forward one hundred years as she explores
American society on the first day of the twenty-first century. What
she discovers is an idealistic, socialized society based upon
"simplicity and sense" where gender distinctions and income
statuses have been eradicated. A new world religion has "enabled
men and women to turn their zeal and energy into practical ethics
and philanthropy, and to believe that if all men are indeed children of
God, and brothers, they must act as such, and we have attained
Universal Peace" (211). Although the inhabitants of this future
century admit they are not perfect, they have successfully abolished
war, channeling their energies instead toward "making life worth
living and this world habitable, in a moral as well as in a material
sense," and they look forward to the eventual discovery of "personal
immortality" for all peaceful inhabitants of earth.

327. De Courcy, Dorothy (with John De Courcy). "Rat Race." Big Book of
      Science Fiction. Ed. Groff Conklin. New York: Crown Publishers,
      1950. 235 – 247.

In this science fiction narrative earth's inhabitants surrender to
invading alien Cafis, whose "weaponry" eradicates all electrical
power on the planet. But the rodent-like Cafis' reign is short-lived,
however. Assuming the race they have just conquered to be civilized,
they are repulsed to discover that the humans who inhabit this planet
are carnivores and have invented weapons with the capability to
destroy life. The humans on this planet may be the first race the
Cafis have ever conquered that is obviously uncivilized, with their
propensity for violence and bloodshed. The disappointing humans,
therefore, are not considered worthy of becoming subjects of the
nonviolent Galactic Empire of Cafis.

328. Finch, Sheila. "Reichs-Peace." Hitler Victorious: Eleven Stories of
      the German Victory in World War II. Ed. George Benford and
      Martin H. Greenberg. New York: Garland, 1986. 221 – 241.

In this fantasy, an American scientist travels to the country where
her Jewish parents, whom she cannot remember, died during their
incarceration in a work camp while she was smuggled out of
Germany and later sent to the United States. Although her mission
is to trade confidential genetic research, Greta discovers when she
arrives that Adolf Hitler's widow has other plans in mind for her.
Greta learns that she has a brother whom Eva Hitler adopted as her
own son during the war. Wolfli has since become an astronaut who
insists on exploring space without radio communication and now
needs to be warned of certain dangers to his life scientists have
monitored. Counting on the reputed telepathic gifts of Romany
bloodkin, Eva arranges for Greta to communicate with her brother

for the first time to guide him safely back to earth. Meanwhile Greta learns through a German official that Wolfli has been selected as the next fuhrer to continue in Hitler's footsteps and carry to completion the master plan his adopted father envisioned. The official explains the proposed strategy:

> "Europe has had forty years of peace—wonderful isn't it? But peace is not necessarily good for people. They grow fat and lazy. They lose the inner strength that made the Fatherland invincible. Some of us see the necessity of rectifying the matter, directing the feet of our nation back to the narrow path of German destiny. We are called upon to be leaders of the world, Fraulein!" (235)

But Frau Hitler has other plans. Burning the confidential papers Greta has brought from the United States, she declares: "Do you not suppose I had enough talk of genetic selection, years ago? It is our destiny and danger to be always thinking of improving the race, you see! But not this way" (240). Her own master plan for the future of Germany envisions progress without the need for war.

329. Fisher, Dorothy Canfield. "Memorial Day." A Harvest of Stories. New York: Harcourt, Brace and Company, 1927. 336 – 344.

Soldiers buried in a cemetery cry out silently to young boys decorating their graves on Memorial Day in this story, but their antiwar proclamations are not heard. As these corpses long to warn successive generations of American youth with romanticized visions of heroism in their heads not to waste their lives in warfare, those very youths are aspiring to military heroism and an eventual burial beside their revered forefathers. John Andrews, who died "screaming his heart out" while his leg was amputated without anesthesia during the Civil War, awakens each Memorial Day and attempts to cry out his warning to the young men he hears walking above his grave:

> But now it was at the little boy he screamed to tell him—to let him know—to warn him. He was horrified by the child's rosy calmness, by his awful unawareness. Yet he could never think of words to warn him. He could only shriek silently from his grave, till the trees quivered to it, till the clouds echoed it back, till the thrush was silenced. But none of the little boys ever heard him. (338)

Through an innovative perspective of retrospective wisdom and experience, Fisher makes a strong antiwar statement through those who have experienced the reality of warfare and yearn to warn future generations against the futility and senselessness of it all.

330. Gearhart, Sally Miller. "The Chipko." Love, Struggle and Change: Stories by Women. Ed. Irene Zahava. Freedom, CA: The Crossing Press, 1982. 169 – 183.

The conflict in this narrative pits nonviolent environmentalists, most of them women, against lumberjacks armed with chain saws, hunting dogs, and a court order in an effort to save a forest of trees. Reciting their haunting chant ("I protect these trees. I protect myself. I protect my comrades. I protect him who attacks us. I will not be moved."), the environmentalists prepare for the inevitable confrontation, remaining "ultimately committed to the oldest strategy of all, if it came to that: hugging individual trees, there to stay until that tree's life was no longer threatened" (174). Against the overwhelming force of the "jacks," the environmentalists have to resort to the "ultimate strategy" but even it proves ineffectual against the sheer number of their assailants. Defeat for the environmental forces—and the trees—seem inevitable until suddenly from above "a war-cry split the air." "Flying furies" of armed women descend upon the forest, bringing with them the hope of survival for the forest and those defending it. Gearhart's story emanates a reverence for nature and life often violated by the aggressive, self-centered motives of earth's inhabitants.

331. Gellhorn, Martha. "About Shorty." 1953. The Honeyed Peace. Freeport, NY: Books for Libraries Press, 1970.

"About Shorty" is a characterization of a woman made unforgettable in the narrator's mind by the events of war and peace that shape her life. The war correspondent-narrator, who cannot remember Shorty's real name, first meets this impressive German woman during the Spanish-Civil War in 1937. Shorty's promiscuity earns her the reputation of a "whore de combat" who loves not only her husband but "all passing men" as well. Her infidelity is forgiven by most journalists in the narrator's social circle until Shorty decides to leave her husband for a Spanish colonel. When her husband later dies in combat, it is as if he has been undeservedly killed twice, once by war and once by his estranged wife, who loses respect among her peers. The narrator leaves Spain at the end of the war, assuming Shorty has become a casualty of war.

When Shorty and the narrator unexpectedly meet in Paris two years later, Shorty's Madonna-like facial expression radiates peace and the approach of motherhood. Her child will be a girl, she predicts, so that she may never be killed at war. Her husband is apolitical. But her peace is short-lived as war intervenes, separating the friends once again for several years. The next time the correspondent hears of Shorty, she learns through a mutual friend that Shorty has left her family in order not to endanger their lives. As a German anti-Fascist, formerly married to a Jew, Shorty would be regarded by the Germans as an enemy. This is the last the narrator hears of Shorty, who remains a tragic figure in her memory.

332. Gilman, Charlotte Perkins. "War." With Her in Ourland. The Forerunner (7) 1916: 38 – 44.

In this chapter of the sequel to <u>Herland</u>, Ellador leaves the utopian Herland with her newly wedded American husband to tour the world, only to discover that Europe, their first destination, is at war. Van describes his wife's reaction:

> Now here was Ellador, daring traveler, leaving her world for mine, and finding herself, not as we three had been, exiled into a wisely ordered, peaceful and beautiful place, with the mothering care of that group of enlightened women; but as one alone in a world of which her first glimpse was of hideous war. As one who had never in her life seen worse evil than misunderstanding, or accident, and not much of these; one to whom universal comfort and beauty was the race habit of a thousand years, the sight of Europe in its present condition was far more of a shock than even I had supposed. (38)

Europeans' acceptance of war as a "normal condition of human life" has created a "social atmosphere of suspicion, distrust, hatred, of ruthless self-aggrandizement and harsh scorn" that is emotionally disturbing to Ellador, who has been reared in a peaceful society all of her life (39). Determined not to be sheltered from the truth of war, however, Ellador insists upon visiting battlefields where she observes firsthand the ruins of war and destruction of human life. It is not the fact that war ends so many lives that Ellador objects to so much, she tells her husband, but the hatred involved. Half the world might die in an earthquake and not do this harm!" she declares. "It is the Hating I mind more than the killing—the perversion of human faculty. It's not humanity dying—it is humanity going mad!" (42). In Gilman's <u>With Her in Ourland</u>, Nan Bowman Albinski explains in her <u>Women's Utopias in British and American Fiction</u>, the "voice of a purely evolved woman comments on our unevolved state, and she concludes that, whatever apparently superior technological progress we might have to offer, it cannot compensate for the violence of war and the misery and exploitation of women and (some) men" (68).

333.   Glendenning, Christina. "Ione." <u>Hurricane Alice</u> Fall-Winter 1988: 1+.

The single, middle-aged American woman who narrates this story travels to Honduras to adopt an illegitimate baby and rescue her from a country where war has become an everyday facet of life. In Honduras she learns that Central Americans harbor resentment against Americans, stemming from the irresponsibility and insensitivity of American military personnel who have been stationed there. One native Honduran explains their antipathy:

> "You Americans come here, make babies, go home. Then other Americans, like you, come and take the babies away. What about the mothers, the grandparents, the other childrens? Does your monies pay for their sorrow? . . . "You

peoples use our womens to make your babies. Then you take
our mens to fight your war in Nicaragua. You kill us." (7)

But the narrator also discovers a kinship of ideology with a
Honduran woman with whom she lives for several months as she
wades through the complex adoption process. This woman has too
lost faith in her government over the issue of war, but not her faith in
humanity.   Similarly, this woman has given her son to an
undeclared war with an uncertain direction, much like the narrator
lost her brother to the Vietnam War 18 years earlier. Glendenning
depicts the instability and disruption of life in Central America
imposed by war as she also illustrates the innate closeness of women
from dissimilar backgrounds whose commitment to the preservation
of life and mutual abhorrence of war supercede any cultural
barriers, bonding them in friendship.

334.   Harper, Rita-Elizabeth. "Survivors" Orbit 21. Ed. Damon Knight.
       New York: Harper and Row, 1980. 151 – 163.

An emerging adolescent female learns the necessary skills and
resourcefulness to insure the survival of her family in the
fantasized postwar community depicted in this bleak science fiction
story. When her mother dies of starvation so that her children may
have more food allotments, rationed by "protectors," the narrator,
who records her thoughts in the form of a journal, is left to care for
four younger brothers and sisters. As food resources dwindle and
scavenging becomes less and less beneficial, protectors continue to
reduce food allotments to stretch limited supplies. Although she
learns from a neighbor that her mother would not compromise
herself in order to secure more food for her family, the narrator
realizes that survival of her family depends upon her own
resourcefulness and ability to provide. The possessions of those who
perish become the life-sustaining resources for those still alive. And
the sexual favors performed by this 13-year-old girl for her
"protector" will insure that her family have enough food to survive
the winter.   Harper's story illustrates the unnatural and often
callous demands placed upon children during war who nevertheless
adapt unquestioningly and follow their instincts of survival.

335.   Henderson, Zenna. "Subcommittee." Young Extraterrestrials. Eds.
       Isaac Asimov, Martin H. Greenberg, and Charles G. Waugh. New
       York: Harper and Row, 1984. 183 – 213.

The play of children illustrates the simplicity of peaceful coexistence
in this science fiction narrative. While peace negotiations between
warring humans and the alien Linjeni come to a stalemate, with
neither side willing to compromise and risk betrayal, a young
human and Linjeni alien secretly play compatibly together with only
limited communication, oblivious to their glaring superficial
differences. It is not until negotiating officials observe this unlikely
friendship that they realize the words of the young human's mother
are indeed true: "Our alikenesses outweigh our differences so far

that it's just foolish to sit here all this time shaking our differences at each other and not finding out a thing about our likenesses. We are fundamentally the same. . ." (208).

336. Hill, Ingrid. "Whistling After Laval." Dixie Church Interstate Blues. New York: Viking, 1989. 1 – 22.

This narrative details the remembrances of a young Southern girl who loses a beloved cousin in the Korean War during her tenth year "when the summer went on with a soft, wanton vengeance, and so did the war" (3). Although the narrator's whistling of the French national anthem had the strange power to lure Laval back from his habit of sleepwalking while he was still alive, it has no magical power to bring him back from death. All that remains of Laval are photographs and memories of a mysterious but alluring young man whose life has been abruptly cut short by war.

337. Inness-Brown, Elizabeth. "War Song." Satin Palms. Canton, NY: Fiction International, 1981. 42 – 48.

"War Song" is a series of antiwar vignettes narrated from varying perspectives, written by an author characterized by one reviewer as a "mosaicist in fiction." In one "fragment," a poet observes that war gives people a reason to live and die—a sense of purpose:

> He notes that all people ask for things they have never requested before; though each phrases if differently, there is a sameness to the longings: to make a picture, a movement of perfect dance, a poem, a song to be remembered and sung on the front lines, a construction to tower for them where they can not tower and to stand when they lie down, a child to sleep when they are gone, a lasting love: in short to be remembered. (44)

In another fragment, a woman who anticipates being drafted makes a strong antiwar statement:

> Here is what I have to say about the war: come try and find me. I am forty pounds underweight. And let me go on record now, while there's still time: the killing of a thing, anything alive, is more abhorrent to me than making love to a dog. It is not making love, to fuck a dog. I would rather die than join the war. (46)

Each mosaic fragment included in this story adds a piece to the collage of antiwar expressions presented by Inness-Brown.

338. Kalpakian, Laura. "The Battle of Manila." The Pushcart Prize, XV: Best of the Small Presses. Ed. Bill Henderson. Wainscott, NY: Pushcart Press, 1990. 490 – 515.

This sensitive story of maternal loss to war is narrated from the viewpoint of an aging woman fighting her own stubborn battle for independence and sanity while she bears the emotional burden of trying to preserve the memory of her third and youngest son killed in combat in the Philippines during World War Two. At 22, "Ben was still too young to die and I am all that keeps him alive," Manila tells herself. "Keeping him alive is my life, but it's hard on you, this living for and loving the dead, it's hard, harder because you can't love death. You have to hate the death while you love the dead and keeping them alive is hard for an old woman like me" (513).

In a recurring dream, Manila reenacts her own fantasized version of Ben's clean and painless death in which she pictures herself in the middle of battle on Manila Bay, oblivious to the "shocks and shells, the blast and shriek all around" while she searches for her son:

> "I am in my old dress like the one I got on now and my old green checked apron that's wore through here and there and I kneel in the mud beside a body I know is Ben. I pull him up on my lap and turn him over slowly. The first few times I have this dream, that's all I do: just kneel and turn him over, glad to see his face in only muddy, no blood or nothing. I am glad they have not shot up his face. But lately in my dream I find fresh water from somewheres and I bathe that mud from his face and I am so happy that with the mud washed off, it is still perfect." (493)

The beginning of another generation's war in faraway Vietnam claims yet another young man who was a close companion to Manila. Danny's disappearance in action allows Manila at long last to share her grief—and persistent dream—with another, much younger mother now in need of solace and compassion. A woman she once referred to as "slut" and considered unworthy of her own son's affection, Manila now holds closely in mutual grieving for their lost sons of war:

> I stroke her hair and back. My grief is not my own anymore. I hold her and tell her over and over about the battle for Manila and the mud and finding the body and how someone will lift Danny from the mud, bathe his face, and find he isn't bloody in the least, just muddy and how when the mud is washed off, he is still perfect and young and beautiful. I tell how she will pull him into her arms and hold him against her shoulder, sing maybe. I tell how he will smile, how he will know the touch even if he don't know the person. I hold Connie Frett and I tell her over and over and we stay on the porch till it's long past dark and the dry red moon rises slow in the night sky. (515)

Kalpakian's story presents a strong characterization of a mother's endless mourning for the loss of her son and the psychological defenses she uses to cope with his loss while the aging process begins to threaten her own mental stability and ultimate survival.

339. Kingston, Maxine Kong. "White Tigers." The Woman Warrior: Memoirs of a Girlhood Among Ghosts. New York: Alfred A. Knopf, 1977. 19 – 53.

In this narrative a Chinese woman reared by her mother on nightly bedtime stories of heroines and swordswomen vows that she will grow up to be a "warrior woman." In her fantasy she becomes a character in one of her mother's legends who is selected at the age of nine to be trained as a warrior. Isolated in the mountains, she spends the next nine years of her life, including several days in the company of white tigers, learning survival skills and offensive tactics until she is ready to join the peasant rebellion. She marries a fellow warrior and remembers withdrawing from combat only once: "I hid from battle only once, when, I gave birth to our baby. In dark and silver dreams I had seen him falling from the sky, each night closer to the earth, his soul a star" (40). Flying the umbilical cord of her infant son as a flag, she makes a sling for her baby and continues to do battle, becoming one of the first generals to lead the rebellion against the reigning Chinese emperors. The young woman emerges as a heroine who discredits the traditional Chinese belief that "girls are maggots in the race. It is more profitable to raise geese than daughters" (43).

Once in the United States the Chinese heroine discovers another kind of war is being waged—a war based on racism against immigrants such as her family. The narrator becomes a different kind of swordswoman on American soil, but a warrior nonetheless seeking revenge for the injustices against herself and her family.

340. Kramer, Kathryn. "Seeds of Conflict." Soldiers and Civilians: Americans at War and at Home. Ed. Tom Jenks. New York: Bantam Books. 44 – 63.

Kramer satirizes the complacency of those who consider themselves immune to war, yet refuse to acknowledge the "seeds of conflict" often sewn on an individual level that comprise the roots of warfare and dissension. In this story Arborville citizens isolate themselves from the outer world, arrogant in their confidence that they are above the reproach of war, even though the warning signs exist: "This might be the most volatile century in the history of the world, but in Arborville people were content just to enjoy life, make some money and have children, give their children the childhoods they themselves had missed" (44). The story focuses on one particular Arborville family—the Quinces—who harbor an unacknowledged "snake in the garden" eating away at their fantasy of peaceful coexistence. The grandfather of the family is often an unwelcome intrusion in the household who causes marital friction and fills the children's heads with "all kind of unrealistic ideas." The father of the family, alternately volatile and loving, demands peace and quiet when he is at home and retains a comfortable distance from his children, abdicating instead to his father whom the children seem to prefer. The mother spends much of her time lying in her darkened bedroom with no one allowed entrance. The birth of a third, defective child further alienates mother and father from each other and their children. The conflict begins to reach a climax when his father decides it is time to institutionalize Lark. The mother accuses her husband of rejecting his own son because "he wasn't perfect enough for Arborville" (63). A war is brewing in the Quinces' household, yet the family remains oblivious to the warning signs within and without, living in potentially volatile complacency and denial.

341. Kress, Nancy. "Peace of Mind." When the Music's Over. Ed. Lewis Shiner. New York: Bantam Books, 1991. 5 – 11.

The continuation of war, the protagonist of this story comes to believe, is due to mankind's "evolutionary valuable compartmentalization"— our innate ability to selectively forget past memories and former considerations. The amount of XAL in each person's brain chemistry determines his ability to compartmentalize. A high level, for examples, permits a politician who once served in Vietnam to vote in favor of a resolution that would move the country closer to war. The end of war will not come by words alone, Martin concludes. "The world is at stake," he declares. "Literally. We have learned—slowly, painfully, over the last thirty years—that if we rely on words alone, there will be war. Again and again. . . ." Words are not enough, he contends, "against guns, not against missiles, not against toxins. And not against ingrained, through-to-the bone, immovable evolution. The kind of evolution that starts wars because a soldier or a camp guard to a politician can wall off in his mind what he's doing from the other human beings he's doing it to. Because he can compartmentalize too well. Too often. Too fatally" (11). The only possible solution to continued war foreseen by this revolutionary is to inject doses of an XAL-inhibitor into the bodies of those in power. He theorizes this strategy will decrease their ability to compartmentalize and thus promote peaceful thinking.

342. Le Guin, Ursula K. "The Ones Who Walk Away from Omelas." The Wind's Twelve Quarters. New York: Harper and Row, 1975. 275 – 284.

Winner of the Hugo award in 1972, this short story imagines a unique utopia set on the northwest coast of the United States where the happiness of its inhabitants is enjoyed at the expense of one young scapegoat. The people of Omelas thrive contentedly with very few rules or laws; the society has no need for bombs or soldiers. They live peacefully as if "the joy built upon successful slaughter is not the right kind of joy; it will not do; it is fearful and it is trivial" (280). But there is a price to pay for this blissful existence. In order to preserve their utopia, the citizens of Omelas are required to keep a retarded child locked in a closet where he communicates with no one:

> They all know it is there, all the people of Omelas. Some of
> them have come to see it, others are content merely to know it

is there. They all know that it has to be there. Some of them understand why, and some do not, but they all understand that their happiness, the beauty of their city, the tenderness of their friendships, the health of their children, the wisdom of their scholars, the skill of their makers, even the abundance of their harvest and the kindly weathers of their skies, depend wholly on this child's abominable misery. (282)

While the majority of inhabitants accept this sacrifice of one individual for the good of the majority, knowing that to try to improve the degrading circumstances in the child's life would jeopardize their happiness, "a few people, however, cannot live with this fact without feeling overcome with guilt, and these few choose to leave the city. The ones who walk away from Omelas exemplify the revolutionary individual who cannot enjoy a prosperity dependent on the suffering of others" (Spivack 84).

Le Guin explains in the introduction to the story that her idea for writing this narrative stems from the unlikely combination of the moral dilemma of the scapegoat discussed by American philosopher William James in "The Moral Philosopher and the Moral Life" and her own propensity to read signs backwards: "Omelas" spelled in reverse becomes Salem, O(regon), a probable location for the utopia described (275 – 276). Her narrative suggests a utopian society where residence may be voluntary but require difficult ethical choices.

343. Le Guin, Ursula K. "The Phoenix." The Compass Rose. New York: Harper and Row, 1982. 128 – 134.

Civil war divides Partisans and Loyalists in this narrative, the Partisans determined to eliminate all evidence of the past as they believe that "Nothing mattered but the future" while Loyalists attempt to preserve "the past that ensures a future." The result is a violent chaos of civil disorder:

> Weeks now, the loudspeakers, the machine guns, the explosions, the helicopters, the fires, the silences; the body politic was incurable, its agony went on and on. You went miles for a cabbage, a kilo of meal. Then next day the sweet shop at the corner was open, children buying orange drink. And the next day it was gone, the corner building blown up, burnt out. The carcass politic. Faces of people like facades of buildings downtown, the great hotels, blank and furtive, all blinds down. (132)

The war includes the burning of books which a Partisan librarian tries to save, not out of ideological conviction, but from a feeling of responsibility only to his position.

344. Mackenroth, Nancy. "To Sleep, Perchance to Dream." The Far Side of Time: Thirteen Original Stories. Ed. Roger Elwood. New York: Dodd, Mead and Company, 1974. 193 – 198.

This fantasy explores one of the causes of war—man's fear of the unknown and his narrow-sightedness toward individual differences. On a distant planet one of the Dreamers of the people of Lith, whose dreams accurately forecast future events, attempts to avert war from his land when he dreams a terrifying vision of war to come: "Fire death, and destruction. The village in flames and the screaming children fleeing into the desert to die, while their elders perished trying to save the village" (197). Waging battle against his own dream, Yalin the Dreamer counters this dream with another of an invasion of visitors from outer space who "journey from a distant star to spread harmony through the universe" and come in the spirit of "peace and friendship" (197). But when their spaceship lands the following day, as YaLin envisioned, he encounters strange creatures from planet earth who have been taught by their "wise men that all thinking creatures in the universe must look much like themselves" (198). Thus, the human who kills YaLin the Dreamer believes he is acting in self-defense when he slays the giant lizardlike creature, not realizing that its savage roar was actually YaLin's welcome.

The death of YaLin must be avenged, however, for Dreamers are sacred among the People of Lith. His fearful dream of fire, death, and destruction which YaLin attempted to prevent from coming true in order to protect the People of Lith now comes to pass, a war born of a human's fear and his overzealous urge to conquer the unknown before he attempts to understand.

345. MacLean, Katherine. "Small War." Saving Worlds. Eds. Roger Elwood and Virginia Kidd. Garden City, NY: Doubleday, 1973. 61 – 67.

An ecological war to save endangered wildlife is waged in this story set during a future time when "small wars" have become sanctioned under permits issued by the government and are considered legal if required rules and regulations are followed. Hunterhunters seek out hunters threatening the existence of animals, and it is rumored that the Society for the Prevention of Cruelty to Animals offers a reward for each human ear delivered. Although the whales endangered in this story are able to escape to safer waters, it is the lives of humans which are now placed in danger in what promises to be many "small wars" to come.

346. Mancuso, Caroline. "What to Do if They Come." Word of Mouth: 150 Short-Short Stories by 90 Women Writers. Ed. Irene Zahova. Freedom, CA: Crossing Press, 1990. 91 – 93.

This short narrative depicts school children practising in fire-drill fashion for an anticipated Communist invasion during which their religious faith will be severely tested, according to their Catholic nun teachers. Following a successful simulated invasion, during which the students crouch under their desks in fear and cling rigidly to their faith as instructed, the sister-teacher of the class warns the students to resist peacefully, should a true invasion occur. "We're looking for martyrs, not heroes," she advises. "Remember you have no chance against the communists. Their guns will be real and loaded, not like the toy I just used. . . . Now sit down quietly and take out your arithmetic books" (92 – 93). This fantasy envisions a future of religious extremism and paranoia where children hold fast to their religious beliefs out of fear rather than inner conviction.

347. Marchant, Charlotte. "Sweet Life." Reweaving the Web of Life: Feminism and Nonviolence. Ed. Pam McAllister. Philadelphia: New Society Publishers, 1982. 306 – 316.

"Sweet Life" is a semi-autobiographical narrative of a young woman who serves a 30-day prison sentence for rioting during a 1960s antiwar demonstration. This story offers a perspective of prison life from the inside out, written from the viewpoint of an idealistic revolutionary with admittedly much to learn about the nature of human beings and social change. The most influential of all the prisoners she encounters is an aging black activist named Sweet Life whom she communicates with through prison vents but never meets face to face. While he dreams of racial equality, Sweet Life embraces a "vision of a future that included so much more patience then mine," the narrator admits, and teaches the narrator that "all my dreams would take lots of work and especially time" (316).

Marchant's writing also explores the fragile boundary between violence and nonviolence often tested during antiwar protests of the 1960s. She explains:

> This story may raise questions for some pacifists around the range of action which can be considered nonviolent. The character in this story is arrested while trying to break "the huge plate glass windows of buildings lining the streets of corporate America. Is this nonviolent action? Is this violent action? Where do we draw the line?" (316)

348. Moffatt, Deborah. "Willie's War." First Fictions: Introduction 9. New York: Faber and Faber, 1986. 25 – 33.

A clash in different generations' attitudes toward war is evidenced in this narrative. A British World War Two veteran who immigrates to peaceful Vermont with his American wife becomes a pacifist who maintains that regardless of circumstance, "Nobody wins a war. . . . Winning a war is all in the mind" (27). Willie's philosophy clashes with those of his college daughter's abrasive Jewish boyfriend who views war in more self-serving terms, protective of Israel and sensitive to the persecution of his Jewish ancestors during World War Two. During one of their verbal confrontations, Willie challenges Jake's simplistic assessment of World War Two as a conflict between only Germans and Jews:

> "The Germans, the Jews! Is that all there was to the war? What about all the soldiers who died? American soldiers,

British soldiers. The ones who came back from the war
without legs or arms or mute or deaf or just plain insane?
What about the gypsies in the concentration camps? The
Catholics, the conscientious Protestants? What about me?" (31)

Disclosing to his family for the first time that he was imprisoned in a
prisoner-of-war camp for four years, Willie reveals a loss of pride and
dignity and a continuing sense of fear still remaining from his war
experience years later. Moffatt's narrative illustrates how cultural
identities and self-centered interests color perceptions toward war
and can precipitate conflicts between generations.

349. Moore, Catherine L. (with Henry Kuttner as Lewis Padgett). "The
Fairy Chessmen." Astounding Science-Fiction Jan. 1946: 7 – 45
and Feb. 1946: 122 – 176.

In this futuristic narrative, citizens of the last two great nations left
on earth—the Americans and the European Falangists—have been
locked in a "see-saw war, each with a knife against the other's
armored throat" for several decades (11). In this highly technological
age, war is directed by technicians who live underground and fought
with robots. "War, these days, was more of a chess game than a
series of battles" (14). To break the stalemate the Falangists have
devised a new kind of bomb that emits hard radiations which produce
a gene mutation that combines genius with insanity. This bizarre
form of insanity affects many of the technicians controlling the
American side of the war. The fate of the United States rests in
finding someone who can break the equation of the enemy, based
upon a complicated, variable logic, without going insane. As the war
ends with the defeat of the Falangists, the advanced weapons and
"technological miracles" of war stand idle, but this interim will
probably be short-lived, for a prolonged period of peace is
recognized as "psychologically unendurable" for nations so
advanced in war technology. It is generally acknowledged among
Americans that "there would always be an enemy." During the
American-Falangist War, space travel was considered frivolous, but
now as earth returns temporarily to a peace state, the American
military looks toward outer space to find a new focus of attack. "The
Enemy stood at the gates of the sky, with the silent challenge it had
given since man first raised his eyes from the ground" (176). If
mankind can create an Enemy somewhere beyond earth's borders in
the hostile universe, the human race might be saved from "fatal
interglobal conflict" and eventual extinction of itself.

350. Metzger, Deena. The Woman Who Slept With Men to Take the War
Out of Them. Culver City, CA: Peace Press, 1978.

This innovative novella, written in a dramatic monologue form that
includes the voices of several men and women, is a fictional study of
the differing ways war is viewed according to gender. In her
introduction to the novella, Barbara Myerhoff explains the symbolic
role of the two main characters—General (representative of males

who espouse war) and the Woman (representative of female pacifists) in the novella:

> In the first piece, the enemy is The General, one who destroys indifferently, without awareness or choice. The Woman sets herself against his deadness. She conquers him by taking him in, absorbing him, using her body to assert the fundamental anatomical truth, that a man and a woman uniting briefly make the two into one. This primordial form of connection is a vanquishment by taming—her body the cauldron that transforms him from the Other into one who is momentarily a part of her, a partner. In a dramatic but quiet moment, the alchemical work is done: he covers her feet against the cold with a rough blanket. The General has developed enough imagination and therefore empathy to feel what she feels. So this is why women have always slept with warriors, even those who have killed their loved ones. Not out of fickleness, envy or attraction to power, not because destructiveness is an aphrodisiac, as some misogynists have suggested. They sleep with the enemy to make him their own, to assert their commitment to life over death, in final refusal to believe that anyone who understands can continue to destroy. (vi – vii)

A chorus of voices in the novella chants the universal symbolism employed by Metzger in the narrative: "Every country is an occupied country. Every woman is an occupied territory. Every woman knows the enemy. Every woman who sleeps with a man sleeps with the general" (18).

Myerhoff describes <u>The Woman Who Slept With Men to Take the War Out of Them</u> as a "Mythic Hero Quest" of a female hero whose experiences help her to realize "her own well-being and the well-being of the outerworld are inseparable" (vi). The novella stresses that we are all a part of each other—a fundamental relationship that is destroyed by the unnatural act of war. In a <u>Small Press Review</u> essay, the reviewer writes that Metzger's "rhythmic voice invokes an ancient, traditional setting in which basic questions seem natural and urgent. She describes a society torn by its refusal to view its conflicts in anything but absolute terms of right and wrong, good and evil" (8) .

351. Norris, Helen. "The Cormorant." <u>Sewanee Review</u> 96.2 (1988): 179 – 204.

A veteran's attempts to bury his war experience through isolation and art therapy are given voice in this sensitive, sensual narrative. Living alone by the seashore, the veteran-protagonist of this short story adopts the carving of bird statues as postwar therapy. This interest eventually evolves into his career, gradually blocking out the past and bringing peace once again into his life:

The years of the war he held at bay. There was an inlet down the coast where the water beneath was cold to touch and full of all manner of rotting stuff. It was overlaid with a layer of warm and sunlit sea. He was the inlet, he deeply knew. His dreams, they never surfaced now. He never waded in and stirred. (181)

But the return of the cormorants with their feathers "black as Satan" and their unmerciful devouring of living things brings disturbing images of the war back again, disrupting his peace. And the sudden appearance of a woman who violates his solitude and rekindles his sexual interest but abruptly disappears from his life assures him that "the war he thought he had left behind had taken him back, was his forever. . ." (203). This veteran's own need for human contact woos him away from the non-threatening security of his world of art but leaves him vulnerable to feelings and emotions, allowing repressed memories of his war experience to surface without a means of escape.

352. Olsen, Tillie. "Hey Sailor, What Ship?" Twenty Years of Stanford Short Stories. Eds. Wallace Stegner and Richard Scowcroft. Stanford: Stanford University Press, 1966. 295 – 313.

Olsen characterizes a war veteran in this narrative who cannot wean himself from his dependence upon alcohol, an addiction acquired during military service. For Whitey, alcoholism is a defense mechanism which enables him to cope with "the memories to forget, the dreams to be stifled, the hopeless hopes to be murdered" leftover from war (312). He vacillates between drunkenness and sobriety, fantasy and reality, stretching the generous patience of his wife to its maximum. "What's going to happen with you, Whitey?" she finally confronts him. "I never know if you'll be back. If you'll be able to be back" (312). It is Whitey's experience with war that has severed him from the real world, making it impossible to predict if he will ever "be able to be back" and readjust to a civilian world.

353. Popkes, Opal Lee. "Zuma Chowt's Cave." The Third Woman: Minority Women Writers of the United States. Ed. Dexter Fisher. Boston: Houghton Mifflin, 1980. 58-69.

American and Indian cultures clash in this narrative in which a World War Two military deserter unexpectedly encounters a hermitic Indian family living a primitive existence in a cave along the polluted California coast, hunting rats and eluding the encroachment of the Indian-hating "white man." The adolescent Indian daughter's first impulse is to kill this strange intruder who has disrupted their solitary peace, but she is halted by her mother, who tries to patiently reason with her protective daughter who has never encountered the white civilization: "I tell you it is a man," she tries to explain. "A man like your father. It is a man like a husband. It is not an animal to be slaughtered for food. It is a man. A man!" (65).

Private Weeks is convinced he must have drifted to Central America when he dived overboard because he has never seen Americans like these before. "How in hell did people like you keep from gitten' civilized?" he asks in disbelief. "Where you been? Don't you know there's a world out there?" (67). These Indians are so isolated they aren't even aware there's a world war ongoing, the white man's hatred now aimed across the ocean at enemies other than Indians.

Although the cultural backgrounds of these Americans differ drastically, the Indian mother views this soldier's sudden appearance as perhaps the only opportunity for the regeneration of her family and her one chance to become a grandmother. She advises her daughter not to kill this white man, once regarded as an enemy, but to accept him instead as a husband, even as he prepares to depart and continue his escape from military duty.

354. Prose, Francine. "Cimmaron." Louder Than Words. Ed. William Shore. New York: Vintage Books, 1989. 236 – 250.

Prose studies how the death of her soldier-husband, killed during an explosion while serving in Beirut, Lebanon, colors the perceptions of a young wife toward the approaching birth of her first child in this story. Like most of Kenny's family and friends, Coral never doubted he would return safely by her expected due date. "At Kenny's going-away party, no one said a word about danger. They pretended his going to Lebanon was just business in another part of the world" (239). Coral buys an issue of Newsweek which contains pictures of the bombing, feeling like a kid examining Playboy clandestinely, to try to bring the reality of war into sharper focus and put her young husband's remote death in clearer context. Kenny's death in military service fosters a more protective feeling in Coral toward her soon-to-be delivered infant and a more realistic perspective on human mortality as well as the disregard for individual life fostered by war. She concludes that no matter whether you're playing on a playground or fighting on a battlefield, "there is no limit to how evil people can be. Everywhere they are just waiting for you to nod off so they can drive into you and blow you up" (250). With this lingering thought, she wraps her arms around herself, as if by her actions she can protect her unborn son or daughter, isolated from danger in a separate planet all its own for the moment, from the inhumanity of war which she has just begun to fully recognize herself.

355. Rafkin, Louise. "Blueprints for Modern Living." Unholy Alliances. Ed. Louise Rakin. San Francisco: Cleis Press, 1988. 65 – 76.

A woman approaching the milestone of her thirtieth birthday shares an unexpected intimacy of emotion with a friend after they take part in an antiwar protest in this story. The protest, well attended by "old, young, families carrying picnics, dogs on and off leashes" takes place on the coast of California, where "our military ships guns and missiles to Nicaragua, the Persian Gulf, and who knows where else? . . . Slipping silently under the Golden Gate Bridge, the weapons—

the marked guns and missiles and whatever else is packed in those crates marked boldly for the world to see—become our offering to the peoples of this planet" (72). The presence of a gray-haired couple at the protest, the woman sporting a "U.S. Out of Central America" button and sharing fried chicken with friends while her husband seeks names on an antiwar petition, reminds the narrator and her friend of their own troubled lives contrasted with such obvious stability and harmony of purpose. "How did you get this far together?" the narrator longs to ask. "How do you keep believing?" (73). While the narrator cries because she is about to "slide over thirty and I have no career, no babies, no husband, no picket fence," her friend cries over his dissolving marriage (75). Both cry together for the continued presence of war in the world and continued United States militarism they have just publicly protested.

356. Reed, Kit. "Songs of War." The New Women of Wonder. Ed. Pamela Sargent. New York: Random House, 1977. 121 – 175.

When the passage of a women's equality law fails to produce substantial gains for women who still shoulder most of the responsibility for dismal domestic chores and child rearing, a band of militant females band together to wage war against the American male populace in this satirical fantasy. Women nationwide leave behind their burned casseroles, unwashed dishes, and perplexed husbands to join the revolution. But there is little agreement among the leaders of the revolution about how to organize their effort or how they will change the country once victory is theirs:

> Rap was advocating a scorched-earth policy; the women would rise like phoenixes from the ashes and build a new nation from the rubble, more or less alone. Sheena raised the idea of an auxiliary made up of male sympathizers. The women would rule, but with men at hand. Margy secretly felt that both Rap and Sheena were too militant; she didn't want things to be completely different, only a little better. Ellen Ferguson wanted to annex all the land surrounding her place. She envisioned it as the capitol city of the new world. The butch sisters wanted special legislation that would outlaw contact, social or sexual, with men, with, perhaps, special provisions for social meetings with their gay brethren. Certain of the straight sisters were made uncomfortable by their association with the butch sisters and wished there were some way the battle could progress without them. At least half of these women wanted their men back, once victory was assured, and the other half were looking into ways of perpetuating the race by means of parthenogenesis, or, at worst, sperm banks and AI techniques. One highly vocal splinter group wanted mandatory sterilization for everybody, and a portion of the lunatic fringe was demanding transsexual operations. Because nobody could agree, the women decided for the time being to skip over the issues and concentrate on the war effort itself. (142 – 143)

Although the all-female forces win a few minor victories and sport certain dismembered part of males as trophies around their necks, their revolution fails for lack of inner cohesion and whole-hearted commitment of participants (some women actually miss the domestic chores they ran away from as well as the company of men). The revolution gradually fades away with few casualties and no significant gains toward equality achieved. "Now that it was over, things went on more or less as they had been before," Reed concludes (175).

357. Russ, Joanna. "When It Changed." Nebula Award Stories. Vol. 8. New York: Harper and Row, 1973. 95 – 105.

Women living in an all-female planet for the past 600 years resist the infiltration of men from Earth in this short story because they fear the integration of males into their lifestyles will mean the loss of sexual equality and probable reintroduction of war that has not been a part of their civilization for 32 generations since the last surviving male died. "When one culture has the big guns and the other has none, there is a certain predictability about the outcome," writes Russ (103). The women of Whileaway fear that if they readmit men into their society their lives will become "one long cry of pain" similar to the lives of their ancestors who were forced to live with war and inequality in the company of men.

358. Sargent, Pamela. "The Broken Hoop." The Best of Pamela Sargent. Ed. Martin H. Greenberg. Chicago: Academy Chicago Publishers, 1987. 214 – 232.

The young Indian woman in this fantasy denies her visions and refuses to step through the "golden circle" of her imagination with other Indians in search of a more peaceful world in which to live, a world where there are no soldiers controlling Indians' lives and threatening their future. Fearing that her visions are but a delusion and that to follow them would be to sacrifice her reason to irrationality, Catherine chooses not to risk passing through the "golden circle" to discover what kind of reality lies beyond. By denying her fantasy, she realizes too late, she will be forced to live in a "white man's world, a prisoner of the world to come" (232)

359. Sargent, Pamela. "Shadows." The Best of Pamela Sargent. Ed. Martin H. Greenberg. Chicago: Academy Chicago Publishers, 1987. 82 – 129.

Alien females descend upon earth to wage war against the human race in this narrative, demanding only that the humans who survive the invasion develop their individual concentration powers. Those humans who respond to the command discover that they, like the alien Aadae, have the ability to mentally transcend the limitations of physical form and journey through time and space in unlimited directions. The Aadae promise the humans:

You will travel with the other minds of space, streaking among the stars with tachyonic beings who have transformed their physical shapes ages ago. You will meet those who abandoned their bodies but live near their worlds, afraid to venture further. And if you are very strong, you may approach a star where the strongest dwell, ready to fight you if you intrude. They will try to fling you far away, but if you contend with them long enough, they will reveal their secrets and allow you to join them. Your mind will grow stronger with each journey, and when you body can no longer hold it, you will leave it behind, a garment which you have outgrown, and journey among the stars. You will learn all one can learn here and then move on to where there is only unending reflection. (126 – 127)

For those humans receptive to the teachings of the Aadae, the responsibility becomes theirs to journey to other worlds, as the Aadae have done, to release other races in the universe from the "oblivion of death" through the undiscovered power of their own mental concentration.

360. Sheldon, Alice Hastings (as James Tiptree, Jr.). "Beam Us Home." Byte Beautiful: Eight Science Fiction Stories. Garden City: Doubleday, 1985. 54 – 65.

A sensitive young American disturbed by the current state of the world, dominated by violence and lack of regard for human needs, rises above the inhumanity and squalor below as he leaves his body on earth to die from bacteriological infection contracted while fighting Guevarrista rebels in Venezuela. Hobie fantasizes himself as a member of the Star Trek crew, allowing his mind to ascend into space where his newly fantasized "home" becomes a sanctuary of peace safely distant from the wartorn earth far below. The characterization of Hobie—"a person so alienated from humankind by his own sympathetic humanity that he prefers to think of himself as an observer from a spaceship—allows Tiptree to make several wickedly-accurate statements about the orientation and thrust of our civilization," writes Gardner Dozois in The Fiction of James Tiptree, Jr. Originally written during the Vietnam War, this story prompted Sheldon to comment concerning the connection between war and her own science fiction: "I just wish history would stop acting as if it were trying to copy me" (Dozois 13).

In this story Sheldon offers a graphic depiction of the anguishing physical and mental states of a soldier's slow, excruciating death. Her writing is also sharply critical of a civilization which considers itself advanced but continues to resort to primitive aggression to resolve conflicts, a civilization in which those who genuinely care for one another are social misfits.

361. Sheldon, Alice Hastings (as James Tiptree, Jr.). "Houston, Houston, Do You Read?" Star Songs of An Old Primate. New York: Ballatine, 1978. 164 – 226.

Three American male astronauts lost in space discover they have been hurled forward in time in this science fiction narrative. While they have been orbiting the universe, a viral epidemic precipitating "riots and fighting which swept the world when humanity found itself sterile" has reduced the population of the planet from eight billion to two million. Only 11,000 of these inhabitants are human beings; the remainder are clones, the astronauts discover to their dismay, and almost all are females who have dismantled the patriarchal structure and created a much simpler, peaceful society where equality is the governing force. The few men left on earth are slowly dying out. The women who now dominate earth fear the reintroduction of male aggression once more would encourage warfare and contribute little to the progress of their civilization. Fighting, a woman explains to one of the astronauts, "ended when you did, I believe. We can hardly turn you loose on Earth, and we simply have no facilities for people with your emotional problems" (225). Masculinity, from the viewpoint of these women, is regarded as a "disease" potentially threatening to the peace which they have established on earth.

362. Sheldon, Alice Hastings (as James Tiptree, Jr.) "The Last Flight of Dr. Ain." SF: Authors' Choice 4. Ed. Harry Harrison. New York: G. P. Putnam's Sons, 1974. 219 – 230.

A bacteriological warfare specialist takes it upon himself to begin wiping out humanity with the creation of a mutated leukemia virus in a one-man war against the world rather than allow earth's inhabitants to destroy the biosphere with pollution in this story. Although Dr. Aim admits that the course he has taken may be morally wrong, he defends himself with an all-encompassing indictment of contemporary society: "We are all wrong. Now it's over" (229). In her introduction to the story, Sheldon laments that by "doing what comes naturally" as "current destructo champs" we who are a "runaway product of the planet Earth" have become "a disease of Earth" (220).

363. Sheldon, Alice Hastings (as James Tiptree, Jr.). "Yanqui Doodle." Crown of Stars. New York: Tom Doherty Associates, 1988. 130 – 169.

In this war fantasy an American soldier fighting to save a South American country from the threat of Communist rule turns his wrath upon visiting American officials in retaliation for the trauma he has endured while attempting to withdraw from a year-long, drug-dependent tour of combat duty sanctioned by the United States military. The issuance of BZs by the United States military removes any reservations Private First Class Donald Still, or any other American soldier, may have had about blowing away anybody, even the "baby-faced Commie Gues" not yet teenagers. In fact these tiny pills make the killing experience "exhilarating." NDs allow sleep without the interruption of nightmares which frequently disturb soldiers in combat, while Ms coat the horrific reality of war with a euphoric sense of "all-rightness" that allows soldiers to float through the experience of war.

But detoxification from these perception-altering substances proves to be a torturously slow process, Still discovers, exacerbated by the insensitive attitude of the military hospital staff where he attempts to recover. During this agonizing ordeal Still begins to conclude it is the American officials directing this war safely from afar, manipulating the lives of fighting men as if they were toy soldiers, who are his real enemies. "Do those men know, can they guess," he wonders, "that the little figures they move around are real live men and boys, boys who bleed?" (169).

Instead of returning to the front, as planned, when he escapes from the hospital, Still aims his M-16 at those who have attempted to control his mind for the past terrifying year of combat. In this narrative Sheldon presents a frightening possibility of the misuse of drugs sanctioned by the military machine, willing to forfeit the freedom of individual thought and inflict long-term suffering on its military forces in return for the short-term gains of war.

364. Short, Gertrude. A Visitor from Venus. New York: William-Frederick Press, 1949.

This novella contrasts a primitive earth, still resorting to the violence of war to resolve conflicts, with an idealized utopia which has developed on the planet Venus where war has been "abandoned as a planetary policy" and government emanates "from within" each individual citizen's conscience. After studying earth's culture, a visitor from Venus concludes that the moral values of those who inhabit earth have been "debased in inverse proportion to their material achievements" and now suffer from "immature destructiveness" (12). She analyzes the Earthites' deficiencies:

> "They have advanced in material knowledge, but are lagging in human relations. They have failed to keep these two developments in step. Had they done so, their findings for the promotion of peace would be in the ascendance rather than their efforts to wipe each other out. They are paying a high price for their failure to keep peace morally and spiritually with their material knowledge and science." (18 – 19)

Among the most glaring defects of Earthites she discovers is their suppression of women's rights. While men continue to wage wars, generation after generation, the feelings of women toward war are never considered. "War is Adam's institution," the visitor discovers. "He starts and stops them. Eve is expected only to bring forth Adam's sons. She may pour a lifetime of devotion into training these children for peaceful pursuits, only to be pushed aside, and made to see all her work undone, in a war" (24). Adam might have avoided many wars had he "let Eve have a voice in Earth's affairs and paid heed to the Earth's greatest teacher of love and brotherhood," she concludes (31).

It is her hope that the women of earth will unite and assert their rights as equal citizens. To put an end to the cycle of war the women of earth must organize a "world-wide education of their children to prevent future conflicts," declares the visitor from Venus. "Surely, none would deny them this solace, nor their right at the peace tables of Earth" (31). When wars on earth end, the visitor explains, "and death and destruction are found to be the real winners," the Adams get together and write treaties. Between wars they "take time out to dream, plan and talk international friendship, world peace organization. They even spend a trifle toward such ends" (27). But in a few years these treaties are forgotten, and the Adams find it easier to fight more wars than honor their past pledges, spending much more money destroying one another than trying to promote world harmony. "Someday Eve will just cut through the red tape and get a job done," predicts the visitor. "Peace insurance should be her contribution" (26). Short's writing represents both a plea to put an end to the barbaric ritual of war on earth and to rectify inequality among the sexes, giving women a stronger voice in such vital issues as war and peace.

365. Sinclair, Jo. "The Medal." Tales of Our People: Great Stories of the Jew in America. Ed. Jerry D. Lewis. New York: Bernard Geis Associates, 1969. 235 – 244.

In this story the 12-year-old Jewish son of a war casualty begins to accept his father's death as he and his mother search together for a reason to justify the medal of valor which Joshua has inherited in honor of his father. Mildred describes to her son a man who loved his home, his street, his country and was willing to do whatever was necessary to protect his freedom of choice from the threat of Nazism. "Sometimes a reason is just there," she explains to her son. "Inside a man. What he thinks and feels—believes—like part of his body" (242). Mother and son begin to feel a sense of mutual healing from their pain of loss as they commit themselves to the same love of home, street, and country which energized the life of the man they both loved and have lost.

366. Smedley, Agnes. "Shan-fei, Communist." Writing Red: An Anthology of American Women Writers, 1930 – 1940. Eds. Charlotte Nekola and Paula Rabinowitz: New York: The Feminist Press, 1987. 30 – 35.

This narrative is a characterization of a Chinese woman whose mother sacrifices herself so that her daughter may lead a free life. The only symbol of enslavement that remains with Shan-fei during her life of revolutionary activity is her deformed feet, bound in traditional Chinese style for the first eleven years of her life under the tyrannical rule of her father. At his funeral Shan-fei's mother unwinds the bandages binding her feet and symbolically sets free her daughter. Shan-fei eventually joins the Communist revolution during the 1920s and loses both a son and husband during the period of White Terror. Despite her losses and imprisonment for two years, Shan-fei continues to work for the liberation of all Chinese people. In answer to the question posed to the author, "Is Shan-fei beautiful?" Smedley writes: "She is squarely built like a peasant and it seems that it would be very difficult to push her off the earth—so elemental is she, so firmly rooted to the earth. Beautiful? I do not know—is the earth beautiful?" (35).

367. St. Clair, Margaret (as Idris Seabright) "Short in the Chest." 17X Infinity. Ed. Groff Conklin. New York: Dell, 1969. 229 – 238.

In this futuristic fantasy, the United States military tries to cure inter-service tension between air, sea, and ground military forces by promoting "dighting" between the sexes. Since dighting is no longer a natural human drive, men and women are issued drugs for tension reduction and sexual arousal. But the future of the military forces looks bleak in this story. A robot-psychologist with confused thought patterns resulting from a short in its electrical wiring begins to advise its female clients to shoot their potential sexual partners instead of dighting with men of rival armed forces whom they regard as inferior, an idea which may ultimately substantially reduce the military population of the country. Through the medium of science fiction St. Clair comments on the self-defeating nature of rivalry within the military and the dangers that can result from too much dependence upon mechanization and artificial stimulants in our lives.

368. Swan, Gladys. "Land of Promise." Of Memory and Desire. Baton Rouge: Louisiana State University Press, 1989. 117 – 130.

This story portrays the self-reliance of the wife of a disturbed veteran who is deserted time and again by her husband who can no longer function in a world "where the rent was to be paid and the tax notices came and there had been sons to be raised and given a stake in the future" (124). Moe slips in and out of Fanny's life, eventually becoming "no more a husband or a father or a man who belonged anywhere," spending most of his time in a fruitless search for valuable rocks he is convinced will bring wealth to his family (125). While her husband wanders the hills of New Mexico, a man without a home whose only real interest is the lure of the land, Fanny dies having established her own business and raised two sons alone but never having known the security and intimacy of a real husband, for hers was lost to war long ago.

369. Vaughn, Stephanie. "Able, Baker, Charlie, Dog." Sweet Talk. New York: Random House, 1990. 3 – 27.

This story describes a father-daughter relationship strained by the emotional distance of a father whose life is dominated by his unyielding military mentality. The career officer Vaughn portrays teaches his preschool daughter the military alphabet—Able, Baker, Charlie, Dog, Easy, Fox, George, How, etc.—and uses mealtimes "to lecture on the mechanics of life" so that his daughter will learn to successfully compete in the civilian world. By the time Gemma reaches elementary school, she knows how to plant tomatoes, load a shotgun shell, gut a dove, explain the principles of crop rotation and the flying buttress, and discuss the Defenestration of Prague. But she still does not know her father.

When Gemma detects her father's military career is falling apart— and his self-esteem along with it, she has no words for him. Even after he trades his military commission for a hardware business venture, her father attempts to control her life with continual rules of conduct and unwanted advice, even calling her at college in the middle of the night to make sure her protein intake is adequate. Following his death, gradually self-inflicted by an overconsumption of alcohol and tobacco, Gemma mourns not for her father but for the intimate relationship they were never able to build because his preoccupation with his military career and rigid personality prohibited such closeness.

370. Vaughn, Stephanie. "Dog Heaven." Sweet Talk. New York: Random House, 1990. 176 – 194.

This narrative is a series of remembrances of a young girl growing up in a military family, living on a series of military posts. The story reaches back to the narrator's initial recognition during her school years that as a daughter of a military officer, her childhood would be much different form that of "civilian kids," who often teased—and considered themselves superior to—the "Army kids." The story illustrates the impact of transient military life on children, forced to part with close friends and beloved pets as their families frequently move. It also contrasts the insular life of families living on a self-contained military post with the lives of civilians outside. Vaughn's narrative, too, traces the emerging political awareness of a young girl who first learns the destructive capabilities of weapons of war. Shown graphic pictures of victims of the atomic bombing of Japan during World War Two by a school teacher, the narrator begins to realize the devastating power locked within the missiles her father commands, just a few miles from their military post.

371. Vilott, Rhondi. "Persephone." Orbit 21. Ed. Damon Knight. New York: Harper and Row, 1980. 101 – 108.

A woman warrior faces a conflict of choice between childbearing and the continuation of her promising military career in this science fiction story. Although Chrystan's clash with the queen of the alien Bharans ends in near victory for the invading human troops, she responds to the "spark of life fighting its own battle" within her body as she makes the decision to return to earth—even at the disapproval of her recently promoted husband eager for victory—rather than take the risk of losing another unborn child, as she has twice previously during battle. The instinct to procreate and nurture life proves stronger than the urge to continue to destroy lives through armed conflict in the characterization of this futuristic woman.

372. Vogan, Sara. "Scenes From the Homefront." The Pushcart Prize, V. Ed. Bill Henderson. Yonkers: Pushcart Press, 1980. 437 – 455.

The attitudes of three generations of males toward war are contrasted in this story. The grandfather, who has lived through five wars in his 93 years, believes himself to be either Robert E. Lee or Clarence Darrow during the last three decades in his life. Burning his granddaughter's history book as a piece of "Yankee propaganda crap," he continually mourns his greatest defeat at Gettysburg. His son, denied entry into World War Two because of an eye defect, becomes obsessed with the study of warfare, converting his den into a war museum and filling his young children's minds with images of war victims while he insists, "You can't understand peace if you don't realize the nature of war. All these people will have died in vain if you won't look at them" (441). Believing that "love of country and our way of life" justifies war, he condemns his son as a "goddamn subversive" when he refuses to fight in the Vietnam War. "You are not my son," his father screams. "You are a cowardly piece of trash. A no-talent lying cheat" (450). While the son resists the draft by deliberately keeping himself underweight, his sister, who narrates the story, aids draft resisters heading to Canada even as their father makes a worldwide tour of battlefields in search of the war experience he never had. This story contrasts the changing viewpoints of three generations of male family members toward war, one so dominated by war he cannot separate his personal identity from the concept of himself as soldier, one so regretful he could not serve he becomes obsessed with an inflated sense of duty, and one who rejects the traditional ideas of his forefathers in his denouncement of the Vietnam War as an unjust mistake in which he refuses to participate.

373. Walters, Anna Lee. "Warriors." The Sun is Not Merciful. Ithaca: Firebrand Books, 1985. 11 – 26.

"Warriors" is a character sketch of a Pawnee warrior "born into the wrong time" from the viewpoint of his niece who vows to carry on his "battle for beauty" after he dies a dejected hobo. By the time Uncle Ralph is born, the "warrior life" he so idolizes is gone. "Uncle Ralph was trapped in a transparent bubble of a new time," the narrator writes. "The bubble bound him tight as it blew around us" (12). The ways and beliefs of the Pawnees live on only in his stories of life and death, both "fierce and gentle" in which "warriors dangled in delicate balance" (12). Uncle Ralph bemoans the loss of devotion to beauty which he feels characterizes contemporary society:

"No one believes in the old ways anymore. They want to believe when it's convenient, when it doesn't cost them anything and they get something in return. There are no more believers. There are no more warriors. They are all gone. Those who are left only want to go to the Moon" (22).

Outnumbered in his individual battle to retain those ideals, he dies a drunken hobo with fantasies of himself as a warrior among thousands, all joined in a common quest for beauty and individuality. His nieces recall not the lonely, disgraceful circumstances of his last days but remember him for the wise advice he gave that "we must live beautifully or not live at all" as they vow to carry on his unfinished battle in their own lives (26).

374. Warren, Rosalind A. "The Inkblot Test." _The Women Who Walk Through Fire: Women's Fantasy and Science Fiction._ Vol. 2. Ed. Susanna J. Sturgia. Freedom,CA: The Crossing Press, 1990. 2 Vols. 23 – 26.

In the futuristic life predicted in this short narrative, a woman's future depends upon her interpretation of a Rorschach inkblot test, but Society dictates the "correct" response and imposes the death penalty for any rebellious ideas. While the protagonist of the story desires to be a poet and interprets the inkblot as a poetic vision, Society judges this to be an incorrect response and prompts her to recite the correct answer: "IT IS A PRODUCTIVE DAY IN THE MISSILE FACTORY. A YOUNG WORKER, CLAD IN OVERALLS, IS STANDING BY HER POST. SHE IS WORKING ON THE DELICATE MECHANISM THAT WILL GUIDE THE MISSILES TO THEIR TARGETS, SMASHING THE ENEMY. THIS VISION GIVES HER MUCH PLEASURE" (23). Society already has enough poets. It now needs her to be a productive missile factor worker to "make the bombs Society so urgently needs" for its war effort. Her only alternative, other than the death penalty, is to volunteer to take the risk to become an outer space explorer, a role reserved for misfits of this repressive Society.

LITERARY CRITICISM AND BIBLIOGRAPHIC SOURCES

Adams, J. Donald. "A Sequel to The Good Earth." Rev. of Sons, by Pearl S. Buck. The New York Times Book Review 25 Sept. 1932: 1.

Albinski, Nan Bowman, Women's Utopias in British and American Fiction. London: Routledge, 1988.

Allen, Bruce. "New fiction with earmarks of 'past' values." Rev. of A Handbook for Visitors from Outer Space, by Kathryn Kramer. Christian Science Monitor 5 Sept. 1984: 21 – 22.

Allen, Paula Gunn. Introduction. Spider Woman's Granddaughters: Traditional Tales and Contemporary Writing by Native American Women. Ed. Paula Gunn Allen. Boston: Beacon Press, 1989. 1 – 21.

Axelsson, Arne. Restrained Response: American Novels of the Cold War and Korea, 1945 – 1962. Westport, CT: Greenwood Press, 1990.

Barr, Marleen S. Future Females: A Critical Anthology. Bowling Green: Bowling Green State University Popular Press, 198.

Bartkowski, Frances. Feminist Utopias. Lincoln: University of Nebraska Press, 1978.

Berkson, Dorothy. "So We All Became Mothers: Harriet Beecher Stowe, Charlotte Perkins Gillman, and the New World of Women's Culture." Feminism, Utopia, and Narrative. Eds. Libby Falk Jones and Sarah Webster Goodwin. Knoxville: University of Tennesse Press, 1990. 100 – 115.

Betsky, Celia. Rev. of Woman on the Edge of Time, by Marge Piercy. New Republic 9 Oct. 1976: 39 – 40.

Blake, Patricia. "In Extreme Cases." Rev. of The Honeyed Peace, by Martha Gellhorn. The New York Times Book Review 30 Aug. 1953: 4.

Blish, James. "Books." Rev. of The Lathe of Heaven, by Ursula K. Le Guin. Magazine of Science Fantasy and Fiction. July 1972: 59 – 64+.

Boos, Florence and Lynn Miller, eds. Bibliography of Women and Literature. 2 vols. New York: Holmes and Meier, 1989.

Buck, Pearl S. Epilogue. The Living Reed. By Buck. New York: John Day Company, 1963. 475 – 478.

Buck, Pearl S. Historical Note. The Living Reed. By Buck. New York: John Day Company, 1963. 9 – 17.

Bucknall, Barbara J. Ursula K. Le Guin. New York: Frederick Ungar, 1981.

Carroll, Berenice A., Clinton F. Fink, and Jane E. Mohraz. Peace and War: A Guide to Bibliographies. Santa Barbara: ABC-Clio, Inc., 1983.

Cheung, King-Kok and Stan Yogi, eds. Asian American Literature, An Annotated Bibliography. New York: The Modern Language Association, 1988.

Cummins, Elizabeth. Understanding Ursula K. Le Guin. Columbia: University of South Carolina Press, 1990.

"Daurella." Rev. of The Battle Months of George Daurella, by Beulah Marie Dix. The New York Times Book Review 21 May 1916: 213.

"Dear Frontiers: Letters from Women Fantasy and Science Fiction Writers." Frontiers 2.3 (1977): 62 – 78.

Delany, Samuel R. "The Kesh in Song and Story." Rev. of Always Coming Home, by Ursula K. Le Guin. The New York Times Book Review 29 Sept. 1985: 31.

Dix, Beulah Marie. Epilogue. The Battle Months of George Daurella. By Dix. New York: Duffield and Company, 1916. 319 – 320.

Doyle, Paul A. Pearl S. Buck. Boston: Twayne Publishers, 1980.

Dozois, Gardner. The Fiction of James Tiptree, Jr. New York: ALGOL Press, 1977.

Du Pont, Denise, ed. Women of Vision. New York: St. Martin's Press, 1988.

Durdin, Peggy. "The Kims Struggle On." Rev. of The Living Reed, by Pearl S. Buck. The New York Times Book Review 22 Sept. 1963: 40.

Easton, Tom. Rev. of Always Coming Home, by Ursula K. Le Guin. Analog Science Fiction-Science Fact. June 1986: 186 – 187.

Franks, Lucinda. Rev. of A Weave of Women, by E. M. Broner. Ms. July 1978: 34.

Freibert, Lucy M. "World Views in Utopian Novels by Women." Journal of Popular Culture. 17.1 (1983): 49 – 59.

Gearhart, Sally Miller. "Future Visions: Today's Politics: Feminist Utopias in Review." Women in Search of Utopia: Mavericks and Mythmakers. Eds. Ruby Rohrlich and Elaine Hoffman Baruch. New York: Schocken Books, 1984. 296 – 309.

Greenland, Colin. "Remaking the World." Times Literary Supplement 3 June 1988: 622.

Hawes, Norma B. "Books in Brief." Rev. of Vida, by Marge Piercy. National Review 30 May 1980: 675 – 676.

Jacobs, Naomi. "Beyond Stasis and Symmetry: Lessing, Le Guin, and the Remodeling of Utopia." Extrapolation 29.1 (1988): 24 – 45.

Jackson, Marni. "A story of bombs and lovers." Rev. of Vida, by Marge Piercy. Macleans 31 March 1980: 47.

Jefferson, Margo. "Future vs. Present." Rev. of Woman on the Edge of Time, by Marge Piercy. Newsweek 7 June 1976: 94 – 95.

Jen, Tai. "Of the Good Earth." Rev. of Sons, by Pearl S. Buck. Saturday Review of Literature 24 Sept. 1932: 123.

Jonas, Gerald. Rev. of A Door Into Ocean, by Joan Slonczewski. The New York Times Book Review 12 Jan. 1986: 22.

Kessler, Carol F. "Communities of Sisters: Utopian Fiction by U.S. Women, 1970 – 1980." Sisterhood Surveyed: Proceedings of the Mid-Atlantic Women's Studies Association, 1982 Conference. Ed. Anne Dzamba Sessa. West Chester, PA: West Chester University, 1983. 79 – 87.

Khanna, Lee Cullen. "Women's Utopias: New Worlds, New Texts." Feminism, Utopia, and Narrative. Eds. Libby Falk Jones and Sarah Webster Goodwin. Knoxville: University of Tennesse Press, 1990. 130 – 140.

Kottner, Ann. "Literature's Black Sheep: Stretching the Definition." Rev. of A Door Into Ocean, by Joan Slonczewski. Belles Lettres. Spring 1989: 4.

Kramer, Kathryn. Afterword and Preface. "The House at World's End." By Kramer. A Handbook for Visitors from Outer Space. New York: A. A. Knopf, 1984.

Lane, Ann J. The Charlotte Perkins Gilman Reader. New York: Pantheon Books, 1980.

Lane, Ann J. Introduction. Herland. By Charlotte Perkins Gilman. New York: Pantheon Books, 1979. v – xxiii.

Lefanu, Sarah. Feminism and Science Fiction. Bloomington: Indiana University Press, 1988.

Leonard, John. "Books of The Times." Rev. of A Weave of Women, by E. M. Broner. New York Times July 25 1978: C6.

Maybon, Richie. "Modern Youth in 'Ancient' China." Rev. of Flame From the Rock, by Adet Lin. Saturday Review 1 Jan. 1944: 20.

Miller, Margaret. "The Ideal Woman in Two Feminist Science Fiction Utopias." Science Fiction Studies 10 (1983): 191 – 197.

Morton, Brian. "History or fantasy." Rev. of Duncan's Colony, by Natalie Petesch. Times Literary Supplement. 15 Oct. 1982: 1142.

Myerhoff, Barbara. Foreword. The Woman Who Slept With Men to Take the War Out of Them. By Deena Metzger. Culver City, CA: Peace Press, 1978. v – vii.

Overton, Jeanne K. Pearl Buck: Bibliography and Criticism. Boston: Simmons College, 1942.

Patai, Daphne. "British and American Utopias by Women (1836 – 1979): An Annotated Bibliography: Part I." Alternative Futures 4.2 – 3 (1981): 184 – 206.

Pearce, Jacqueline. "Feminist Utopian Vision and Social Change." Alternatives 16.3 (1989): 50 – 54.

Pearson, Carol. "Coming Home: Four Feminist Utopias and Patriarchal Experience." Future Females: A Critical Anthology. Ed. Marleen S. Barr. Bowling Green, OH: Bowling Green State University Popular Press, 1981: 63 – 70.

Pearson, Carol. "Women's Fantasies and Feminist Utopias." Frontiers 2.3 (1977) : 50 – 61.

Prescott, Peter S. "Dream Fiction." Rev. of The Lathe of Heaven, by Ursula K. Le Guin. Newsweek 29 Nov. 1971: 104 – 106.

Rev. of The Woman Who Slept With Men to Take the War Out of Them by Deena Metzger. Small Press Review Oct. 1982: 8.

Rev. of Vida, by Marge Piercy. The Atlantic. Feb. 1980: 96.

Rock, Roger O. The Native American in American Literature: A Selectively Annotated Bibliography. Westport, CT: Greenwood Press, 1985.

Rohrlich, Ruby and Elaine Hoffman Baruch. Women in Search of Utopia: Mavericks and Mythmakers. New York: Schocken Books, 1984.

Russ, Joanna. "Recent Feminist Utopias." Future Females: A Critical Anthology. Ed. Marleen S. Barr. Bowling Green, OH: Bowling Green State University Popular Press, 1981: 71 – 85.

Sale, Roger. Rev. of Woman on the Edge of Time, by Marge Piercy. The New York Times Book Review 20 June 1976: 6.

Sargent, Lyman Tower. British and American Utopias 1516 – 1975: An Annotated Bibliography. Boston: G. K. Hall, 1979.

Sauber, Dorothy. "Historical Context/Literary Content: Women Write About War and Women." Thesis. Hamline University, 1988.

Scharnhorst, Gary. Charlotte Perkins Gilman. Boston: G. K. Hall, 1985.

Shinn, Thelma J. Worlds Within Women: Myth and Mythmaking in Fantastic Literature by Women. Westport, CT: Greenwood Press, 1986.

Spivack, Charlotte. Ursula K. Le Guin. Boston: G.K. Hall, 1984.

Sternhell, Carol. "Before or After the End of the World." Rev. of A Handbook for Visitors from Outer Space, by Kathryn Kramer. The New York Times Book Review 5 Aug. 1984: 10.

Walzer, Judith B. Rev. of Vida, by Marge Piercy. The New Republic, 9 Feb. 1980: 38 – 40.

Watson, Carole McAlpine. Prologue: The Novels of Black American Women, 1891 – 1965. Westport, CT: Greenwood Press, 1985.

Weaver, Mary Jo. Rev. of A Weave of Women, by E. M. Broner. Commonweal 25 Feb. 1983: 118 – 119.

Woods, Katherine. "Pearl Buck's Stirring Novel on China's Invasion." Rev. of The Patriot, by Pearl S. Buck. The New York Times Book Review 5 March 1939: 2.

Author Index

Authors are listed alphabetically by last name. Numbers refer to bibliographic entries.

Title Index

Short fictions entries are enclosed in quotation marks. All other entries are novels. Numbers refer to bibliographic entries.

Subject Index

All numbers refer to item numbers in the bibliography except those in parentheses which refer to page numbers of chapter introductions.

About the Author

SUSANNE CARTER is the microforms supervisor at Southwest Missouri State University Library. She has also published several essays on Vietnam War literature written by American women.